by WOMEN: AN ANTHOLOGY of LITERATURE

Marcia McClintock folsom

Linda Heinlein Kirschner

Houghton Mifflin Company · Boston
atlanta dallas geneva, illinois hopewell, new jersey palo alto

Acknowledgments

"A Dream," by Bella Akhmadulina from *Poets on Street Corners* by Olga Carlisle. Copyright © 1968 by Random House, Inc. Reprinted by permission of the publisher.

"In the Evening," by Anna Akhmatova from *Poets on Street Corners* by Olga Carlisle. Copyright © 1968 by Random House, Inc. Reprinted by permission of the publisher.

"Eden Is a Zoo," by Margaret Atwood from *Procedures for Underground.* Copyright © 1970 by Oxford University Press, Canadian branch. All rights reserved. Published by permission of Little, Brown & Co. in association with the Atlantic Monthly Press.

"The Meeting," by Louise Bogan from *The Blue Estuaries* by Louise Bogan. Copyright © 1957, 1958, 1962, 1963, 1964, 1965, 1966, 1967, 1968 by Louise Bogan. Reprinted by permission of Farrar, Straus & Giroux.

"The Demon Lover," by Elizabeth Bowen from *Ivy Gripped the Steps and Other Stories* by Elizabeth Bowen. Copyright 1946 and renewed 1974 by Elizabeth Bowen. Reprinted by permission of Alfred A. Knopf, Inc. and Jonathan Cape, Ltd.

"Beverly Hills, Chicago," by Gwendolyn Brooks from *The World of Gwendolyn Brooks* by Gwendolyn Brooks. Copyright 1949 by Gwendolyn Brooks Blakely. Reprinted by permission of Harper & Row, Publishers, Inc.

"Seminary," by Constance Carrier from *The Middle Voice*, Swallow Press, 1955. Originally in *The New Yorker*. Reprinted by permission; © 1949 The New Yorker Magazine, Inc.

"The Sentimentality of William Tavener," by Willa Cather from *Willa Cather's Collected Short Fiction, 1892–1912*, edited by Virginia Faulkner. Introduction by Mildred Bennett. Revised edition © 1970 by the University of Nebraska Press.

"On Seeing My Great-Aunt in a Funeral Parlor," by Diana Chang. Reprinted from *The American Scholar*, vol. 28, number 1, winter 1958/59. Copyright © 1958 by the United Chapters of Phi Beta Kappa. By permission of the publishers.

"The Little Bouilloux Girl," by Colette from *My Mother's House* by Colette, translated by Una Vicenzo Trowbridge and Enid McLeod. Copyright 1953 by Farrar, Straus & Young, Inc. Reprinted with the permission of Farrar, Straus & Giroux.

"Further Notes for the Alumni Bulletin," by Patricia Cumming. Copyright 1974 by Patricia Cumming. First published in *Quartet*, vol. vi, nos. 15–16, winter-spring 1974.

"Natural Law," by Babette Deutsch from *The Collected Poems of Babette Deutsch*. Copyright by Babette Deutsch. Reprinted with permission of the author.

Acknowledgments continued on page 475.

About the editors

Marcia McClintock Folsom is an Instructor in English at Wheelock College where she is also Director of Freshman Advisement. She has also taught English literature at Boston College. She is a graduate of Wellesley College and the University of California, Berkeley. She is presently completing work on her doctoral dissertation.

Linda Heinlein Kirschner is teaching English at The Hun School of Princeton as an Edward E. Ford Foundation Visiting Scholar. She has been both Dean of Girls and Chairperson of the English Department when teaching in New York City. She attended The College of Wooster and Hamline University and has published several books. Ms. Kirschner is included in the current edition of *Who's Who of American Women*.

CONTENTS

vi

like ✓ confronts isolation by death
fynds restrictions, convent, etiquette, But bracing for
future embraces the solace that
conventions afford

POETRY

bREAkiNG fREE

INTRODUCTION

Why does a woman write? What in the human spirit motivates a person to rebel against her traditional role? Why, through the centuries, have so many women defied the opinions of their contemporaries in order to put words on paper? These larger questions were in our minds as we approached our reading for this book. But also a personal question loomed. How, we wondered, would we feel about women writers, and yes, women themselves, after a year spent reading as much writing by women as we could? The answer is simple: our admiration for their perseverance, for their courage, for their writing, has been enhanced.

Women's writing is finer than we imagined. Here is literature that represents the creative energies of women who have written through the ages. Some were ostracized for daring to speak out in what was considered a man's world. Perhaps worse, many were simply ignored. We could see among these writers a common bond: each felt a need to express herself, to affirm her existence. The women represented in this book, and others like them, have made it easier for us to write and to be heard today. They have, in affirming their existences, validated ours as well. To all these women, we extend our gratitude. They have enriched our lives. May they enrich yours.

Women hold a place in lit. far back recorded time
Irrespective of wheth author. male/female, women
frequently emerge as strong individs. capable of
independence, courage, growth, honesty self assertion
+ self realisation.
 — Bible introduces to
 — Homer develops sev. story w. characters among them
 — The portraits of women Shakespeare presents lesforceful
   nor w/out moments of strength
 — View of w. as rendered by woman writers more subjective
   flavor
exp self discovery

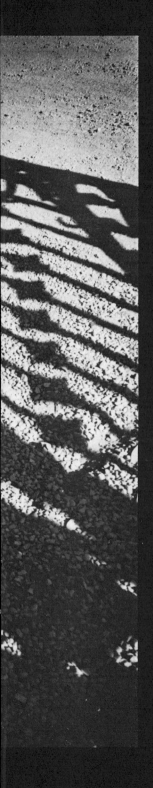

Short Stories

Short stories have been around a long time. Their origin is ancient, reaching back into the nearly mythical past. In the middle of the nineteenth century, writers began to think of the tale as a special kind of art, and to discover astonishing possibilities for presenting characters and exploring problems in short narratives. Writers have found in the compressed size of short stories an opportunity to transform ordinary life and ideas into the dense, illuminating experience of fiction.

Any short story deserves to be read first in an open, submitting, hungry way. We read a story to find out what happens, to experience its mood. In remembering and rereading it, however, we become more aware of how it works. It makes a difference, for example, if the story is told by a character who participates in the action, or by a character who observes it, or if the author herself is the narrator. Identifying the story's point of view is a good way to begin to understand its construction. Some stories make the reader hurry ahead to discover the outcome of the plot, others make the reader linger over the details which create its mood. Sometimes the events of a story take place in a very short time, as in Kate Chopin's "The Story of an Hour." The action in other stories covers many years. Learning to recognize how an author handles time and sequence within a short narrative helps the reader understand the story.

Often the most rewarding way to think about a group of stories is thematically. The stories we have selected here fit together in a number of ways. For example, one theme common to these stories is marriage, and the contrast of marriage with romance. In Katherine Anne Porter's narrative, Granny Weatherall still feels anguish over a romance, an engagement, a heartbreak, which happened decades ago. The jilting stands against her later marriage to someone else, her children, grandchildren, her many triumphs. Both realities persist—the loss, the riches of a full life. In this story, and in the Willa Cather story as well, the costs of compromise in marriage are paid in daily external adjustments and private suffering. But we also feel how deeply these writers value the exchanges of everyday life, the romance of prosaic routine. During the evening described in Cather's story, the Taveners uncover the love which always lay at the heart of their marriage; and the discovery has "all the miracle of romance."

In Elizabeth Bowen's ghost story, everyday arrangements explicitly stand for something amazingly precious. The wife remembering her children's jackets, putting sheets on stored furniture, expresses a continuing love which contrasts with an old romantic promise she once made—a promise which now seems foolish, and fatal. Chopin's heroine simultaneously discovers the meaning of romantic promises and marriage compromises when she becomes a widow. The most troubling exploration of married intimacy is the old man Revere's attempt to understand his wife's death, his children's lives, to reconstruct their past out of his own hazy, blinking memory. How little he has known about the life he has lived!

Finally, in one of these stories, the simplest facts of marriage: a woman and man living together, cooking food, building a fire, sleeping in a big bed, working, having a child; these primary elements of being married are transformed into luminous truths. Marriage itself has all the mystery of romance in Welty's story, where an outsider—a traveling salesman—whose perceptions have been made fresh, vulnerable, and alive by a terrible sickness, can see a woman and man linked together as a breathtaking revelation.

2 *Marcia Folsom*

THE STORY OF AN HOUR

Kate Chopin

Knowing that Mrs. Mallard was afflicted with a heart trouble, great care was taken to break to her as gently as possible the news of her husband's death.

It was her sister Josephine who told her, in broken sentences; veiled hints that revealed in half concealing. Her husband's friend Richards was there, too, near her. It was he who had been in the newspaper office when intelligence of the railroad disaster was received, with Brently Mallard's name leading the list of "killed." He had only taken the time to assure himself of its truth by a second telegram, and had hastened to forestall any less careful, less tender friend in bearing the sad message.

She did not hear the story as many women have heard the same, with a paralyzed inability to accept its significance. She wept at once, with sudden, wild abandonment, in her sister's arms. When the storm of grief had spent itself she went away to her room alone. She would have no one follow her.

There stood, facing the open window, a comfortable, roomy arm-chair. Into this she sank, pressed down by a physical exhaustion that haunted her body and seemed to reach into her soul.

She could see in the open square before her house the tops of trees that were all aquiver with the new spring life. The delicious breath of rain was in the air. In the street below a peddler was crying his wares. The notes of a distant song which some one was singing reached her faintly, and countless sparrows were twittering in the eaves.

There were patches of blue sky showing here and there through the clouds that had met and piled one above the other in the west facing her window.

She sat with her head thrown back upon the cushion of the chair, quite motionless, except when a sob came up into her throat and shook her, as a child who has cried itself to sleep continues to sob in its dreams.

She was young, with a fair, calm face, whose lines bespoke repression and even a certain strength. But now there was a dull stare in her eyes, whose gaze was fixed away off yonder on one of those patches of blue sky. It was not a glance of reflection, but rather indicated a suspension of intelligent thought.

There was something coming to her and she was waiting for it, fearfully. What was it? She did not know; it was too subtle and elusive to name. But she felt it, creeping out of the sky, reaching toward her through the sounds, the scents, the color that filled the air.

Now her bosom rose and fell tumultuously. She was beginning to recognize this thing that was approaching to possess her, and she was striving to beat it back with her will—as powerless as her two white slender hands would have been.

When she abandoned herself a little whispered word escaped her slightly parted lips. She said it over and over under her breath: "free, free, free!" The vacant stare and the look of terror that had followed it went from her eyes. They stayed keen and bright. Her pulses beat fast, and the coursing blood warmed and relaxed every inch of her body.

She did not stop to ask if it were or were not a monstrous joy that held her. A clear and exalted perception enabled her to dismiss the suggestion as trivial.

She knew that she would weep again when she saw the kind, tender hands folded in death; the face that had never looked save with love upon her, fixed and gray and dead. But she saw beyond that bitter moment a long procession of years to come that would belong to her absolutely. And she opened and spread her arms out to them in welcome.

There would be no one to live for her during those coming years; she would live for herself. There would be no powerful will bending hers in that blind persistence with which men and women believe they have a right to impose a private will upon a fellow-creature. A kind intention or a cruel intention made the act seem no less a crime as she looked upon it in that brief moment of illumination.

And yet she had loved him—sometimes. Often she had not. What did it matter! What could love, the unsolved mystery, count for in face of this possession of self-assertion which she suddenly recognized as the strongest impulse of her being!

"Free! Body and soul free!" she kept whispering.

Josephine was kneeling before the closed door with her lips to the keyhole, imploring for admission. "Louise, open the door! I beg; open the door—you will make yourself ill. What are you doing, Louise? For heaven's sake open the door."

"Go away. I am not making myself ill." No; she was drinking in a very elixir of life through that open window.

Her fancy was running riot along those days ahead of her. Spring days, and summer days, and all sorts of days that would be her own. She breathed a quick prayer that life might be long. It was only yesterday she had thought with a shudder that life might be long.

She arose at length and opened the door to her sister's importunities. There was a feverish triumph in her eyes, and she carried herself unwittingly like a goddess of Victory. She clasped her sister's waist, and together they descended the stairs. Richards stood waiting for them at the bottom.

Some one was opening the front door with a latchkey. It was Brently Mallard who entered, a little travel-stained, composedly carrying his grip-sack and umbrella. He had been far from the scene of accident, and did not even know there had been one. He stood amazed at Josephine's piercing cry; at Richards' quick motion to screen him from the view of his wife.

But Richards was too late.

When the doctors came they said she had died of heart disease—of joy that kills.

Insight

1. Mrs. Mallard exults in her new-found freedom. What specifically does this freedom represent for her? Do you sympathize with her joyous sense of freedom, or do you consider her feelings selfish and "monstrous"? Explain.

2. *Irony.* Irony always involves incongruity of some kind, usually between what appears to be and what really is. The simplest form of irony is *verbal irony*—saying one thing and meaning another, as in a sarcastic remark. On a more complex level, there is *irony of situation*—incongruity between what is expected to happen and what actually happens, between what appears to be true and what is true. Irony is a common literary device because life itself is full of irony.

   There is much irony in "The Story of an Hour." Mrs. Mallard's reaction to her husband's death is ironic in that she feels an exhilarating sense of freedom rather than the expected emotion of paralyzed grief. The major irony of the story comes from the incongruity between what was expected to cause Mrs. Mallard's heart attack and what actually caused it. What is that incongruity? What further irony is there in the ending? *not death but life* *joy that kills : no — loss of freedom*

THE SENTIMENTALITY
OF WILLIAM TAVENER

Willa Cather

It takes a strong woman to make any sort of success of living in the West, and Hester undoubtedly was that. When people spoke of William Tavener as the most prosperous farmer in McPherson County, they usually added that his wife was a "good manager." She was an executive woman, quick of tongue and something of an imperatrix.[1] The only reason her husband did not consult her about his business was that she did not wait to be consulted.

It would have been quite impossible for one man, within the limited sphere of human action, to follow all Hester's advice, but in the end William usually acted upon some of her suggestions. When she incessantly denounced the "shiftlessness" of letting a new threshing machine stand unprotected in the open, he eventually built a shed for it. When she sniffed contemptuously at his notion of fencing a hog corral with sod walls, he made a spiritless beginning on the structure—merely to "show his temper," as she put it—but in the end he went off quietly to town and bought enough barbed wire to complete the fence. When the first heavy rains came on, and the pigs rooted down the sod wall and made little paths all over it to facilitate their ascent, he heard his wife relate with relish the story of the little pig that built a mud house, to the minister at the dinner table, and William's gravity never relaxed for an instant. Silence, indeed, was William's refuge and his strength.

William set his boys a wholesome example to respect their mother. People who knew him very well suspected that he even admired her. He was a hard man towards his neighbors, and even towards his sons: grasping, determined and ambitious.

There was an occasional blue day about the house when William went over the store bills, but he never objected to items relating to his wife's gowns or bonnets. So it came about that many of the foolish, unnecessary little things that Hester bought for her boys, she had charged to her personal account.

One spring night Hester sat in a rocking chair by the sitting room window, darning socks. She rocked violently and sent her long needle vigorously back and forth over her gourd, and it took only a very

[1] IMPERATRIX: female emperor.

casual glance to see that she was wrought up over something. William sat on the other side of the table reading his farm paper. If he had noticed his wife's agitation, his calm, clean-shaven face betrayed no sign of concern. He must have noticed the sarcastic turn of her remarks at the supper table, and he must have noticed the moody silence of the older boys as they ate. When supper was but half over little Billy, the youngest, had suddenly pushed back his plate and slipped away from the table, manfully trying to swallow a sob. But William Tavener never heeded ominous forecasts in the domestic horizon, and he never looked for a storm until it broke.

After supper the boys had gone to the pond under the willows in the big cattle corral, to get rid of the dust of plowing. Hester could hear an occasional splash and a laugh ringing clear through the stillness of the night, as she sat by the open window. She sat silent for almost an hour reviewing in her mind many plans of attack. But she was too vigorous a woman to be much of a strategist, and she usually came to her point with directness. At last she cut her thread and suddenly put her darning down, saying emphatically:

"William, I don't think it would hurt you to let the boys go to that circus in town tomorrow."

William continued to read his farm paper, but it was not Hester's custom to wait for an answer. She usually divined his arguments and assailed them one by one before he uttered them.

"You've been short of hands all summer, and you've worked the boys hard, and a man ought use his own flesh and blood as well as he does his hired hands. We're plenty able to afford it, and it's little enough our boys ever spend. I don't see how you can expect 'em to be steady and hard workin', unless you encourage 'em a little. I never could see much harm in circuses, and our boys have never been to one. Oh, I know Jim Howley's boys get drunk an' carry on when they go, but our boys ain't that sort, an' you know it, William. The animals are real instructive, an' our boys don't get to see much out here on the prairie. It was different where we were raised, but the boys have got no advantages here, an' if you don't take care, they'll grow up to be greenhorns."

Hester paused a moment, and William folded up his paper, but vouchsafed no remark. His sisters in Virginia had often said that only a quiet man like William could ever have lived with Hester Perkins. Secretly, William was rather proud of his wife's "gift of speech," and of the fact that she could talk in prayer meeting as fluently as a man. He confined his own efforts in that line to a brief prayer at Covenant meetings.

Hester shook out another sock and went on.

"Nobody was ever hurt by goin' to a circus. Why, law me! I remember I went to one myself once, when I was little. I had most forgot about it. It was over at Pewtown, an' I remember how I had set my heart on going. I don't think I'd ever forgiven my father if he hadn't taken me, though that red clay road was in a frightful way after the rain. I mind they had an elephant and six poll parrots, an' a Rocky Mountain lion, an' a cage of monkeys, an' two camels. My! but they were a sight to me then!"

Hester dropped the black sock and shook her head and smiled at the recollection. She was not expecting anything from William yet, and she was fairly startled when he said gravely, in much the same tone in which he announced the hymns in prayer meeting:

"No, there was only one camel. The other was a dromedary."

She peered around the lamp and looked at him keenly.

"Why, William, how come you to know?"

William folded his paper and answered with some hesitation, "I was there, too."

Hester's interest flashed up. "Well, I never, William! To think of my finding it out after all these years! Why, you couldn't have been much bigger'n our Billy then. It seems queer I never saw you when you was little, to remember about you. But then you Back Creek folks never have anything to do with us Gap people. But how come you to go? Your father was stricter with you than you are with your boys."

"I reckon I shouldn't 'a gone," he said slowly, "but boys will do foolish things. I had done a good deal of fox hunting the winter before, and father let me keep the bounty money. I hired Tom Smith's Tap to weed the corn for me, an' I slipped off unbeknownst to father an' went to the show."

Hester spoke up warmly: "Nonsense, William! It didn't do you no harm, I guess. You was always worked hard enough. It must have been a big sight for a little fellow. That clown must have just tickled you to death."

William crossed his knees and leaned back in his chair.

"I reckon I could tell all that fool's jokes now. Sometimes I can't help thinkin' about 'em in meetin' when the sermon's long. I mind I had on a pair of new boots that hurt me like the mischief, but I forgot all about 'em when that fellow rode the donkey. I recall I had to take them boots off as soon as I got out of sight o' town, and walked home in the mud barefoot."

"O poor little fellow!" Hester ejaculated, drawing her chair nearer and leaning her elbows on the table. "What cruel shoes they did use to make for children. I remember I went up to Back Creek to see the circus wagons go by. They came down from Romney, you know. The circus men stopped at the creek to water the animals, an' the elephant got stubborn an' broke a big limb off the yellow willow tree that grew there by the toll house porch, an' the Scribners were 'fraid as death he'd pull the house down. But this much I saw him do; he waded in the creek an' filled his trunk with water and squirted it in at the window and nearly ruined Ellen Scribner's pink lawn dress that she had just ironed an' laid out on the bed ready to wear to the circus."

"I reckon that must have been a trial to Ellen," chuckled William, "for she was mighty prim in them days."

Hester drew her chair still nearer William's. Since the children had begun growing up, her conversation with her husband had been almost wholly confined to questions of economy and expense. Their relationship had become purely a business one, like that between landlord and tenant. In her desire to indulge her boys she had unconsciously assumed a defensive and almost hostile attitude towards her husband. No debtor ever haggled with his usurer more doggedly than did Hester with her husband in behalf of her sons. The strategic contest had gone on so long that it had almost crowded out the memory of a closer relationship. This exchange of confidences tonight, when common recollections took them unawares and opened their hearts, had all the miracle of romance. They talked on and on; of old neighbors, of old familiar faces in the valley where they had grown up, of long forgotten incidents of their youth—weddings, picnics, sleighing parties and baptizings. For years they had talked of nothing else but butter and eggs and the prices of things, and now they had as much to say to each other as people who meet after a long separation.

When the clock struck ten, William rose and went over to his walnut secretary and unlocked it. From his red leather wallet he took out a ten-dollar bill and laid it on the table beside Hester.

"Tell the boys not to stay late, an' not to drive the horses hard," he said quietly, and went off to bed.

Hester blew out the lamp and sat still in the dark a long time. She left the bill lying on the table where William had placed it. She had a painful sense of having missed something, or lost something; she felt that somehow the years had cheated her.

The little locust trees that grew by the fence were white with blossoms. Their heavy odor floated in to her on the night wind and recalled a night long ago, when the first whippoorwill of the Spring was heard, and the rough, buxom girls of Hawkins Gap had held her laughing and struggling under the locust trees, and searched in her bosom for a lock of her sweetheart's hair, which is supposed to be on every girl's breast when the first whippoorwill sings. Two of those same girls had been her bridesmaids. Hester had been a very happy bride. She rose and went softly into the room where William lay. He was sleeping heavily, but occasionally moved his hand before his face to ward off the flies. Hester went into the parlor and took the piece of mosquito net from the basket of wax apples and pears that her sister

The Sentimentality of William Tavener

had made before she died. One of the boys had brought it all the way from Virginia, packed in a tin pail, since Hester would not risk shipping so precious an ornament by freight. She went back to the bedroom and spread the net over William's head. Then she sat down by the bed and listened to his deep, regular breathing until she heard the boys returning. She went out to meet them and warn them not to waken their father.

"I'll be up early to get your breakfast, boys. Your father says you can go to the show." As she handed the money to the eldest, she felt a sudden throb of allegiance to her husband and said sharply, "And you be careful of that, an' don't waste it. Your father works hard for his money."

The boys looked at each other in astonishment and felt that they had lost a powerful ally.

she sees her on their side

but gained a whole family

renewal of their relationship. for love. Importance of communication. Import of common memories (lack of)

Insight

1. At the end of the story the boys feel they have "lost a powerful ally." Why do they feel that way?
2. Hester's soft, almost uncharacteristic gestures at the end of the story represent a change in Hester herself. What is this change, and what has caused it?
3. *Tone.* Tone is the attitude the author takes toward his or her subject. That attitude is revealed through choice of words and selection of details, and by emphasis and comments that are made. The tone of a story may be that of any human emotion or mental attitude—anger, bitterness, tenderness, humor, regret.

   At the beginning of the story Cather's tone is detached, almost businesslike, as she describes Hester and William. How does the tone change in the course of the story?

contemptuous, sarcastic, maternal loving appreciative

intimate loving — open nostalgic

THE jilting of GRANNY WEATHERALL

Katherine Anne Porter

She flicked her wrist neatly out of Doctor Harry's pudgy careful fingers and pulled the sheet up to her chin. The brat ought to be in knee breeches. Doctoring around the country with spectacles on his nose! "Get along now, take your schoolbooks and go. There's nothing wrong with me."

Doctor Harry spread a warm paw like a cushion on her forehead where the forked green vein danced and made her eyelids twitch. "Now, now, be a good girl, and we'll have you up in no time."

"That's no way to speak to a woman nearly eighty years old just because she's down. I'd have you respect your elders, young man."

"Well, Missy, excuse me." Doctor Harry patted her cheek. "But I've got to warn you, haven't I? You're a marvel, but you must be careful or you're going to be good and sorry."

"Don't tell me what I'm going to be. I'm on my feet now, morally speaking. It's Cornelia. I had to go to bed to get rid of her."

Her bones felt loose, and floated around in her skin, and Doctor Harry floated like a balloon around the foot of the bed. He floated and pulled down his waistcoat and swung his glasses on a cord. "Well, stay where you are, it certainly can't hurt you."

"Get along and doctor your sick," said Granny Weatherall. "Leave a well woman alone. I'll call for you when I want you. . . . Where were you forty years ago when I pulled through milk-leg[1] and double pneumonia? You weren't even born. Don't let Cornelia lead you on," she shouted, because Doctor Harry appeared to float up to the ceiling and out. "I pay my own bills, and I don't throw my money away on nonsense!"

She meant to wave good-by, but it was too much trouble. Her eyes closed of themselves, it was like a dark curtain drawn around the bed. The pillow rose and floated under her, pleasant as a hammock in a light wind. She listened to the leaves rustling outside the window. No, somebody was swishing newspapers: no, Cornelia and Doctor Harry were whispering together. She leaped broad awake, thinking they whispered in her ear.

11   [1] MILK-LEG: swelling of the legs after childbirth.

"She was never like this, *never* like this!" "Well, what can we expect?" "Yes, eighty years old. . . ."

Well, and what if she was? She still had ears. It was like Cornelia to whisper around doors. She always kept things secret in such a public way. She was always being tactful and kind. Cornelia was dutiful; that was the trouble with her. Dutiful and good: "So good and dutiful," said Granny, "that I'd like to spank her." She saw herself spanking Cornelia and making a fine job of it.

"What'd you say, Mother?"

Granny felt her face tying up in hard knots.

"Can't a body think, I'd like to know?"

"I thought you might want something."

"I do. I want a lot of things. First off, go away and don't whisper."

She lay and drowsed, hoping in her sleep that the children would keep out and let her rest a minute. It had been a long day. Not that she was tired. It was always pleasant to snatch a minute now and then. There was always so much to be done, let me see: tomorrow.

Tomorrow was far away and there was nothing to trouble about. Things were finished somehow when the time came; thank God there was always a little margin over for peace: then a person could spread out the plan of life and tuck in the edges orderly. It was good to have everything clean and folded away, with the hair brushes and tonic bottles sitting straight on the white embroidered linen: the day started without fuss and the pantry shelves laid out with rows of jelly glasses and brown jugs and white stone-china jars with blue whirligigs and words painted on them: coffee, tea, sugar, ginger, cinnamon, allspice: and the bronze clock with the lion on top nicely dusted off. The dust that lion could collect in twenty-four hours! The box in the attic with all those letters tied up, well, she'd have to go through that tomorrow. All those letters—George's letters and John's letters and her letters to them both—lying around for the children to find afterwards made her uneasy. Yes, that would be tomorrow's business. No use to let them know how silly she had been once.

While she was rummaging around she found death in her mind and it felt clammy and unfamiliar. She had spent so much time preparing for death there was no need for bringing it up again. Let it take care of itself now. When she was sixty she had felt very old, finished, and went around making farewell trips to see her children and grandchildren, with a secret in her mind: This is the very last of your mother, children! Then she made her will and came down with a long fever. That was all just a notion like a lot of other things, but it was lucky too, for she had once for all got over the idea of dying for a long time. Now she couldn't be worried. She hoped she had better sense now. Her father had lived to be one hundred and two years old and had drunk a noggin of strong hot toddy on his last birthday.

He told the reporters it was his daily habit, and he owed his long life to that. He had made quite a scandal and was very pleased about it. She believed she'd just plague Cornelia a little.

"Cornelia! Cornelia!" No footsteps, but a sudden hand on her cheek. "Bless you, where have you been?"

"Here, mother."

"Well, Cornelia, I want a noggin of hot toddy."

"Are you cold, darling?"

"I'm chilly, Cornelia. Lying in bed stops the circulation. I must have told you that a thousand times."

Well, she could just hear Cornelia telling her husband that Mother was getting a little childish and they'd have to humor her. The thing that most annoyed her was that Cornelia thought she was deaf, dumb, and blind. Little hasty glances and tiny gestures tossed around her and over her head saying, "Don't cross her, let her have her way, she's eighty years old," and she sitting there as if she lived in a thin glass cage. Sometimes Granny almost made up her mind to pack up and move back to her own house where nobody could remind her every minute that she was old. Wait, wait, Cornelia, till your own children whisper behind your back!

In her day she had kept a better house and had got more work done. She wasn't too old yet for Lydia to be driving eighty miles for advice when one of the children jumped the track, and Jimmy still dropped in and talked things over: "Now, Mammy, you've a good business head, I want to know what you think of this? . . ." Old. Cornelia couldn't change the furniture around without asking. Little things, little things! They had been so sweet when they were little. Granny wished the old days were back again with the children young and everything to be done over. It had been a hard pull, but not too much for her. When she thought of all the food she had cooked, and all the clothes she had cut and sewed, and all the gardens she had made—well, the children showed it. There they were, made out of her, and they couldn't get away from that. Sometimes she wanted to see John again and point to them and say, Well, I didn't do so badly, did I? But that would have to wait. That was for tomorrow. She used to think of him as a man, but now all the children were older than their father, and he would be a child beside her if she saw him now. It seemed strange and there was something wrong in the idea. Why, he couldn't possibly recognize her. She had fenced in a hundred acres once, digging the post holes herself and clamping the wires with just a Negro boy to help. That changed a woman. John would be looking for a young woman with the peaked Spanish comb in her hair and the painted fan. Digging post holes changed a woman. Riding country roads in the winter when women had their babies was another thing: sitting up nights with sick horses and sick Negroes and sick children and hardly ever losing one. John, I hardly ever lost one of them! John would see that in a minute, that would be something he could understand, she wouldn't have to explain anything!

It made her feel like rolling up her sleeves and putting the whole place to rights again. No matter if Cornelia was determined to be everywhere at once, there were a great many things left undone on this place. She would start tomorrow and do them. It was good to be strong enough for everything, even if all you made melted and changed and slipped under your hands, so that by the time you finished you almost forgot what you were working for. What was it I set out to do? she asked herself intently, but she could not remember. A fog rose over the valley, she saw it marching across the creek swallowing the trees and moving up the hill like an army of ghosts. Soon it would be at the near edge of the orchard, and then it was time to go in and light the lamps. Come in, children, don't stay out in the night air.

Lighting the lamps had been beautiful. The children huddled up to her and breathed like little calves waiting at the bars in the twilight. Their eyes followed the match and watched the flame rise and settle in a blue curve, then they moved away from her. The lamp was lit, they didn't have to be scared and hang on to mother any more. Never, never, never more. God, for all my life I thank Thee. Without Thee, my God, I could never have done it. Hail, Mary, full of grace.

I want you to pick all the fruit this year and see that nothing is wasted. There's always someone who can use it. Don't let good things rot for want of using. You waste life when you waste good food. Don't let things get lost. It's bitter to lose things. Now, don't let me get to thinking, not when I am tired and taking a little nap before supper. . . .

The pillow rose about her shoulders and pressed against her heart and the memory was being squeezed out of it: oh, push down the pillow, somebody: it would smother her if she tried to hold it. Such a fresh breeze blowing and such a green day with no threats in it. But he had not come, just the same. What does a woman do when she has put on the white veil and set out the white cake for a man and he doesn't come? She tried to remember. No, I swear he never harmed me but in that. He never harmed me but in that . . . and what if he did? There was the day, the day, but a whirl of dark smoke rose and covered it, crept up and over into the bright field where everything was planted so carefully in orderly rows. That was hell, she knew hell when she saw it. For sixty years she had prayed against remembering him and against losing her soul in the deep pit of hell, and now the two things were mingled in one and the thought of him was a smoky cloud from hell that moved and crept in her head when she had just got rid of Doctor Harry and was trying to rest a minute.

Wounded vanity, Ellen, said a sharp voice in the top of her mind. Don't let your wounded vanity get the upper hand of you. Plenty of girls get jilted. You were jilted, weren't you? Then stand up to it. Her eyelids wavered and let in streamers of blue-gray light like tissue paper over her eyes. She must get up and pull the shades down or she'd never sleep. She was in bed again and the shades were not down. How could that happen? Better turn over, hide from the light, sleeping in the light gave you nightmares. "Mother, how do you feel now?" and a stinging wetness on her forehead. But I don't like having my face washed in cold water!

Hapsy? George? Lydia? Jimmy? No, Cornelia, and her features were swollen and full of little puddles. "They're coming, darling, they'll all be here soon." Go wash your face, child, you look funny.

Instead of obeying, Cornelia knelt down and put her head on the pillow. She seemed to be talking but there was no sound. "Well, are you tongue-tied? Whose birthday is it? Are you going to give a party?"

Cornelia's mouth moved urgently in strange shapes. "Don't do that, you bother me, daughter."

"Oh, no, Mother. Oh, no. . . ."

Nonsense. It was strange about children. They disputed your every word. "No what, Cornelia?"

"Here's Doctor Harry."

"I won't see that boy again. He just left five minutes ago."

"That was this morning, Mother. It's night now. Here's the nurse."

"This is Doctor Harry, Mrs. Weatherall. I never saw you look so young and happy!"

"Ah, I'll never be young again—but I'd be happy if they'd let me lie in peace and get rested."

She thought she spoke up loudly, but no one answered. A warm weight on her forehead, a warm bracelet on her wrist, and a breeze went on whispering, trying to tell her something. A shuffle of leaves in the everlasting hand of God, He blew on them and they danced and rattled. "Mother, don't mind, we're going to give you a little hypodermic." "Look here, daughter, how do ants get in this bed? I saw sugar ants yesterday." Did you send for Hapsy too?

It was Hapsy she really wanted. She had to go a long way back through a great many rooms to find Hapsy standing with a baby on her arm. She seemed to herself to be Hapsy also, and the baby on Hapsy's arm was Hapsy and himself and herself, all at once, and there was no surprise in the meeting. Then Hapsy melted from within and turned flimsy as gray gauze and the baby was a gauzy shadow, and Hapsy came up close and said, "I thought you'd never come," and looked at her very searchingly and said, "You haven't changed a bit!" They leaned forward to kiss, when Cornelia began whispering from a long way off, "Oh, is there anything you want to tell me? Is there anything I can do for you?"

Yes, she had changed her mind after sixty years and she would like to see George. I want you to find George. Find him and be sure to tell him I forgot him. I want him to know I had my husband just the same and my children and my house like any other woman. A good house too and a good husband that I loved and fine children out of him. Better than I hoped for even. Tell him I was given back everything he took away and more. Oh, no, oh, God, no, there was something else besides the house and the man and the children. Oh, surely they were not all? What was it? Something not given back. . . . Her breath crowded down under her ribs and grew into a monstrous frightening shape with cutting edges; it bored up into her head, and the agony was unbelievable: Yes, John, get the Doctor now, no more talk, my time has come.

When this one was born it should be the last. The last. It should have been born first, for it was the one she had truly wanted. Everything came in good time. Nothing left out, left over. She was strong, in three days she would be as well as ever. Better. A woman needed milk in her to have her full health.

"Mother, do you hear me?"

"I've been telling you—"

"Mother, Father Connolly's here."

"I went to Holy Communion only last week. Tell him I'm not so sinful as all that."

"Father just wants to speak to you."

He could speak as much as he pleased. It was like him to drop in and inquire about her soul as if it were a teething baby, and then stay on for a cup of tea and a round of cards and gossip. He always had a funny story of some sort, usually about an Irishman who made his little mistakes and confessed them, and the point lay in some absurd thing he would blurt out in the confessional showing his struggles between native piety and original sin. Granny felt easy about her soul. Cornelia, where are your manners? Give Father Connolly a chair. She had her secret comfortable understanding with a few favorite saints who cleared a straight road to God for her. All as surely signed and sealed as the papers for the new Forty Acres. Forever . . . heirs and assigns forever. Since the day the wedding cake was not cut, but thrown out and wasted. The whole bottom dropped out of the world, and there she was blind and sweating with nothing under her feet and the walls falling away. His hand had caught her under the breast, she had not fallen, there was the freshly polished floor with the green rug on it, just as before. He had cursed like a sailor's parrot and said, "I'll kill him for you." Don't lay a hand on him, for my sake leave something to God. "Now, Ellen, you must believe what I tell you. . . ."

So there was nothing, nothing to worry about any more, except sometimes in the night one of the children screamed in a nightmare, and they both hustled out shaking and hunting for the matches and calling, "There, wait a minute, here we are!" John, get the doctor now, Hapsy's time has come. But there was Hapsy standing by the bed in a white cap. "Cornelia, tell Hapsy to take off her cap. I can't see her plain."

Her eyes opened very wide and the room stood out like a picture she had seen somewhere. Dark colors with the shadows rising towards the ceiling in long angles. The tall black dresser gleamed with nothing on it but John's picture, enlarged from a little one, with John's eyes very black when they should have been blue. You never saw him, so how do you know how he looked? But the man insisted the copy was perfect, it was very rich and handsome. For a picture, yes, but it's not my husband. The table by the bed had a linen cover and a candle and a crucifix. The light was blue from Cornelia's silk lampshades. No sort of light at all, just frippery. You had to live forty years with kerosene lamps to appreciate honest electricity. She felt very strong and she saw Doctor Harry with a rosy nimbus around him.

"You look like a saint, Doctor Harry, and I vow that's as near as you'll ever come to it."

"She's saying something."

"I heard you, Cornelia. What's all this carrying-on?"

"Father Connolly's saying—"

Cornelia's voice staggered and bumped like a cart in a bad road. It rounded corners and turned back again and arrived nowhere. Granny stepped up in the cart very lightly and reached for the reins, but a man sat beside her and she knew him by his hands, driving the cart. She did not look in his face, for she knew without seeing, but looked instead down the road where the trees leaned over and bowed to each other and a thousand birds were singing a Mass. She felt like singing too, but she put her hand in the bosom of her dress and pulled out a rosary, and Father Connolly murmured Latin in a very solemn voice and tickled her feet. My God, will you stop that nonsense? I'm a married woman. What if he did run away and leave me to face the priest by myself? I found another a whole world better. I wouldn't have exchanged my husband for anybody except St. Michael himself, and you may tell him that for me with a thank you in the bargain.

Light flashed on her closed eyelids, and a deep roaring shook her. Cornelia, is that lightning? I hear thunder. There's going to be a storm. Close all the windows. Call the children in. . . . "Mother, here we are, all of us." "Is that you, Hapsy?" "Oh, no, I'm Lydia. We drove as fast as we could." Their faces drifted above her, drifted away. The rosary fell out of her hands and Lydia put it back. Jimmy tried to help, their hands fumbled together, and Granny closed two fingers around Jimmy's thumb. Beads wouldn't do, it must be something alive. She was so amazed her thoughts ran round and round. So, my dear Lord, this is my death and I wasn't even thinking about it. My children have come to see me die. But I can't, it's not time. Oh, I always hated surprises. I wanted to give Cornelia the amethyst set —Cornelia, you're to have the amethyst set, but Hapsy's to wear it when she wants, and, Doctor Harry, do shut up. Nobody sent for you. Oh, my dear Lord, do wait a minute. I meant to do something about the Forty Acres, Jimmy doesn't need it and Lydia will later on, with that worthless husband of hers. I meant to finish the altar cloth and send six bottles of wine to Sister Borgia for her dyspepsia. I want to send six bottles of wine to Sister Borgia, Father Connolly, now don't let me forget.

Cornelia's voice made short turns and tilted over and crashed. "Oh, Mother, oh, Mother, oh, Mother. . . ."

"I'm not going, Cornelia. I'm taken by surprise. I can't go."

You'll see Hapsy again. What about her? "I thought you'd never come." Granny made a long journey outward, looking for Hapsy. What if I don't find her? What then? Her heart sank down and down, there was no bottom to death, she couldn't come to the end of it. The blue light from Cornelia's lampshade drew into a tiny point in the center of her brain, it flickered and winked like an eye, quietly it fluttered and dwindled. Granny lay curled down within herself, amazed and watchful, staring at the point of light that was herself; her body was now only a deeper mass of shadow in an endless darkness and this darkness would curl around the light and swallow it up. God, give a sign!

For the second time there was no sign. Again no bridegroom and the priest in the house. She could not remember any other sorrow because this grief wiped them all away. Oh, no, there's nothing more cruel than this—I'll never forgive it. She stretched herself with a deep breath and blew out the light.

Insight

1. *Stream of consciousness.* Porter frequently employs a technique called stream of consciousness. In this technique ideas are revealed as they occur in the mind without any apparent order and often mixing past and present. Why is use of this technique particularly effective in this story? What thoughts run through Granny's mind on this last day of her life? What do these thoughts reveal about her life and character?

2. "There's nothing more cruel than this," Granny cries to herself at the end of the story. What is the grief she is referring to, and why is it worse than any other?

THE dEMON lOVER

Elizabeth Bowen

Towards the end of her day in London Mrs. Drover went round to her shut-up house to look for several things she wanted to take away. Some belonged to herself, some to her family, who were by now used to their country life. It was late August; it had been a steamy, showery day: at the moment the trees down the pavement glittered in an escape of humid yellow afternoon sun. Against the next batch of clouds, already piling up ink-dark, broken chimneys and parapets stood out. In her once familiar street, as in any unused channel, an unfamiliar queerness had silted up; a cat wove itself in and out of railings, but no human eye watched Mrs. Drover's return. Shifting some parcels under her arm, she slowly forced round her latchkey in an unwilling lock, then gave the door, which had warped, a push with her knee. Dead air came out to meet her as she went in.

The staircase window having been boarded up, no light came down into the hall. But one door, she could just see, stood ajar, so she went quickly through into the room and unshuttered the big window in there. Now the prosaic woman, looking about her, was more perplexed than she knew by everything that she saw, by traces of her long former habit of life—the yellow smoke-stain up the white marble mantelpiece, the ring left by a vase on the top of the escritoire; the bruise in the wallpaper where, on the door being thrown open widely, the china handle had always hit the wall. The piano, having gone away to be stored, had left what looked like claw-marks on its part of the parquet. Though not much dust had seeped in, each object wore a film of another kind; and, the only ventilation being the chimney, the whole drawing room smelled of the cold hearth. Mrs. Drover put down her parcels on the escritoire and left the room to proceed upstairs; the things she wanted were in the bedroom chest.

She had been anxious to see how the house was—the part-time caretaker she shared with some neighbors was away this week on his holiday, known to be not yet back. At the best of times he did not look in often, and she was never sure that she trusted him. There were some cracks in the structure, left by the last bombing, on which she was anxious to keep an eye. Not that one could do anything—

A shaft of refracted daylight now lay across the hall. She stopped dead and stared at the hall table—on this lay a letter addressed to her.

She thought first—then the caretaker *must* be back. All the same, who, seeing the house shuttered, would have dropped a letter in at the box? It was not a circular, it was not a bill. And the post office redirected, to the address in the country, everything for her that came through the post. The caretaker (even if he *were* back) did not know she was due in London today—her call here had been planned to be a surprise—so his negligence in the matter of this letter, leaving it to wait in the dusk and dust, annoyed her. Annoyed, she picked up the letter, which bore no stamp. But it cannot be important, or they would know. . . . She took the letter rapidly upstairs with her, without a stop to look at the writing till she reached what had been her bedroom, where she let in light. The room looked over the garden and other gardens: the sun had gone in; as the clouds sharpened and lowered, the trees and rank lawns seemed already to smoke with dark. Her reluctance to look again at the letter came from the fact that she felt intruded upon—and by someone contemptuous of her ways. However, in the tenseness preceding the fall of rain she read it: it was a few lines.

Dear Kathleen,
You will not have forgotten that today is our anniversary, and the day we said. The years have gone by at once slowly and fast. In view of the fact that nothing has changed, I shall rely upon you to keep your promise. I was sorry to see you leave London, but was satisfied that you would be back in time. You may expect me, therefore, at the hour arranged.

Until then . . .

K.

Mrs. Drover looked for the date: it was today's. She dropped the letter on to the bedsprings, then picked it up to see the writing again—her lips, beneath the remains of lipstick, beginning to go white. She felt so much the change in her own face that she went to the mirror, polished a clear patch in it and looked at once urgently and stealthily in. She was confronted by a woman of forty-four, with eyes staring out under a hat brim that had been rather carelessly pulled down. She had not put on any more powder since she left the shop where she ate her solitary tea. The pearls her husband had given her on their marriage hung loose round her now rather thinner throat, slipping into the V of the pink wool jumper her sister knitted last autumn as they sat round the fire. Mrs. Drover's most normal expression was one of controlled worry, but of assent. Since the birth of the third of her little boys, attended by a quite serious illness, she had had an intermittent muscular flicker to the left of her mouth, but in spite of this she could always sustain a manner that was at once energetic and calm.

Turning from her own face as precipitately as she had gone to meet it, she went to the chest where the things were, unlocked it, threw up the lid and knelt to search. But as the rain began to come crashing down she could not keep from looking over her shoulder at the stripped bed on which the letter lay. Behind the blanket of rain the clock of the church that still stood struck six—with rapidly heightening apprehension she counted each of the slow strokes. "The hour arranged. . . . My God," she said, "*what* hour? How should I . . . ? After twenty-five years . . ."

The young girl talking to the soldier in the garden had not ever completely seen his face. It was dark; they were saying goodbye under a tree. Now and then—for it felt, from not seeing him at this intense moment, as though she had never seen him at all—she verified his presence for these few moments longer by putting out a hand, which he each time pressed, without very much kindness, and painfully, on to one of the breast buttons of his uniform. That cut of the button on the palm of her hand was, principally, what she was to carry away. This was so near the end of a leave from France that she could only wish him already gone. It was August 1916. Being not kissed, being drawn away from and looked at intimidated Kathleen till she imagined spectral glitters in the place of his eyes. Turning away and looking back up the lawn she saw, through branches of trees, the drawing room window alight: she caught a breath for the moment when she could go running back there into the safe arms of her mother and sister, and cry: "What shall I do, what shall I do? He has gone."

Hearing her catch her breath, her fiancé said, without feeling: "Cold?"

"You're going away such a long way."

"Not so far as you think."

"I don't understand?"

"You don't have to," he said. "You will. You know what we said."

"But that was—suppose you—I mean, suppose."

"I shall be with you," he said, "sooner or later. You won't forget that. You need do nothing but wait."

Only a little more than a minute later she was free to run up the silent lawn. Looking in through the window at her mother and sister, who did not for the moment perceive her, she already felt that unnatural promise drive down between her and the rest of all human kind. No other way of having given herself could have made her feel so apart, lost and forsworn. She could not have plighted a more sinister troth.

Kathleen behaved well when, some months later, her fiancé was reported missing, presumed killed. Her family not only supported her but were able to praise her courage without stint because they could not regret, as a husband for her, the man they knew almost nothing about. They hoped she would, in a year or two, console herself—and had it been only a question of consolation things might have gone much straighter ahead. But her trouble, behind just a little grief, was a complete dislocation from everything. She did not reject other lovers, for these failed to appear: for years she failed to attract men— and with the approach of her thirties she became natural enough to share her family's anxiousness on this score. She began to put herself out, to wonder; and at thirty-two she was very greatly relieved to find herself being courted by William Drover. She married him, and the two of them settled down in this quiet, arboreal part of Kensington: in this house the years piled up, her children were born and they all lived till they were driven out by the bombs of the next war. Her movements as Mrs. Drover were circumscribed, and she dismissed any idea that they were still watched.

As things were—dead or living the letter-writer sent her only a threat. Unable, for some minutes, to go on kneeling with her back exposed to the empty room, Mrs. Drover rose from the chest to sit on an upright chair whose back was firmly against the wall. The desuetude of her former bedroom, her married London home's whole air of being a cracked cup from which memory, with its reassuring power, had either evaporated or leaked away, made a crisis—and at just this crisis the letter-writer had, knowledgeably, struck. The hollowness of the house this evening cancelled years on years of voices, habits and steps. Through the shut windows she only heard rain fall on the roofs around. To rally herself, she said she was in a mood— and, for two or three seconds shutting her eyes, told herself that she had imagined the letter. But she opened them—there it lay on the bed.

On the supernatural side of the letter's entrance she was not permitting her mind to dwell. Who, in London, knew she meant to call at the house today? Evidently, however, this had been known. The caretaker, *had* he come back, had had no cause to expect her: he would have taken the letter in his pocket, to forward it, at his own time, through the post. There was no other sign that the caretaker had been in—but, if not? Letters dropped in at doors of deserted houses do not fly or walk to tables in halls. They do not sit on the dust of empty tables with the air of certainty that they will be found. There is needed some human hand—but nobody but the caretaker had a key. Under circumstances she did not care to consider, a house can be entered without a key. It was possible that she was not alone now. She might be being waited for, downstairs. Waited for—until when? Until "the hour arranged." At least that was not six o'clock: six had struck.

She rose from the chair and went over and locked the door.

The thing was, to get out. To fly? No, not that: she had to catch her train. As a woman whose utter dependability was the keystone of her family life she was not willing to return to the country, to her husband, her little boys and her sister, without the objects she had come up to fetch. Resuming work at the chest she set about making up a number of parcels in a rapid, fumbling-decisive way. These, with her shopping parcels, would be too much to carry; these meant a taxi—at the thought of the taxi her heart went up and her normal breathing resumed. I will ring up the taxi now; the taxi cannot come too soon: I shall hear the taxi out there running its engine, till I walk calmly down to it through the hall. I'll ring up— But no: the telephone is cut off. . . . She tugged at a knot she had tied wrong.

The idea of flight . . . He was never kind to me, not really. I don't remember him kind at all. Mother said he never considered me. He was set on me, that was what it was—not love. Not love, not meaning a person well. What did he do, to make me promise like that? I can't remember.—But she found that she could.

She remembered with such dreadful acuteness that the twenty-five years since then dissolved like smoke and she instinctively looked for the weal left by the button on the palm of her hand. She remembered not only all that he said and did but the complete suspension of *her* existence during that August week. I was not myself—they all told me so at the time. She remembered—but with one white burning blank as where acid has dropped on a photograph: *under no conditions* could she remember his face.

So, wherever he may be waiting, I shall not know him. You have no time to run from a face you do not expect.

The thing was to get to the taxi before any clock struck what could be the hour. She would slip down the street and round the side of the square to where the square gave on the main road. She would return in the taxi, safe, to her own door, and bring the solid driver into the house with her to pick up the parcels from room to room. The idea of the taxi driver made her decisive, bold: she unlocked her door, went to the top of the staircase and listened down.

She heard nothing—but while she was hearing nothing the *passé* air of the staircase was disturbed by a draught that travelled up to her face. It emanated from the basement: down there a door or window was being opened by someone who chose this moment to leave the house.

The rain had stopped; the pavements steamily shone as Mrs. Drover let herself out by inches from her own front door into the empty street. The unoccupied houses opposite continued to meet her look with their damaged stare. Making towards the thoroughfare and the taxi, she tried not to keep looking behind. Indeed, the silence was so intense—one of those creeks of London silence exaggerated this summer by the damage of war—that no tread could have gained on hers unheard. Where her street debouched on the square where people went on living she grew conscious of and checked her unnatural pace. Across the open end of the square two buses impassively passed each other; women, a perambulator, cyclists, a man wheeling a barrow signalized, once again, the ordinary flow of life. At the square's most populous corner should be—and was—the short taxi rank. This evening, only one taxi—but this, although it presented its blank rump, appeared already to be alertly waiting for her. Indeed, without looking round the driver started his engine as she panted up from behind and put her hand on the door. As she did so, the clock struck seven. The taxi faced the main road: to make the trip back to her house it would have to turn—she had settled back on the seat and the taxi *had* turned before she, surprised by its knowing movement, recollected that she had not "said where." She leaned forward to scratch at the glass panel that divided the driver's head from her own.

The driver braked to what was almost a stop, turned round and slid the glass panel back: the jolt of this flung Mrs. Drover forward till her face was almost into the glass. Through the aperture driver and passenger, not six inches between them, remained for an eternity eye to eye. Mrs. Drover's mouth hung open for some seconds before she could issue her first scream. After that she continued to scream freely and to beat with her gloved hands on the glass all round as the taxi, accelerating without mercy, made off with her into the hinterland of deserted streets.

Insight
1. *Setting.* A story's setting is its background of time and place. It may influence the action of a character; it may create an atmosphere which forces the character to react in a specific manner. What is the setting in this story? How important is the setting to the events of the story?
2. Although the action of the story is confined to a few brief hours in Mrs. Drover's life, much about her past is revealed. What are some of the important details about her past? Which of these details have contributed to her present psychological condition? How would you characterize her present state of mind?

death of a
traveling salesman

Eudora Welty

heat of sun
makes him angry

drumming up
business

R. J. Bowman, who for fourteen years had traveled for a shoe company through Mississippi, drove his Ford along a rutted dirt path. It was a long day! The time did not seem to clear the noon hurdle and settle into soft afternoon. The sun, keeping its strength here even in winter, stayed at the top of the sky, and every time Bowman stuck his head out of the dusty car to stare up the road, it seemed to reach a long arm down and push against the top of his head, right through his hat—like the practical joke of an old drummer, long on the road. It made him feel all the more angry and helpless. He was feverish, and he was not quite sure of the way.

This was his first day back on the road after a long siege of influenza. He had had very high fever, and dreams, and had become weakened and pale, enough to tell the difference in the mirror, and he could not think clearly. . . . All afternoon, in the midst of his anger, and for no reason, he had thought of his dead grandmother. She had been a comfortable soul. Once more Bowman wished he could fall into the big feather bed that had been in her room. . . . Then he forgot her again.

This desolate hill country! And he seemed to be going the wrong way—it was as if he were going back, far back. There was not a house in sight. . . . There was no use wishing he were back in bed, though. By paying the hotel doctor his bill he had proved his recovery. He had not even been sorry when the pretty trained nurse said goodbye. He did not like illness, he distrusted it, as he distrusted the road without signposts. It angered him. He had given the nurse a really expensive bracelet, just because she was packing up her bag and leaving.

But now—what if in fourteen years on the road he had never been ill before and never had an accident? His record was broken, and he had even begun almost to question it. . . . He had gradually put up at better hotels, in the bigger towns, but weren't they all, eternally, stuffy in summer and drafty in winter? Women? He could only remember little rooms within little rooms, like a nest of Chinese paper boxes, and if he thought of one woman he saw the worn loneliness that the furniture of that room seemed built of. And he himself—he was a man who always wore rather wide-brimmed black hats, and in the wavy hotel mirrors had looked something like a bullfighter, as he paused for that inevitable instant on the landing, walking downstairs to supper.... He leaned out of the car again, and once more the sun pushed at his head.

Bowman had wanted to reach Beulah by dark, to go to bed and sleep off his fatigue. As he remembered, Beulah was fifty miles away from the last town, on a graveled road. This was only a cow trail. How had he ever come to such a place? One hand wiped the sweat from his face, and he drove on.

He had made the Beulah trip before. But he had never seen this hill or this petering-out path before—or that cloud, he thought shyly, looking up and then down quickly—any more than he had seen this day before. Why did he not admit he was simply lost and had been for miles? . . . He was not in the habit of asking the way of strangers, and these people never knew where the very roads they lived on went to; but then he had not even been close enough to anyone to call out. People standing in the fields now and then, or on top of the haystacks, had been too far away, looking like leaning sticks or weeds, turning a little at the solitary rattle of his car across their countryside, watching the pale sobered winter dust where it chunked out behind like big squashes down the road. The stares of these distant people had followed him solidly like a wall, impenetrable, behind which they turned back after he had passed.

The cloud floated there to one side like the bolster on his grandmother's bed. It went over a cabin on the edge of a hill, where two bare chinaberry trees clutched at the sky. He drove through a heap of dead oak leaves, his wheels stirring their weightless sides to make a silvery melancholy whistle as the car passed through their bed. No car had been along this way ahead of him. Then he saw that he was on the edge of a ravine that fell away, a red erosion, and that this was indeed the road's end.

He pulled the brake. But it did not hold, though he put all his strength into it. The car, tipped toward the edge, rolled a little. Without doubt, it was going over the bank.

He got out quietly, as though some mischief had been done him and he had his dignity to remember. He lifted his bag and sample case out, set them down, and stood back and watched the car roll over the edge. He heard something—not the crash he was listening for, but a slow, unuproarious crackle. Rather distastefully he went to look over, and he saw that his car had fallen into a tangle of immense grapevines as thick as his arm, which caught it and held it, rocked it like a grotesque child in a dark cradle, and then, as he watched, concerned somehow that he was not still inside it, released it gently to the ground.

He sighed.

Where am I? he wondered with a shock. Why didn't I do something? All his anger seemed to have drifted away from him. There

[handwritten margin notes: hallucin- atory mind floating freely]

[handwritten margin notes: even car has cradle]

[handwritten margin note: philosophical]

was the house back on the hill. He took a bag in each hand and with almost childlike willingness went toward it. But his breathing came with difficulty, and he had to stop to rest.

It was a shotgun house, two rooms and an open passage between, perched on the hill. The whole cabin slanted a little under the heavy heaped-up vine that covered the roof, light and green, as though forgotten from summer. A woman stood in the passage.

He stopped still. Then all of a sudden his heart began to behave strangely. Like a rocket set off, it began to leap and expand into uneven patterns of beats which showered into his brain, and he could not think. But in scattering and falling it made no noise. It shot up with great power, almost elation, and fell gently, like acrobats into nets. It began to pound profoundly, then waited irresponsibly, hitting in some sort of inward mockery first at his ribs, then against his eyes, then under his shoulder blades, and against the roof of his mouth when he tried to say, "Good afternoon, madam." But he could not hear his heart—it was as quiet as ashes falling. This was rather comforting; still, it was shocking to Bowman to feel his heart beating at all.

Stock-still in his confusion, he dropped his bags, which seemed to drift in slow bulks gracefully through the air and to cushion themselves on the gray prostrate grass near the doorstep.

As for the woman standing there, he saw at once that she was old. Since she could not possibly hear his heart, he ignored the pounding and now looked at her carefully, and yet in his distraction dreamily, with his mouth open.

She had been cleaning the lamp, and held it, half blackened, half clear, in front of her. He saw her with the dark passage behind her. She was a big woman with a weather-beaten but unwrinkled face; her lips were held tightly together, and her eyes looked with a curious dulled brightness into his. He looked at her shoes, which were like bundles. If it were summer she would be barefoot. . . . Bowman, who automatically judged a woman's age on sight, set her age at fifty. She wore a formless garment of some gray coarse material, rough-dried from a washing, from which her arms appeared pink and unexpectedly round. When she never said a word, and sustained her quiet pose of holding the lamp, he was convinced of the strength in her body.

"Good afternoon, madam," he said.

She stared on, whether at him or at the air around him he could not tell, but after a moment she lowered her eyes to show that she would listen to whatever he had to say.

"I wonder if you would be interested—" He tried once more. "An accident—my car . . ."

Her voice emerged low and remote, like a sound across a lake. "Sonny he ain't here."

"Sonny?"

"Sonny ain't here now."

Her son—a fellow able to bring my car up, he decided in blurred relief. He pointed down the hill. "My car's in the bottom of the ditch. I'll need help."

"Sonny ain't here, but he'll be here."

She was becoming clearer to him and her voice stronger, and Bowman saw that she was stupid.

He was hardly surprised at the deepening postponement and tedium of his journey. He took a breath, and heard his voice speaking over the silent blows of his heart. "I was sick. I am not strong yet. . . . May I come in?"

He stooped and laid his big black hat over the handle on his bag. It was a humble motion, almost a bow, that instantly struck him as absurd and betraying of all his weakness. He looked up at the woman, the wind blowing his hair. He might have continued for a long time in this unfamiliar attitude; he had never been a patient man, but when he was sick he had learned to sink submissively into the pillows, to wait for his medicine. He waited on the woman.

Then she, looking at him with blue eyes, turned and held open the door, and after a moment Bowman, as if convinced in his action, stood erect and followed her in.

Inside, the darkness of the house touched him like a professional hand, the doctor's. The woman set the half-cleaned lamp on a table in the center of the room and pointed, also like a professional person, a guide, to a chair with a yellow cowhide seat. She herself crouched on the hearth, drawing her knees up under the shapeless dress.

At first he felt hopefully secure. His heart was quieter. The room was enclosed in the gloom of yellow pine boards. He could see the other room, with the foot of an iron bed showing, across the passage. The bed had been made up with a red-and-yellow pieced quilt that looked like a map or a picture, a little like his grandmother's girlhood painting of Rome burning.

He had ached for coolness, but in this room it was cold. He stared at the hearth with dead coals lying on it and iron pots in the corners. The hearth and smoked chimney were of the stone he had seen ribbing the hills, mostly slate. Why is there no fire? he wondered.

And it was so still. The silence of the fields seemed to enter and move familiarly through the house. The wind used the open hall. He felt that he was in a mysterious, quiet, cool danger. It was necessary to do what? . . . To talk.

"I have a nice line of women's low-priced shoes . . ." he said.

30

But the woman answered, "Sonny 'll be here. He's strong. Sonny 'll move your car."

"Where is he now?"

"Farms for Mr. Redmond."

Mr. Redmond. Mr. Redmond. That was someone he would never have to encounter, and he was glad. Somehow the name did not appeal to him. . . . In a flare of touchiness and anxiety, Bowman wished to avoid even mention of unknown men and their unknown farms.

"Do you two live here alone?" He was surprised to hear his old voice, chatty, confidential, inflected for selling shoes, asking a question like that—a thing he did not even want to know.

"Yes. We are alone." *sense of isolation / wrong impression*

alone together

He was surprised at the way she answered. She had taken a long time to say that. She had nodded her head in a deep way too. Had she wished to affect him with some sort of premonition? he wondered unhappily. Or was it only that she would not help him, after all, by talking with him? For he was not strong enough to receive the impact of unfamiliar things without a little talk to break their fall. He had lived a month in which nothing had happened except in his head and his body—an almost inaudible life of heartbeats and dreams that came back, a life of fever and privacy, a delicate life which had left him weak to the point of—what? Of begging. The pulse in his palm leapt like a trout in a brook.

human, not commercial relationship surprise / unknown

He wondered over and over why the woman did not go ahead with cleaning the lamp. What prompted her to stay there across the room, silently bestowing her presence upon him? He saw that with her it was not a time for doing little tasks. Her face was grave; she was feeling how right she was. Perhaps it was only politeness. In docility he held his eyes stiffly wide: they fixed themselves on the woman's clasped hands as though she held the cord they were strung on.

Then, "Sonny's coming," she said.

He himself had not heard anything, but there came a man passing the window and then plunging in at the door, with two hounds beside him. Sonny was a big enough man, with his belt slung low about his hips. He looked at least thirty. He had a hot, red face that was yet full of silence. He wore muddy blue pants and an old military coat stained and patched. World War? Bowman wondered. Great God, it was a Confederate coat. On the back of his light hair he had a wide filthy black hat which seemed to insult Bowman's own. He pushed down the dogs from his chest. He was strong, with dignity and heaviness in his way of moving. . . . There was the resemblance to his mother.

They stood side by side. . . . He must account again for his presence here.

"Sonny, this man, he had his car to run off over the prec'pice an' wants to know if you will git it out for him," the woman said after a few minutes.

Bowman could not even state his case.

Sonny's eyes lay upon him.

He knew he should offer explanations and show money—at least appear either penitent or authoritative. But all he could do was to shrug slightly.

Sonny brushed by him going to the window, followed by the eager dogs, and looked out. There was effort even in the way he was looking, as if he could throw his sight out like a rope. Without turning Bowman felt that his own eyes could have seen nothing: it was too far.

"Got me a mule out there an' got me a block an' tackle," said Sonny meaningfully. "I *could* catch me my mule an' git me my ropes, an' before long I'd git your car out the ravine."

He looked completely around the room, as if in meditation, his eyes roving in their own distance. Then he pressed his lips firmly and yet shyly together, and with the dogs ahead of him this time, he lowered his head and strode out. The hard earth sounded, cupping to his powerful way of walking—almost a stagger.

Mischievously, at the suggestion of those sounds, Bowman's heart leapt again. It seemed to walk about inside him.

"Sonny's goin' to do it," the woman said. She said it again, singing it almost, like a song. She was sitting in her place by the hearth.

Without looking out, he heard some shouts and the dogs barking and the pounding of hoofs in short runs on the hill. In a few minutes Sonny passed under the window with a rope, and there was a brown mule with quivering, shining, purple-looking ears. The mule actually looked in the window. Under its eyelashes it turned target-like eyes into his. Bowman averted his head and saw the woman looking serenely back at the mule, with only satisfaction in her face.

She sang a little more, under her breath. It occurred to him, and it seemed quite marvelous, that she was not really talking to him, but rather following the thing that came about with words that were unconscious and part of her looking.

So he said nothing, and this time when he did not reply he felt a curious and strong emotion, not fear, rise up in him.

This time, when his heart leapt, something—his soul—seemed to leap too, like a little colt invited out of a pen. He stared at the woman while the frantic nimbleness of his feeling made his head sway. He could not move; there was nothing he could do, unless perhaps he might embrace this woman who sat there growing old and shapeless before him.

But he wanted to leap up, to say to her, I have been sick and I found out then, only then, how lonely I am. Is it too late? My heart

Minds others can hear his heart

puts up a struggle inside me, and you may have heard it, protesting against emptiness. . . . It should be full, he would rush on to tell her, thinking of his heart now as a deep lake, it should be holding love like other hearts. It should be flooded with love. There would be a warm spring day . . . Come and stand in my heart, whoever you are, and a whole river would cover your feet and rise higher and take your knees in whirlpools, and draw you down to itself, your whole body, your heart too.

But he moved a trembling hand across his eyes, and looked at the placid crouching woman across the room. She was still as a statue. He felt ashamed and exhausted by the thought that he might, in one more moment, have tried by simple words and embraces to communicate some strange thing—something which seemed always to have just escaped him . . . *love*

pulls back to reality & next day

Sunlight touched the furthest pot on the hearth. It was late afternoon. This time tomorrow he would be somewhere on a good graveled road, driving his car past things that happened to people, quicker than their happening. Seeing ahead to the next day, he was glad, and knew that this was no time to embrace an old woman. He could feel in his pounding temples the readying of his blood for motion and for hurrying away.

"Sonny's hitched up your car by now," said the woman. "He'll git it out the ravine right shortly."

"Fine!" he cried with his customary enthusiasm.

hospitality

Yet it seemed a long time that they waited. It began to get dark. Bowman was cramped in his chair. Any man should know enough to get up and walk around while he waited. There was something like guilt in such stillness and silence.

But instead of getting up, he listened. . . . His breathing restrained, his eyes powerless in the growing dark, he listened uneasily for a warming sound, forgetting in wariness what it would be. Before long he heard something—soft, continuous, insinuating.

"What's that noise?" he asked, his voice jumping into the dark. Then wildly he was afraid it would be his heart beating so plainly in the quiet room, and she would tell him so.

"You might hear the stream," she said grudgingly.

Her voice was closer. She was standing by the table. He wondered why she did not light the lamp. She stood there in the dark and did not light it.

Bowman would never speak to her now, for the time was past. I'll sleep in the dark, he thought, in his bewilderment pitying himself.

Heavily she moved on to the window. Her arm, vaguely white, rose straight from her full side and she pointed out into the darkness.

"That white speck's Sonny," she said, talking to herself.

He turned unwillingly and peered over her shoulder; he hesitated to rise and stand beside her. His eyes searched the dusky air. The white speck floated smoothly toward her finger, like a leaf on a river, growing whiter in the dark. It was as if she had shown him something secret, part of her life, but had offered no explanation. He looked away. He was moved almost to tears, feeling for no reason that she had made a silent declaration equivalent to his own. His hand waited upon his chest.

Then a step shook the house, and Sonny was in the room. Bowman felt how the woman left him there and went to the other man's side.

"I done got your car out, mister," said Sonny's voice in the dark. "She's settin' a-waitin' in the road, turned to go back where she come from."

"Fine!" said Bowman, projecting his own voice to loudness. "I'm surely much obliged—I could never have done it myself—I was sick. . . ."

"I could do it easy," said Sonny.

Bowman could feel them both waiting in the dark, and he could hear the dogs panting out in the yard, waiting to bark when he should go. He felt strangely helpless and resentful. Now that he could go, he longed to stay. From what was he being deprived? His chest was rudely shaken by the violence of his heart. These people cherished something here that he could not see, they withheld some ancient promise of food and warmth and light. Between them they had a conspiracy. He thought of the way she had moved away from him and gone to Sonny, she had flowed toward him. He was shaking with cold, he was tired, and it was not fair. Humbly and yet angrily he stuck his hand into his pocket.

"Of course I'm going to pay you for everything—"

"We don't take money for such," said Sonny's voice belligerently.

"I want to pay. But do something more . . . Let me stay—tonight. . . ." He took another step toward them. If only they could see him, they would know his sincerity, his real need! His voice went on, "I'm not very strong yet, I'm not able to walk far, even back to my car, maybe, I don't know—I don't know exactly where I am—"

He stopped. He felt as if he might burst into tears. What would they think of him!

Sonny came over and put his hands on him. Bowman felt them pass (they were professional too) across his chest, over his hips. He could feel Sonny's eyes upon him in the dark.

"You ain't no revenuer come sneakin' here, mister, ain't got no gun?"

To this end of nowhere! And yet *he* had come. He made a grave answer. "No."

"You can stay."

"Sonny," said the woman, "you'll have to borry some fire."

"I'll go git it from Redmond's," said Sonny.

"What?" Bowman strained to hear their words to each other.

"Our fire, it's out, and Sonny's got to borry some, because it's dark an' cold," she said.

"But matches—I have matches—"

"We don't have no need for 'em," she said proudly. "Sonny's goin' after his own fire."

"I'm goin' to Redmond's," said Sonny with an air of importance, and he went out.

After they had waited a while, Bowman looked out the window and saw a light moving over the hill. It spread itself out like a little fan. It zigzagged along the field, darting and swift, not like Sonny at all. . . . Soon enough, Sonny staggered in, holding a burning stick behind him in tongs, fire flowing in his wake, blazing light into the corners of the room.

"We'll make a fire now," the woman said, taking the brand.

When that was done she lit the lamp. It showed its dark and light. The whole room turned golden-yellow like some sort of flower, and the walls smelled of it and seemed to tremble with the quiet rushing of the fire and the waving of the burning lampwick in its funnel of light.

The woman moved among the iron pots. With the tongs she dropped hot coals on top of the iron lids. They made a set of soft vibrations, like the sound of a bell far away.

She looked up and over at Bowman, but he could not answer. He was trembling. . . .

"Have a drink, mister?" Sonny asked. He had brought in a chair from the other room and sat astride it with his folded arms across the back. Now we are all visible to one another, Bowman thought, and cried, "Yes sir, you bet, thanks!"

"Come after me and do just what I do," said Sonny.

It was another excursion into the dark. They went through the hall, out to the back of the house, past a shed and a hooded well. They came to a wilderness of thicket.

"Down on your knees," said Sonny.

"What?" Sweat broke out on his forehead.

He understood when Sonny began to crawl through a sort of tunnel that the bushes made over the ground. He followed, startled in spite of himself when a twig or a thorn touched him gently without making a sound, clinging to him and finally letting him go.

Sonny stopped crawling and, crouched on his knees, began to dig with both his hands into the dirt. Bowman shyly struck matches and made a light. In a few minutes Sonny pulled up a jug. He poured out some of the whisky into a bottle from his coat pocket, and buried the jug again. "You never know who's liable to knock at your door," he said, and laughed. "Start back," he said, almost formally. "Ain't no need for us to drink outdoors, like hogs."

At the table by the fire, sitting opposite each other in their chairs, Sonny and Bowman took drinks out of the bottle, passing it across. The dogs slept; one of them was having a dream.

"This is good," said Bowman. "This is what I needed." It was just as though he were drinking the fire off the hearth.

"He makes it," said the woman with quiet pride.

She was pushing the coals off the pots, and the smells of corn bread and coffee circled the room. She set everything on the table before the men, with a bone-handled knife stuck into one of the potatoes, splitting out its golden fiber. Then she stood for a minute looking at them, tall and full above them where they sat. She leaned a little toward them.

"You all can eat now," she said, and suddenly smiled.

Bowman had just happened to be looking at her. He set his cup back on the table in unbelieving protest. A pain pressed at his eyes. He saw that she was not an old woman. She was young, still young. He could think of no number of years for her. She was the same age as Sonny, and she belonged to him. She stood with the deep dark corner of the room behind her, the shifting yellow light scattering over her head and her gray formless dress, trembling over her tall body when it bent over them in its sudden communication. She was young. Her teeth were shining and her eyes glowed. She turned and walked slowly and heavily out of the room, and he heard her sit down on the cot and then lie down. The pattern on the quilt moved.

"She's goin' to have a baby," said Sonny, popping a bite into his mouth.

Bowman could not speak. He was shocked with knowing what was really in this house. A marriage, a fruitful marriage. That simple thing. Anyone could have had that.

Somehow he felt unable to be indignant or protest, although some sort of joke had certainly been played upon him. There was nothing remote or mysterious here—only something private. The only secret was the ancient communication between two people. But the memory of the woman's waiting silently by the cold hearth, of the man's stubborn journey a mile away to get fire, and how they finally brought out their food and drink and filled the room proudly with all they had to show, was suddenly too clear and too enormous within him for response. . . .

"You ain't as hungry as you look," said Sonny.

The woman came out of the bedroom as soon as the men had finished, and ate her supper while her husband stared peacefully into the fire.

Then they put the dogs out, with the food that was left.

"I think I'd better sleep here by the fire, on the floor," said Bowman.

He felt that he had been cheated, and that he could afford now to be generous. Ill though he was, he was not going to ask them for their bed. He was through with asking favors in this house, now that he understood what was there.

"Sure, mister."

But he had not known yet how slowly he understood. They had not meant to give him their bed. After a little interval they both rose and looking at him gravely went into the other room.

He lay stretched by the fire until it grew low and dying. He watched every tongue of blaze lick out and vanish. "There will be special reduced prices on all footwear during the month of January," he found himself repeating quietly, and then he lay with his lips tight shut.

How many noises the night had! He heard the stream running, the fire dying, and he was sure now that he heard his heart beating, too, the sound it made under his ribs. He heard breathing, round and deep, of the man and his wife in the room across the passage. And that was all. But emotion swelled patiently within him, and he wished that the child were his.

He must get back to where he had been before. He stood weakly before the red coals and put on his overcoat. It felt too heavy on his shoulders. As he started out he looked and saw that the woman had never got through with cleaning the lamp. On some impulse he put all the money from his billfold under its fluted glass base, almost ostentatiously.

Ashamed, shrugging a little, and then shivering, he took his bags and went out. The cold of the air seemed to lift him bodily. The moon was in the sky.

On the slope he began to run, he could not help it. Just as he reached the road, where his car seemed to sit in the moonlight like a boat, his heart began to give off tremendous explosions like a rifle, bang bang bang.

He sank in fright onto the road, his bags falling about him. He felt as if all this had happened before. He covered his heart with both hands to keep anyone from hearing the noise it made.

But nobody heard it.

Insight

1. At the beginning of the story we learn that this is Bowman's first day back on the road after a long siege of the flu. This illness was his first in fourteen years on the road. How has the illness affected him? What is his physical and mental state when he arrives at the couple's house?

2. For most of the story, Bowman believes that the woman is old and Sonny is her child. What is his emotional reaction to her while he is under that impression? *submisse drawn stupid*

3. The key event in the story is Bowman's shocked discovery that what is really in the house is "a fruitful marriage." Until that discovery Bowman believes that what the two people have is remote and mysterious. "Between them they had a conspiracy ... it was not fair." When he discovers that the woman and Sonny are husband and pregnant wife, he considers that what they have is a simple thing. "Anyone could have had that." Why does this realization overwhelm him and ultimately kill him?

4. *Point of view.* The position from which a story is told is its point of view. Telling a story from the *personal* point of view, the narrator consistently assumes the identity of a particular character in the story. The action is then revealed as seen and felt by that character. Using the *omniscient* point of view, the narrator stands outside the story knowing what each character is doing and thinking at any moment. Determine the point of view in "Death of a Traveling Salesman" and what the advantage is of using that particular point of view. In the last line of the story, there is a shift in point of view. Why is that shift necessary?

by THE NORTH GATE

Joyce Carol Oates

The first time something strange happened to him, the old man, Revere, had felt it descend down upon him like an opaque white mist, something which was still part of his dream and would not let him wake. He had been dreaming of the past again that night, and his dream had been fragmented and confused, like pieces of a jigsaw puzzle spilled across his mind.

He had dreamed first of the winter his wife had died—not of her death, really, but of the house as she lay dying, with her two sisters at her bedside, whispering, and whispering at mealtimes, strangers to him—and he had dreamed of his childhood, oddly, so long ago, and of the schoolteacher in the old schoolhouse down the road. These memories had flattened as if they were no more than photographs, and he saw them from a distance, until all the land he owned, and the road, and the jungle-like expanse of the countryside lay before him. It was not the daylight world but another world, and at first he thought it must be his picture of what the land had been like before anyone had come to it. He sometimes thought about things like that —his grandfather had been one of the first settlers here—and Revere, though he could hardly remember the old man, felt a strange kinship with him. But then he saw in his dream that there were already people there: men working in fields, children dawdling to school, and that all of them were surrounded by the great pressure of the forest and of weeds, acres of weeds, pressing in on them. He remembered thinking clearly: I spent sixty-eight years fighting those weeds—sixty-eight years. Then the discomforting scene changed to a fine white mist, and he felt himself rising through it as if through water; rising, soaring to air, to life, having cheated death at least one more day. He knew before he woke that something strange had happened. Maybe in the house, maybe outside. And, later, as he groped around in the near dark—the sun would not rise for another half hour—he heard the hound whining, and his fingers froze to the cold buttons of his shirt. It was Nell. He could hear her in the shed, whining, scratching against the screen door. When he opened the door the dog crawled across the threshold to him, shivering. "Hey, what's wrong with the hound? Too cold for you?" he laughed, but then his laughter stopped. He stooped and saw what was wrong: The dog's ears had been slit, neatly and viciously, and were now crusted with dried blood. Revere held the dog trembling against him, trembling himself, and looked off to

39

the screen door and beyond to the grass blurred with dew, and to his farm buildings and the outer blur of his land, just waking to light.

That had been the day before. Now Revere stood in the shed by his house and stared in bewilderment at his barn. Somehow the sight of the white smoke rising slowly behind the barn and the memory of the dog's ears, its anxious eyes, came to him at the same time: He saw them together, and he both realized something and doubted everything.

At first he had thought the barn was on fire, but running out as far as the pump he could see that only the grass in the field behind the barn was burning. The wind came from the northwest, from the mountains far to the north, and gently fanned the flames. Sometimes the narrow fire would die down, and white smoke would rise in a puff; but in the next instant the flames would reappear, slyly, slanting up over the top of the grass, bent flat by the wind. Revere grabbed both wooden buckets and filled them at the pump; then he set them down and ran back to the shed, muttering to himself, and got a broom that was propped up in a corner with a fine network of cobwebs about it. Running back again, he thought; I ought to of fired that field myself. But I guess I would of done it when there wasn't all that wind.

Behind the barn the fire inched away from him. The field seemed to be dissolving in white smoke; and, sometimes hidden from him, sometimes piercing to his eyes, toothlike flames flared upward. Far to the right the hay barn tilted, looking as if it were leaning away in fear. Revere stared at it as he stumbled across the field. "It ain't gettin' to you," he muttered. He began beating wildly at the flames with the broom, now and then looking around at the hay barn. It was still safe. He worked for some time. "Least I'll get this field cleaned," he thought, but he could not fool himself with such thoughts for long; as he stood with his heels in the dirt, slamming at the flames, his breath searing his throat, he knew that he could not fool himself. Nothing he might think up later, nothing he could contrive into words, would make up for what he must endure now. The air had turned to shimmering heat, the broom was smoldering, and there was a black burnt spot on his trousers that he thought might be widening; but it was all right. The fire was nearly out now, and he was all right —there was only a patch of it left, small flames licking at the dry tufts of grass near the ground. He poured water on it. The milky smoke curled up. He was turning, the creaking bucket in his hand, when something happened. A great wave of heat struck him, conspiring with the weariness inside his head; something slammed against his back and he lay still.

He woke at about noon. He was lying on his back where he had fallen. He got stiffly to his feet, blinking in confusion and shame, and when he looked at the field he was astonished at how small the fire had been. It had come nowhere near the hay barn or even the fence on the other side. He stared at it almost as if he were disappointed. In that moment the world shimmered about him, hot and opaque and gently mocking. He could not remember falling; he could not think how it had happened. But when he felt the familiar weariness in his back and legs he understood; he understood why he had fallen there and why he had fallen the other time—on the road coming from the store when some children had been running after him and throwing pieces of dried mud, shouting, "Old Revere! Old man Revere!"

He looked around at his land. The summer sky looked hardened by heat, and beneath it the land lay still, save for where the wind prodded it—fluttering of leaves and slow, graceful eclipsing of light by shadow. When he turned back, the hound, Nell, rose from where she had been lying and ran to him. "Yes, it's all right," he said, stroking the dog's head. He looked around as if he thought someone might be watching. "Don't you worry about me. I'm feelin' better now." He went back to the house.

Now he sat on the bench by the shed door and rested in the sunlight, looking at the barn and thinking about the smoke and the dog's ears. Around the corner blackbirds were rioting in the cherry tree, but he did not have the strength to get up to chase them away. Not that it mattered, for he had given up picking the cherries long ago, and besides they were small and often wormy. Thinking of cherries ought to have made him hungry and he felt a vague dutiful notion to go in and eat; but he did not move. Overhead the sun moved past the peak of the house, and the shadow in which he sat extended to his feet. The dog lay before him, sleeping, and sometimes stretched out her legs as if she were pushing something away.

Revere watched the hound and thought about what had happened. He knew that something had happened. And there had to be a reason for it—a reason he must try to discover. He had always had faith in understanding and knowledge, the kind of thinking found in books, though Heaven knew he had never been good at it himself. He had never read a word until he was thirty, and only then when the schoolteacher had taken such pains with him, acting serious all the time, refusing to give in and laugh at a grown man doing a child's lessons. Revere felt a sudden flash of warmth for the man; he had liked him fine. But after so long, after such work, he had forgotten everything; he found one day, when he tried to read again, that it had slipped away from him. He was as ashamed of that now, thirty-eight years later, as he had been on that day. So much time wasted. He used to go over to the schoolhouse after the children left, every afternoon, and the schoolteacher—a young man afraid of the big boys—would talk to him and show him books, books he would like Revere to read later on, books with colored bindings, with gold letters in a glass case at the front of the room. Chalk dust would hang in the silent air. When Revere spoke it would be slowly and politely, not the way he bawled orders at home. He could never understand why the young man did not laugh at him. He wanted to learn; he felt the young man's strange desire to teach him; but when it was time to speak or read—why, Revere would stare at the print and at his big thumbs on either page, and everything would get mixed up. Revere, filled with shame, could not look up at the teacher.

One winter there was trouble: A boy had struck the teacher; he had fallen. Revere never found out how seriously he was hurt, or what happened to him after he left. The schoolhouse was boarded up for a while, then opened again a few years later, for the winter months. But now it was closed again and had been closed for about three years. If children wanted to go to school, they had to go somewhere else, miles away. On his walks Revere often crossed the fields to the school, and there he would sit on the stone steps and think. His feet would sprawl idly before him. The old building was in disrepair, its windows boarded up crazily, and looking at it made Revere feel bad. He would sit and think of the past and of the school on those dark winter afternoons, of the young man's careful, friendly voice. . . . The schoolhouse was the key to one of his secrets. It was there that his saddest failure had occurred; but that failure was not really something he wanted to forget. As if he felt the necessity to remember, he would return again and again to the ruined school and, sitting on the steps, stare dreamily out at the wild grass and the dirt road and the field beyond. Sometimes a farmer would be in the field working a team, and he would come to the fence and lean over, settling himself for a talk. Revere always felt that he must know the man, but at that distance he could not be sure—his eyes were not so good any more— and he had to smile and nod as if he understood everything well.

"You, Revere," the man would say. His face was broad and tanned, and snatches of yellow hair showed beneath his straw hat. "Ain't you got nothin' to do at home? Ain't there somethin' there you should see to?"

Revere supposed this was a joke, so he would laugh an old man's cackle and answer, "It goes on by itself."

"Is that so?" the man would say, spitting toward the ditch. "You sure of that now?"

"Always was like that," Revere would say. He felt both cheerful and discomforted, but he would laugh just the same, as if the man's words struck him as funny.

"You watch out life don't catch up with you," the farmer would say.

42

"I stood it sixty-eight years now," Revere would answer.

Dorothea Lange Collection, The Oakland Museum.

After a while the man's eyes would move away and he would gradually seem to forget Revere, as if the old man did not matter. His hands would be busy pulling absently and viciously at stalks of grass growing by the fence posts, pulling them out and shredding them in his strong fingers, and letting the wind blow the pieces away.

When Revere went home the sight of the farm always discouraged him; he could not believe it had fallen into such disrepair. The barns looked tilted—they did for a fact—and the yard was wild with grass gone to seed, and chickens running loose that did not know him, and pieces of wire and stones and old wheels lying around: chicken fencing, boards, sheets of asbestos, things for which there were no longer any names, all lying around, telling lazily of failure. He would go around them to the house. This at least looked better, though Heaven knew it would never be the same as it had been when his wife was alive and there were the children—the two boys and Nancy, his daughter. It seemed to have changed as if by magic—the shed and the house and the whole look of the land—as soon as he was finally left alone.

Now he stirred on the bench. The dog woke at once. One of her ears had fallen back, showing the pink, scarred inside. As Revere looked at the dog he realized slowly, and with the sense of approaching a revelation of sorts, that he was very tired, deathly tired. Only a few years ago he and the boys used to fire the fields, the one behind the barn and the long one by the creek, and then he had been able to work all morning and afternoon and feel nothing except hunger; maybe a little weariness, but mostly hunger. How the boys worked with him, shouting and running with brooms! They had not even worn shirts. . . . But that must have been more than only a few years ago, he thought. His boys Frank and Will, with the blackened brooms over their shoulders, big strong boys, taller than he already, with their dirty faces slit by grins, cuffing each other when he wasn't looking, arguing even at the supper table with their faces washed and their big feet sticking out from under the table. . . . Was it possible that he was their father, that he had made possible their lives, their strength, their fierce awkward affection for him? Later Frank had got into trouble with that knife he had been so proud of buying. The boy he had fought with had died; people said he just lay down and bled as if there was no end to it, and Frank had run, run off on foot, and Revere had never heard from him again. Sometimes his wife would forget that and talk about Frank as if he were still home, and when she lay in her final sickness she often spoke of him, whining that he hadn't come to kiss her good-by, and her going on such a long journey (though he had never kissed her when he was home; they never did such things). Revere had waited for a few years before he began to think of Frank as dead.

When Will left home he wrote letters back, he wrote five or six of them; and Revere still had them somewhere around the house. In his last letter he said he was traveling somewhere west, to find work with a lot of other men; but they had heard no more from him. Revere remembered Will as the slighter of the two boys, the dark one, the one he had never really gotten to know, and then it was too late. The history of the boy's life with them seemed a mystery, as if a stranger had lived with them, and Revere too stupid to find out much about him. . . . When Frank had run off, it was Will who told him. They had stood outside, right by the shed, and Will's face was wet and his dark hair looked wild and comic. "Frank tole me to tell you he got in some trouble." Will had said. "He—he got in some trouble back there. . . ." The boy's eyes got big and wet, and Revere had been astonished and ready to tell him that boys never cried—until he heard the news. Behind Will one of the big lilac trees was moving a little in the wind, all its flowers shriveled and brown, and around it some chickens were picking in their brisk, alert, ridiculous way, jerking their heads up now and then as if someone had called to them.

Then in Revere's daydream the time changed, and it was later: a wintertime, inside the house. Revere tried to remember which time this was, and why his daughter Nancy was standing by the big bedroom door, and why she looked so stupidly at him. Then he remembered that his wife was sick and that her sisters were in the room, and they must have said something to Nancy; she had run out with her face tightened in anger. "Now you don't pay any attention to them," he had told her, "they're just old—" The Nancy of that day had been married just the summer before and lived with her husband and his folks; she seemed suddenly a stranger; she looked at him as though he were a stranger.

"Oh, and you too! I'm sick of you all!" she had cried. Then she stopped and looked funny and ran to him and took both his hands. "Oh, Pa," she said. Revere's face ached as if it wanted to smile or something, but when he opened his mouth to talk he had nothing to say. He remembered having lifted Nancy high into the air when she was a baby, and swinging her around while the boys shouted and stamped in excitement and his wife pleaded with him to stop; but the memory was only his, not Nancy's; they did not share it; she cared nothing for it. As she held his hands, looking at him, he was about to smile but somehow never did. . . .

Then the time changed again, and it was later still—another incident. This time Nancy was talking to him as if it were she and not he who was older. Nancy wanted him to come to live with them in Pools Brook—that was it—but he couldn't keep his mind still enough to think about it; he couldn't quite understand it. "I never expected to be eaten up by things, one after the other," he had said to them. Nancy's husband was both embarrassed and impatient; he must have hated to talk to an old man like this, to argue with him about something so trivial. "I wouldn't know how to start over again in another house," he had said. His words had made sense to him, but Nancy had gone on with something different as if she had not even been listening. After a while she had left, angry, and her husband with her; Revere remembered staring after the man, watching them out of his kitchen window. The young man had light hair and small nervous eyes; he too was a stranger, and he and Nancy, walking fast alongside each other but not touching, seemed to be strangers to each other as well. Revere felt a pang of guilt, as if he had betrayed Nancy, as

By the North Gate

he had betrayed his sons, by bringing them all into a world of strangers. There was something perplexing about it, but it was too difficult for him to think of and made him feel bad, and already his mind was confused with other things.

Like hungry flies, his thoughts buzzed around inside his head. Now it was an old unfinished argument with the schoolteacher he was thinking of, and now his wife; now, a handsaw someone had borrowed and never returned; now, his wife's sisters jealously guarding her death amid a smell of moth balls, with the curtains moving in that spring's late, sickly light. . . .

Then Revere woke with a start. His heart pounded furiously. He was slouched on the bench, but he straightened and stared about the cluttered yard as if ready to jump up and challenge anyone who was there. The yard was empty. Behind the barn the field was blurred. He rubbed his eyes, but he could see no better; green grass and burnt grass melted into one another. He looked at things closer to him, safer to look at. Nell had gone, and the grass was still flattened where she had been lying. "Well," he said, yawning, "I s'pose I am gettin' old, to need sleep like that after such a little fire. . . . Only a little fire . . ." He mumbled to himself without listening. He was going to stand, and his legs were tensed for the effort; but for some reason he did not stand. He remained on the bench, his head bowed, his eyes on the dust at his feet. There was something he must think of, something he must understand; but he was not sure just what it was. At last he stood up and went inside the house. There he listened for the dog, for the sound of her toenails on the rough planking of the shed. After a while, as he put together something to eat, moving wearily from place to place, grunting aloud, he forgot what he had been listening for.

When Revere had finished the meal, he stayed seated at the old table, his arms out before him, staring at the window with its blind, dull orange glow. Then he happened to look around and saw someone standing at the door. He only happened to look around; he had not heard any sound. A young boy stood peering through the loose screen of the door. For a moment Revere and the boy stared at each other. Then the boy said, "Mister, could you come out here a minute?"

Revere was angry that his heart was pounding so. He got up and went to the door. "What do you want?" he said. He and the boy glanced toward the shed doorway, as if both knew there was someone else out there. The boy was smiling in a broad, peculiar way. "Somebody to see me? Your pa, maybe?" Revere asked. But he did not know who the boy was. There were so many young people around, boys growing up, nearly men, he could no longer keep track of them all. "Your pa out there?" he said.

"Ain't my pa," said the boy. He came up to about Revere's chin—a heavy, strong boy, about twelve, with a tanned face and dirty blond hair. He went ahead of Revere.

Outside stood two other boys. Revere shaded his eyes. "Anything I can do for you?" he said. He supposed he knew their fathers or grandfathers, but no names came to mind. The tallest of the three stood with a grimy bare foot on Revere's bench. He had almost white hair and pale eyebrows and eyelashes; he was smiling at Revere. "You want to fish off my land?" Revere said, though he saw before the words were out that they carried no poles. "You can take that path there—"

"Ain't fish we're interested in today," the tall boy said. "We wondered if we could . . ." He looked at Revere evenly, while the other two smiled identically and gazed up past Revere's head to the roof of the house. "We wondered if we could use some of your water there."

"You never needed to ask," said Revere.

He waved toward the pump. But the boys did not move, and the tallest one leaned over the bench and spat into the dust as if he was tired of waiting for something. The heavy one—the one who had come to Revere's door, the one with a careful blank face and a round stomach, prominent under his overalls—simply watched. And the third boy, the youngest, stood with his two upper front teeth catching his lower lip in a precarious, tickled smile. "It's right there. You go ahead," said Revere. Running to the pump, the two bigger boys poked at the other, not looking back at Revere. He watched as the fat boy took hold of the pump handle as if testing it and began pumping. Water splashed down onto the wooden planks. Revere waited, and he saw with a strange, weakening sense of dismay—a sense of something within him dissolving, collapsing—that they had no bottles or buckets, that they simply stood around the glistening platform while the fat boy pumped, the old pump handle creaking, the water splashing down onto the planks. The fat boy was jerking the pump handle up as high as it would go, even jumping a little with it, looking so funny that the other two laughed—the little boy especially, laughing with his eyes pinched blind, his hands slapping at his thighs like a grown man's. After about five minutes they lost interest.

They whispered together and looked back at Revere. Revere was conscious of himself: an old man standing before his rotting house, his thin white hair wild about his head, his arms raised in an absurd gesture of alarm. The boys jumped off the pump platform and started back. The fat one came first. He was smiling now, and as he neared Revere the old man could see drops of water on his face, as though the boy had been out in the rain. "My brothers an' me want to thank you kindly," he said. The other boys laughed. The fat boy did not glance at them but wiped his forehead importantly. The back of his hand, suddenly uplifted, was smeared with dirt and something red, maybe paint. Revere did not know what to say. "We were all hot before," the fat boy said chattily.

"We been walkin'," the little boy said.

"Yes," said the fat boy. "That will fix us up fine."

Revere waited. There seemed to be something they expected of him. "I don't understand," he said.

"Well, you got them-there white whiskers," the fat boy said. The others laughed, and the fat boy laughed too, suddenly, as if he hadn't meant to but couldn't help it. He looked past Revere, up to the roof of the house or to the sky. "Well, I guess we'll be goin' now."

"We got to eat supper," the little boy said.

"We can't stay," the fat boy said. "I guess we'll be back, though. We'll be back tomorrow."

They turned and went back along the path. Revere watched them. He watched them with a dull pain beginning in his chest, maybe in his heart. By the pump the boys looked around. "You got yourself some flies there," the fat boy called in a high, singsong voice.

"What?" said Revere. "What?"

"Some flies there." The boys laughed together, their faces blurred across the distance. "Lots of flies around the corner there. That corner there." They turned and ran. Revere stood with his heart pounding madly as before. Then he went to the corner of the shed. The ground was barren and stony there and had eroded sharply away from the house. A few feet away stood the lilac tree that had always been stunted, stunted in the shade of the house. . . . Revere stopped suddenly. He was about to call to the dog, when he noticed the deep gash in her stomach, and the blood, and the glinting circle of flies buzzing around her. He ran, sliding on the rocky ground, to her side. As he bent over, flies grazed his face. He touched the dog's head; her eyes were open and wet and seemed to be looking at him.

He got up, scrambling, knocking pebbles downhill, and went back to the corner of the house. His eyes had turned so weak, it did not seem possible they could betray him like this when he needed them so desperately. He stumbled on down the path. He thought of what he would say to the boys when he found them, how he would shout, how sternly, with what furious strength he would confront them, how they would cringe—they were only boys! But when he began shouting hoarsely, "You there! You boys! Come back here . . ." he felt he did not know what else to say. He was hurrying, stumbling. He could not always see the ground; it seemed to jerk beneath him. He stopped by a rusty overturned barrel to catch his breath.

How weak his eyes had become! Revere knew what his land and barns looked like, so he could fill in details that were now blurred and gone; but he could not really see them. Or the grass either. It was made of millions of little stalks, moving in the wind, but to Revere it looked like a solid green river. The boys were gone. "Why did you do that?" he cried. He shook his fist. "Why did you? Why did you come on my land to do that?" A skinny white chicken darted away, clucking in terror. "You tell me why you did it!" Revere shouted. "I never done nothin' to any man, not a one of them. I never got born to fight. . . ." He stared in anger at his own trembling hands. The sunlight was quiet about him but—try though he did—he could not see the boys anywhere, not hiding in the grass or looking at him around the corner of his barn. He thought of the children running after him on the road that day, and how he had joked with them at first and then had seen that they were not laughing with him, but only staring at him, their little hands raised and about to throw something at him. "You old Revere!" they had cried, but it was not because he was a Revere, not because he was who he was—there was no reason for their behavior. Now he stared at the fine golden glow that had begun to descend upon the countryside, on the tops of the waving blades of grass, imparting a strange soft light to his own familiar land, as if an answer to his questions might somehow come from out of nowhere. To the wavering abstract pictures of the boys that remained in his memory, he shouted, "You come back! Come back here! All my life I done battle against it: that life don't mean nothin'! That it don't make sense! Sixty-eight years of a battle, so you come back! You listen to me! You ain't goin' to change my mind now, an' me grown so old an' come so far. . . ."

The wind eased upon him from the northwest again. It touched his tearful squinting eyes and his raised fist. "All of sixty-eight years," he said, this time to himself, with the air of one telling a secret. "Sixty-eight years I fought it . . . an' I never give in, not once. Not with Frank even. . . . I never give in." He believed there was something he should do, something a man ought to do, even an old man; but it would never get to the beginning of things. It would never get through. At the rim of his consciousness the faces of the boys floated, but they no longer possessed any identity, any individuality. By an effort of the will that exhausted him, that strained his mind and even his heart, he saw them enveloped by a greater darkness beyond them, the darkness of this wild land itself; he saw them caught within the accidental pattern of a fate in which he himself would be caught. "But they ain't no judgment upon the world," he said scornfully. "They ain't anything but boys, no more. No more than that. They don't stand for anything s'post to change my mind about life."

His thoughts built up and collapsed about him. He stood on the path and stared at his blackened shoes while his hand groped along the side of the rusted barrel, coming away flecked with soft rust. He sat down heavily. The barrel rolled a little forward and stopped, then rolled back to its groove in the earth; and Revere sat with his feet out before him, his legs stiff and tensed and weak all at once. "This here ain't no more than a accident," he mumbled, and then to his slow delight everything seemed clear. He felt he was arguing with the young man who had taught school down the road so long ago. It was in such a way they had argued, argued about life, about strange things —no one else had ever talked to Revere like that, not even his wife, not even his father—and Revere would give his side and, knowing all along he was right, would leave out parts so that the teacher could fill them in. What had they talked about—with the schoolroom warm and dusty around them, emptied of the children, and the windows already showing dark at five-thirty, and the schoolteacher with his worried eyes, his abstract gaze, who thought so long before he spoke —what was it they had talked about?

One time, one winter afternoon, they had talked about stories, in particular about a story Revere had just finished reading (it had taken him about a week to do so, trying to figure out the words before the teacher told him what they were, reading painfully aloud). The story was about magic and things happening in a past time, in another world; it was about a young girl, and death and disorder that befell her, that came to her in the form of a dark man. "It don't make no sense," Revere had said, pretending more scorn than he felt and looking slyly up at the teacher, " 'cause things don't happen that way in the world." The teacher had had an answer, but Revere could not remember it. He did remember that time, though, and the smell of chalk and dust and the coal burning in the stove at his back, and it seemed good to remember just the same, good to remember. All the strange failures of his life, all its picking torment, even this final vexatious waiting for death—all shrank before his memory of that time, the way his childhood nightmares had shrunk back, vanquished, before the clear empty sunshine of the day.

Insight

1. Although the killing of Revere's dog is a shocking event, Oates has prepared the reader for it by giving us hints that something strange and evil is going to happen. Point out some of the passages in the story where these hints are given. How do these suggestions of strangeness and evil affect the atmosphere of the story? How did this atmosphere affect you, the reader?

2. The old man Revere is alone on his decaying farm; he can hardly see anymore; his wife is dead, and his children are gone from home and strangers to him; he is ridiculed by his neighbors. Despite all this, the old man is determined to believe that life has meaning. What is his reaction when his dog's ears are slit? When the dog is killed?

3. At the end of the story Revere remembers one winter afternoon in the schoolhouse with the teacher. "All the strange failures of his life, all its picking torment, even this final vexatious waiting for death—all shrank before his memory of that time...." What is it about that memory that comforts him?

4. *Character.* Usually a short story focuses on one central character and what happens to him or her. To engage our interest, a writer must create characters that we can recognize as believable and perhaps even identify with. An author reveals character by describing what the person says, does, and thinks, and how others react to the person.

   In "By the North Gate" how does Oates develop the character of Revere? How would you describe his character? Use specific references to the story to support your characterization.

iN SUMMARY

Insight and Composition

1. Writers often concern themselves with the question of values. Are we living our best life? What is wrong with our existence? All of the stories in this unit imply that various values are worthy of us. The warmth that comes from closeness in marriage is prized in "The Sentimentality of William Tavener." Examine some of the values in these stories. Which seem to you the most worthy?

2. Both Granny in "The Jilting of Granny Weatherall" and Bowman in "Death of a Traveling Salesman" are seen on the final day of their lives. Contrast their thoughts as they approach death. Which of the two do you feel has come to a clearer acceptance of death? Which of the two has had a happier life? Explain your answer.

3. In "By the North Gate" Revere sees his own children as "strangers" to him. What other characters from the stories in this unit might be viewed as "strangers" to themselves or to those who love them?

4. Compare the setting of "The Demon Lover" with that of "The Story of an Hour." To what extent do you think the setting of each is a controlling factor in the determination of the plot?

5. Carl Jung, the noted psychologist, has written that "There is no coming to consciousness without pain," as Bowman realizes in "Death of a Traveling Salesman." Discuss the relevance and appropriateness of this statement to the characters in these stories.

6. All of the stories in this unit are concerned with the state of marriage. Discuss the views of marriage presented here and explain the effect the marriage had upon the characters involved.

SEARCH FOR SELF

"Who am I?" What a strange question it is! Who am I?
Children ask "who am I?" just to hear their names.
"You are Mikala, you are Shango." But there comes
a moment when your name alone does not answer the
question. Suddenly, your own name sounds flat or
foreign or fake. That's only my name! Is my face me?
Is my body me? Would I still be myself if I had a different
mother, a different father? Would I still be me if I were
the oldest child in my family? the youngest? What does
it mean: "I am black," "I am female"? Is my skin or
my sex me?

Anyone can experience this odd distance between
inner feelings and outside self. Anyone can chronicle
thoughts like these: Who is this person walking along?
I look down and see feet in brown shoes, stepping
over puddles. I go inside, sit in an empty classroom,

dig in a dirty pocketbook to find a pen. Here are my hands on the paper. My rings, my bitten nails, the old half-moon scar on my left hand. Somehow I cut my hand there when I was very young. I can remember how hard I looked at that scar when I was four years old riding in a double stroller with my sister. I remember staring at it when I was sitting in the last row in music class, next to the radiators, in second grade. This is the same hand but I am not the same.

Someone talks to me and I answer. "Hi. Fine." What does he see when he looks at me? He sees my face, my blue raincoat. What do I look like? I know a lot of different mirrors. The oval one at home turns me into a portrait, a cameo. In tall department store mirrors I look surprised and raw and alone. I look and look, but none of the mirrors really tell me. I still want to know who is this person. Other people reflect my self. I catch a glimpse at parties, when someone hurries to meet me—and when someone hurries not to meet me.

The search for self pushes us back into childhood. Was I me when I was born? The search pushes us back to ancestors. What did my grandfather do for a living? Did my great-grandmother speak English? Some of the most painful moments come when you are no longer a child and yet not a grown-up: hanging back, sneaking forward, suspicious of anyone a year older, full of longing for old comforts, yearning for new, imagined delights. But the search goes on after twenties, thirties, after middle age.

These are stories, poems, and reflections of writers describing the search for self. In these selections the search takes characters into mirrors, where they try to fathom the mild, tormenting image of their own faces. Some characters here search for identity in the reflecting surface of other people's eyes. At a party, at a dance, on a train, in the subway, on a country lane, characters in these selections look at other people to find a reflection of who they are. Am I someone's double? Am I beautiful? Do they like me? Am I old? Will they laugh at me? Am I good? Was I like that when I was young?

In the half-remembered scenes and feelings of childhood, other characters search for the lost self who still lives somehow, buried in the adult each has become. Growing old gives us a new self. What becomes of the old one? Looking at children, adults see their old, young selves: in adults, children see their future selves. In the light of dimly understood stories about her ancestors, one character here tries to illuminate the meaning of her own developing life and identity.

The search for self never really stops. George Eliot, warning her readers against hasty judgments about people either young or old, observed, "character too is a process and an unfolding." We are not finished. Our changes create in us new selves to be discovered and acknowledged.

54   *Marcia Folsom*

portrait of girl with comic book

Phyllis McGinley

Thirteen's no age at all. Thirteen is nothing.
It is not wit, or powder on the face,
Or Wednesday matinées, or misses' clothing,
Or intellect, or grace.
Twelve has its tribal customs. But thirteen   5
Is neither boys in battered cars nor dolls,
Not *Sara Crewe*,* or movie magazine,
Or pennants on the walls.

Thirteen keeps diaries and tropical fish
(A month, at most); scorns jumpropes in the spring;   10
Could not, would fortune grant it, name its wish;
Wants nothing, everything;
Has secrets from itself, friends it despises;
Admits none to the terrors that it feels;
Owns half a hundred masks but no disguises;   15
And walks upon its heels.

Thirteen's anomalous*—not that, not this:
Not folded bud, or wave that laps a shore,
Or moth proverbial from the chrysalis.
Is the one age defeats the metaphor.   20
Is not a town, like childhood, strongly walled
But easily surrounded; is no city.
Nor, quitted once, can it be quite recalled—
Not even with pity.

---

[7] SARA CREWE: a novel for young children by Frances Eliza Burnett written in 1887. [17] ANOMALOUS: changing from an accepted or expected order or form.

Nikki-Roasa

Nikki Giovanni

childhood rememberances are always a drag
if you're Black
you always remember things like living in Woodlawn
with no inside toilet
and if you become famous or something   5
they never talk about how happy you were to have your
                                 mother
all to yourself and
how good the water felt when you got your bath from one
                                 of those
big tubs that folk in chicago barbecue in
and somehow when you talk about home   10
it never gets across how much you
understood their feelings
as the whole family attended meetings about Hollydale
and even though you remember
your biographers never understand   15
your father's pain as he sells his stock
and another dream goes
and though you're poor it isn't poverty that
concerns you
and though they fought a lot   20
it isn't your father's drinking that makes any difference
but only that everybody is together and you
and your sister have happy birthdays and very good christ-
masses and I really hope no white person ever has cause to
write about me because they never understand Black love   25
is Black wealth and they'll probably talk about my hard
childhood and never understand that all the while I was
quite happy

Nikki Giovanni

Insight
1. "Thirteen's no age at all," asserts the speaker in the McGinley poem. What are some of the things wrong with age thirteen as suggested in the poem? What does the poem suggest are some examples of ambivalent behavior at this age? Would you agree with McGinley's characterization?
2. In Giovanni's poem, "Nikki-Roasa," childhood is portrayed through contrasts between how the speaker feels about her childhood and how other people, no doubt, will evaluate her childhood. What are some of these contrasts? How would you define the speaker's attitude toward her childhood?
3. Although treating a similar situation, these two poems present quite different pictures of that situation. Which view appears to be the more personal one? Which, the more realistic? Which poem do you prefer? Why?

from THE diARy of ANAÏS NiN

Reflecting on herself [handwritten]

from [March, 1937]

I cannot remember what I saw in the mirror as a child. Perhaps a child never looks at a mirror. Perhaps a child, like a cat, is so much inside of himself that he does not see himself in the mirror. He sees a child. The child does not remember what he looks like. Later I remembered what I looked like. But when I look at photographs of myself one, two, three, four, five years old, I do not recognize myself. The child is *one*. At one with himself. Never outside of himself. I can remember what I did but not the reflection of what I did. No reflections. Six years old. Seven years old. Eight years old. Nine. Ten. Eleven. No images. No reflections. Feelings. I can feel what I felt about my father's white mice, the horror they inspired in me, the revolting odor, the taste of a burnt omelette my father made for us while my mother was sick and expecting Joaquin in Berlin. The feel of the beach in Barcelona, the feel of the balcony there, the fear of death and the writing of a testament, the feelings in church, in the street. Sounds in the Spanish courtyard, singing, a memory of a gaiety which was to haunt me all my life, totally absent from America. The face of the maid Ramona, the music in the streets, children dancing on the sidewalks. Voices. The appearance of others, the long black mustache of Granados, the embrace of the nuns, drowning me in veils as they leaned over. No picture in the mind's eye of what I wore. The long black stockings of Spanish children I saw in a photograph. I do remember my passion for penny "surprise" packages, the passion for surprise. Yet at the age of six the perfection of the blue bow on my hair, shaped like a butterfly, preoccupied me, since I insisted that my godmother tie it because she tied it better than anyone else. I must have seen this bow in the mirror then. I do not remember whether I saw this bow, the little girl in the very short white-lace-edged dress, or again a photograph taken in Havana where all my cousins and I stood in a row according to our heights, all wearing enormous ribbons and short white dresses. In the mirror there never was a child. The first mirror had a frame of white wood. In it there is no Anaïs Nin, but Marie Antoinette with a white lace cap, a long black dress, standing on a pile of chairs, the chariot, riding to her beheading. No Anaïs Nin. An actress playing all the parts of characters in French history. I am Charlotte Corday plunging a knife into

58

the tyrant Marat. I am, of course, Joan of Arc. At fourteen, the portrayal of a Joan burning at the stake was my brother's favorite horror story.

The first mirror in which the self appears is very large, it is inlaid inside of a brown wood wall in the room of a brownstone house. Next to it the window pours down so strong a light that the rest of the room is not reflected in the mirror. The image of the girl who approaches it is brought into luminous relief. Against a foggy darkness, the girl of fifteen stands with frightened eyes. She is looking at her dress, a dress of shiny worn blue serge, which was fixed up for her out of an old one belonging to a cousin. It does not fit her. It is meager. It looks poor. The girl is looking at the worn shiny dark-blue serge dress with shame. It is the day she has been told in school that she is gifted for writing. They had come purposely into the class to tell her. In spite of being a foreigner, in spite of having to use the dictionary, she had written the best essay in the class. She who was always quiet and who did not wish to be noticed, was told to come up the aisle and speak to the English teacher before everyone, to hear the compliment. And the joy, the dazzling joy which had first struck her was instantly killed by the awareness of the dress. I did not want to get up, to be noticed. I was ashamed of this meager dress with a shine on it, its worn air, its orphan air, its hand-me-down air.

There is another mirror framed in brown wood. The girl is looking at the new dress which transfigures her. What an extraordinary change. She leans over very close to look at the humid eyes, the humid mouth, the moisture and luminousness brought about by the change of dress. She walks up very slowly to the mirror, very slowly, as if she did not want to frighten reflections away. Several times, at fifteen, she walks very slowly towards the mirror. Every girl of fifteen has put the same question to a mirror: "Am I beautiful?" The face is masklike. It does not smile. It does not want to charm the mirror, or deceive the mirror, or flirt with it and gain a false answer. The girl is in a trance. She does not want to frighten the reflection away herself. Someone has said she is very pale. She approaches the mirror and stands very still like a statue. Immobile. Waxy. She never makes a gesture. Surprised. Somnambulistic? She only moves to become someone else, impersonating Sara Bernhardt, Mélisande, *La Dame aux Camélias*, Madame Bovary, Thaïs. She is never Anaïs Nin who goes to school, and grows vegetables and flowers in her backyard. She is immobile, haunting, like a figure moving in a dream. She is decomposed before the mirror into a hundred personages, recomposed into paleness and immobility. Silence. She is watching for an expression which will betray the spirit. You can never catch the face alive, laughing, or loving. At sixteen she is looking at the mirror with her hair up for the first time. There is always the question. The mirror is not going to answer it. She will have to look for the answer in the eyes and faces of the boys who dance with her, men later, and above all the painters.

Insight

1. Anaïs Nin, remembering youthful reflections of herself in the mirror, notes that each time a different person was reflected. What is this young girl like in each reflection? How does her view of herself change?

2. What does the author mean by her comment, "In the mirror there never was a child"?

THE NEW MIRROR

Ann Petry

My mother said, "Where is your father?" She was standing outside the door of the downstairs bathroom. Even if she had been farther away, I would have understood what she said, because her voice had a peculiar quality just this side of harshness, which made it carry over longer distances than other people's voices.

From inside the bathroom, I said, "He's in the backyard listening to the bees."

"Please tell him that breakfast is ready."

"Right away," I said. But I didn't tell him right away. I didn't move. We had had a late, cold spring, with snow on the ground until the end of April. Then in May the weather turned suddenly warm and the huge old cherry trees in our yard blossomed almost overnight. There were three of them, planted in a straight line down the middle of the backyard. As soon as the sun was up, it seemed as though all the honeybees in Wheeling, New York, came to the trees in swarms. Every sunny morning, my father stood under one of those bloom-filled cherry trees and listened to the hum of the bees. My mother knew this just as well as I did, but she was sending a bathroom dawdler to carry a message to a cherry-tree dawdler so that she would finally have both of us in the dining room for breakfast at the same time.

I spent the next ten minutes looking at myself in the new plate-glass mirror that had been hung over the basin just the day before. A new electrical fixture had been installed over the mirror. My mother had had these changes made so that my father could shave downstairs. She said this would be more convenient for him, because it placed him closer to the drugstore while he shaved. Our drugstore was in the front of the building where we lived.

The bathroom walls were white, and under the brilliant, all-revealing light cast by the new fixture I looked like all dark creatures impaled on a flat white surface: too big, too dark. My skin was a muddy brown, not the clear, dark brown I had always supposed it to be. I turned my head and the braid of hair that reached halfway down my back looked like a thick black snake. It even undulated slightly as I moved. I grabbed the braid close to my head and looked around for a pair of scissors, thinking I would cut the braid off, because it was an absolutely revolting hair style for a fifteen-year-old girl. But there weren't any scissors, so I released my grip on the braid and took another look at myself—head-on in the glittering mirror. I decided that the way I looked in that white-walled bathroom was the way our family looked in the town of Wheeling, New York. We were the only admittedly black family in an all-white community and we stood out; we looked strange, alien. There was another black family—the Granites—but they claimed to be Mohawk Indians. Whenever my father mentioned them, he laughed until tears came to his eyes, saying, "Mohawks? Ha, ha, ha. Well, five or six generations of Fanti tribesmen must have caught five or six generations of those Mohawk females named Granite under a bush somewhere. Ha, ha, ha."

He never said things like that in the drugstore. He and my mother and my aunts kept their private lives and their thoughts about people inside the family circle, deliberately separating the life of the family from the life of the drugstore. But it didn't work the other way around, for practically everything we did was decided in terms of whether it was good or bad for the drugstore. I liked the store, and I liked working in it on Saturdays and after school, but it often seemed to me a monstrous, mindless, sightless force that shaped our lives into any old pattern it chose, and it chose the patterns at random.

I turned out the light and went to tell my father that breakfast was ready. He was standing motionless under the first big cherry tree. He had his back turned, but I could tell from the way he held his head that he was listening intently. He was short, and seen from the back like that, his torso looked as though it had been designed for a bigger man.

"Yoo-hoo!" I shouted, as though I were calling someone at least two hundred feet away from me. "Break-fast. Break-fast." In my mind, I said, "Sam-u-el, Sam-u-el." But I didn't say that out loud.

He did not turn around. He lifted his hand in a gesture that pushed the sound of my voice away, indicating that he had heard me and that I was not to call him again.

I sat down on the back steps to wait for him. Though the sun was up, it was cool in the yard. The air was filled with a delicate fragrance that came from all the flowering shrubs, from the cherry blossoms and the pear blossoms, and from the small plants—violets and daffodils. A song sparrow was singing somewhere close by. I told myself that if I were a maker of perfumes I would make one and call it "Spring," and it would smell like this cool, sweet, early-morning air and I would let only beautiful young brown girls use it, and if I could sing I would sing like the song sparrow and I would let only beautiful young brown boys hear me.

When we finally went into the house and sat down to breakfast, my father said (just as he did every spring) that the honeybees buzzed on one note and that it was E-flat just below middle C but with a

difference. He said he had never been able to define this in the musical part of his mind and so had decided that it was the essential difference in the sound produced by the buzzing of a bee and the sound produced by a human voice lifted in song. He also said that he wouldn't want to live anywhere else in the world except right here in Wheeling, New York, in the building that housed our drugstore, with that big backyard with those cherry trees in it, so that in the spring of the year, when the trees were in full bloom, he could stand under them smelling that cherry-blossom sweet air and listening to those bees holding that one note—E-flat below middle C. Then he said, "When I was out there just now, that first cherry tree was so aswarm with life, there were so many bees moving around bumping into the blossoms and making that buzzing sound, that hum . . ." He touched his forehead lightly with one of his big hands, as though he were trying to stimulate his thinking processes. "You know, I could have sworn that tree spoke to me."

I leaned toward him, waiting to hear what he was going to say. I did not believe the tree had said anything to him, but I wanted to know what it was he *thought* the tree had said. It seemed to me a perfect moment for this kind of revelation. We had just finished eating an enormous breakfast: grapefruit and oatmeal and scrambled eggs and sausage and hot cornmeal muffins. This delicious food and this sunny room in which we had eaten it were pleasant segments of the private part of our life, totally separated from the drugstore, which was the public part. I relished the thought that the steady stream of white customers who went in and out of our drugstore did not know what our dining room was like, did not even know if we had one. It was like having a concealed weapon to use against your enemy.

The dining room was a square-shaped, white-walled room on the east side of the building. The brilliant light of the morning sun was reflected from the walls so that the whole room seemed to shimmer with light and the walls were no longer white but a pale yellow. I thought my father looked quite handsome in this room. His skin was a deep reddish brown and he was freshly shaved. He had used an after-shave lotion, and it gave his face a shiny look. He was bald-headed, and in this brilliantly sunlit room the skin on his face and on his head looked as though it had been polished.

The dining room table was oak. It was square, well suited to the square shape of the room. The chairs had tall backs and there was a design across the top of each one. The design looked as though it had been pressed into the wood by some kind of machine.

My mother sat at one end of the table and my father sat at the other end, in armchairs. I sat on one side of the table, and my Aunt Sophronia sat on the other side. She was my mother's youngest sister. She and my mother looked very much alike, though she was lighter in color than my mother. They were both short, rather small-boned women. Their eyes looked black, though they were a very dark brown. They wore their hair the same way—piled up on top of their heads. My mother's hair was beginning to turn gray, but Aunt Sophronia's was black. There was a big difference in their voices. Aunt Sophronia's voice was low-pitched, musical—a very gentle voice.

My aunt and my mother and father were drinking their second cups of coffee and I was drinking my second glass of milk when my father said he thought the cherry tree had spoken to him. They both looked at him in surprise.

I asked, "What did the tree say?"

"It bent down toward me and it said . . ." He paused, beckoned to me to lean toward him a little more. He lowered his voice. "The tree said, 'Child of the sun—' " He stopped talking and looked directly at me. In that sun-washed room, his eyes were reddish brown, almost the same color as his skin, and I got the funny feeling that I had never really looked right at him before, and that he believed the tree had said something to him, and I was shocked. He whispered, "The tree said, 'It will soon be time to go and open the drugstore!' "

I scowled at him and he threw his head back and laughed, making a roaring, explosive sound. It was just as though he had said, "Got you, you idiot—you—ha, ha, ha." He opened his mouth so wide I could see his gums, red and moist, see the three teeth that he had left, one in the upper jaw and two in the lower jaw, even see his tonsils. I began muttering to him in my mind, "How do you chew your food, old toothless one with the red-brown skin and the bald head. Go up, thou bald head. Go up, thou bald-headed black man."

Right after breakfast, I helped my father open the drugstore for the day. I was still annoyed that he had been able to fool me into thinking he believed a cherry tree had spoken to him, but I so enjoyed working in the drugstore that I would not deny myself that pleasure simply because he had deliberately talked nonsense and I had been stupid enough to believe him.

He swept the floor with a big soft-bristled broom. Then he went outside and swept off the long, wooden steps that ran all the way across the front of the building. He left the front door open, and the cool, sweet-smelling early-morning air dispelled the heavy odor of cigars, the sticky vanilla smell from the soda fountain and the medicinal smell of the prescription room—part alcohol, part spicy things, part disinfectant.

I put change in both the cash registers—the one in the store proper and the one behind the fountain. The fountain was in a separate room, rather like a porch with a great many windows. I put syrups in the fountain—chocolate, Coca-Cola, root beer, lemon, cherry, vanilla. The chocolate syrup had a mouth-watering smell, and the cherry and the lemon syrups smelled like a fruit stand on a hot summer day, but the root beer and the Coca-Cola syrups smelled like metal.

Our black and white cat sat in the doorway and watched my father. The cat yawned, opening his mouth wide, and I could see his wonderful flexible pink tongue and his teeth—like the teeth of a tiger, only smaller, of course. I wondered if cats ever became practically toothless, like my father. He wouldn't have cavities filled because he said all that silver or amalgam or gold or whatever it was, and all that X-raying that butter-fingered dentists do, and all that use of Novocain was what made people develop cancer of the jaw. When his teeth hurt and the dentist said the pain was due to a big cavity, he simply had the tooth pulled out without an anesthetic. Once I asked him if it hurt to have teeth pulled without Novocain or gas. He said, "Of course it hurts. But it is a purely temporary hurt. The roots of my teeth go straight down and it is a very simple matter to pull them out. I've pulled some of them out myself."

I sorted the newspapers, looked at the headlines, quickly skimmed the inside of the Buffalo *News*. I saw a picture of a man, obviously an actor, wearing a straw hat. I wanted the picture because of his tooth-revealing grin, and I reminded myself to cut it out. The newspapers that didn't sell were returned for credit. Quite often I snipped out items that interested me. I always hunted for articles that dealt with the importance of chewing food thoroughly, and for pictures of men with no teeth, and for pictures of very handsome men exposing a great many teeth. I intended to leave this particular picture on the prescription counter, where my father would be sure to see it.

When Aunt Sophronia came to work at nine o'clock, the store was clean and it smelled good inside. Like my father, she was a pharmacist, and when he was not in the store, she was there. She wore dark skirts and white shirtwaists when she was working, and she put on a gray cotton store coat so that people would know she worked in the store and would not think she was a customer.

One other person worked in the drugstore—Pedro, a twelve-year-old Portuguese boy. He was supposed to arrive at nine on Saturdays and Sundays. He was always prompt and the first stroke of the town clock had not yet sounded when he came hurrying into the store. He was a very sturdily built boy, with big dark eyes. He had an enormous quantity of tangled black hair. He couldn't afford to have his hair cut at the barbershop, so my father cut it for him. The first time I saw him cutting Pedro's hair out in the back room, I asked him if he knew how to cut hair.

He said, "No."

I said, "Well, how do you know what to do?"

"I don't," he said, snipping away with the scissors. "But I can shorten it some. Otherwise, he'll look like a girl."

Though Pedro was fond of all of us, he had a special feeling about my father. He told my father that he would like to stay in the store all the time—he could sleep in the back room, and all he needed was a blanket and a mattress and he could bring those from home, and he would provide his own food and clothes. There were eleven kids in his family, and I imagine he preferred being part of a family in which there were fewer people, and so decided to become a member of our family. My father wouldn't let him sleep in the back room, but Pedro did manage to spend most of his waking hours (when he wasn't in school, of course) at the store. He provided his own food. He ate oranges, sucking out the juice and the pulp. He hung a big smoked sausage from one of the rafters in the back room and sliced off pieces of it for his lunch. He loved fresh pineapple, and he was always saying that the only thing in the world he'd ever steal if he couldn't get it any other way would be a ripe pineapple.

At one minute after nine, my father went to the post office. When he left, he was holding some letters that he was going to mail. I thought his hand looked big and very dark holding all those white envelopes. I went to the door and watched him as he walked up the street, past the elm trees, past the iron urn on the village green, past the robins and the tender green young grass on each side of the gravel path. He had a stiff straw hat tilted just a little toward the back of his head. As he moved off up the street, he was whistling "Ain't goin' to study war no more, no more, no more."

We were so busy in the store that morning that I did not realize what time it was until my mother called up to find out why my father had not been home for his noon meal. There was such a sharp line of demarcation between house and store that my mother always telephoned the drugstore when she had a message for my father.

Aunt Sophronia answered the phone. I heard her say, "He's not in the store right now—he's probably in the cellar. We'll send him right along." After she hung up the receiver, she said, "See if your father is in the cellar unpacking stock or way down in the yard burning rubbish."

He wasn't in the cellar and he wasn't in the backyard. The burner was piled high with the contents of the wastebasket from the prescription room (junk mail, empty pillboxes, old labels) and the contents of the rubbish box from the fountain (straws, paper napkins, Popsicle wrappers).

All three cherry trees were still filled with bees, and they were buzzing on their one note. I walked from one tree to the next, pausing to listen, looking up into the white blossoms, and the trees seemed to be alive in a strange way because of the comings and goings of the bees. As I stood there, I felt it would be very easy to believe that those trees could speak to me.

I went back to the drugstore, and Aunt Sophronia said, "You didn't see him?"

"No. And I don't think he ever came back from the post office. Each time someone asked for him, I thought he was in the back room or down in the cellar or outside in the yard. And each time, whoever it was wanted him said they'd come back later, and I never really had to look for him."

"I'll call the post office and ask if he's picked up our packages, and that way I'll find out if he's been there without actually saying that we're looking for him."

I could hear her end of the conversation, and obviously he hadn't been in the post office at all that morning. She hung up the telephone and called the railroad station and asked if Mr. Layen had been there to get an express package. The stationmaster had a big booming voice, and I could hear him say, "No." Aunt Sophronia said, "You would have seen him if he had been at the station?" He said, "I certainly would."

Pedro and I wanted to go and look for my father. Aunt Sophronia snapped at us, saying, "Don't be foolish. Where would you look? In the river? In the taverns? Your father wouldn't kill himself, and he doesn't drink . . ."

She frightened me. She had frightened Pedro, too; he was pale and his eyes looked bigger. I had thought my father was late for dinner because he had stopped somewhere to talk and got involved in a long-winded conversation, and that if Pedro and I had walked up or down the street we would have found him and told him his dinner was ready. Aunt Sophronia obviously thought something dreadful had happened to him. Now we began to think so, too.

We kept waiting on the customers just as though there was no crisis in our family. I kept saying to myself, "Your father dies, your mother dies, you break your leg or your back, you stand in a pool of cold sweat from a fever, you stand in a pool of warm blood from a wound, and you go out in the store and smile and say, 'Fine, just fine, we're all fine, nothin's ever wrong with us cull-ed folks.'"

Whenever the store was empty, my aunt would say nervously, "What could have happened to him?" And then clear her throat two or three times in quick succession—a sure sign that she was upset and frightened. Later in the afternoon she said in a queer way, just as though he had passed out of our lives and she was already reminiscing about him, "He did everything at exactly the same time every day. He always said that was the only way you could run a store—have a certain time for everything and stick to it."

This was true. He opened the drugstore promptly at eight, he went to get the mail promptly at nine, and he ate his dinner at twelve. At four in the afternoon, he drank a bottle of Moxie—the only soda pop that he regarded as fit for human consumption. (He said if that were ever taken off the market he would have to drink tea, which upset his stomach because it was a drink suited to the emotional needs of the Chinese, the East Indians, the English, the Irish, and nervous American females, and it had, therefore, no value for him, representing as he did a segment of a submerged population group only a few generations out of Africa, where his ancestors had obviously been witch doctors.)

On Sundays he went to church. He went in through the rear entrance and into the choir loft from the back about two minutes after the service started. There was a slight stir as the ladies of the choir and the other male singer (a tall, thin man who sang bass) rearranged themselves to make room for him. He sang a solo almost every Sunday, for he had a great big, beautiful tenor voice. On Sundays he smelled strongly of after-shave lotion, and on weekdays he smelled faintly of after-shave lotion.

My aunt kept saying, "Where would he go? Where would he go?"

I said, "Maybe he went to Buffalo." I didn't believe this, but she'd have to stop clearing her throat long enough to contradict me.

"What would he go there for? Why wouldn't he say so? How would he get there?"

"He could go on the bus," I said. "Maybe he went to get new eyeglasses. He buys his eyeglasses in the five-and-ten. He likes five-and-tens."

"He hates buses. He says they smell and they lurch."

I laughed. "He says they stink and they lurch in such a way they churn the contents of your belly upside down." She made no comment, so I said again, "He buys his glasses in the five-and-ten in Buffalo and—"

"What?" she said. "I don't believe it."

"It's true. You ask Mother. She said that the last time they went to Buffalo . . ." I tried to remember how long ago that would have been.

"Well?"

"Well, Mother said she wanted to get a new hat and he said that he'd be in the five-and-ten, and there was Samuel and an old black man with him, and they were bent practically double over a counter. She told me, 'Your father had a piece of newspaper in his hand and he had on a pair of glasses, and he was looking at this newspaper, saying, "No, not strong enough," and he moved on and picked up another pair of glasses and put them on and said, "Let's see. Ah! Fine!" Then he turned to this old black man, a dreadful-looking old man, ragged and dirty and unshaven and smelling foully of whiskey, and he said to him, "You got yours?" ' Mother said, 'Samuel, whatever are you doing?' Even when she told it, she sounded horrified. He said, 'I'm getting my glasses.' Then he asked the old man if he'd got his, and the old man nodded and looked at Mother and sort of slunk away. I suppose she had on one of those flowered hats and white gloves. Mother said she looked at the counter and there were rows and rows of glasses and they were all fifty cents apiece. And that's what Samuel uses—that's what he's always used. He says that he doesn't need special lenses, that he hasn't anything unusual the matter with his eyes. All he needs is some magnifying glass so that he can see to read small printed matter, and so that's why he buys his glasses in the five-and-ten." I stopped talking.

My aunt didn't say anything. She frowned at me.

So I started again. "He gets two pair at a time. Sometimes he loses them. Sometimes he breaks them. You know he likes to push them up high on top of his forehead, out of the way when he isn't using them, and his bald head is always greasy or sweaty and the glasses slide off on the floor and quite often they break. Didn't you know that?"

She said, "No, and I wish you'd stop calling your father Samuel." She went to wait on a customer.

I sat down on the high stool in front of the prescription counter. I didn't believe that my father had gone to Buffalo. He wouldn't go away without leaving any message. I wondered if he'd been kidnapped, and dismissed the idea as ridiculous. Something must have happened to him.

My mother called the store again, and right afterward Aunt Sophronia told Pedro to go in through the kitchen door and get coffee and sandwiches that Mrs. Layen had made and bring them into the store. We ate in the back room, one at a time. We didn't eat very much. I didn't like the smell of the coffee. It has always seemed to me that the human liver doesn't like coffee, that it makes the liver shiver. But all my family drank coffee and so did Pedro, and they didn't like to have me tell them how I felt about it.

I sat in the back room with that liver-shivering smell in my nose and looked out the back door. It was a pleasant place to sit and eat. It was a big room, and the rafters in the ceiling were exposed. True, there was a lot of clutter—pots and pans and mops and brooms, and big copper kettles stuck in corners or hanging from the rafters, and piles of old newspapers and magazines stacked on empty cartons. The walls were lined with small boxes that contained herbs. Some wholesale druggist had thrown them out, and my father had said he'd take them, because a dried herb would be good a hundred years from now; if it were properly dried, it would not lose its special properties. The back room always smelled faintly of aromatic substances—a kind of sneeze-making smell. The door was open, and I could look out into the backyard and see the cherry trees and the forsythia and all the flowering shrubs and the tender new grass.

We were very busy in the store all that afternoon. At five o'clock, my mother came in through the back door and sat down in the prescription room. She kept looking out of the window, toward the green. She had on a hat—a dark blue straw hat with small white flowers across the front—and her best black summer suit and white gloves. She was obviously dressed for an emergency, for disaster, prepared to identify Samuel Layen in hospital or morgue or police station.

The customers came in a steady stream. They bought the afternoon papers, cigarettes, tobacco. Men on their way home from work stopped to get ice cream for dessert. As the afternoon wore along, the shadows from the elm trees lengthened until they were as long as the green was wide. The iron urn in the middle looked chalk white. As the daylight slowly diminished, the trunks of the trees—that great expanse of trunk without branches, characteristic of the elms—seemed to be darkening and darkening.

I turned on the lights in the store and the student lamp on the prescription counter. It wasn't really quite dark enough to justify turning on the lights and I thought my aunt would say this, but she didn't. She asked my mother if she would like a glass of ginger ale.

"That would be very nice, thank you," my mother said. Her voice was deeper and harsher, and its carrying quality seemed to have increased.

"Pedro, get Mrs. Layen a glass of ginger ale."

When Pedro brought the ginger ale, Mother took a sip of it and then put it on the windowsill. It stayed there—bubbles forming, breaking, breaking, forming, breaking, until finally it was just a glass of yellowish liquid sitting forgotten on the windowsill.

When there weren't any customers in the store, we all went into the prescription room and sat down and waited with my mother. We sat in silence—Pedro and Aunt Sophronia and my mother and I. I kept thinking, But my father wouldn't leave us of his own free will. Only this morning at breakfast he said he wouldn't want to live anywhere else in the world except right here where we live. It could be suicide, or he could have been murdered. Certainly not kidnapped for ransom. What do we own? We don't own a car. There's the old building where we live and there's the store with its ancient mahogany-colored fixtures and glass-enclosed cases and the fountain room. But if it were all put together with our clothes and our household goods—pots and pans and chairs and tables and sofas and beds and mirrors—it wouldn't add up to anything to kidnap a man for.

Then I thought, Perhaps he left my mother for another woman. Preposterous. He was always saying that the first time he saw her she was sixteen and he decided right then and there he was going to marry her; she had big, black, snappy eyes, and her skin was so brown and so beautiful. His friends said he would be robbing the cradle, because he was twenty-four. He did marry her when she was eighteen. He said that whenever he looked at her he always thought, Black is the color of my true love's hair.

Aunt Sophronia said, "Perhaps we should put something in the newspaper—something . . ."

My mother said, "No," harshly. "The Layens would descend like a horde of locusts, crying, 'Samuel! Samuel! Samuel!' No. They all read the Buffalo *Recorder* and they would be down from Buffalo before we could turn around twice. Sometimes I think they use some form of astral projection. No. We won't put anything in the newspapers, not even if . . ."

I knew she was going to say, or had stopped herself from saying, "even if he is dead," though I did not see how she could keep an account of his death out of the newspapers.

My mother said my father's family was like a separate and warlike tribe—arrogant, wary, hostile. She thought they were probably descended from the Watusi. In Buffalo, they moved through the streets in groups of three or four. She always had the impression they were stalking something. Their voices were very low in pitch, almost guttural, and unless you listened closely you got the impression they were not speaking English but were simply making an accented sound —uh-uh-uh-*uh*—that only they could understand.

Whenever my great-grandfather, the bearded patriarch of the family, went out on the streets of Buffalo, he was accompanied by one of his grandsons, a boy about fourteen, tall, quick-moving. The boy was always given the same instructions: "Anything happen to your grandfather, anybody say anything to him, you come straight back here, straight back here." "Anybody say anything to him" meant if anyone called him "out of his name." If this occurred, my mother said the boy would go straight home with the old man and emerge in the company of Uncle Joe, Uncle Bill, Uncle Bobby, Uncle John, Uncle George, my father, Aunt Kate, and Aunt Hal—all of them hellbent on vengeance.

They had lived in New Jersey—they always said "Jersey"—at the foot of a mountain they called Sour Mountain. When they first came to New York State, they lived in Albany. The whole clan—Great-Grandma, Great-Grandpa, Grandma and Grandpa, and all eight children including my father, Samuel, and a baby—came to Albany on one of the Hudson River boats. They had six ducks in wooden cages going splat all over the deck, a huge, woolly black dog—ancestry unknown, temper vicious—and six painted parlor chairs that Great-Grandma insisted on bringing with her. The men and boys wore black felt hats, and the skin on their faces and hands was almost as dark as the felt of the hats. They wore heavy black suits that Great-Grandma had made for them. Whenever anyone approached them on the boat, they executed a kind of flanking motion and very quickly formed a circle, the men facing the outside, the women on the inside.

My mother once told me she knew all the details about the arrival of these black strangers in Albany, because her family had known a black man who worked on the Hudson River boats and he had told her father about it. When the boat approached the dock, it had to be maneuvered into position, and so it started to move back down the river. It did not go very far, but there was an ever-increasing length of water between the boat and the dock. The sun was out, the brass railings gleamed in the sunlight, and the white paint sparkled as the boat edged away from the dock. The dark-skinned, fierce-looking men held a conference. The old bearded man who was my great-grandfather gave a cry—a trumpeting kind of cry—and took a long running leap off the boat and landed on the dock, hitting it with his cane and bellowing, "You ain't takin' us back now, you know! Throw that baby down to me! Throw that baby down to me!" There were outraged cries from the people on the deck. One of the Layens threw the baby down to the old man and he caught it. He glared up at the scowling deckhands and the staring people and shouted, "Ain't goin' to take us back now, you know! We paid to get here. Ain't going to take us back now. Jump!" he roared. "All of you, jump!"

My mother said the black man told her father this story, and he ended it by saying, "You know, those people jumped off that boat— even the women. They picked up all their stuff, even those damn ducks and that vicious dog and those chairs, and they took these long running leaps and landed on the dock. I never saw anything like it. And that old bearded black man kept walking up and down on the dock, hitting it with his cane, and he's got this baby, dangling it by one foot, and he's hollering out and hollering out, 'We paid to get here! Ain't goin' to take us back now, you know!' "

I sat in the prescription room staring at my mother and thinking again, If my father died, she would not tell his family? Even if he died? She would be afraid to tell them for fear they would arrive in Wheeling and attack all the inhabitants—they would be as devastating as a gang of professional stranglers. Old as he was now, my great-grandfather wouldn't ride in an automobile and he didn't like trains, so he would probably walk down to Wheeling from Buffalo, muttering to himself, intractable, dangerous, his beard quivering with rage, his little eyes blazing with the light of battle.

Customers kept coming into the store. Pedro and I waited on them. Once, when we were both behind the tobacco counter, he said, "I could just walk around in the town and look for him. I wouldn't tell people he was lost."

I shook my head. "Aunt Sophronia wouldn't like it."

Each time the phone rang, I answered it. I left the door of the phone booth open, so they could all hear what I said, in case it was some kind of news about my father. It never was. It was always somebody who wanted some of his chocolate syrup, or his special-formula cold cream, or his lotion for acne. I kept saying the same thing in reply. "He isn't here right now. We expect him, we expect him. When? Later. We expect him later."

There was an automatic closing device on the screen door which kept it from banging shut. It made a hissing sound when the door was opened. Each time we heard that hiss, we all looked toward the door expectantly, thinking perhaps this time it would be Samuel. Finally, Aunt Sophronia turned on a small radio on the prescription counter. There was a great deal of static, voices came in faintly, and there was a thin thread of music in the background—a confusion of sounds. I had never known my aunt to turn on the radio in the store. My father said that only certain kinds of decaying drugstores had radios blatting in them, and that the owners turned them on hoping to distract the customers' attention away from the leaks in the roof, the holes in the floor, the flyblown packages, and the smell of cat.

Aunt Sophronia sat on the high stool in front of the prescription counter, bent forward a little, listening. We all listened. My mother looked down at her hands, Pedro looked at the floor, Aunt Sophronia looked at the black and white linoleum on the counter. I thought, We're waiting to hear one of those fudge-voiced announcers say that a short thick-bodied black man has been found on the railroad track, train gone over him, or he's been found hanging or shot or drowned. Why drowned? Well, the river's close by.

I practiced different versions of the story. "Young woman finds short, thick-bodied, unidentified black man." "School children find colored druggist in river." "Negro pharmacist lost in mountains." "Black man shot by white man in love duel." Colored druggist. Negro pharmacist. Black man. My father? I hovered in the doorway listening to the radio—world news roundup, weather, terrible music. Nothing about unidentified black men.

Aunt Sophronia turned toward my mother and said something in a low voice.

"Police?" my mother said in a very loud voice, and repeated it. "Police?"

"He's been gone since nine o'clock this morning. What else can we do except call the police?"

"No!" My mother's voice was louder and harsher than I had ever heard it. "There's no need to go to the police. We don't know where Samuel is, but if we wait patiently we'll find out." Her eyes were open very wide and they glistened. It occurred to me that they might be luminous in the dark, like a cat's eyes.

"He might have had an accident."

"We would have been informed," my mother said firmly. "His name is engraved on the inside of his watch. His name is on his shirt and on his underwear and his handkerchiefs. I mark everything with indelible ink."

"But if it happened in Buffalo—"

"If what happened? What are you talking about?"

Aunt Sophronia began to cry. Right there in the prescription room. She made so much noise you could hear her out in the store. I was appalled. The private part of our life had suddenly and noisily entered the public part—or perhaps it was the other way around. When people cry and try to talk at the same time, their words come out jerkily and they have to speak between the taking of big convulsive breaths, and so they cannot control the volume of their speech and they shout, and that is what my quiet-voiced Aunt Sophronia was doing. She was shouting right there in the drugstore. Someone came into the store and turned to look toward the prescription room to see what was going on. Pedro ran out of the room to wait on the customer.

"I'm just as fond of him as you are!" Aunt Sophronia shouted between sobs and gasps and agonized-sounding crying noises. "Just as worried as you are! You can't just sit there and let him disappear! And not do anything about it!"

My mother stood up, looked at me, and said, "Call a taxi." Then she turned to my aunt and said, "We will go to the Tenyeck Barracks and discuss this with the state police." Her voice was pitched so low and it was so loud that it sounded like a man's voice.

When the town taxi came, I stood in the doorway and watched them go down the front steps. It was perfectly obvious that my aunt had been crying, for her eyelids were red and swollen. My mother looked ill. They both seemed to have shrunk in size. They were bent over and so looked smaller and shorter than they actually were. When they reached the sidewalk, they turned and glanced up at me. I felt like crying, too. The flowered hat had slipped so far back on my mother's head that it made her look as though she were bald. Aunt Sophronia had a yellow pencil stuck in her hair, and she had put on an old black coat that hung in the back room. The coat was too big for her; the sleeves were too long and it reached almost to her ankles. Under it, she was still wearing the gray cotton store coat. They looked like little old women—humble, questing, moving slowly. When they turned, I could see the white part of their eyes under the irises, and I had to look away from them.

Aunt Sophronia said, "If there are any prescriptions, I'll fill them later." Then she took my mother by the arm and they went toward the taxi. The driver got out and held the door open for them and closed it behind them.

I wondered what my mother would say to the state police. "My husband is missing. He is a short, broad-shouldered black man, bald-headed, forty-eight years old?" Would the state police snicker and say, "Yes, we would hardly expect you, with your dark brown skin, to be married to a white man. Wearing what when last seen?" "Light gray summer suit and polka-dot bow tie, highly polished black shoes." The gravel path that bisects the village green was very dry this morning—no mud. So there would still have been polish on his shoes. But not if he were drowned. But who would drown him, and why?

Might have drowned himself. Drowned himself? Surely she will say that he has only three teeth, three teeth only—one in the upper jaw and two in the lower jaw.

Then I thought, But why did they have to *go* to the police? Why couldn't they have telephoned? Because someone might have overheard the conversation. So what difference would that make? Did they think the police would send out a silent and invisible bloodhound to hunt for the black druggist from Wheeling? Did they think the police would send out invisible men to search the morgues in Buffalo, to fish for a fresh black corpse in the streams and coves and brooks in and around Wheeling?

We didn't even hunt for him the way white people would have hunted for their father. It was all indirect. Has he been to the post office? . . . "Oh, oh, oh." Has he been to the railroad station to pick up an express package? . . . "I see, I see, I see."

Between customers I thought, We've even infected Pedro, who is Portuguese, with this disease, whatever it is. Why did we have to hunt for my father this way? Because there is something scandalous about a disappearance, especially if it is a black man who disappears. Could be caused by a shortage of funds (What funds? His own?), a shortage of narcotics, unpaid bills, a mistake made in a prescription—scandal, scandal, scandal. Black druggist, mixed up with police, disappears. Mixed up with police.

It wasn't until Miss Rena Randolph handed me an empty prescription bottle to be refilled that I realized what my aunt had done. I held the sticky bottle in my hand, the label all over gravy drips, as my father was wont to say, and I thought, Why, I'm in charge of the drugstore and I am only fifteen. The only other person working in the store is Pedro, and he is only twelve. All my life I'd heard conversations about "uncovered" drugstores—drugstores without a pharmacist on the premises. For the first time, our store was "uncovered." Suppose something happened . . .

Miss Randolph leaned against the counter and coughed and coughed and coughed. "I won't need it until morning," she said, pointing at the bottle that I held. "I have more at home. I always keep two bottles ahead."

My father told me once that he thought she looked as though she had just been dug up out of her grave. She was a very unhealthy-looking old woman. She was tall and very thin. Her skin was gray, her clothes were gray, and her hair was gray. But her teeth were yellow. She wore eyeglasses with no rims. Just last week when my father was refilling this same prescription for her, he said, "I don't know what Doc keeps giving her this stuff for. Perfectly obvious what's the matter with her, and this isn't going to cure it."

"What *is* the matter with her?" I asked.

He shrugged his shoulders and said evasively, "Your guess is just as good as mine—or Doc's."

"I can get it in the morning," she repeated now.

"Yes, ma'am. It will be ready in the morning."

"Quiet in here tonight. Where's your aunt?"

"Outside," I said, and the way I said it made it sound as though I meant "transported" or "sold down the river."

She looked around the store as though she were a stranger, seeing it for the first time. She said, "It's a nice night. I suppose she's working in the garden."

After Miss Randolph left, I looked around the store, too. What had she seen that made her say it was a nice night and that my aunt would be working in the garden? You couldn't really see what was on the shelves—just the gleam of bottles and jars inside the dark-mahogany, glass-enclosed cases. The corners lay in deep shadow. It might have been a conjurer's shop, except, of course, for the cigarettes and the candy and the soda fountain. The bottles gleaming darkly along the walls could have held wool of bat and nose of Turk, root of the mandrake and dust of the toad. I went out in the back room and looked into the yard. It seemed to go on forever, reaching into a vast, mysterious distance, unexplored, silent—not even the twitter of a bird. It was pitch black. I couldn't see the blossoms on the cherry trees, I couldn't tell what shape the yard was. But I now knew what was wrong with Miss Rena Randolph. She was crazy.

As the evening wore along, we got fewer and fewer customers. They bought cigarettes and cigars, candy, magazines. Very few cars went past. The town clock struck nine, and this surprised me, because I hadn't realized it was so late. My father always closed the store at nine-thirty. I had never closed it—or opened it, for that matter. I did not know where the keys to the front door were kept. I watched the clock, wondering what I should do at nine-thirty.

At quarter past nine, there was only one customer in the store—a woman who had purchased a box of candy. I was wrapping it up for her when someone pulled the screen door open with an abrupt, yanking movement and Pedro said, "Ah—"

I looked up and saw my father standing in the doorway, swaying back and forth, his arms extended. As I watched, he reached out and supported himself by leaning against the doorjamb. His appearance was so strange, he seemed so weak, so unlike himself, that I thought, He's been wounded. I peered at him, hunting for bruises on his face or his hands. As he entered the store, he kept looking around, blinking. He was wearing his light gray suit, and his newest boater hat, and the bow tie that I remembered. But the tie was twisted around to one side and it was partly untied, and his suit looked rumpled and so did his shirt.

I escorted the customer to the door, held it open for her, and then went to my father and said, "We—we didn't know where you were. Are you all right?"

He patted my hand. He said, "Look," and he smiled, revealing a set of glittering, horrible, wolfish-looking false teeth. There was a dribble of dried blood at the corner of his mouth. "I got my teeth."

I could barely understand what he said. He sounded as though he were speaking through or around a formidable obstruction that prevented his tongue and his lips from performing their normal function. The teeth glistened like the white porcelain fixtures in the downstairs bathroom.

I said, "Oh," weakly.

Pedro patted my father's arm. He said, "I worried—"

"Am I always going to sound like this?"

"I don't think so," I said.

He went into the prescription room and sat down in the chair by the window. Pedro stood beside him. I sat down on the high stool in front of the counter.

"Where's Sophy?"

I jumped off the stool. "They've gone to the police. I must telephone them—"

"Police? Police?" He made whistling noises when he said this. "Jesus Christ! For what?"

"They thought you were lost. I've got to call the Barracks—"

"Lawth?" he said, angrily. "Loweth?" he roared. "Lowerth? How could I we lowerth?" He stopped talking, reached up and took out the new false teeth, and wrapped them in his handkerchief. When he spoke again, he sounded just like himself. "I read about this place in Norwich where they take all your teeth out at once and put the false teeth in—make them for you and put them in all the same day. That's where I was. In Norwich. Getting my teeth. How could I get lost?"

"Oh!" I said and put my hand over my mouth, keeping the pain away. "Didn't it hurt? Don't the teeth hurt?"

"Hurt?" he shouted. "Of course they hurt!"

"But why didn't you tell Mother you were going?"

"I didn't think I'd be gone more than two hours. I got on a bus up at the corner, and it didn't take long to get there. They pulled the teeth out. Then they took impressions. They wouldn't let me have the teeth right away, said they had to wait to make sure the jaw had stopped bleeding, and so the whole process took longer than I thought it would."

"What made you finally get false teeth?" I didn't think it was pictures of the Valentino types, with their perfect white teeth, that I'd left around for him to see, and I didn't think it was the sight of Gramps Fender, the old man who took care of the house next door and whose false teeth hung loose in his mouth, or the fact that my Aunt Sophronia and my mother kept talking about the importance of chewing as an aid to the digestion of food. So if it wasn't any of these things, then what was it?

He sighed and said that that morning, while he was shaving, he had run through a solo he was to sing in church on Sunday. He stood in front of that new plate-glass mirror in the downstairs bathroom under all that brilliant white light, and he opened his mouth wide, and he saw himself in the mirror—the open mouth all red and moist inside, and the naked gums with a tooth here and there, and it was the mouth of an idiot out of Shakespeare, it was the mouth of the nurse in *Romeo and Juliet*, the mouth of the gravediggers in *Hamlet*, but most shocking of all, it was the mouth of Samuel Layen. This was what the congregation looked at and into on Sunday mornings. He said he couldn't bear the thought that that was what all those white people saw when he sang a solo. If he hadn't seen his mouth wide open like that in the new mirror under that new light . . .

I thought, But the congregation couldn't possibly see the inside of his mouth—he's in the choir loft when he sings, and he's much too far away from them. But I didn't say this.

He said it was while he was standing under the first cherry tree, looking up at the sky and listening to the hum of the bees, that he decided he would take a bus and head for Norwich and get himself some false teeth that very day without saying anything about it to anyone. He put the teeth back in his mouth and turned to Pedro and said, in that mumbling, full-of-pebbles voice, "How do I look?" and he smiled.

Pedro said, "You look beautiful, Mr. Layen," and touched him gently on the shoulder.

I went into the phone booth and closed the door. I started to dial the number of the state police. It was on a card up over the phone, along with the telephone numbers of the local doctors and the firehouse. I hesitated. The phone booth smelled of all its recent users—of cigar smoke, perfume, sweat. I felt as constrained as though all of these people were in the booth with me: politicians, idle females, workmen. I couldn't imagine myself saying, "We thought my father was missing. He's been gone all day and my mother and my aunt have now reported him as missing, but he's back." Why didn't I feel free to say this? Was it the presence of those recent users of the phone booth, who might ask, "Where'd he go?" "Has he done this before?" "Has he got a girl friend?" I dialed the number, and a gruff voice said, "State Police. Tenyeck Barracks. Officer O'Toole speaking."

I didn't know what to say to him, so I didn't say anything.

The voice sounded loud, impatient, in my ear. "Hullo! Hello? Speak up! Speak up!"

If I said that we thought my father was missing but he isn't, he's found, he's back, then wouldn't this Officer O'Toole want to know where he'd been? I said, "Well—"

The voice said, "Hello? Hello?" and "Yes?" and "What is it?" It was a very gruff voice and it had a barking quality.

I shook my head at the voice. I was not free to speak openly to that gruff policeman's voice. I thought, Well, now, perhaps the reason my father hadn't wanted to replace his teeth was that one of the images of the black man that the white man carries around with him is of white teeth flashing in a black and grinning face. So my father went toothless to destroy that image. But then there is toothless old Uncle Tom, and my old black mammy with her head rag is toothless, too, and without teeth my father fitted *that* image of the black man, didn't he?

So he was damned either way. Was he not? And so was I. And so was I.

Then I thought, Why bother? Why not act just like other people, just this once, just like white people—come right out and say the lost is found. My hand, my own hand, had in response to some order from my subconscious reached for a pencil that was securely fastened to a nail in the booth, tied there by a long red string. The pencil hung next to a big white pad. This was where we wrote down telephone orders. I was doodling on the big white pad. The skin on my hand was so dark in contrast to the white pad that I stared, because that was the second time that day that I had taken a good look at the color of my skin against something stark white. I looked at my dark brown hand and thought, Throw that baby down to me, you ain't goin' to take us back now, you know; all of us people with this dark skin must help hold the black island inviolate. I said, "This is Mr. Layen's daughter, at Layen's Drugstore in Wheeling. Mrs. Layen and her sister, Miss Bart, are on their way over there. Will you tell them that Mr. Layen found his watch—"

"Found his watch? He lost it, did he? Valuable watch, I suppose. Wait a minute. They're just coming up the steps now, just coming in the door. Wait a minute. I'll let you talk to Mrs. Layen yourself."

Everybody knew us for miles around. We were those rare laboratory specimens the black people who ran the drugstore in the white town of Wheeling, New York, only black family in town except for the Granites, who, ha, ha, ha—

"Wait a minute," the gruff, barking voice said again.

I closed my eyes and I could see my mother and my aunt—two bent-over little women, going up the steps of the state-police barracks in Tenyeck, humble, hesitant, the whites of their eyes showing under the irises.

My mother's voice sounded in my ear. "Yes?" Harsh, loud.

I said, "Father is so happy. He found his watch. He thinks he dropped it in Norwich, where he went to get his new false teeth." It sounded as though he'd always had false teeth—or at least Officer O'Toole, who was undoubtedly listening in, would think so.

Insight

1. How would you describe the narrator of this story? Does she appear to be perceptive? Mature? What is her relationship with her father? In what ways are these two people similar?

2. What reaction does the girl have upon seeing herself in the new mirror? Compare this reaction with that of her father as he views himself in the same mirror. What new ideas about themselves has each gained from the images they now receive?

3. Why is it so important to the Layens that they separate "the life of the family from the life of the drugstore"? What is implied by the narrator's comment that the totally separate life "was like having a concealed weapon to use against your enemy"? *meredith scrutiny*

4. Explain the meaning and implications of the paragraph, "So he was damned either way. Was he not? And so was I. And so was I."

iN MiNd

Denise Levertov

There's in my mind a woman
of innocence, unadorned but

fair-featured, and smelling of
apples or grass. She wears

a utopian smock or shift, her hair   5
is light brown and smooth, and she

is kind and very clean without
ostentation—
                    but she has
no imagination.   10
                    And there's a
turbulent moon-ridden girl

or old woman, or both,
dressed in opals and rags, feathers

and torn taffeta,   15
who knows strange songs—

but she is not kind.

MIRROR

Sylvia Plath

[handwritten: A sustained metaphor mirror / lake]
[handwritten: pt. of view mirror + lake]

I am silver and exact. I have no preconceptions.
Whatever I see I swallow immediately
Just as it is, unmisted by love or dislike.
I am not cruel, only truthful—
The eye of a little god, four-cornered. *[handwritten: showing things as are]* 5
Most of the time I meditate on the opposite wall.
It is pink, with speckles. I have looked at it so long
I think it is a part of my heart. But it flickers.
Faces and darkness separate us over and over.

[handwritten left margin: This is who I am, what I do]

Now I am a lake. A woman bends over me, 10
Searching my reaches for what she really is.
Then she turns to those liars, the candles or the moon.
I see her back, and reflect it faithfully.
She rewards me with tears and an agitation of hands. *[handwritten: breaks up water]*
I am important to her. She comes and goes. 15
Each morning it is her face that replaces the darkness.
In me she has drowned a young girl, and in me an old woman
Rises toward her day after day, like a terrible fish. *[handwritten: figure of speech]*

[handwritten left margin: Brings in a person / lake is faithful + truthful]

[handwritten notes:]
lifelong companion, honest / shows us w/out bias
2 of beauty standard. double

5

Comes out of water
reminds us in charge daily
human truth — shows reflection as is read
truth, sometimes not wanting truth.
Power of truth

THE double GOER

Dilys Laing

The woman took a train
away away from herself.
She thought: I need a change
and wheels make revolutions.
I'm half a century old   5
and must be getting somewhere.
And so she futured on
away from her own presence.

The landscape boiled around her
like a pan of beans.   10
A man without a face
made her ticket holy.
Adventure thrilled her nerves
restless rapture shook her.
Love is in the next seat,   15
she mused, and strength and glory
are over the hill, and I
grow younger as I leave
my me behind.

The telephone wires were staves   20
of a quintet score.
The hills were modulations
through the circle of keys.
Freedom is music, she thought,
smiling at the conductor.   25
This is your station, lady,
he snapped, and on the downbeat
she stepped to the vita nuova.*

A crowd had come to meet her
and they were fond in greeting: 30
husband, child, and father,
mother, and all the neighbors.

[28] VITA NUOVA: new life.

They travel as fast as I do,
she thought, and turned to climb
back to freedom's flying.   35
The door was shut. The train
streamed off like spilled water.

She faced the crowd and cried:
I love you all but one:
the one who wears my face.   40
She is the one I fled from.

They said: You took her with you
and brought her back again.
You look sick. Welcome home.

Insight
1. Characterize the women in each of these three poems. What details
   do you learn about each? How do these details contribute to the
   meaning of the poem?
2. Which woman appears to know herself best? What evidence is
   there to support your answer?

SAMUEL

Grace Paley

Some boys are very tough. They're afraid of nothing. They are the ones who climb a wall and take a bow at the top. Not only are they brave on the roof, but they make a lot of noise in the darkest part of the cellar where even the super hates to go. They also jiggle and hop on the platform between the locked doors of the subway cars.

Four boys are jiggling on the swaying platform. Their names are Alfred, Calvin, Samuel, and Tom. The men and the women in the cars on either side watch them. They don't like them to jiggle or jump but don't want to interfere. Of course some of the men in the cars were once brave boys like these. One of them had ridden the tail of a speeding truck from New York to Rockaway Beach without getting off, without his sore fingers losing hold. Nothing happened to him then or later. He had made a compact with other boys who preferred to watch: Starting at Eighth Avenue and Fifteenth Street, he would get to some specified place, maybe Twenty-third and the river, by hopping the tops of the moving trucks. This was hard to do when one truck turned a corner in the wrong direction and the nearest truck was a couple of feet too high. He made three or four starts before succeeding. He had gotten this idea from a film at school called *The Romance of Logging*. He had finished high school, married a good friend, was in a responsible job and going to night school.

These two men and others looked at the four boys jumping and jiggling on the platform and thought, It must be fun to ride that way, especially now the weather is nice and we're out of the tunnel and way high over the Bronx. Then they thought, These kids do seem to be acting sort of stupid. They *are* little. Then they thought of some of the brave things they had done when they were boys and jiggling didn't seem so risky.

The ladies in the car became very angry when they looked at the four boys. Most of them brought their brows together and hoped the boys could see their extreme disapproval. One of the ladies wanted to get up and say, Be careful you dumb kids, get off that platform or I'll call a cop. But three of the boys were Negroes and the fourth was something else she couldn't tell for sure. She was afraid they'd be fresh and laugh at her and embarrass her. She wasn't afraid they'd hit her, but she was afraid of embarrassment. Another lady thought, Their mothers never know where they are. It wasn't true in this particular case. Their mothers all knew that they had gone to see the missile exhibit on Fourteenth Street.

89

Out on the platform, whenever the train accelerated, the boys would raise their hands and point them up to the sky to act like rockets going off, then they rat-tat-tatted the shatterproof glass pane like machine guns, although no machine guns had been exhibited.

For some reason known only to the motorman, the train began a sudden slowdown. The lady who was afraid of embarrassment saw the boys jerk forward and backward and grab the swinging guard chains. She had her own boy at home. She stood up with determination and went to the door. She slid it open and said, "You boys will be hurt. You'll be killed. I'm going to call the conductor if you don't just go into the next car and sit down and be quiet."

Two of the boys said, "Yes'm," and acted as though they were about to go. Two of them blinked their eyes a couple of times and pressed their lips together. The train resumed its speed. The door slid shut, parting the lady and the boys. She leaned against the side door because she had to get off at the next stop.

The boys opened their eyes wide at each other and laughed. The lady blushed. The boys looked at her and laughed harder. They began to pound each other's back. Samuel laughed the hardest and pounded Alfred's back until Alfred coughed and the tears came. Alfred held tight to the chain hook. Samuel pounded him ever harder when he saw the tears. He said, "Why you bawling? You a baby, huh?" and laughed. One of the men whose boyhood had been more watchful than brave became angry. He stood up straight and looked at the boys for a couple of seconds. Then he walked in a citizenly way to the end of the car, where he pulled the emergency cord. Almost at once, with a terrible hiss, the pressure of air abandoned the brakes and the wheels were caught and held.

People standing in the most secure places fell forward, then backward. Samuel had let go of his hold on the chain so he could pound Tom as well as Alfred. All the passengers in the cars whipped back and forth, but he pitched only forward and fell head first to be crushed and killed between the cars.

The train had stopped hard, halfway into the station, and the conductor called at once for the trainmen who knew about this kind of death and how to take the body from the wheels and brakes. There was silence except for passengers from other cars who asked, What happened! What happened! The ladies waited around wondering if he might be an only child. The men recalled other afternoons with very bad endings. The little boys stayed close to each other, leaning and touching shoulders and arms and legs.

When the policeman knocked at the door and told her about it, Samuel's mother began to scream. She screamed all day and moaned all night, though the doctors tried to quiet her with pills.

Oh, oh, she hopelessly cried. She did not know how she could ever find another boy like that one. However, she was a young woman and she became pregnant. Then for a few months she was hopeful. The child born to her was a boy. They brought him to be seen and nursed. She smiled. But immediately she saw that this baby wasn't Samuel. She and her husband together have had other children, but never again will a boy exactly like Samuel be known.

Insight

1. The men on the train are classified into two groups—the "brave" and the "watchful." How does each group react to the boys' behavior? What explanation can you suggest for the different attitudes?

2. While Samuel's behavior may appear foolhardy, the author appears to be evaluating it positively. What hints do you find in the story that she does not disapprove of his behavior?

MY FIRST TWO WOMEN

Nadine Gordimer

I have been trying to remember when and where I saw my father's second wife for the first time. I must have seen her frequently, without singling her out or being aware of her, at many of those houses, full of friends, where my father and I were guests in the summer of 1928. My father had many friends, and it seems to me (I was not more than four years old at the time) that, at weekends at least, we were made much of at a whole roster of houses, from tiny shacks, which young couples had "fixed up" for themselves, to semi-mansions, where we had two guest rooms and a bathroom all to ourselves. Whether we sat under a peach tree on painted homemade chairs at a shack, or around the swimming pool on cane chaises-longues at a mansion, the atmosphere of those Saturdays and Sundays was the same: the glasses of warm beer, full of sun, into which I sometimes stuck a finger; the light and color of a Johannesburg summer, with thousands of midges, grasshoppers and other weightless leaping atoms exploding softly over your face as you lay down on the grass; the laughter and voices of the men and women, as comforting and pleasant as the drunken buzz of the great bluebottles that fell sated from rotting fruit, or bees that hung a moment over your head, on their way to and fro between elaborate flowering rockeries. She must have been there often—one of the women who would help me into the spotted rubber Loch Ness[1] monster that kept me afloat, or bring me a lemonade with a colored straw to drink it through—so often that I ceased to see her.

During the months of that summer, I lived at one or another of those friends' houses, along with the children of the house; sometimes my father stayed there with me, and sometimes he did not. But even if he was not actually living in the same place with me, he was in and out every day, and the whole period has in my mind the blurring change and excitement of a prolonged holiday—children to play with, a series of affectionate women who arranged treats, settled fights, and gave me presents. The whereabouts of my mother were vague to me and not particularly troubling. It seems to me that I believed her not to be back yet from her visit to my grandmother in Kenya, and yet I have the recollection of once speaking to her on the telephone, as if

---

[1] LOCH NESS: a lake in Scotland noted for repeated unconfirmed reports of a monster inhabiting it.

she were in Johannesburg after all. I remember saying, "When are you coming back?" and then not waiting for her to answer but going on, "Guess what I've got in my hand?" (It was a frog, which had just been discovered to have completed its metamorphosis from a tadpole in a tin basin full of stones and water.)

The previous winter, when my mother had gone to Kenya, my father and I had lived in our house, my parents' own house, alone. This was not unusual; I am aware that I had been alone with him, in the care of servants, time and again before that. In fact, any conception I have in my mind of my mother and father and me living together as a family includes her rather as a presence—rooms that were hers, books and trinkets belonging to her, the mute testimony of her grand piano—rather than a flesh-and-blood actuality. Even if she *was* there she did little or nothing of an intimate nature for me; I do not connect her with meal or bath times. So it came about, I suppose, that I scarcely understood, that summer, that there was a real upheaval and change over my head. My father and I were never to go back to that house together. In fact, we both had left it for good; even though I, before the decision was to be made final for me, was to return for a few weeks, it was not to the *same house,* in any but the brick-and-mortar sense, and my position in it and the regrouping of its attention in relation to me were so overwhelmingly changed that they wiped out, in a blaze of self-importance and glory, the dim near babyhood that had gone before.

For, suddenly, in a beautiful autumn month (it must have been March), I found myself back in our house with my mother. The willows around the lawn were fountains spouting pale-yellow leaves on the grass that was kept green all year round. I slept with my mother, in her bed. Surely I had not done so before. When I said to her, "Mummy, didn't I used to sleep in the nursery before you went to Kenya?" she pushed up my pajama jacket and blew in my navel and said, "Darling, I really have no idea where your Daddy put you to sleep while I was away."

She had short, shiny black hair cut across her forehead in a fringe. She took me to the barber and had my hair, my black hair, cut in a fringe. (Daddy used to brush my hair back, first dipping the brush in water. "Water dries out the hair," she said.) We would get out of her car together, at the houses of friends, and she would walk with me slowly up the path toward them, hand in hand. We looked exactly alike, they all said, exactly alike; it was incredible that a small boy could look so much the image of his mother.

My mother would put me up on the long stool beside her while she played the piano; I had never been so close to a piano while it was being played, and sometimes the loud parts of the music swelled through my head frighteningly, like the feeling once when I slipped through my Loch Ness monster and went under in a swimming pool. Then I got used to the sensation and found it exciting, and I would say to her, "Play loudly, Mummy. Make it boom." Sometimes she would stop playing suddenly and whirl around and hold me tight, looking out over my head at the guests who had been listening. I would hear the last reverberation die away in the great rosewood shape behind us while silence held in the room.

My mother walked up and down a room when she talked, and she talked a great deal, to people who seemed to have no chance to answer her, but were there to listen. Once, in the bathroom, I threw a wet toy and it hit my African nanny on the mouth, and when she smacked my behind and I yelled, my mother rushed in and raged at her, yelling as loudly as I did. My mother was beautiful when she was angry, for she was one of those women who cry with anger, and her eyes glistened and her natural pallor was stained bright with rising blood.

She took me to a circus. She took me to a native mineworkers' "war" dance. She came home from town with a pile of educational toys and sat over me, watching, while I hesitated, caught her long, black, urging eye, brilliant as the eye of an animal that can see in the dark, and then, with a kind of hypnotized instinct born of the desire to please, fitted the right shape on the right peg.

There were still a few leaves, like droplets not yet shaken off, on the twigs of the willows when my clothes and toys were packed up again and my father came to fetch me away.

This time I went to the sea, with the family of three little boys and their mother, with whom I had stayed before. I had a wonderful time, and when I came back, it was to a new house that I had never seen. In it were my father and his second wife.

I was not surprised to see this woman, and, as I have said, she was not a stranger to me. I liked her, and, made gregarious by the life of the past year, asked, "How much days can Deb stay with us?"

"For always," said my father.

"Doesn't she ever have to go home?"

"This is her home, and yours, and Daddy's."

"Why?"

"Because she is married to me now, Nick. She is my wife, and husbands and wives love each other and live together in the same house."

There was a pause, and when I spoke again, what I said must have been very different from what they expected. They did not know that while I was on holiday at the sea I had been taken, one rainy afternoon, along with the older children, to the cinema. There I had seen, in all the rose and crystalline blur of Technicolor, a man and woman dance out beneath the chandeliers of a ballroom. When I had asked what they were doing, I was told that this was a wedding—the man and the woman had just been married.

"Do you mean like this?" I asked my father and my stepmother, taking my father's hand, bending my knees, and shaping out my arms in a jiglike posture. I hopped around solemnly, dragging him with me.

"Dancing?" guessed my father, mystified and affectionate, appealing to his wife.

"Oh, that's wonderful!" she cried in sudden delight. "Bless his formal heart! A real wedding!"

There followed a confusion of hugging, all around. I was aware only that in some way I had pleased them.

I was now nearly five years old and due to begin going to school. My stepmother took me to town with her, and together we bought the supplies for my birthday party, and my school uniform, and a satchel with a fancy lock—soon to be stained as greasy as an old fish-and-chip wrapping with the print of successive school lunches—and the elaborate equipment of pencil sharpeners, erasers and rulers indispensable to the child who has not yet learned to write. Deb understood what a birthday party for a five-year-old boy should be like. She had ideas of her own, and could sway a wavering torment of indecision between candleholders in the guise of soldiers or elephants, imparting to the waverer a comforting sense of the rightness of the final choice, but she also knew when to efface her own preferences entirely and let me enjoy my own choice for my own unexplained reasons. In fact, she was so good at the calm management of the practical details of my small life that I suppose I quickly assumed this stability as my right, and took it altogether for granted, as children, in their fierce unconscious instinct for personal salvation, take all those rights which, if withheld from them, they cannot consciously remark, but whose lack they exhibit and revenge with equal unconscious ferocity. Of course Deb bought neat and comfortable clothes for me, found the books I would best like to hear her read from, took me with her on visits that would be interesting to me, but left me at home to play when she was going where there would be nothing to amuse me; she always had, hadn't she, right from the first day?

The children at school wanted to know why I called my mother "Deb." When I said that she was not my mother, they insisted that she must be. "Are you my mother now, Deb?" I asked her.

"No," she said. "You know that you have your own mother."

"They say you must be, because you live with Daddy and me."

"I'm your second mother," she said, looking to see if that would do.

"Like my godmother?"

"That's right."

I dashed off to play; it was perfectly satisfactory.

There came a stage when school, the preparation for which had been so enjoyable, palled. I suppose there must have been some incident there, some small failure which embarrassed or shamed me. I do not remember. But I know that, suddenly, I didn't want to go to school. Deb was gentle but insistent. I remember my own long, sullen silence one day, after a wrangle of "Whys?" from me and firm explanations from her. At last I said, "When I'm at my mother's I stay home all the time."

My stepmother was squatting on her heels in front of a low cupboard, and her eyes opened up toward me like the eyes of those sleeping dolls which girl children alternately lower and raise by inclining the doll's body, but her voice was the same as usual. "If you lived with your mother now, you would go to school just as you do here," she said.

I stood right in front of her. She looked up at me again, and I said, "No I wouldn't." I waited. Then I said, "She lets me do what I like." I waited again. "I can even play her piano. She's got a big piano. As big as this room."

My stepmother went on slowly putting back into the cupboard the gramophone records she had been sorting and cleaning. Standing over her, I could see the top of her head, an unfamiliar aspect of a grownup. It was then, I think, that I began to see her for the first time, not as one of the succession of pretty ladies who petted and cared for me, but as Deb, as someone connected in wordless depths with my father and me, as my father and I and, yes, my mother were connected. Someone who had entered, irrevocably, the atavistic tension of that cunning battle for love and supremacy that exists between children and parents sometimes even beyond the grave, when one protagonist is dead and mourned, and lives on in the fierce dissatisfaction of the other's memory.

She was a fair woman, this Deb, this woman beloved of my father; on all faces there is some feature, some plane that catches the light in characteristic prominence of that face, and on her face, at that moment and always, it was her long golden eyebrows, shining. They were bleached from much swimming, but her dull, curly hair, always protected from sun and water by a cap, hung colorless and nowhere smooth enough to shine. The face was broad and brown across strong cheekbones, and she had a big, orange-painted mouth, the beautiful underlip of which supported the upper as calmly as a carved pediment. Her eyes, moving from record to cupboard, lowered under my presence, were green or blue, depending upon what color she wore. As she squatted, her knees, with thighs and calves showing under the short skirt, closed back against each other like the blades of a knife, were particularly pretty—smooth and pink-skinned, with a close speckling of dainty freckles, like the round tops of her arms and her long calves. She was the sort of fair woman who would never be called a blonde.

Deb. I knew what it smelled like in that pink freckled neck. I knew the stiff and ugly ears that she kept hidden under that hair, and that sometimes, when she was hot and lifted her hair off her neck a moment for coolness, were suddenly discovered.

I shall never forget the feeling I had as I stood there over her. If I search my adult experience as a man to approximate it, I can only say that now it seems to me that physically it was rather like the effect of the first drink you take after a long wet day of some strenuous exercise—rowing or hunting. It was a feeling of power that came like an inflow of physical strength. I was only five years old, but power is something of which I am convinced there is no innocence this side of the womb, and I knew what it was, all right; I understood, without a name for it, what I had. And with it came all the weapons—that bright, clinical set that I didn't need to have explained to me, as my father had had to explain to me the uses of the set of carpenter's tools I had been given for my birthday. My hand would go out unfalteringly for these drills and probes, and the unremembered pain of where they had been used on me would guide me to their application.

"Deb," I said, "why didn't Daddy marry my mother?"

"He did," she said. "Once he was married to her. But they were not happy with each other. Not like Daddy and me—and you. Not happy together like us." She did not ask me if I remembered this, but her voice suggested the question, in spite of her.

Daddy. My mother. My mother was simply a word I was using at that moment. I could not see her in my head. She was a mouth moving, singing; for a second she sat at the piano, smiled at me, one of her swift, startling smiles that was like someone jumping out of concealment and saying "Boo!" Inside me, it gave me a fright. If my dog had been there, I would have pulled back his ears, hard, to hear him yelp. There was Deb, squatting in front of me. I said, "My mother's got a piano as big as this house. I want to go and stay with her."

Deb got up from the floor and rubbed down her thighs. "Soon," she said. "You'll go on a visit soon, I'm sure. Let's see if tea's ready." We did not take each other's hand, but walked out onto the porch side by side, with a space between us.

It was after that day that I began to be conscious of the relationship between my father and Deb. This was not the way he and those others—the pretty, helpful friends who were the mothers of my friends—had behaved toward each other. I watched with unbiased interest, as I would have watched a bird bringing his mate tidbits where she balanced on our paling fence, when my father ate an apple bite-and-bite-about with this woman, or, passing her chair at breakfast, after he had kissed me good-by in the morning, paused to press his cheek silently, and with closed eyes, against hers. In the car, I noticed that she rested her hand on his knee as he drove. Sometimes, in the evenings, both she and I sat on his lap at once.

There were no images in my memory to which to match these. They were married, Deb and my father. This behavior was marriage. Deb herself had told me that marriage once had existed between my father and my mother. One day I came home from a visit to my mother and remarked, conversationally, in the bedroom Deb and my father shared, "My mother's got a bed just like yours, Deb, and that's where Daddy and she used to sleep when he lived there, didn't you, Daddy?"

It was Sunday, and my father still lay in bed, reading the paper, though Deb's place was empty and she was gathering her clothes together before she went off to the bathroom. He said, "No, son. Don't you remember? Mine was the room with the little balcony."

"Oh, yes," I said. "Of course, I know." All at once I remembered the smell of that rather dark, high room, a smell of shirts fresh from the iron, of the two leather golf bags in the corner, and some chemical with which the carpet had been cleaned. All this—the smell of my father—had disappeared under the warmer, relaxing and polleny scents of the room he now shared with a woman, where peach-colored dust from her powder settled along his hairbrushes, and the stockings she peeled off retained the limp, collapsed semblance of her legs, like the newly shed skin of a snake I had come upon in the bush when I was on holiday at the sea.

I think that there must have been something strongly attractive to me in the ease of this feminine intimacy to which my father and I found ourselves admitted with such naturalness. Yet because it was unfamiliar, the very seductiveness of its comfort seemed, against the confusion of my short life, a kind of disloyalty, to which I was party and of which I was guilty. Disloyalty—to what? Guilty—of what?

I was too young for motives; I could only let them bubble up, manifest in queer little words and actions. I know that that Sunday morning I said stoutly, as if I were explaining some special system of living, "There we each had our *own* rooms. Everybody slept in their own room."

Before the end of the first year of the marriage that power that had come to me like a set of magical weapons, the day when my stepmother knelt before me at the record cupboard, became absolute. It crushed upon my little-boy's head the vainglory and triumph of the tyrant, crown or thorn. I was to wear it as my own for the rest of my childhood.

I was cuddling Deb, secure in her arms one day, when I said, out of some gentle honey of warmth that I felt peacefully within me, "I'm going to call you Mummy because I love you best." I am sure that she knew that the statement was not quite so stunning and meaningful as it sounds now, out of the context of childhood. Quite often, she had heard me say of an animal or a new friend, "You know whom I love. I love only Eddie." (Or "Sam," or "Chris.") Sometimes the vehement preference was expressed not out of real feeling for the friend or animal in question, but out of pique toward some other child or animal. At other times it was merely an unreasonable welling up of well-being that had to find an object. But I had never before said this particular thing to her. I felt her thighs tighten suddenly beneath me; all four fingers and the thumb of her hand seized round my arm. She shook back her hair fumblingly and held her face away from mine to look at me; she was awkward with joy. I looked up into the stare of her eyes— grown-up eyes that fell before mine—and in me, like milk soured by a flash of lightning, the sweet secretion of affection became insipid in the fearful, amazed thrill of victim turned victor.

That was our story, really, for many years. My father and Deb were deeply in love and theirs was a serene marriage. The three of us lived together in amity; it was a place of warmth for a child to grow in. I visited my mother at regular, if widely spaced, intervals. I went to her for short periods at Christmas, birthdays, and during holidays. Thus along with her, with that elegant black head and those hard wrists volatile with all the wonderful bracelets she had picked up all over the world, went excitement and occasion, treats and parties, people who exclaimed over me, and the abolishment of that guillotine of joys, bedtime. Sometimes the tide of grown-up activities would pass on over my head and leave me stranded and abandoned on a corner of somebody's sofa, rubbing my eyes against the glare of forgotten lights. It did not matter; the next day, or the day after that, I was sure to be delivered back to Deb and my father and the comfort of my child's pace.

Thus it was, too, that along with home and Deb and my father went everyday life, the greater part of life, with time for boredom, for transgressions and punishments. When I visited my mother for a weekend or a day I was on my best behavior, befitting a treat or an occasion; I was never with her long enough to need chastisement. So when, at home, I was naughty and my father or Deb had to punish me, I would inflame myself against them with the firm belief that my mother would never punish me. At these times of resentment and injury, I would see her clearly and positively, flaming in the light of a Christmas tree or the fiery ring of candles on a birthday cake, my champion against a world that would not bend entirely to my own will. In the same way, for the first few days after my return from a visit to her, everything about the way she lived and the things about her were lit up by the occasion with which my visit had coincided;

her flat (when I was seven or eight she moved into a luxurious pent-house in a block overlooking a country club) was like the glowing cardboard interior of the king's castle, carried away in my mind from a pantomime matinee. "There's a swimming pool right on top of the building, on the roof garden," I would tell Deb. "I swim there every morning. Once I swam at night. My mother lets me. The lift doesn't go up to the top—you have to walk the last flight of stairs from the twelfth floor." "My mother's got a car with an overhead drive. Do you know what that is, Deb? It means you don't have to change the gears with your hands." "I wish we had a swimming pool here. I don't like this old house without even a swimming pool."

Deb always answered me quietly and evenly. Never, even when I was very young, did she try to point out rival attractions at home. But in time, when I grew older and was perhaps eleven or twelve, I struggled against something that went more than quiet—went dead—in her during these one-sided conversations. I felt not that she was not listening, but that she was listless, without interest in what I said. And then I did not know at whom the resentment I suddenly felt was directed, whether at my mother—that glossy-haired kingfisher flashing in and out of my life—for having a roof-garden swimming pool and a car without gears, or at Deb, for her lack of attention and negative reaction to my relation of these wonders. This reaction of hers was all the more irking, and in some vague, apprehensive way dismaying, when one remembered the way she watched and listened to me sometimes, with that look in her eyes that wanted something from me, wondered, hesitated, hopeful—that look I had known how to conjure up ever since the first day when I suggested I would call her my mother, and that, in perverse, irresistible use of the same power, I had also known how never to allow to come to articulacy, to emotional fulfillment, between us. The business of my calling her mother, for instance; it had come up several times again, while I was small. But she, in the silence that followed, had never managed anything more than, once, an almost unintelligibly murmured "If you like." And I, once the impulsive, casually pronounced sentence had exploded and left its peculiar after-silence, had dropped my avowal as I left a toy, here or there, for someone else to pick up in house or garden. I never did call her mother; in time, I think I should have been surprised to hear that there had ever been any question that she should be anything else but "Deb."

I was strongly attached to her, and when, at twelve or thirteen, I entered adolescence and boarding school at the same time, there was in fact a calm friendship between us unusual between a woman, and a boy walking the knife edge dividing small-boy scorn of the feminine from awakening sex interest. I suppose if she had been truly in the position of a mother, this relationship would not have been possible.

Her position must have been curiously like that of the woman who, failing to secure as a lover the man with whom she has fallen in love, is offered instead his respect and his confidences.

I was fifteen when I asked the question that had taken a thousand different forms—doubts, anxieties, and revenges—all through my life but had never formulated itself directly. The truth was, I had never known what that question *was*—only felt it, in all my blood and bones, fumbled toward it under the kisses of people who loved me, asked it with my seeking of my father's hands, the warmth of Deb's lap, the approval of my form master's eye, the smiles of my friends. Now it came to me matter-of-factly, in words.

I was home from school for the weekend, and there had been guests at lunch. They had discussed the divorce of a common friend and the wrangle over the custody of the children of the marriage. One of the guests was a lawyer, and he had gone into the legal niceties in some detail. After the guests had gone, my father went off for his nap and Deb and I dragged our favorite canvas chairs out onto the lawn. As I settled mine at a comfortable angle, I asked her, curiously, "Deb, how was it that my mother didn't get me? The custody of me, I mean."

She thought for a moment, and I thought she must be trying how best to present some legal technicality in a way that both she and I would understand.

"I mean, their divorce was an arranged thing, wasn't it—one of those things arranged to look like desertion that Derrick spoke about? Why didn't my mother get me?" The lawyer had explained that where parents contested the custody, unless there was some strong factor to suggest that the mother was unsuitable to rear a child, a young child was usually awarded to her care.

Then quite suddenly Deb spoke. Her face was red and she looked strange, and she spoke so fast that what she said was almost blurted. "She gave you up."

Her face and tone so astonished me that the impact of what she had said missed its mark. I stared at her, questioning.

She met my gaze stiffly, with a kind of jerky bravado, intense, looking through me.

"How do you mean?"

"Voluntarily. She gave you over to your father."

The pressure in her face died slowly down; her hands moved, as if released, on the chair arms. "I should never have told you," she said flatly. "I'd promised myself I never should."

"You mean she didn't want me?"

"We don't know what her reasons were, Nick. We can't know them."

"Didn't try to get me?"

There was a long silence. "We made up our minds. We decided it was best. We decided we would try and make your relationship with her as normal as possible. Never say anything against her. I promised myself I wouldn't try—for myself. I often wanted to tell you—oh, lots of things. I wanted to punish you for what I withheld for your sake. I wanted to hurt you; I suppose I forgot you were a child. . . . Well, what does it matter anyway? It's all worked itself out, long ago. Only I shouldn't have told you now. It's pointless." She smiled at me, as at a friend who can be counted on to understand a confession. "It didn't even give me any pleasure."

My stepmother talked about this whole situation in which we had all lived as if it were something remembered from the past, instead of a living situation out of the continuity of which I was then, at that moment, beginning my life as a man. All worked itself out, long ago. Perhaps it had. Yes, she was right. All worked itself out, without me. Above and about me, over my head, saving me the risk and the opportunity of my own volition.

My mother? That black-haired, handsome woman become rather fleshy, who, I discovered while I sat, an awkward visitor among her admiring friends (I had inherited her love of music), sang off-key.

But it was not toward her that I felt anger, regret, and a terrible, mournful anguish of loss, which brought up from somewhere in my tall, coarse, half-man's, half-child's body what I was alarmed to recognize as the raking turmoil that precedes tears.

"We're really good friends, aren't we?" said my stepmother lovingly, with quiet conviction.

It was true: that was what we were—all we were.

I have never forgiven her for it.

Insight

1. What feelings does the boy appear to have toward his mother before Deb's arrival? How does he view her after Deb's arrival? Has this view changed at the end of the story? Explain.
2. How would you characterize the boy's mother? How deep do her feelings toward her son appear to be? Explain.
3. Describe and account for Deb's response to the boy's question, "Are you my mother now, Deb?" and to his statement, "I'm going to call you Mummy because I love you best."
4. Both the boy and Deb suffer deeply from unmet emotional needs. What are these needs? Why are they not fulfilled?
5. Do you agree with Deb's evaluation, "Well, what does it matter anyway? It's all worked itself out, long ago. Only I shouldn't have told you now. It's pointless"? Explain.
6. How do you account for the boy's feelings toward Deb? To what extent do you feel she is to blame for these feelings?

TWO POEMS

Sappho

This way, that way

I do not know
what to do: I
am of two minds

I ask you, sir, to

Stand face to face
with me as a friend
would: show me the
favor of your eyes

A White Heron

Sarah Orne Jewett

Sylvia = wood-nymph

I

The woods were already filled with shadows one June evening, just
before eight o'clock, though a bright sunset still glimmered faintly
among the trunks of the trees. A little girl was driving home her cow,
a plodding, dilatory, provoking creature in her behavior, but a valued
companion for all that. They were going away from the western light,
and striking deep into the dark woods, but their feet were familiar
with the path, and it was no matter whether their eyes could see it or
not.

There was hardly a night the summer through when the old cow
could be found waiting at the pasture bars; on the contrary, it was her
greatest pleasure to hide herself away among the high huckleberry
bushes, and though she wore a loud bell she had made the discovery
that if one stood perfectly still it would not ring. So Sylvia had to
hunt for her until she found her, and call Co'! Co'! with never an
answering Moo, until her childish patience was quite spent. If the
creature had not given good milk and plenty of it, the case would
have seemed very different to her owners. Besides, Sylvia had all the
time there was, and very little use to make of it. Sometimes in
pleasant weather it was a consolation to look upon the cow's pranks
as an intelligent attempt to play hide and seek, and as the child had no
playmates she lent herself to this amusement with a good deal of zest.
Though this chase had been so long that the wary animal herself had
given an unusual signal of her whereabouts, Sylvia had only laughed
when she came upon Mistress Moolly at the swamp-side, and urged
her affectionately homeward with a twig of birch leaves. The old cow
was not inclined to wander farther, she even turned in the right direction for once as they left the pasture, and stepped along the road at
a good pace. She was quite ready to be milked now, and seldom
stopped to browse. Sylvia wondered what her grandmother would
say because they were so late. It was a great while since she had left
home at half past five o'clock, but everybody knew the difficulty of
making this errand a short one. Mrs. Tilley had chased the hornéd
torment too many summer evenings herself to blame any one else for
lingering, and was only thankful as she waited that she had Sylvia,
nowadays, to give such valuable assistance. The good woman suspected that Sylvia loitered occasionally on her own account; there
never was such a child for straying about out-of-doors since the world
was made! Everybody said that it was a good change for a little maid

*all her relation-
ships with
creatures*

dilatory   causing delay

who had tried to grow for eight years in a crowded manufacturing town, but, as for Sylvia herself, it seemed as if she never had been alive at all before she came to live at the farm. She thought often with wistful compassion of a wretched dry geranium that belonged to a town neighbor.

"'Afraid of folks,'" old Mrs. Tilley said to herself, with a smile, after she had made the unlikely choice of Sylvia from her daughter's houseful of children, and was returning to the farm. "'Afraid of folks,' they said! I guess she won't be troubled no great with 'em up to the old place!" When they reached the door of the lonely house and stopped to unlock it, and the cat came to purr loudly, and rub against them, a deserted pussy, indeed, but fat with young robins, Sylvia whispered that this was a beautiful place to live in, and she never should wish to go home.

The companions followed the shady woodroad, the cow taking slow steps, and the child very fast ones. The cow stopped long at the brook to drink, as if the pasture were not half a swamp, and Sylvia stood still and waited, letting her bare feet cool themselves in the shoal water, while the great twilight moths struck softly against her. She waded on through the brook as the cow moved away, and listened to the thrushes with a heart that beat fast with pleasure. There was a stirring in the great boughs overhead. They were full of little birds and beasts that seemed to be wide-awake, and going about their world, or else saying good-night to each other in sleepy twitters. Sylvia herself felt sleepy as she walked along. However, it was not much farther to the house, and the air was soft and sweet. She was not often in the woods so late as this, and it made her feel as if she were a part of the gray shadows and the moving leaves. She was just thinking how long it seemed since she first came to the farm a year ago, and wondering if everything went on in the noisy town just the same as when she was there; the thought of the great red-faced boy who used to chase and frighten her made her hurry along the path to escape from the shadow of the trees.

Suddenly this little woods-girl is horror-stricken to hear a clear whistle not very far away. Not a bird's whistle, which would have a sort of friendliness, but a boy's whistle, determined, and somewhat aggressive. Sylvia left the cow to whatever sad fate might await her, and stepped discreetly aside into the bushes, but she was just too late. The enemy had discovered her, and called out in a very cheerful and persuasive tone, "Halloa, little girl, how far is it to the road?" and trembling Sylvia answered almost inaudibly, "A good ways."

She did not dare to look boldly at the tall young man, who carried a gun over his shoulder, but she came out of her bush and again followed the cow, while he walked alongside.

"I have been hunting for some birds," the stranger said kindly, "and I have lost my way, and need a friend very much. Don't be afraid," he added gallantly. "Speak up and tell me what your name is, and whether you think I can spend the night at your house, and go out gunning early in the morning."

Sylvia was more alarmed than before. Would not her grandmother consider her much to blame? But who could have foreseen such an accident as this? It did not appear to be her fault, and she hung her head as if the stem of it were broken, but managed to answer "Sylvy," with much effort when her companion again asked her name.

Mrs. Tilley was standing in the doorway when the trio came into view. The cow gave a loud moo by way of explanation.

"Yes, you'd better speak up for yourself, you old trial! Where'd she tucked herself away this time, Sylvy?" Sylvia kept an awed silence; she knew by instinct that her grandmother did not comprehend the gravity of the situation. She must be mistaking the stranger for one of the farmer-lads of the region.

The young man stood his gun beside the door, and dropped a heavy game-bag beside it; then he bade Mrs. Tilley good-evening, and repeated his wayfarer's story, and asked if he could have a night's lodging.

"Put me anywhere you like," he said. "I must be off early in the morning, before day; but I am very hungry, indeed. You can give me some milk at any rate, that's plain."

"Dear sakes, yes," responded the hostess, whose long slumbering hospitality seemed to be easily awakened. "You might fare better if you went out on the main road a mile or so, but you're welcome to what we've got. I'll milk right off, and you make yourself at home. You can sleep on husks or feathers," she proffered graciously. "I raised them all myself. There's good pasturing for geese just below here towards the ma'sh. Now step round and set a plate for the gentleman, Sylvy!" And Sylvia promptly stepped. She was glad to have something to do, and she was hungry herself.

It was a surprise to find so clean and comfortable a little dwelling in this New England wilderness. The young man had known the horrors of its most primitive housekeeping, and the dreary squalor of that level of society which does not rebel at the companionship of hens. This was the best thrift of an old-fashioned farmstead, though on such a small scale that it seemed like a hermitage. He listened eagerly to the old woman's quaint talk, he watched Sylvia's pale face and shining gray eyes with ever growing enthusiasm, and insisted that this was the best supper he had eaten for a month; then, afterward, the new-made friends sat down in the doorway together while the moon came up.

Soon it would be berry-time, and Sylvia was a great help at picking. The cow was a good milker, though a plaguy thing to keep track of, the hostess gossiped frankly, adding presently that she had buried four children, so that Sylvia's mother, and a son (who might be dead) in California were all the children she had left. "Dan, my boy, was a great hand to go gunning," she explained sadly. "I never wanted for pa'tridges or gray squer'ls while he was to home. He's been a great wand'rer, I expect, and he's no hand to write letters. There, I don't blame him, I'd ha' seen the world myself if it had been so I could."

"Sylvia takes after him," the grandmother continued affectionately, after a minute's pause. "There ain't a foot o' ground she don't know her way over, and the wild creatur's counts her one o' themselves. Squer'ls she'll tame to come an' feed right out o' her hands, and all sorts o' birds. Last winter she got the jay-birds to bangeing here, and I believe she'd 'a' scanted herself of her own meals to have plenty to throw out amongst 'em, if I had n't kep' watch. Anything but crows, I tell her, I'm willin' to help support,—though Dan he went an' tamed one o' them that did seem to have reason same as folks. It was round here a good spell after he went away. Dan an' his father they did n't hitch,—but he never held up his head ag'in after Dan had dared him an' gone off."

The guest did not notice this hint of family sorrows in his eager interest in something else.

"So Sylvy knows all about birds, does she?" he exclaimed, as he looked round at the little girl who sat, very demure but increasingly sleepy, in the moonlight. "I am making a collection of birds myself. I have been at it ever since I was a boy." (Mrs. Tilley smiled.) "There are two or three very rare ones I have been hunting for these five years. I mean to get them on my own ground if they can be found."

"Do you cage 'em up?" asked Mrs. Tilley doubtfully, in response to this enthusiastic announcement.

"Oh, no, they're stuffed and preserved, dozens and dozens of them," said the ornithologist, "and I have shot or snared every one myself. I caught a glimpse of a white heron three miles from here on Saturday, and I have followed it in this direction. They have never been found in this district at all. The little white heron, it is," and he turned again to look at Sylvia with the hope of discovering that the rare bird was one of her acquaintances.

But Sylvia was watching a hop-toad in the narrow footpath.

"You would know the heron if you saw it," the stranger continued eagerly. "A queer tall white bird with soft feathers and long thin legs. And it would have a nest perhaps in the top of a high tree, made of sticks, something like a hawk's nest."

Sylvia's heart gave a wild beat; she knew that strange white bird, and had once stolen softly near where it stood in some bright green swamp grass, away over at the other side of the woods. There was an open place where the sunshine always seemed strangely yellow and hot, where tall, nodding rushes grew, and her grandmother had warned her that she might sink in the soft black mud underneath and never be heard of more. Not far beyond were the salt marshes and beyond those was the sea, the sea which Sylvia wondered and dreamed about, but never had looked upon, though its great voice could often be heard above the noise of the woods on stormy nights.

"I can't think of anything I should like so much as to find that heron's nest," the handsome stranger was saying. "I would give ten dollars to anybody who could show it to me," he added desperately, "and I mean to spend my whole vacation hunting for it if need be. Perhaps it was only migrating, or had been chased out of its own region by some bird of prey."

Mrs. Tilley gave amazed attention to all this, but Sylvia still watched the toad, not divining, as she might have done at some calmer time, that the creature wished to get to its hole under the door-step, and was much hindered by the unusual spectators at that hour of the evening. No amount of thought, that night, could decide how many wished-for treasures the ten dollars, so lightly spoken of, would buy.

The next day the young sportsman hovered about the woods, and Sylvia kept him company, having lost her first fear of the friendly lad, who proved to be most kind and sympathetic. He told her many things about the birds and what they knew and where they lived and what they did with themselves. And he gave her a jack-knife, which she thought as great a treasure as if she were a desert-islander. All day long he did not once make her troubled or afraid except when he brought down some unsuspecting singing creature from its bough. Sylvia would have liked him vastly better without his gun; she could not understand why he killed the very birds he seemed to like so much. But as the day waned, Sylvia still watched the young man with loving admiration. She had never seen anybody so charming and de-lightful; the woman's heart, asleep in the child, was vaguely thrilled by a dream of love. Some premonition of that great power stirred and swayed these young foresters who traversed the solemn woodlands with soft-footed silent care. They stopped to listen to a bird's song; they pressed forward again eagerly, parting the branches,—speaking to each other rarely and in whispers; the young man going first and Sylvia following, fascinated, a few steps behind, with her gray eyes dark with excitement.

She grieved because the longed-for white heron was elusive, but she did not lead the guest, she only followed, and there was no such thing as speaking first. The sound of her own unquestioned voice would have terrified her,—it was hard enough to answer yes or no when there was need of that. At last evening began to fall, and they drove the cow home together, and Sylvia smiled with pleasure when they came to the place where she heard the whistle and was afraid only the night before.

II

Half a mile from home, at the farther edge of the woods, where the land was highest, a great pine-tree stood, the last of its generation. Whether it was left for a boundary mark, or for what reason, no one could say; the woodchoppers who had felled its mates were dead and gone long ago, and a whole forest of sturdy trees, pines and oaks and maples, had grown again. But the stately head of this old pine towered above them all and made a landmark for sea and shore miles and miles away. Sylvia knew it well. She had always believed that whoever climbed to the top of it could see the ocean; and the little girl had often laid her hand on the great rough trunk and looked up wistfully at those dark boughs that the wind always stirred, no matter how hot and still the air might be below. Now she thought of the tree with a new excitement, for why, if one climbed it at break of day, could not one see all the world, and easily discover whence the white heron flew, and mark the place, and find the hidden nest?

What a spirit of adventure, what wild ambition! What fancied triumph and delight and glory for the later morning when she could make known the secret! It was almost too real and too great for the childish heart to bear.

All night the door of the little house stood open, and the whippoorwills came and sang upon the very step. The young sportsman and his old hostess were sound asleep, but Sylvia's great design kept her broad awake and watching. She forgot to think of sleep. The short summer night seemed as long as the winter darkness, and at last when the whippoorwills ceased, and she was afraid the morning would after all come too soon, she stole out of the house and followed the pasture path through the woods, hastening toward the open ground beyond, listening with a sense of comfort and companionship to the drowsy twitter of a half-awakened bird, whose perch she had jarred in passing. Alas, if the great wave of human interest which flooded for the first time this dull little life should sweep away the satisfactions of an existence heart to heart with nature and the dumb life of the forest!

There was the huge tree asleep yet in the paling moonlight, and small and hopeful Sylvia began with utmost bravery to mount to the top of it, with tingling, eager blood coursing the channels of her whole frame, with her bare feet and fingers, that pinched and held like bird's claws to the monstrous ladder reaching up, up, almost to the sky itself. First she must mount the white oak tree that grew alongside, where she was almost lost among the dark branches and the green leaves heavy and wet with dew; a bird fluttered off its nest, and a red squirrel ran to and fro and scolded pettishly at the harmless housebreaker. Sylvia felt her way easily. She had often climbed there, and knew that higher still one of the oak's upper branches chafed against the pine trunk, just where its lower boughs were set close together. There, when she made the dangerous pass from one tree to the other, the great enterprise would really begin.

She crept out along the swaying oak limb at last, and took the daring step across into the old pine-tree. The way was harder than she thought; she must reach far and hold fast, the sharp dry twigs caught and held her and scratched her like angry talons, the pitch made her thin little fingers clumsy and stiff as she went round and round the tree's great stem, higher and higher upward. The sparrows and robins in the woods below were beginning to wake and twitter to the dawn, yet it seemed much lighter there aloft in the pine-tree, and the child knew that she must hurry if her project were to be of any use.

The tree seemed to lengthen itself out as she went up, and to reach farther and farther upward. It was like a great main-mast to the voyaging earth; it must truly have been amazed that morning through all its ponderous frame as it felt this determined spark of human spirit creeping and climbing from higher branch to branch. Who knows how steadily the least twigs held themselves to advantage this light, weak creature on her way! The old pine must have loved his new dependent. More than all the hawks, and bats, and moths, and even the sweet-voiced thrushes, was the brave, beating heart of the solitary gray-eyed child. And the tree stood still and held away the winds that June morning while the dawn grew bright in the east.

Sylvia's face was like a pale star, if one had seen it from the ground, when the last thorny bough was past, and she stood trembling and tired but wholly triumphant, high in the tree-top. Yes, there was the sea with the dawning sun making a golden dazzle over it, and toward that glorious east flew two hawks with slow-moving pinions. How low they looked in the air from that height when before one had only seen them far up, and dark against the blue sky. Their gray feathers were as soft as moths; they seemed only a little way from the tree, and Sylvia felt as if she too could go flying away among the clouds. Westward, the woodlands and farms reached miles and miles into the distance; here and there were church steeples, and white villages; truly it was a vast and awesome world.

The birds sang louder and louder. At last the sun came up bewilderingly bright. Sylvia could see the white sails of ships out at sea, and the clouds that were purple and rose-colored and yellow at first began to fade away. Where was the white heron's nest in the sea of green

Tree comes alive ↓ mw

change of person

branches, and was this wonderful sight and pageant of the world the only reward for having climbed to such a giddy height? Now look down again, Sylvia, where the green marsh is set among the shining birches and dark hemlocks; there where you saw the white heron once you will see him again; look, look! a white spot of him like a single floating feather comes up from the dead hemlock and grows larger, and rises, and comes close at last, and goes by the landmark pine with steady sweep of wing and outstretched slender neck and crested head. And wait! wait! do not move a foot or a finger, little girl, do not send an arrow of light and consciousness from your two eager eyes, for the heron has perched on a pine bough not far beyond yours, and cries back to his mate on the nest, and plumes his feathers for the new day!

The child gives a long sigh a minute later when a company of shouting cat-birds comes also to the tree, and vexed by their fluttering and lawlessness the solemn heron goes away. She knows his secret now, the wild, light, slender bird that floats and wavers, and goes back like an arrow presently to his home in the green world beneath. Then Sylvia, well satisfied, makes her perilous way down again, not daring to look far below the branch she stands on, ready to cry sometimes because her fingers ache and her lamed feet slip. Wondering over and over again what the stranger would say to her, and what he would think when she told him how to find his way straight to the heron's nest.

"Sylvy, Sylvy!" called the busy old grandmother again and again, but nobody answered, and the small husk bed was empty, and Sylvia had disappeared.

The guest waked from a dream, and remembering his day's pleasure hurried to dress himself that it might sooner begin. He was sure from the way the shy little girl looked once or twice yesterday that she had at least seen the white heron, and now she must really be persuaded to tell. Here she comes now, paler than ever, and her worn old frock is torn and tattered, and smeared with pine pitch. The grandmother and the sportsman stand in the door together and question her, and the splendid moment has come to speak of the dead hemlock-tree by the green marsh.

But Sylvia does not speak after all, though the old grandmother fretfully rebukes her, and the young man's kind appealing eyes are looking straight in her own. He can make them rich with money; he has promised it, and they are poor now. He is so well worth making happy, and he waits to hear the story she can tell.

No, she must keep silence! What is it that suddenly forbids her and makes her dumb? Has she been nine years growing, and now, when the great world for the first time puts out a hand to her, must she thrust it aside for a bird's sake? The murmur of the pine's green branches is in her ears, she remembers how the white heron came flying through the golden air and how they watched the sea and the morning together, and Sylvia cannot speak; she cannot tell the heron's secret and give its life away.

Dear loyalty, that suffered a sharp pang as the guest went away disappointed later in the day, that could have served and followed him and loved him as a dog loves! Many a night Sylvia heard the echo of his whistle haunting the pasture path as she came home with the loitering cow. She forgot even her sorrow at the sharp report of his gun and the piteous sight of thrushes and sparrows dropping silent to the ground, their songs hushed and their pretty feathers stained and wet with blood. Were the birds better friends than their hunter might have been,—who can tell? Whatever treasures were lost to her, woodlands and summer-time, remember! Bring your gifts and graces and tell your secrets to this lonely country child!

Insight

1. How would you characterize Sylvia? What specific lines can you cite from the story which suggest that Mrs. Tilley's "unlikely choice . . . from her daughter's houseful of children" was a wise one?
2. What mixed feelings does Sylvia have toward the stranger throughout the story? How would you account for these feelings?
3. What psychological reasons motivate Sylvia to climb the tree? In what way does her perspective change upon reaching the top?
4. How do you account for Sylvia's remaining silent about the heron at the end of the story? How believable do you find her change of attitude? Explain.
5. What painful conflict does Sylvia suffer at the end of the story? What is meant by the phrase "Dear loyalty"?

effort at speech
between two people

Muriel Rukeyser

Speak to me.   Take my hand.   What are you now?
I will tell you all.   I will conceal nothing.
When I was three, a little child read a story about a rabbit
who died, in the story, and I crawled under a chair   :
a pink rabbit   :   it was my birthday, and a candle   5
burnt a sore spot on my finger, and I was told to be happy.

Oh, grow to know me.   I am not happy.   I will be open:
Now I am thinking of white sails against a sky like music,
like glad horns blowing, and birds tilting, and an arm about me.
There was one I loved, who wanted to live, sailing.   10

Effort at Speech Between Two People

Speak to me.   Take my hand.   What are you now? *crying at what*
When I was nine, I was fruitily sentimental. *was beautiful*
fluid   :   and my widowed aunt played Chopin,
and I bent my head to the painted woodwork, and wept.
I want now to be close to you.   I would   15
link the minutes of my days close, somehow, to your days.

I am not happy.   I will be open.
I have liked lamps in evening corners, and quiet poems.
? There has been fear in my life.   Sometimes I speculate on what
a tragedy his life was, really.   20

deeper regues   Take my hand.   *more intense holding* Fist my mind in your hand.   What are you now?
death   When I was fourteen, I had dreams of suicide,
end   I stood at a steep window, at sunset, hoping toward death   :
beauty saved   if the light had not melted clouds and plains to beauty,
from death   if light had not transformed that day, I would have leapt.   25
I am unhappy.   I am lonely.   Speak to me.

I will be open.   I think he never loved me:
he loved the bright beaches, the little lips of foam
that ride small waves, he loved the veer of gulls:
not sincere   he said with a gay mouth   :   I love you.   Grow to know me.   30
mocking

information
What are you now? If we could touch one another,   *communicate*
if these our separate entities could come to grips,
recent   clenched like a Chinese puzzle ...   yesterday.   *no conclusion to if*
I stood in a crowded street that was live with people,   *we could*
and no one spoke a word, and the morning shone.   35
no communica-   Everyone silent, moving ...   Take my hand.   Speak to me.
tion

*3 L's of comm: person to woman speaks to self - starts + end
trying to move outside of self. 2. two people talking unable to
communicate. 3. someone speaking to another who doesn't
respond*

*Nor sure who you he or I is. Someone w feelings + memories
try to get in touch w them + shaving them*

Insight

1. What do we find out about the two people who are speaking? What are they seeking? Do they attain what they seek?
2. How would you describe the mood of this poem? Which lines are particularly effective in establishing the mood?

116

a cry for recognition

Her first ball

Katherine Mansfield

Exactly when the ball began Leila would have found it hard to say. Perhaps her first real partner was the cab. It did not matter that she shared the cab with the Sheridan girls and their brother. She sat back in her own little corner of it, and the bolster on which her hand rested felt like the sleeve of an unknown young man's dress suit; and away they bowled, past waltzing lamp-posts and houses and fences and trees.

"Have you really never been to a ball before, Leila? But, my child, how too weird—" cried the Sheridan girls.

"Our nearest neighbour was fifteen miles," said Leila softly, gently opening and shutting her fan.

Oh, dear, how hard it was to be indifferent like the others! She tried not to smile too much; she tried not to care. But every single thing was so new and exciting . . . Meg's tuberoses, Jose's long loop of amber, Laura's little dark head, pushing above her white fur like a flower through snow. She would remember for ever. It even gave her a pang to see her cousin Laurie throw away the wisps of tissue paper he pulled from the fastenings of his new gloves. She would like to have kept those wisps as a keepsake, as a remembrance. Laurie leaned forward and put his hand on Laura's knee.

"Look here, darling," he said. "The third and the ninth as usual. Twig?"

Oh, how marvellous to have a brother! In her excitement Leila felt that if there had been time, if it hadn't been impossible, she couldn't have helped crying because she was an only child, and no brother had ever said "Twig?" to her; no sister would ever say, as Meg said to Jose that moment, "I've never known your hair go up more successfully than it has to-night!"

But, of course, there was no time. They were at the drill hall already; there were cabs in front of them and cabs behind. The road was bright on either side with moving fan-like lights, and on the pavement gay couples seemed to float through the air; little satin shoes chased each other like birds.

"Hold on to me, Leila; you'll get lost," said Laura.

"Come on, girls, let's make a dash for it," said Laurie.

Leila put two fingers on Laura's pink velvet cloak, and they were somehow lifted past the big golden lantern, carried along the passage, and pushed into the little room marked "Ladies." Here the crowd was so great there was hardly space to take off their things; the noise was deafening. Two benches on either side were stacked high with wraps. Two old women in white aprons ran up and down tossing fresh armfuls. And everybody was pressing forward trying to get at the little dressing-table and mirror at the far end.

A great quivering jet of gas lighted the ladies' room. It couldn't wait; it was dancing already. When the door opened again and there came a burst of tuning from the drill hall, it leaped almost to the ceiling.

Dark girls, fair girls were patting their hair, tying ribbons again, tucking handkerchiefs down the fronts of their bodices; smoothing marble-white gloves. And because they were all laughing it seemed to Leila that they were all lovely.

"Aren't there any invisible hair-pins?" cried a voice. "How most extraordinary! I can't see a single invisible hair-pin."

"Powder my back, there's a darling," cried some one else.

"But I must have a needle and cotton. I've torn simply miles and miles of the frill," wailed a third.

Then, "Pass them along, pass them along!" The straw basket of programmes was tossed from arm to arm. Darling little pink-and-silver programmes, with pink pencils and fluffy tassels. Leila's fingers shook as she took one out of the basket. She wanted to ask some one, "Am I meant to have one too?" but she had just time to read: "Waltz 3. *Two, Two in a Canoe*. Polka 4. *Making the Feathers Fly*," when Meg cried, "Ready, Leila?" and they pressed their way through the crush in the passage towards the big double doors of the drill hall.

Dancing had not begun yet, but the band had stopped tuning, and the noise was so great it seemed that when it did begin to play it would never be heard. Leila, pressing close to Meg, looking over Meg's shoulder, felt that even the little quivering coloured flags strung across the ceiling were talking. She quite forgot to be shy; she forgot how in the middle of dressing she had sat down on the bed with one shoe off and one shoe on and begged her mother to ring up her cousins and say she couldn't go after all. And the rush of longing she had had to be sitting on the veranda of their forsaken up-country home, listening to the baby owls crying "More pork" in the moonlight, was changed to a rush of joy so sweet that it was hard to bear alone. She clutched her fan, and, gazing at the gleaming, golden floor, the azaleas, the lanterns, the stage at one end with its red carpet and gilt chairs and the band in a corner, she thought breathlessly, "How heavenly; how simply heavenly!"

All the girls stood grouped together at one side of the doors, the men at the other, and the chaperones in dark dresses, smiling rather foolishly, walked with little careful steps over the polished floor towards the stage.

"This is my little country cousin Leila. Be nice to her. Find her partners; she's under my wing," said Meg, going up to one girl after another.

Strange faces smiled at Leila—sweetly, vaguely. Strange voices answered, "Of course, my dear." But Leila felt the girls didn't really see her. They were looking towards the men. Why didn't the men begin? What were they waiting for? There they stood, smoothing their gloves, patting their glossy hair and smiling among themselves. Then, quite suddenly, as if they had only just made up their minds that that was what they had to do, the men came gliding over the parquet. There was a joyful flutter among the girls. A tall, fair man flew up to Meg, seized her programme, scribbled something; Meg passed him on to Leila. "May I have the pleasure?" He ducked and smiled. There came a dark man wearing an eyeglass, then cousin Laurie with a friend, and Laura with a little freckled fellow whose tie was crooked. Then quite an old man—fat, with a big bald patch on his head—took her programme and murmured, "Let me see, let me see!" And he was a long time comparing his programme, which looked black with names, with hers. It seemed to give him so much trouble that Leila was ashamed. "Oh, please don't bother," she said eagerly. But instead of replying the fat man wrote something, glanced at her again. "Do I remember this bright little face?" he said softly. "Is it known to me of yore?" At that moment the band began playing; the fat man disappeared. He was tossed away on a great wave of music that came flying over the gleaming floor, breaking the groups up into couples, scattering them, sending them spinning. . . .

Leila had learned to dance at boarding school. Every Saturday afternoon the boarders were hurried off to a little corrugated iron mission hall where Miss Eccles (of London) held her "select" classes. But the difference between that dusty-smelling hall—with calico texts on the walls, the poor terrified little woman in a brown velvet toque with rabbit's ears thumping the cold piano, Miss Eccles poking the girls' feet with her long white wand—and this was so tremendous that Leila was sure if her partner didn't come and she had to listen to that marvellous music and to watch the others sliding, gliding over the golden floor, she would die at least, or faint, or lift her arms and fly out of one of those dark windows that showed the stars.

"Ours, I think—" Some one bowed, smiled, and offered her his arm; she hadn't to die after all. Some one's hand pressed her waist, and she floated away like a flower that is tossed into a pool.

"Quite a good floor, isn't it?" drawled a faint voice close to her ear.

"I think it's most beautifully slippery," said Leila.

"Pardon!" The faint voice sounded surprised. Leila said it again. And there was a tiny pause before the voice echoed, "Oh, quite!" and she was swung round again.

He steered so beautifully. That was the great difference between dancing with girls and men, Leila decided. Girls banged into each other, and stamped on each other's feet; the girl who was gentleman always clutched you so.

The azaleas were separate flowers no longer; they were pink and white flags streaming by.

"Were you at the Bells' last week?" the voice came again. It sounded tired. Leila wondered whether she ought to ask him if he would like to stop.

"No, this is my first dance," said she.

Her partner gave a little gasping laugh. "Oh, I say," he protested.

"Yes, it is really the first dance I've ever been to." Leila was most fervent. It was such a relief to be able to tell somebody. "You see, I've lived in the country all my life up until now. . . ."

At that moment the music stopped, and they went to sit on two chairs against the wall. Leila tucked her pink satin feet under and fanned herself, while she blissfully watched the other couples passing and disappearing through the swing doors.

"Enjoying yourself, Leila?" asked Jose, nodding her golden head.

Laura passed and gave her the faintest little wink; it made Leila wonder for a moment whether she was quite grown up after all. Certainly her partner did not say very much. He coughed, tucked his handkerchief away, pulled down his waistcoat, took a minute thread off his sleeve. But it didn't matter. Almost immediately the band started, and her second partner seemed to spring from the ceiling.

"Floor's not bad," said the new voice. Did one always begin with the floor? And then, "Were you at the Neaves' on Tuesday?" And again Leila explained. Perhaps it was a little strange that her partners were not more interested. For it was thrilling. Her first ball! She was only at the beginning of everything. It seemed to her that she had never known what the night was like before. Up till now it had been dark, silent, beautiful very often—oh, yes—but mournful somehow. Solemn. And now it would never be like that again—it had opened dazzling bright.

"Care for an ice?" said her partner. And they went through the swing doors, down the passage, to the supper room. Her cheeks burned, she was fearfully thirsty. How sweet the ices looked on little glass plates, and how cold the frosted spoon was, iced too! And when they came back to the hall there was the fat man waiting for her by the door. It gave her quite a shock again to see how old he was; he ought to have been on the stage with the fathers and mothers. And when Leila compared him with her other partners he looked shabby. His waistcoat was creased, there was a button off his glove, his coat looked as if it was dusty with French chalk.

"Come along, little lady," said the fat man. He scarcely troubled to clasp her, and they moved away so gently, it was more like walking than dancing. But he said not a word about the floor. "Your first dance, isn't it?" he murmured.

put down

"How *did* you know?"

"Ah," said the fat man, "that's what it is to be old!" He wheezed faintly as he steered her past an awkward couple. "You see, I've been doing this kind of thing for the last thirty years."

"Thirty years?" cried Leila. Twelve years before she was born!

"It hardly bears thinking about, does it?" said the fat man gloomily. Leila looked at his bald head, and she felt quite sorry for him.

disillusioned

"I think it's marvellous to be still going on," she said kindly.

"Kind little lady," said the fat man, and he pressed her a little closer, and hummed a bar of the waltz. "Of course," he said, "you can't hope to last anything like as long as that. No-o," said the fat man, "long before that you'll be sitting up there on the stage, looking on, in your nice black velvet. And these pretty arms will have turned into little short fat ones, and you'll beat time with such a different kind of fan—a black bony one." The fat man seemed to shudder. "And you'll smile away like the poor old dears up there, and point to your daughter, and tell the elderly lady next to you how some dreadful man tried to kiss her at the club ball. And your heart will ache, ache"—the fat man squeezed her closer still, as if he really was sorry for that poor heart—"because no one wants to kiss you now. And you'll say how unpleasant these polished floors are to walk on, how dangerous they are. Eh, Mademoiselle Twinkletoes?" said the fat man softly.

Leila gave a light little laugh, but she did not feel like laughing. Was it—could it all be true? It sounded terribly true. Was this first ball only the beginning of her last ball after all? At that the music seemed to change; it sounded sad, sad; it rose upon a great sigh. Oh, how quickly things changed! Why didn't happiness last for ever? For ever wasn't a bit too long. *I step closer to wisdom, it doesn't*

"I want to stop," she said in a breathless voice. The fat man led her to the door.

"No," she said, "I won't go outside. I won't sit down. I'll just stand here, thank you." She leaned against the wall, tapping with her foot, pulling up her gloves and trying to smile. But deep inside her a little girl threw her pinafore over her head and sobbed. Why had he spoiled it all? *The little girl dies a bit - death of childhood*

"I say, you know," said the fat man, "you mustn't take me seriously, little lady."

"As if I should!" said Leila, tossing her small dark head and sucking her underlip. . . . *pulls away from put down*

121

Her First Ball

Again the couples paraded. The swing doors opened and shut. Now new music was given out by the bandmaster. But Leila didn't want to dance any more. She wanted to be home, or sitting on the veranda listening to those baby owls. When she looked through the dark windows at the stars, they had long beams like wings. . . .

But presently a soft, melting, ravishing tune began, and a young man with curly hair bowed before her. She would have to dance, out of politeness, until she could find Meg. Very stiffly she walked into the middle; very haughtily she put her hand on his sleeve. But in one minute, in one turn, her feet glided, glided. The lights, the azaleas, the dresses, the pink faces, the velvet chairs, all became one beautiful flying wheel. And when her next partner bumped her into the fat man and he said, "Par*don*," she smiled at him more radiantly than ever. She didn't even recognize him again.

Insight

1. Trace the changing moods experienced by Leila from her initial anticipation of the ball to her final failure to recognize the fat man.
2. How would you summarize the fat man's words to Leila? What reasons do you suppose he has for speaking as he does? Do you think he meant his remarks cruelly?
3. "Was this first ball only the beginning of her last ball after all?" thinks Leila. What is the meaning of her question? How would you answer it?

122

IN SUMMARY

Insight and Composition

1. The initiation of a young person into the adult world, as in "My First Two Women," is one of the oldest and most common themes in literature. Which stories in this unit might be classified as "initiation stories"? What basic similarities can be noted in each story?

2. Naive, gullible, or inexperienced characters in their search for self often encounter disillusioning experiences, experiences which contribute to the eventual maturing of the individual. What disillusionment is encountered by Leila in "Her First Ball" and by the characters in the other selections in this unit? What maturity do you think is gained through experiencing these disillusionments?

3. In searching for self, young people frequently select an older person to serve as a model for present or future behavior. Sometimes the models are worthy of emulation; sometimes, not. Which characters in these stories have focused on models whom they seek to emulate? How worthy of emulation does each model appear to be?

4. While knowing one's self should be every individual's goal, such knowledge is often painful and even at times destructive. Examine the degree of self-knowledge the characters in the selections in this unit exhibit. Which characters appear to know themselves most fully? Does that self-knowledge prove painful? Explain.

DRAMA

Dreams and trifles. These two plays are about dreams of altering everyday life, and about the trivial tasks which take up time and trivial objects which fill up houses. But in these plays, dreams and trifles are not shadowy or insignificant. One play shows that dreams sometimes shape the most momentous decisions, and the other suggests that trifling facts and events sometimes lie behind powerful feeling and drastic action.

In all drama, our interest is focused on characters, their motives and their conflicts. Since plays are meant to be produced—to be acted and seen—we must read plays in a different way than we read poetry, for example. A reader has to visualize how a character should look, to imagine what tone of voice would fit with an assigned speech, to think how words from one character might affect another. When we see a play, we confront the physical presence of living human beings, and from their words, their gestures, their actions, their clothes and the setting we find them in, we judge who they are and what motivates them. But when we read a play, we have to participate actively in the creation of the play's world—the reader's dramatic imagination is needed here to help create the Youngers' Chicago living room, the Wrights' prairie kitchen, and to fill out from speeches and stage directions alone what the characters are like and what motivates them.

The title of Lorraine Hansberry's play is taken from a poem by Langston Hughes which answers in various ways the question, "What happens to a dream deferred?" What happens when a person cannot make a vital dream come true? If fulfillment is postponed too long, what happens? The four main adult characters in the play are motivated primarily by their dreams of how to change the wearying pressure of their cramped, explosive confinement in a little apartment. Walter Younger dreams of owning a liquor store, which he thinks will assure him of what he really wants—plenty of money, in a world which has made him value money as life itself. His sister Beneatha, struggling to figure out her identity in clothes, school, and dates, dreams of becoming a doctor. Ruth Younger dreams of a happier marriage with Walter and of a little more security than life lived at the edge of exasperation, poverty and despair. And Lena Younger, mother of Walter and Beneatha, dreams of owning a comfortable house. But even more, she dreams of seeing her children grow up into courageous, dignified adults. Within the play, these dreams clash, blow up, fade, rise again, fail, come true, or wait.

Susan Keating Glaspell's "Trifles" also concentrates intensely upon understanding character and motive, but the two people—a married couple—whose characters and motives we want most to understand, never appear in the play. One is dead—murdered probably, and the other is in jail—the murder suspect. The play is a kind of detective story: we watch the investigators assemble the clues which help define the personalities of husband and wife, and which establish a motive for murder. The clues are all trifles: the look of homemade jellies in a kitchen cupboard, stitches in a handmade quilt, something hidden in a sewing basket. The mystery is solved by two women's imaginative comprehension of the woman who is not there, because they understand from their own experience how the "trifles" of domestic married life, and the conventional attitudes of men who condescend to women, may discourage or burden or even maim a woman's spirit. What the two women do with this knowledge makes the surprising ending of the play.

These two dramatists consider in their plays longings, rage, disappointment, triumph, and endurance. Additionally in each of these plays we also find a profound, intimate grasp of the influence of domestic realities upon human experience.

Marcia Folsom

TRifLES

Susan Glaspell

Characters

MR. PETERS	*the sheriff.*
MR. HENDERSON	*the county attorney.*
MR. HALE	*a neighbor.*
MRS. HALE	*wife of* MR. HALE.
MRS. PETERS	*wife of* SHERIFF PETERS.

SCENE: The kitchen in the now abandoned farmhouse of JOHN WRIGHT, a gloomy kitchen, and left without having been put in order—unwashed pans under the sink, a loaf of bread outside the breadbox, a dish towel on the table—other signs of uncompleted work. At the rear the outer door opens, and the SHERIFF comes in, followed by the COUNTY ATTORNEY and HALE. The SHERIFF and HALE are men in middle life, the COUNTY ATTORNEY is a young man; all are much bundled up and go at once to the stove. They are followed by the two women —the SHERIFF'S WIFE first; she is a slight wiry woman, with a thin nervous face. MRS. HALE is larger and would ordinarily be called more comfortable looking, but she is disturbed now and looks fearfully about as she enters. The women have come in slowly and stand close together near the door.

COUNTY ATTORNEY (*rubbing his hands*): This feels good. Come up to the fire, ladies.

MRS. PETERS (*after taking a step forward*): I'm not—cold.

SHERIFF (*unbuttoning his overcoat and stepping away from the stove as if to mark the beginning of official business*): Now, Mr. Hale, before we move things about, you explain to Mr. Henderson just what you saw when you came here yesterday morning.

COUNTY ATTORNEY: By the way, has anything been moved? Are things just as you left them yesterday?

SHERIFF (*looking about*): It's just the same. When it dropped below zero last night, I thought I'd better send Frank out this morning to make a fire for us—no use getting pneumonia with a big case on; but I told him not to touch anything except the stove— and you know Frank.

COUNTY ATTORNEY: Somebody should have been left here yesterday.

SHERIFF: Oh—yesterday. When I had to send Frank to Morris Center for that man who went crazy—I want you to know I had my hands full yesterday. I knew you could get back from Omaha by today, and as long as I went over everything here myself—

COUNTY ATTORNEY: Well, Mr. Hale, tell just what happened when you came here yesterday morning.

HALE: Harry and I had started to town with a load of potatoes. We came along the road from my place; and as I got here, I said, "I'm going to see if I can't get John Wright to go in with me on a party telephone." I spoke to Wright about it once before, and he put me off, saying folks talked too much anyway, and all he asked was peace and quiet—I guess you know about how much he talked himself; but I thought maybe if I went to the house and talked about it before his wife, though I said to Harry that I didn't know as what his wife wanted made much difference to John—

COUNTY ATTORNEY: Let's talk about that later, Mr. Hale. I do want to talk about that, but tell now just what happened when you got to the house.

HALE: I didn't hear or see anything; I knocked at the door, and still it was all quiet inside. I knew they must be up, it was past eight o'clock. So I knocked again, and I thought I heard somebody say, "Come in." I wasn't sure, I'm not sure yet, but I opened the door—this door (*Indicating the door by which the two women are still standing.*) and there in that rocker—(*Pointing to it.*) sat Mrs. Wright. [*They all look at the rocker.*]

COUNTY ATTORNEY: What—was she doing?

HALE: She was rockin' back and forth. She had her apron in her hand and was kind of—pleating it.

COUNTY ATTORNEY: And how did she—look?

HALE: Well, she looked queer.

COUNTY ATTORNEY: How do you mean—queer?

HALE: Well, as if she didn't know what she was going to do next. And kind of done up.

COUNTY ATTORNEY: How did she seem to feel about your coming?

HALE: Why, I don't think she minded—one way or other. She didn't pay much attention. I said, "How do, Mrs. Wright, it's cold, ain't it?" And she said, "Is it?"—and went on kind of pleating at her apron. Well, I was surprised; she didn't ask me to come up to the stove, or to set down, but just sat there, not even looking at me, so I said, "I want to see John." And then she—laughed. I guess you would call it a laugh. I thought of Harry and the team outside, so I said a little sharp: "Can't I see John?" "No," she says, kind o' dull like. "Ain't he home?" says I. "Yes," says she, "he's home." "Then why can't I see him?" I asked her, out of patience. " 'Cause he's dead," says she. "*Dead?*" says I. She just nodded her head, not gettin' a bit excited, but rockin' back and forth. "Why—where is he?" says I, not knowing what to say. She just pointed upstairs—like that (*Himself pointing to the room above.*) I got up, with the idea of going up there. I walked from there to here—then I says, "Why, what did he die of?" "He died of a rope around his neck," says she, and just went on pleatin' at her apron. Well, I went out and called Harry. I thought I might—need help. We went upstairs, and there he was lyin'—

COUNTY ATTORNEY: I think I'd rather have you go into that upstairs, where you can point it all out. Just go on now with the rest of the story.

HALE: Well, my first thought was to get that rope off. I looked . . . (*Stops, his face twitches.*) . . . but Harry, he went up to him, and he said, "No, he's dead all right, and we'd better not touch anything." So we went back downstairs. She was still sitting that same way. "Has anybody been notified?" I asked. "No," says she, unconcerned. "Who did this, Mrs. Wright?" said Harry. He said it businesslike—and she stopped pleatin' of her apron. "I don't know," she says. "You don't *know*?" says Harry. "No," says she. "Weren't you sleepin' in the bed with him?" says Harry. "Yes," says she, "but I was on the inside." "Somebody slipped a rope round his neck and strangled him, and you didn't wake up?" says Harry. "I didn't wake up," she said after him. We must 'a looked as if we didn't see how that could be, for after a minute she said, "I sleep sound." Harry was going to ask her more questions, but I said maybe we ought to let her tell her story first to the coroner, or the sheriff, so Harry went fast as he could to Rivers' place, where there's a telephone.

COUNTY ATTORNEY: And what did Mrs. Wright do when she knew that you had gone for the coroner?

HALE: She moved from that chair to this over here . . . (*Pointing to a small chair in the corner.*) . . . and just sat there with her hands held together and looking down. I got a feeling that I ought to make some conversation, so I said I had come in to see if John wanted to put in a telephone, and at that she started to laugh, and then she stopped and looked at me— scared. (*The* COUNTY ATTORNEY, *who has had his notebook out, makes a note.*) I dunno, maybe it wasn't scared. I wouldn't like to say it was.

Soon Harry got back, and then Dr. Lloyd came, and you, Mr. Peters, and so I guess that's all I know that you don't.

COUNTY ATTORNEY (*looking around*): I guess we'll go upstairs first—and then out to the barn and around there. (*To the* SHERIFF.) You're convinced that there was nothing important here —nothing that would point to any motive?

SHERIFF: Nothing here but kitchen things.

[*The* COUNTY ATTORNEY, *after again looking around the kitchen, opens the door of a cupboard closet. He gets up on a chair and looks on a shelf. Pulls his hand away, sticky.*]

COUNTY ATTORNEY: Here's a nice mess. [*The women draw nearer.*]

MRS. PETERS (*to the other woman*): Oh, her fruit; it did freeze. (*To the* LAWYER.) She worried about that when it turned so cold. She said the fire'd go out and her jars would break.

SHERIFF: Well, can you beat the women! Held for murder and worryin' about her preserves.

COUNTY ATTORNEY: I guess before we're through she may have something more serious than preserves to worry about.

HALE: Well, women are used to worrying over trifles.

[*The two women move a little closer together.*]

COUNTY ATTORNEY (*with the gallantry of a young politician*): And yet, for all their worries, what would we do without the ladies? (*The women do not unbend. He goes to the sink, takes a dipperful of water from the pail and, pouring it into a basin, washes his hands. Starts to wipe them on the roller towel, turns it for a cleaner place.)* Dirty towels! *(Kicks his foot against the pans under the sink.)* Not much of a housekeeper, would you say, ladies?

MRS. HALE *(stiffly)*: There's a great deal of work to be done on a farm.

COUNTY ATTORNEY: To be sure, and yet ... *(With a little bow to her.)* ... I know there are some Dickson county farmhouses which do not have such roller towels.

[He gives it a pull to expose its full length again.]

MRS. HALE: Those towels get dirty awful quick. Men's hands aren't always as clean as they might be.

COUNTY ATTORNEY: Ah, loyal to your sex, I see. But you and Mrs. Wright were neighbors. I suppose you were friends, too.

MRS. HALE *(shaking her head)*: I've not seen much of her of late years. I've not been in this house—it's more than a year.

COUNTY ATTORNEY: And why was that? You didn't like her?

MRS. HALE: I like her well enough. Farmers' wives have their hands full, Mr. Henderson. And then—

COUNTY ATTORNEY: Yes—?

MRS. HALE *(looking about)*: It never seemed a very cheerful place.

COUNTY ATTORNEY: No—it's not cheerful. I shouldn't say she had the homemaking instinct.

MRS. HALE: Well, I don't know as Wright had, either.

COUNTY ATTORNEY: You mean that they didn't get on very well?

MRS. HALE: No, I don't mean anything. But I don't think a place'd be any cheerfuler for John Wright's being in it.

COUNTY ATTORNEY: I'd like to talk more of that a little later. I want to get the lay of things upstairs now.

[He goes to the left, where three steps lead to a stair door.]

SHERIFF: I suppose anything Mrs. Peters does'll be all right. She was to take in some clothes for her, you know, and a few little things. We left in such a hurry yesterday.

COUNTY ATTORNEY: Yes, but I would like to see what you take, Mrs. Peters, and keep an eye out for anything that might be of use to us.

MRS. PETERS: Yes, Mr. Henderson.

[The women listen to the men's steps on the stairs, then look about the kitchen.]

MRS. HALE: I'd hate to have men coming into my kitchen, snooping around and criticizing.

[She arranges the pans under sink which the LAWYER had shoved out of place.]

MRS. PETERS: Of course it's no more than their duty.

MRS. HALE: Duty's all right, but I guess that deputy sheriff that came out to make the fire might have got a little of this on. *(Gives the roller towel a pull.)* Wish I'd thought of that sooner. Seems mean to talk about her for not having things slicked up when she had to come away in such a hurry.

MRS. PETERS *(who has gone to a small table in the left rear corner of the room, and lifted one end of a towel that covers a pan)*: She had bread set.

[Stands still.]

MRS. HALE (*eyes fixed on a loaf of bread beside the breadbox, which is on a low shelf at the other side of the room. Moves slowly toward it.*): She was going to put this in there. (*Picks up loaf, then abruptly drops it. In a manner of returning to familiar things.*) It's a shame about her fruit. I wonder if it's all gone. (*Gets up on the chair and looks.*) I think there's some here that's all right, Mrs. Peters. Yes—here; (*Holding it toward the window.*) this is cherries, too. (*Looking again.*) I declare I believe that's the only one. (*Gets down, bottle in her hand. Goes to the sink and wipes it off on the outside.*) She'll feel awful bad after all her hard work in the hot weather. I remember the afternoon I put up my cherries last summer.

[*She puts the bottle on the big kitchen table, center of the room. With a sigh, is about to sit down in the rocking chair. Before she is seated realizes what chair it is; with a slow look at it, steps back. The chair, which she has touched, rocks back and forth.*]

MRS. PETERS: Well, I must get those things from the front-room closet. (*She goes to the door at the right, but after looking into the other room steps back.*) You coming with me, Mrs. Hale? You could help me carry them.
[*They go in the other room; reappear, Mrs. PETERS carrying a dress and skirt, Mrs. HALE following with a pair of shoes.*]
MRS. PETERS: My, it's cold in there.
[*She puts the clothes on the big table, and hurries to the stove.*]

MRS. HALE (*examining the skirt*): Wright was close. I think maybe that's why she kept so much to herself. She didn't even belong to the Ladies' Aid. I suppose she felt she couldn't do her part, and then you don't enjoy things when you feel shabby. She used to wear pretty clothes and be lively, when she was Minnie Foster, one of the town girls singing in the choir. But that—oh, that was thirty years ago. This all you was to take in?
MRS. PETERS: She said she wanted an apron. Funny thing to want, for there isn't much to get you dirty in jail, goodness knows. But I suppose just to make her feel more natural. She said they was in the top drawer in this cupboard. Yes, here. And then her little shawl that always hung behind the door. (*Opens stair door and looks.*) Yes, here it is.
[*Quickly shuts door leading upstairs.*]
MRS. HALE (*abruptly moving toward her*): Mrs. Peters?
MRS. PETERS: Yes, Mrs. Hale?
MRS. HALE: Do you think she did it?
MRS. PETERS (*in a frightened voice*): Oh, I don't know.
MRS. HALE: Well, I don't think she did. Asking for an apron and her little shawl. Worrying about her fruit.
MRS. PETERS (*starts to speak, glances up, where footsteps are heard in the room above. In a low voice*): Mr. Peters says it looks bad for her. Mr. Henderson is awful sarcastic in a speech, and he'll make fun of her sayin' she didn't wake up.
MRS. HALE: Well, I guess John Wright didn't wake when they was slipping that rope under his neck.

MRS. PETERS: No, it's strange. It must have been done awful crafty and still. They say it was such a—funny way to kill a man, rigging it all up like that.

MRS. HALE: That's just what Mr. Hale said. There was a gun in the house. He says that's what he can't understand.

MRS. PETERS: Mr. Henderson said coming out that what was needed for the case was a motive; something to show anger, or—sudden feeling.

MRS. HALE (*who is standing by the table*): Well, I don't see any signs of anger around here. (*She puts her hand on the dish towel which lies on the table, stands looking down at the table, one half of which is clean, the other half messy.*) It's wiped here. (*Makes a move as if to finish work, then turns and looks at loaf of bread outside the breadbox. Drops towel. In that voice of coming back to familiar things.*) Wonder how they are finding things upstairs? I hope she had it a little more red-up there. You know, it seems kind of *sneaking*. Locking her up in town and then coming out here and trying to get her own house to turn against her!

MRS. PETERS: But, Mrs. Hale, the law is the law.

MRS. HALE: I s'pose 'tis. (*Unbuttoning her coat.*) Better loosen up your things, Mrs. Peters. You won't feel them when you go out.

[MRS. PETERS *takes off her fur tippet, goes to hang it on hook at back of room, stands looking at the under part of the small corner table.*]

MRS. PETERS: She was piecing a quilt.

[*She brings the large sewing basket, and they look at the bright pieces.*]

MRS. HALE: It's log cabin pattern. Pretty, isn't it? I wonder if she was goin' to quilt it or just knot it?

[*Footsteps have been heard coming down the stairs. The* SHERIFF *enters, followed by* HALE *and the* COUNTY ATTORNEY.]

SHERIFF: They wonder if she was going to quilt it or just knot it.

[*The men laugh, the women look abashed.*]

COUNTY ATTORNEY (*rubbing his hands over the stove*): Frank's fire didn't do much up there, did it? Well, let's go out to the barn and get that cleared up.

[*The men go outside.*]

MRS. HALE (*resentfully*): I don't know as there's anything so strange, our takin' up our time with little things while we're waiting for them to get the evidence. (*She sits down at the big table, smoothing out a block with decision.*) I don't see as it's anything to laugh about.

MRS. PETERS (*apologetically*): Of course they've got awful important things on their minds.

[*Pulls up a chair and joins* MRS. HALE *at the table.*]

MRS. HALE (*examining another block*): Mrs. Peters, look at this one. Here, this is the one she was working on, and look at the sewing! All the rest of it has been so nice and even. And look at this! It's all over the place! Why, it looks as if she didn't know what she was about!

[*After she has said this, they look at each other, then start to glance back at the door. After an instant* MRS. HALE *has pulled at a knot and ripped the sewing.*]

Dorothea Lange Collection, The Oakland Museum.

MRS. PETERS: Oh, what are you doing, Mrs. Hale?

MRS. HALE (*mildly*): Just pulling out a stitch or two that's not sewed very good. (*Threading a needle.*) Bad sewing always made me fidgety.

MRS. PETERS (*nervously*): I don't think we ought to touch things.

MRS. HALE: I'll just finish up this end. (*Suddenly stopping and leaning forward.*) Mrs. Peters?

MRS. PETERS: Yes, Mrs. Hale?

MRS. HALE: What do you suppose she was so nervous about?

MRS. PETERS: Oh—I don't know. I don't know as she was nervous. I sometimes sew awful queer when I'm just tired. (*Mrs. Hale starts to say something, looks at Mrs. Peters, then goes on sewing.*) Well, I must get these things wrapped up. They may be through sooner than we think. (*Putting apron and other things together.*) I wonder where I can find a piece of paper, and string.

MRS. HALE: In that cupboard, maybe.

MRS. PETERS (*looking in cupboard*): Why, here's a birdcage. (*Holds it up.*) Did she have a bird, Mrs. Hale?

MRS. HALE: Why, I don't know whether she did or not—I've not been here for so long. There was a man around last year selling canaries cheap, but I don't know as she took one; maybe she did. She used to sing real pretty herself.

MRS. PETERS (*glancing around*): Seems funny to think of a bird here. But she must have had one, or why should she have a cage? I wonder what happened to it?

MRS. HALE: I s'pose maybe the cat got it.

MRS. PETERS: No, she didn't have a cat.

She's got that feeling some people have about cats—being afraid of them. My cat got in her room, and she was real upset and asked me to take it out.

MRS. HALE: My sister Bessie was like that. Queer, ain't it?

MRS. PETERS (*examining the cage*): Why, look at this door. It's broke. One hinge is pulled apart.

MRS. HALE (*looking, too*): Looks as if someone must have been rough with it.

MRS. PETERS: Why, yes.

[*She brings the cage forward and puts it on the table.*]

MRS. HALE: I wish if they're going to find any evidence they'd be about it. I don't like this place.

MRS. PETERS: But I'm awful glad you came with me, Mrs. Hale. It would be lonesome for me sitting here alone.

MRS. HALE: It would, wouldn't it? (*Dropping her sewing.*) But I tell you what I do wish, Mrs. Peters. I wish I had come over sometimes when *she* was here. I—(*Looking around the room.*)—wish I had.

MRS. PETERS: But of course you were awful busy, Mrs. Hale—your house and your children.

MRS. HALE: I could've come. I stayed away because it weren't cheerful—and that's why I ought to have come. I—I've never liked this place. Maybe because it's down in a hollow, and you don't see the road. I dunno what it is, but it's a lonesome place and always was. I wish I had come over to see Minnie Foster sometimes. I can see now—

[*Shakes her head.*]

MRS. PETERS: Well, you mustn't reproach yourself, Mrs. Hale. Somehow we just don't see how it is with other folks until—something comes up.

MRS. HALE: Not having children makes less work—but it makes a quiet house, and Wright out to work all day, and no company when he did come in. Did you know John Wright, Mrs. Peters?

MRS. PETERS: Not to know him; I've seen him in town. They say he was a good man.

MRS. HALE: Yes—good; he didn't drink, and kept his word as well as most, I guess, and paid his debts. But he was a hard man, Mrs. Peters. Just to pass the time of day with him. (*Shivers.*) Like a raw wind that gets to the bone. (*Pauses, her eye falling on the cage.*) I should think she would 'a wanted a bird. But what do you suppose went wrong with it?

MRS. PETERS: I don't know, unless it got sick and died.

[*She reaches over and swings the broken door, swings it again; both women watch it.*]

MRS. HALE: You weren't raised round here, were you? (*Mrs. Peters shakes her head.*) You didn't know—her?

MRS. PETERS: Not till they brought her yesterday.

MRS. HALE: She—come to think of it, she was kind of like a bird herself—real sweet and pretty, but kind of timid and—fluttery. How—she—did—change. (*Silence; then as if struck by a happy thought and relieved to get back to everyday things.*) Tell you what, Mrs. Peters, why don't you take the quilt in with you? It might take up her mind.

MRS. PETERS: Why, I think that's a real

nice idea, Mrs. Hale. There couldn't possibly be any objection to it, could there? Now, just what would I take? I wonder if her patches are in here—and her things.

[*They look in the sewing basket.*]

MRS. HALE: Here's some red. I expect this has got sewing things in it. (*Brings out a fancy box.*) What a pretty box. Looks like something somebody would give you. Maybe her scissors are in here. (*Opens box. Suddenly puts her hand to her nose.*) Why—(*Mrs. Peters bends nearer, then turns her face away.*) There's something wrapped up in this piece of silk.

MRS. PETERS: Why, this isn't her scissors.

MRS. HALE (*lifting the silk*): Oh, Mrs. Peters—it's—

[MRS. PETERS *bends closer.*]

MRS. PETERS: It's the bird.

MRS. HALE (*jumping up*): But, Mrs. Peters—look at it. Its neck! Look at its neck! It's all—other side *to.*

MRS. PETERS: Somebody—wrung—its neck.

[*Their eyes meet. A look of growing comprehension of horror. Steps are heard outside. Mrs. Hale slips box under quilt pieces, and sinks into her chair. Enter Sheriff and County Attorney. Mrs. Peters rises.*]

COUNTY ATTORNEY (*as one turning from serious things to little pleasantries*): Well, ladies, have you decided whether she was going to quilt it or knot it?

MRS. PETERS: We think she was going to —knot it.

COUNTY ATTORNEY: Well, that's interesting, I'm sure. (*Seeing the birdcage.*)

Has the bird flown?

MRS. HALE (*putting more quilt pieces over the box*): We think the—cat got it.

COUNTY ATTORNEY (*preoccupied*): Is there a cat?

[MRS. HALE *glances in a quick covert way at* MRS. PETERS.]

MRS. PETERS: Well, not now. They're superstitious, you know. They leave.

COUNTY ATTORNEY (*to* SHERIFF PETERS, *continuing an interrupted conversation*): No sign at all of anyone having come from the outside. Their own rope. Now let's go up again and go over it piece by piece. (*They start upstairs.*) It would have to have been someone who knew just the—

[MRS. PETERS *sits down. The two women sit there not looking at one another, but as if peering into something and at the same time holding back. When they talk now, it is in the manner of feeling their way over strange ground, as if afraid of what they are saying, but as if they cannot help saying it.*]

MRS. HALE: She liked the bird. She was going to bury it in that pretty box.

MRS. PETERS (*in a whisper*): When I was a girl—my kitten—there was a boy took a hatchet, and before my eyes—and before I could get there—(*Covers her face an instant.*) If they hadn't held me back, I would have—(*Catches herself, looks upstairs where steps are heard, falters weakly.*)—hurt him.

MRS. HALE (*with a slow look around her*): I wonder how it would seem never to have had any children around. (*Pause.*) No, Wright wouldn't like the bird—a thing that sang. She used to sing. He killed that, too.

MRS. PETERS (*moving uneasily*): We don't know who killed the bird.

MRS. HALE: I knew John Wright.

MRS. PETERS: It was an awful thing was done in this house that night, Mrs. Hale. Killing a man while he slept, slipping a rope around his neck that choked the life out of him.

MRS. HALE: His neck. Choked the life out of him.

[*Her hand goes out and rests on the birdcage.*]

MRS. PETERS (*with rising voice*): We don't know who killed him. We don't *know*.

MRS. HALE (*her own feeling not interrupted*): If there'd been years and years of nothing, then a bird to sing to you, it would be awful—still, after the bird was still.

MRS. PETERS (*something within her speaking*): I know what stillness is. When we homesteaded in Dakota, and my first baby died—after he was two years old, and me with no other then—

MRS. HALE (*moving*): How soon do you suppose they'll be through, looking for evidence?

MRS. PETERS: I know what stillness is. (*Pulling herself back.*) The law has got to punish crime, Mrs. Hale.

MRS. HALE (*not as if answering that*): I wish you'd seen Minnie Foster when she wore a white dress with blue ribbons and stood up there in the choir and sang. (*A look around the room.*) Oh, I *wish* I'd come over here once in a while! That was a crime! That was a crime! Who's going to punish that?

MRS. PETERS (*looking upstairs*): We mustn't—take on.

MRS. HALE: I might have known she needed help! I know how things can be—for women. I tell you, it's queer, Mrs. Peters. We live close together, and we live far apart. We all go through the same things—it's all just a different kind of the same thing. (*Brushes her eyes, noticing the bottle of fruit, reaches out for it.*) If I was you, I wouldn't tell her her fruit was gone. Tell her it *ain't*. Tell her it's all right. Take this in to prove it to her. She—she may never know whether it was broke or not.

MRS. PETERS (*takes the bottle, looks about for something to wrap it in; takes petticoat from the clothes brought from the other room, very nervously begins winding this around the bottle. In a false voice*): My, it's a good thing the men couldn't hear us. Wouldn't they just laugh! Getting all stirred up over a little thing like a —dead canary. As if that could have anything to do with—with—wouldn't they *laugh*!

[*The men are heard coming downstairs.*]

MRS. HALE (*under her breath*): Maybe they would—maybe they wouldn't.

COUNTY ATTORNEY: No, Peters, it's all perfectly clear except a reason for doing it. But you know juries when it comes to women. If there was some definite thing. Something to show— something to make a story about—a thing that would connect up with this strange way of doing it.

[*The women's eyes meet for an instant. Enter HALE from outer door.*]

HALE: Well, I've got the team around. Pretty cold out there.

COUNTY ATTORNEY: I'm going to stay

here awhile by myself. (*To the* Sheriff.) You can send Frank out for me,
can't you? I want to go over everything. I'm not satisfied that we can't
do better.

Sheriff: Do you want to see what Mrs.
Peters is going to take in?

[*The* Attorney *goes to the table,
picks up the apron, laughs.*]

County Attorney: Oh, I guess they're
not very dangerous things the ladies
have picked up. (*Moves a few things
about, disturbing the quilt pieces
which cover the box. Steps back.*)
No, Mrs. Peters doesn't need super-
vising. For that matter, a sheriff's
wife is married to the law. Ever think
of it that way, Mrs. Peters?

Mrs. Peters: Not—just that way.

Sheriff (*chuckling*): Married to the law.
(*Moves toward the other room.*) I
just want you to come in here a minute, George. We ought to take a look
at these windows.

County Attorney (*scoffingly*): Oh,
windows!

Sheriff: We'll be right out, Mr. Hale.

[Hale *goes outside. The* Sheriff *follows the*
County Attorney *into the other room.
Then* Mrs. Hale *rises, hands tight together,
looking intensely at* Mrs. Peters, *whose
eyes make a slow turn, finally meeting* Mrs.
Hale's. *A moment* Mrs. Hale *holds her,
then her own eyes point the way to where
the box is concealed. Suddenly* Mrs. Peters
*throws back quilt pieces and tries to put
the box in the bag she is wearing. It is too
big. She opens box, starts to take bird out,
cannot touch it, goes to pieces, stands there
helpless. Sound of a knob turning in the
other room.* Mrs. Hale *snatches the box
and puts it in the pocket of her big coat.
Enter* County Attorney *and* Sheriff.]

County Attorney (*facetiously*): Well,
Henry, at least we found out that she
was not going to quilt it. She was going to—what is it you call it, ladies?

Mrs. Hale (*her hand against her
pocket*): We call it—knot it, Mr.
Henderson.

Curtain

Insight

1. How would you characterize each of the Wrights? How do those describing them appear to feel about them?

2. Mrs. Peters and Mrs. Hale are the two main characters in the play. In what ways are they different? Which appears to you to be the stronger of the two?

3. The attitude of the men toward the women in the play is a factor in the men's unsuccessful search for a "motive." How would you characterize their attitude? In what way does this attitude contribute to their failure? How do the women appear to react to the comments made by the men? Which woman seems less tolerant toward the men?

4. What clues toward the solving of the murder do the women uncover? How and why do they deal with each clue in the manner they do?

A RAISIN IN THE SUN

Lorraine Hansberry

What happens to a dream deferred?
Does it dry up
Like a raisin in the sun?
Or fester like a sore—
And then run?
Does it stink like rotten meat?
Or crust and sugar over—
Like a syrupy sweet?

Maybe it just sags
Like a heavy load.

Or does it explode?

Langston Hughes

Characters
(in order of appearance)

RUTH YOUNGER
TRAVIS YOUNGER
WALTER LEE YOUNGER (BROTHER)
BENEATHA YOUNGER
LENA YOUNGER (MAMA)

JOSEPH ASAGAI
GEORGE MURCHISON
KARL LINDNER
BOBO
MOVING MEN

The action of the play is set in Chicago's Southside, sometime between World War II and the present.

ACT I

SCENE 1. FRIDAY MORNING.
SCENE 2. THE FOLLOWING MORNING.

ACT II

SCENE 1. LATER, THE SAME DAY.
SCENE 2. FRIDAY NIGHT, A FEW WEEKS LATER.
SCENE 3. MOVING DAY, ONE WEEK LATER.

ACT III

AN HOUR LATER.

ACT I

SCENE 1

The YOUNGER living room would be a comfortable and well-ordered room if it were not for a number of indestructible contradictions to this state of being. Its furnishings are typical and undistinguished, and their primary feature now is that they have clearly had to accommodate the living of too many people for too many years—and they are tired. Still, we can see that at some time, a time probably no longer remembered by the family (except perhaps for MAMA), the furnishings of this room were actually selected

Lorraine Hansberry

with care and love and even hope—and brought to this apartment and arranged with taste and pride.

That was a long time ago. Now the once loved pattern of the couch upholstery has to fight to show itself from under acres of crocheted doilies and couch covers which have themselves finally come to be more important than the upholstery. And here a table or a chair has been moved to disguise the worn places in the carpet; but the carpet has fought back by showing its weariness, with depressing uniformity, elsewhere on its surface.

Weariness has, in fact, won in this room. Everything has been polished, washed, sat on, used, scrubbed too often. All pretenses but living itself have long since vanished from the very atmosphere of this room.

Moreover, a section of this room, for it is not really a room unto itself, though the landlord's lease would make it seem so, slopes backward to provide a small kitchen area where the family prepares the meals that are eaten in the living room proper, which must also serve as dining room. The single window that has been provided for these "two" rooms is located in this kitchen area. The sole natural light the family may enjoy in the course of a day is only that which fights its way through this little window.

At Left, a door leads to a bedroom which is shared by MAMA and her daughter, BENEATHA. At Right, opposite, is a second room (which in the beginning of the life of this apartment was probably a breakfast room) which serves as a bedroom for WALTER and his wife, RUTH.

AT RISE: It is morning dark in the living room. TRAVIS is asleep on the makedown bed at Center. An alarm clock sounds from within the bedroom at Right, and presently RUTH enters from that room and closes the door behind her. She crosses sleepily toward the window. As she passes her sleeping son, she reaches down and shakes him a little. At the window she raises the shade, and a dusky Southside morning light comes in feebly. She fills a pot with water and puts it on to boil. She calls to the boy, between yawns, in a slightly muffled voice.

RUTH is about thirty. We can see that she was a pretty girl, even exceptionally so, but now it is apparent that life has been little that she expected, and disappointment has already begun to hang in her face. In a few years, before thirty-five even, she will be known among her people as a "settled woman."

She crosses to her son and gives him a good, final, rousing shake.

RUTH: Come on now, boy, it's seven-thirty! (*Her son sits up at last, in a stupor of sleepiness.*) I say hurry up, Travis! You ain't the only person in the world got to use a bathroom!

[*The child, a sturdy, handsome little boy of ten or eleven, drags himself out of the bed and almost blindly takes his towels and "today's clothes" from drawers and a closet and goes out to the bathroom, which is in an outside hall and which is shared by another family or families on the same floor. RUTH crosses to the bedroom door at Right and opens it and calls in to her husband.*]

RUTH: Walter Lee! . . . It's after seven-thirty! Lemme see you do some waking up in there now! (*She waits.*) You better get up from there, man! It's after seven-thirty, I tell you. (*She waits again.*) All right, you just go ahead and lay there, and next thing you know Travis be finished and Mr. Johnson'll be in there and you'll be fussing and cussing round here like a madman! And be late, too! (*She waits, at the end of patience.)* Walter Lee—it's time for you to get up!

[*She waits another second and then starts to go into the bedroom, but is apparently satisfied that her husband has begun to get up. She stops, pulls the door to, and returns to the kitchen area. She wipes her face with a moist cloth and runs her fingers through her sleep-disheveled hair in a vain effort and ties an apron around her house-coat. The bedroom door at Right opens, and her husband stands in the doorway in his pajamas, which are rumpled and mis-mated. He is a lean, intense young man in his middle thirties, inclined to quick ner-vous movements and erratic speech habits —and always in his voice there is a quality of indictment.]*

WALTER: Is he out yet?

RUTH: What you mean, *out?* He ain't hardly got in there good yet.

WALTER (*wandering in, still more ori-ented to sleep than to a new day*): Well, what was you doing all that yelling for if I can't even get in there yet? (*Stopping and thinking.*) Check coming today?

RUTH: They *said* Saturday, and this is just Friday, and I hopes to God you ain't going to get up here first thing this morning and start talking to me 'bout no money—'cause I 'bout don't want to hear it.

WALTER: Something the matter with you this morning?

RUTH: No—I'm just sleepy as the devil. What kind of eggs you want?

WALTER: Not scrambled. (RUTH *starts to scramble eggs.*) Paper come? (RUTH *points impatiently to the rolled up Tribune on the table, and he gets it and spreads it out and vaguely reads the front page.*) Set off another bomb yesterday.

RUTH (*maximum indifference*): Did they?

WALTER (*looking up*): What's the matter with you?

RUTH: Ain't nothing the matter with me. And don't keep asking me that this morning.

WALTER: Ain't nobody bothering you. (*Reading the news of the day ab-sently again.*) Say Colonel McCormick is sick.

RUTH (*affecting tea-party interest*): Is he now? Poor thing.

WALTER (*sighing and looking at his watch*): Oh, me. (*He waits.*) Now what is that boy doing in that bath-room all this time? He just going to have to start getting up earlier. I can't be being late to work on ac-count of him fooling around in there.

RUTH (*turning on him*): Oh, no, he ain't going to be getting up no earlier; no such thing! It ain't his fault that he can't get to bed no earlier nights 'cause he got a bunch of crazy good-for-nothing clowns sitting up running their mouths in what is supposed to be his bedroom after ten o'clock at night. . . .

WALTER: That's what you mad about, ain't it? The things I want to talk about with my friends just couldn't be important in your mind, could they?

[*He rises and finds a cigarette in her hand-bag on the table and crosses to the little window and looks out, smoking and deeply enjoying this first one.*]

RUTH (*almost matter-of-factly, a com-plaint too automatic to deserve em-phasis*): Why you always got to smoke before you eat in the morning?

WALTER (*at the window*): Just look at 'em down there ... running and racing to work.... (*He turns and faces his wife and watches her a moment at the stove, and then, suddenly*) You look young this morning, baby.

RUTH (*indifferently*): Yeah?

WALTER: Just for a second—stirring them eggs. It's gone now—just for a second it was—you looked real young again. (*Then, drily*) It's gone now—you look like yourself again.

RUTH: Man, if you don't shut up and leave me alone.

WALTER (*looking out to the street again*): First thing a man ought to learn in life is not to make love to no colored woman first thing in the morning. You-all some evil people at eight o'clock in the morning.

[TRAVIS *appears in the hall doorway, almost fully dressed and quite wide awake now, his towels and pajamas across his shoulders. He opens the door and signals for his father to make the bathroom in a hurry.*]

TRAVIS (*watching the bathroom*): Daddy, come on!

[WALTER *gets his bathroom utensils and flies out to the bathroom.*]

RUTH: Sit down and have your breakfast, Travis.

TRAVIS: Mama, this is Friday. (*Gleefully.*) Check coming tomorrow, huh?

RUTH: You get your mind off money and eat your breakfast.

TRAVIS (*eating*): This is the morning we supposed to bring the fifty cents to school.

RUTH: Well, I ain't got no fifty cents this morning.

TRAVIS: Teacher say we have to.

RUTH: I don't care what teacher say. I ain't got it. Eat your breakfast, Travis.

TRAVIS: I *am* eating.

RUTH: Hush up now and just eat!

[*The boy gives her an exasperated look for her lack of understanding, and eats grudgingly.*]

TRAVIS: You think Grandmama would have it?

RUTH: No! And I want you to stop asking your grandmother for money, you hear me?

TRAVIS (*outraged*): Gaaaleee! I don't ask her; she just gimme it sometimes!

RUTH: Travis Willard Younger—I got too much on me this morning to be....

TRAVIS: Maybe Daddy....

RUTH: *Travis!*

[*The boy hushes abruptly. They are both quiet and tense for several seconds.*]

TRAVIS (*presently*): Could I maybe go carry some groceries in front of the supermarket for a little while after school, then?

RUTH: Just hush, I said.

[*Travis jabs his spoon into his cereal bowl viciously and rests his head in anger upon his fists.*]

RUTH: If you through eating, you can get over there and make up your bed.

[*The boy obeys stiffly and crosses the room, almost mechanically, to the bed, and more or less carefully folds the covering. He carries the bedding into his mother's room and returns with his books and cap.*]

TRAVIS (*sulking and standing apart from her unnaturally*): I'm gone.

RUTH (*looking up from the stove to inspect him automatically*): Come here. (*He crosses to her and she studies his head*). If you don't take this comb and fix this here head, you better! (TRAVIS *puts down his books with a great sigh of oppression and crosses to the mirror. His mother mutters under her breath about his "slubbornness."*) 'Bout to march out of here with that head looking just like chickens slept in it! I just don't know where you get your slubborn ways. ... And get your jacket, too. Looks chilly out this morning.

TRAVIS (*with conspicuously brushed hair and jacket*): I'm gone.

RUTH: Get carfare and milk money—(*Waving one finger.*)—and not a single penny for no caps, you hear me?

TRAVIS (*with sullen politeness*): Yes'm.

[*He turns in outrage to leave. His mother watches after him as in his frustration he approaches the door almost comically. When she speaks to him, her voice has become a very gentle tease.*]

RUTH (*mocking; as she thinks he would say it*): Oh, Mama makes me so mad sometimes, I don't know what to do! (*She waits and continues to his back as he stands stock-still in front of the door.*) I wouldn't kiss that woman good-bye for nothing in this world this morning!

[*The boy finally turns around and rolls his eyes at her, knowing the mood has changed and he is vindicated; he does not, however, move toward her yet.*]

RUTH: Not for nothing in this world!

[*She finally laughs aloud at him and holds out her arms to him, and we see that it is a way between them, very old and practiced. He crosses to her and allows her to embrace him warmly but keeps his face fixed with masculine rigidity. She holds him back from her presently and looks at him and runs her fingers over the features of his face.*]

RUTH (*with utter gentleness*): Now—whose little old angry man are you?

TRAVIS (*the masculinity and gruffness start to fade at last*): Aw gaalee—Mama ...

RUTH (*mimicking*): Aw—gaaaaalleeeee, Mama! (*She pushes him, with rough playfulness and finality, toward the door.*) Get on out of here or you going to be late.

TRAVIS (*in the face of love, new aggressiveness*): Mama, could I *please* go carry groceries?

RUTH: Honey, it's starting to get so cold evenings.

WALTER (*coming in from the bathroom and drawing a make-believe gun from a make-believe holster and shooting at his son*): What is it he wants to do?

RUTH: Go carry groceries after school at the supermarket.

WALTER: Well, let him go. ...

TRAVIS (*quickly, to the ally*): I have to —she won't gimme the fifty cents. ...

WALTER (*to his wife only*): Why not?

RUTH (*simply, and with flavor*): 'Cause we don't have it.

WALTER (*to RUTH only*): What you tell the boy things like that for? (*Reaching down into his pants with a rather important gesture.*) Here, son ...

[*He hands the boy the coin, but his eyes are directed to his wife's. TRAVIS takes the money happily.*]

Lorraine Hansberry

TRAVIS: Thanks, Daddy.

[He starts out. RUTH watches both of them with murder in her eyes. WALTER stands and stares back at her with defiance and suddenly reaches into his pocket again on an afterthought.]

WALTER (without even looking at his son, still staring hard at his wife): In fact, here's another fifty cents.... Buy yourself some fruit today—or take a taxicab to school or something!

TRAVIS: Whoopee—

[He leaps up and clasps his father around the middle with his legs, and they face each other in mutual appreciation; slowly WALTER LEE peeks around the boy to catch the violent rays from his wife's eyes and draws his head back as if shot.]

WALTER: You better get down now— and get to school, man.

TRAVIS (at the door): O.K. Good-bye.

[He exits.]

WALTER (after him, pointing with pride): That's my boy.

[She looks at him in disgust and turns back to her work.]

WALTER: You know what I was thinking 'bout in the bathroom this morning?

RUTH: No.

WALTER: How come you always try to be so pleasant!

RUTH: What is there to be pleasant 'bout!

WALTER: You want to know what I was thinking 'bout in the bathroom or not!

RUTH: I know what you thinking 'bout.

WALTER (ignoring her): 'Bout what me and Willy Harris was talking about last night.

RUTH (immediately—a refrain): Willy Harris is a good-for-nothing loud mouth.

WALTER: Anybody who talks to me has got to be a good-for-nothing loud mouth, ain't he? And what you know about who is just a good-for-nothing loud mouth? Charlie Atkins was just a "good-for-nothing loud mouth" too, wasn't he! When he wanted me to go in the dry-cleaning business with him. And now—he's grossing a hundred thousand a year. A hundred thousand dollars a year! You still call him a loud mouth!

RUTH (bitterly): Oh, Walter Lee.... (She folds her head on her arms over the table.)

WALTER (rising and coming to her and standing over her): You tired, ain't you? Tired of everything. Me, the boy, the way we live—this beat-up hole—everything. Ain't you?

[She doesn't look up, doesn't answer.]

WALTER: So tired—moaning and groaning all the time, but you wouldn't do nothing to help, would you? You couldn't be on my side that long for nothing, could you?

RUTH: Walter, please leave me alone.

WALTER: A man needs for a woman to back him up....

RUTH: Walter....

WALTER: Mama would listen to you. You know she listen to you more than she do me and Bennie. She think more of you. All you have to do is just sit down with her when you drinking your coffee one morning and talking 'bout things like you do and— (He sits down beside her and demonstrates graphically what he thinks her *methods and tone should be.*)—you just sip your coffee, see, and say easy like that you been thinking 'bout that deal Walter Lee is so interested in, 'bout the store and all, and sip some more coffee, like what you saying ain't really that important to you—And the next thing you know, she be listening good and asking you questions and when I come home—I can tell her the details. This ain't no fly-by-night proposition, baby. I mean we figured it out, me and Willy and Bobo.

RUTH (*with a frown*): Bobo?

WALTER: Yeah. You see, this little liquor store we got in mind cost seventy-five thousand, and we figured the initial investment on the place be 'bout thirty thousand, see. That be ten thousand each. Course, there's a couple of hundred you got to pay so's you don't spend your life just waiting for them clowns to let your license get approved. . . .

RUTH: You mean graft?

WALTER (*frowning impatiently*): Don't call it that. See there, that just goes to show you what women understand about the world. Baby, don't *nothing* happen for you in this world 'less you pay *somebody* off!

RUTH: Walter, leave me alone! (*She raises her head and stares at him vigorously—then says, more quietly*) Eat your eggs; they gonna be cold.

WALTER (*straightening up from her and looking off*): That's it. There you are. Man say to his woman: I got me a dream. His woman say: Eat your eggs. (*Sadly, but gaining in power.*) Man say: I got to take hold of this here world, baby! And a woman will

say: Eat your eggs and go to work. (*Passionately now.*) Man say: I got to change my life, I'm choking to death, baby! And his woman say—(*In utter anguish as he brings his fists down on his thighs.*)—Your eggs is getting cold!

RUTH (*softly*): Walter, that ain't none of our money.

WALTER (*not listening at all or even looking at her*): This morning, I was lookin' in the mirror and thinking about it . . . I'm thirty-five years old; I been married eleven years and I got a boy who sleeps in the living room—(*Very, very quietly.*)—and all I got to give him is stories about how rich white people live. . . .

RUTH: Eat your eggs, Walter.

WALTER: *Damn my eggs . . . damn all the eggs that ever was!*

RUTH: Then go to work.

WALTER (*looking up at her*): See—I'm trying to talk to you 'bout myself—(*Shaking his head with the repetition.*)—and all you can say is eat them eggs and go to work.

RUTH (*wearily*): Honey, you never say nothing new. I listen to you every day, every night and every morning, and you never say nothing new. (*Shrugging.*) So you would rather *be* Mr. Arnold than be his chauffeur. So —I would *rather* be living in Buckingham Palace.

WALTER: That is just what is wrong with the colored woman in this world. . . . Don't understand about building their men up and making 'em feel like they somebody. Like they can do something.

RUTH (*drily, but to hurt*): There *are* colored men who do things.

WALTER: No thanks to the colored woman.

RUTH: Well, being a colored woman, I guess I can't help myself none.

[*She rises and gets the ironing board and sets it up and attacks a huge pile of rough-dried clothes, sprinkling them in preparation for the ironing and then rolling them into tight fat balls.*]

WALTER (*mumbling*): We one group of men tied to a race of women with small minds.

[*His sister* BENEATHA *enters. She is about twenty, as slim and intense as her brother. She is not as pretty as her sister-in-law, but her lean, almost intellectual face has a handsomeness of its own. She wears a bright-red flannel nightie, and her thick hair stands wildly about her head. Her speech is a mixture of many things; it is different from the rest of the family's insofar as education has permeated her sense of English—and perhaps the Midwest rather than the South has finally—at last—won out in her inflection; but not altogether, because over all of it is a soft slurring and transformed use of vowels which is the decided influence of the Southside. She passes through the room without looking at either* RUTH *or* WALTER *and goes to the outside door and looks, a little blindly, out to the bathroom. She sees that it has been lost to the Johnsons. She closes the door with a sleepy vengeance and crosses to the table and sits down a little defeated.*]

BENEATHA: I am going to start timing those people.

WALTER: You should get up earlier.

BENEATHA (*her face in her hands. She is still fighting the urge to go back to bed.*): Really—would you suggest dawn? Where's the paper?

WALTER (*pushing the paper across the table to her as he studies her almost clinically, as though he has never seen her before*): You a horrible-looking chick at this hour.

BENEATHA (*drily*): Good morning, everybody.

WALTER (*senselessly*): How is school coming?

BENEATHA (*in the same spirit*): Lovely. Lovely. And you know, biology is the greatest. (*Looking up to him.*) I dissected something that looked just like you yesterday.

WALTER: I just wondered if you've made up your mind and everything.

BENEATHA (*gaining in sharpness and impatience*): And what did I answer yesterday morning—and the day before that?

RUTH (*from the ironing board, like someone disinterested and old*): Don't be so nasty, Bennie.

BENEATHA (*still to her brother*): And the day before that and the day before that!

WALTER (*defensively*): I'm interested in you. Something wrong with that? Ain't many girls who decide. . . .

WALTER AND BENEATHA (*in unison*):— "to be a doctor."

[*Silence.*]

WALTER: Have we figured out yet just exactly how much medical school is going to cost?

RUTH: Walter Lee, why don't you leave that girl alone and get out of here to work?

BENEATHA (*exits to the bathroom and bangs on the door*): Come on out of there, please! (*She comes back into the room.*)

WALTER (*looking at his sister intently*): You know the check is coming tomorrow.

BENEATHA (*turning on him with a sharpness all her own*): That money belongs to Mama, Walter, and it's for her to decide how she wants to use it. I don't care if she wants to buy a house or a rocket ship or just nail it up somewhere and look at it. It's hers. Not ours—*hers*.

WALTER (*bitterly*): Now ain't that fine! You just got your mother's interest at heart, ain't you, girl? You such a nice girl—but if Mama got that money she can always take a few thousand and help you through school too—can't she?

BENEATHA: I have never asked anyone around here to do anything for me!

WALTER: No! And the line between asking and just accepting when the time comes is big and wide—ain't it!

BENEATHA (*with fury*): What do you want from me, Brother—that I quit school or just drop dead, which!

WALTER: I don't want nothing but for you to stop acting holy 'round here. Me and Ruth done made some sacrifices for you—why can't you do something for the family?

RUTH: Walter, don't be dragging me in it.

WALTER: You are in it—Don't you get up and go work in somebody's kitchen for the last three years to help put clothes on her back?

RUTH: Oh, Walter—that's not fair. . . .

WALTER: It ain't that nobody expects you to get on your knees and say thank you, Brother; thank you, Ruth; thank you, Mama—and thank you, Travis, for wearing the same pair of shoes for two semesters. . . .

BENEATHA (*dropping to her knees*): Well —I *do*—all right?—thank everybody . . . and forgive me for ever wanting to be anything at all . . . forgive me, forgive me!

RUTH: Please stop it! Your mama'll hear you.

WALTER: Who the hell told you you had to be a doctor? If you so crazy 'bout messing 'round with sick people— then go be a nurse like other women —or just get married and be quiet. . . .

BENEATHA: Well—you finally got it said. . . . It took you three years, but you finally got it said. Walter, give up; leave me alone—it's Mama's money.

WALTER: *He was my father, too!*

BENEATHA: So what? He was mine, too —and Travis's grandfather—but the insurance money belongs to Mama. Picking on me is not going to make her give it to you to invest in any liquor stores—(*Underbreath, dropping into a chair.*)—and I for one say, God bless Mama for that!

WALTER (*to* RUTH): See—did you hear? Did you hear!

RUTH: Honey, please go to work.

WALTER: Nobody in this house is ever going to understand me.

BENEATHA: Because you're a nut.

WALTER: Who's a nut?

BENEATHA: You—you are a nut. Thee is mad, boy.

WALTER (*looking at his wife and his sister from the door, very sadly*): The world's most backward race of people, and that's a fact.

BENEATHA (*turning slowly in her chair*): And then there are all those prophets who would lead us out of the wilderness—(WALTER *slams out of the house.*)—into the swamps!

RUTH: Bennie, why you always gotta be pickin' on your brother? Can't you be a little sweeter sometimes?

[*Door opens.* WALTER *walks in.*]

WALTER (*to* RUTH): I need some money for carfare.

RUTH (*looks at him, then warms; teasing, but tenderly*): Fifty cents? (*She goes to her bag and gets money.*) Here, take a taxi.

[WALTER *exits.* MAMA *enters. She is a woman in her early sixties, full-bodied and strong. She is one of those women of a certain grace and beauty who wear it so unobtrusively that it takes a while to notice. Her dark brown face is surrounded by the total whiteness of her hair, and, being a woman who has adjusted to many things in life and overcome many more, her face is full of strength. She has, we can see, wit and faith of a kind that keep her eyes lit and full of interest and expectancy. She is, in a word, a beautiful woman. Her bearing is perhaps most like the noble bearing of the women of the Hereros of Southwest Africa—rather as if she imagines that as she walks she still bears a basket or a vessel upon her head. Her speech, on the other hand, is as careless as her carriage is precise—she is inclined to slur everything—but her voice is perhaps not so much quiet as simply soft.*]

MAMA: Who that round here slamming doors at this hour?

[*She crosses through the room, goes to the window, opens it, and brings in a feeble little plant growing doggedly in a small pot on the window sill. She feels the dirt and puts it back out.*]

RUTH: That was Walter Lee. He and Bennie was at it again.

MAMA: My children and they tempers. Lord, if this little old plant don't get more sun than it's been getting, it ain't never going to see spring again. (*She turns from the window.*) What's the matter with you this morning, Ruth? You looks right peaked. You aiming to iron all them things? Leave some for me. I'll get to 'em this afternoon. Bennie honey, it's too drafty for you to be sitting round half dressed. Where's your robe?

BENEATHA: In the cleaners.

MAMA: Well, go get mine and put it on.

BENEATHA: I'm not cold, Mama, honest.

MAMA: I know—but you so thin. . . .

BENEATHA (*irritably*): Mama, I'm not cold.

MAMA (*seeing the makedown bed as* TRAVIS *has left it*): Lord have mercy, look at that poor bed. Bless his heart —he tries, don't he? (*She moves to the bed* TRAVIS *has sloppily made up.*)

RUTH: No—he don't half try at all 'cause he knows you going to come along behind him and fix everything. That's just how come he don't know how to do nothing right now—you done spoiled that boy so.

MAMA: Well—he's a little boy. Ain't supposed to know 'bout housekeeping. My baby, that's what he is. What you fix for his breakfast this morning?

RUTH (*angrily*): I feed my son, Lena!

MAMA: I ain't meddling—(*Underbreath; busy-bodyish.*) I just noticed all last week he had cold cereal, and when it starts getting this chilly in the fall a child ought to have some hot grits or something when he goes out in the cold. . . .

RUTH (*furious*): I gave him hot oats—is that all right!

MAMA: I ain't meddling. (*Pause.*) Put a lot of nice butter on it?

[RUTH *shoots her an angry look and does not reply.*]

MAMA: He likes lots of butter.

RUTH (*exasperated*): Lena. . . .

MAMA (*to* BENEATHA. MAMA *is inclined to wander conversationally sometimes.*): What was you and your brother fussing 'bout this morning?

BENEATHA: It's not important, Mama.

[*She gets up and goes to look out at the bathroom, which is apparently free, and she picks up her towels and rushes out.*]

MAMA: What was they fighting about?

RUTH: Now you know as well as I do.

MAMA (*shaking her head*): Brother still worrying hisself sick about that money?

RUTH: You know he is.

MAMA: You had breakfast?

RUTH: Some coffee.

MAMA: Girl, you better start eating and looking after yourself better. You almost thin as Travis.

RUTH: Lena. . . .

MAMA: Uh-hunh?

RUTH: What are you going to do with it?

MAMA: Now don't you start, child. It's too early in the morning to be talking about money. It ain't Christian.

RUTH: It's just that he got his heart set on that store. . . .

MAMA: You mean that liquor store that Willy Harris want him to invest in?

RUTH: Yes. . . .

MAMA: We ain't no business people, Ruth. We just plain working folks.

RUTH: Ain't nobody business people till they go into business. Walter Lee say colored people ain't never going to start getting ahead till they start gambling on some different kinds of things in the world—investments and things.

MAMA: What done got into you, girl? Walter Lee done finally sold you on investing.

RUTH: No. Mama, something is happening between Walter and me. I don't know what it is—but he needs something—something I can't give him anymore. He needs this chance, Lena.

MAMA (*frowning deeply*): But liquor, honey. . . .

RUTH: Well—like Walter say—I 'spec' people going to always be drinking themselves some liquor.

MAMA: Well—whether they drinks it or not ain't none of my business. But whether I go into business selling it to 'em *is*, and I don't want that on my ledger this late in life. (*Stopping suddenly and studying her daughter-in-law.*) Ruth Younger, what's the matter with you today? You look like you could fall over right there.

RUTH: I'm tired.

MAMA: Then you better stay home from work today.

RUTH: I can't stay home. She'd be calling up the agency and screaming at them, "My girl didn't come in today —send me somebody! My girl didn't come in!" Oh, she just have a fit. . . .

MAMA: Well, let her have it. I'll just call her up and say you got the flu—

RUTH (*laughing*): Why the flu?

MAMA: 'Cause it sounds respectable to 'em. Something white people get, too. They know 'bout the flu. Otherwise they think you been cut up or something when you tell 'em you sick.

RUTH: I got to go in. We need the money.

MAMA: Somebody would of thought my children done all but starved to death the way they talk about money here late. Child, we got a great big old check coming tomorrow.

RUTH (sincerely, but also self-righteously): Now, that's your money. It ain't got nothing to do with me. We all feel like that—Walter and Bennie and me—even Travis.

MAMA (thoughtfully, and suddenly very far away): Ten thousand dollars. . . .

RUTH: Sure is wonderful.

MAMA: Ten thousand dollars.

RUTH: You know what you should do? Miss Lena? You should take yourself a trip somewhere. To Europe or South America or someplace. . . .

MAMA (throwing up her hands at the thought): Oh, child!

RUTH: I'm serious. Just pack up and leave! Go on away and enjoy yourself some. Forget about the family, and have yourself a ball for once in your life—

MAMA (drily): You sound like I'm just about ready to die. Who'd go with me? What I look like v andering round Europe by myself?

RUTH: Shoot—these here rich white women do it all the time. They don't think nothing of packing up they suitcases and piling on one of them big steamships and—swoosh!—they gone, child.

MAMA: Something always told me I wasn't no rich white woman.

RUTH: Well—what are you going to do with it, then?

MAMA: I ain't rightly decided. (Thinking. She speaks now with emphasis.) Some of it got to be put away for Beneatha and her schoolin'—and ain't nothing going to touch that part of it. Nothing. (She waits several seconds, trying to make up her mind about something, and looks at RUTH a little tentatively before going on.) Been thinking that we maybe could meet the notes on a little old two-story somewhere, with a yard where Travis could play in the summertime, if we use part of the insurance for a down payment and everybody kind of pitch in. I could maybe take on a little day work again, few days a week. . . .

RUTH (studying her mother-in-law furtively and concentrating on her ironing, anxious to encourage without seeming to): Well, Lord knows, we've put enough rent into this here rat trap to pay for four houses by now. . . .

MAMA (looking up at the words rat trap and then looking around and leaning back and sighing—in a suddenly reflective mood—): "Rat trap" —yes, that's all it is. (Smiling.) I remember just as well the day me and Big Walter moved in here. Hadn't been married but two weeks and wasn't planning on living here no more than a year. (She shakes her head at the dissolved dream.) We was going to set away, little by little, don't you know, and buy a little place out in Morgan Park. We had even picked out the house. (Chuckling a little.) Looks right dumpy today. But Lord, child, you should know all the dreams I had 'bout buying that house and fixing it up and making me a little garden in the back—(She waits *and stops smiling.*) And didn't none of it happen. (*Dropping her hands in a futile gesture.*)

RUTH (*keeps her head down, ironing*): Yes, life can be a barrel of disappointments, sometimes.

MAMA: Honey, Big Walter would come in here some nights back then and slump down on that couch there and just look at the rug, and look at me and look at the rug and then back at me—and I'd know he was down then . . . really down. (*After a second very long and thoughtful pause; she is seeing back to times that only she can see.*) And then, Lord, when I lost that baby—little Claude—I almost thought I was going to lose Big Walter, too. Oh, that man grieved hisself! He was one man to love his children.

RUTH: Ain't nothin' can tear at you like losin' your baby.

MAMA: I guess that's how come that man finally worked hisself to death like he done. Like he was fighting his own war with this here world that took his baby from him.

RUTH: He sure was a fine man, all right. I always liked Mr. Younger.

MAMA: Crazy 'bout his children! God knows there was plenty wrong with Walter Younger—hard-headed, mean, kind of wild with women—plenty wrong with him. But he sure loved his children. Always wanted them to have something—be something. That's where Brother gets all these notions, I reckon. Big Walter used to say, he'd get right wet in the eyes sometimes, lean his head back with the water standing in his eyes and say, "Seem like God didn't see fit to give

the black man nothing but dreams—but He did give us children to make them dreams seem worthwhile." (*She smiles.*) He could talk like that, don't you know.

RUTH: Yes, he sure could. He was a good man, Mr. Younger.

MAMA: Yes, a fine man—just couldn't never catch up with his dreams, that's all.

[BENEATHA *comes in, brushing her hair and looking up to the ceiling, where the sound of a vacuum cleaner has started up.*]

BENEATHA: What could be so dirty on that woman's rugs that she has to vacuum them every single day?

RUTH: I wish certain young women round here who I could name would take inspiration about certain rugs in a certain apartment I could also mention.

BENEATHA (*shrugging*): How much cleaning can a house need, for Christ's sakes.

MAMA (*not liking the Lord's name used thus*): Bennie!

RUTH: Just listen to her—just listen!

BENEATHA: Oh, God!

MAMA: If you use the Lord's name just one more time—

BENEATHA (*a bit of a whine*): Oh, Mama. . . .

RUTH: Fresh—just fresh as salt, this girl!

BENEATHA (*drily*): Well—if the salt loses its savor. . . .

MAMA: Now that will do. I just ain't going to have you round here reciting the scriptures in vain—you hear me?

BENEATHA: How did I manage to get on everybody's wrong side by just walking into a room?

RUTH: If you weren't so fresh. . . .

BENEATHA: Ruth, I'm twenty years old.

MAMA: What time you be home from school today?

BENEATHA: Kind of late. (*With enthusiasm.*) Madeline is going to start my guitar lessons today.

[MAMA *and* RUTH *look up with the same expression.*]

MAMA: Your *what* kind of lessons?

BENEATHA: Guitar.

RUTH: Oh, Father!

MAMA: How come you done taken it in your mind to learn to play the guitar?

BENEATHA: I just want to, that's all.

MAMA (*smiling*): Lord, child, don't you know what to do with yourself? How long it going to be before you get tired of this now—like you get tired of that little play-acting group you joined last year? (*Looking at* RUTH.) And what was it the year before that?

RUTH: The horseback-riding club for which she bought that fifty-five-dollar riding habit that's been hanging in the closet ever since!

MAMA (*to* BENEATHA): Why you got to flit so from one thing to another, baby?

BENEATHA (*sharply*): I just want to learn to play the guitar. Is there anything wrong with that?

MAMA: Ain't nobody trying to stop you. I just wonders sometimes why you has to flit so from one thing to another all the time. You ain't never done nothing with all that camera equipment you brought home . . .

BENEATHA: I don't flit! I—I experiment with different forms of expression. . . .

RUTH: Like riding a horse?

BENEATHA: People have to express themselves one way or another.

MAMA: What is it you want to express?

BENEATHA (*angrily*): Me!

[MAMA *and* RUTH *look at each other and burst into raucous laughter.*]

BENEATHA: Don't worry—I don't expect you to understand.

MAMA (*to change the subject*): Who you going out with tomorrow night?

BENEATHA (*with displeasure*): George Murchison again.

MAMA (*pleased*): Oh—you getting a little sweet on him?

RUTH: You ask me, this child ain't sweet on nobody but herself—(*Underbreath.*) Express herself! (*They laugh.*)

BENEATHA: Oh—I like George all right, Mama. I mean I like him enough to go out with him and stuff, but—

RUTH (*for devilment*): What does *and stuff* mean?

BENEATHA: Mind your own business.

MAMA: Stop picking at her now, Ruth. (*A thoughtful pause, and then a suspicious sudden look at her daughter as she turns in her chair for emphasis.*) What *does* it mean?

BENEATHA (*wearily*): Oh, I just mean I couldn't ever really be serious about George. He's—he's so shallow.

RUTH: Shallow—what do you mean he's shallow? He's *rich*!

MAMA: Hush, Ruth.

BENEATHA: I know he's rich. He knows he's rich, too.

RUTH: Well—what other qualities a man got to have to satisfy you, little girl?

BENEATHA: You wouldn't even begin to understand. Anybody who married Walter could not possibly understand.

MAMA (*outraged*): What kind of way is that to talk about your brother?

BENEATHA: Brother is a flip—let's face it.

MAMA (*to* RUTH, *helplessly*): What's a flip?

RUTH (*glad to add kindling*): She's saying he's crazy.

BENEATHA: Not crazy. Brother isn't really crazy yet—he—he's an elaborate neurotic.

MAMA: Hush your mouth!

BENEATHA: As for George. Well. George looks good—he's got a beautiful car and he takes me to nice places and, as my sister-in-law says, he is probably the richest boy I will ever get to know, and I even like him sometimes—but if the Youngers are sitting around waiting to see if their little Bennie is going to tie up the family with the Murchisons, they are wasting their time.

RUTH: You mean you wouldn't marry George Murchison if he asked you someday? That pretty, rich thing? Honey, I knew you was odd. . . .

BENEATHA: No, I would not marry him if all I felt for him was what I feel now. Besides, George's family wouldn't really like it.

MAMA: Why not?

BENEATHA: Oh, Mama—The Murchisons are honest-to-God-real-*live*-rich colored people, and the only people in the world who are more snobbish than rich white people are rich colored people. I thought everybody knew that. I've met Mrs. Murchison. She's a scene!

MAMA: You must not dislike people 'cause they well off, honey.

BENEATHA: Why not? It makes just as much sense as disliking people 'cause they are poor, and lots of people do that.

RUTH (*a wisdom-of-the-ages manner. To* MAMA.): Well, she'll get over some of this. . . .

BENEATHA: Get over it? What are you talking about, Ruth? Listen, I'm going to be a doctor. I'm not worried about who I'm going to marry yet—if I ever get married.

MAMA AND RUTH: *If!*

MAMA: Now, Bennie . . . .

BENEATHA: Oh, I probably will . . . but first I'm going to be a doctor, and George, for one, still thinks that's pretty funny. I couldn't be bothered with that. I am going to be a doctor, and everybody around here better understand that!

MAMA (*kindly*): 'Course you going to be a doctor, honey, God willing.

BENEATHA (*drily*): God hasn't got a thing to do with it.

MAMA: Beneatha—that just wasn't necessary.

BENEATHA: Well—neither is God. I get sick of hearing about God.

MAMA: Beneatha!

BENEATHA: I mean it! I'm just tired of hearing about God all the time. What has He got to do with anything? Does He pay tuition?

MAMA: You 'bout to get your fresh little jaw slapped!

RUTH: That's just what she needs, all right!

BENEATHA: Why? Why can't I say what I want to around here, like everybody else?

MAMA: It don't sound nice for a young girl to say things like that—you wasn't brought up that way. Me and your father went to trouble to get you and Brother to church every Sunday.

BENEATHA: Mama, you don't understand. It's all a matter of ideas, and God is just one idea I don't accept. It's not important. I am not going out and be immoral or commit crimes because I don't believe in God. I don't even think about it. It's just that I get tired of Him getting credit for all the things the human race achieves through its own stubborn effort. There simply is no blasted God—there is only man and it is he who makes miracles!

[MAMA *absorbs this speech, studies her daughter and rises slowly and crosses to* BENEATHA *and slaps her powerfully across the face. After, there is only silence, and the daughter drops her eyes from her mother's face, and* MAMA *is very tall before her.*]

MAMA: Now—you say after me, in my mother's house there is still God. (*There is a long pause, and* BENEATHA *stares at the floor wordlessly.* MAMA *repeats the phrase with precision and cool emotion.*) In my mother's house there is still God.
BENEATHA: In my mother's house there is still God.

[*A long pause.*]

MAMA (*walking away from* BENEATHA, *too disturbed for triumphant posture. Stopping and turning back to her daughter*): There are some ideas we ain't going to have in this house. Not long as I am at the head of this family.
BENEATHA: Yes, ma'am.

[MAMA *walks out of the room.*]

RUTH (*almost gently, with profound understanding*): You think you a woman, Bennie—but you still a little girl. What you did was childish—so you got treated like a child.

BENEATHA: I see. (*Quietly.*) I also see that everybody thinks it's all right for Mama to be a tyrant. But all the tyranny in the world will never put a God in the heavens!

[*She picks up her books and goes out.*]

RUTH (*goes to* MAMA's *door*): She said she was sorry.
MAMA (*coming out, going to her plant*): They frightens me, Ruth. My children.
RUTH: You got good children, Lena. They just a little off sometimes—but they're good.
MAMA: No—there's something come down between me and them that don't let us understand each other, and I don't know what it is. One done almost lost his mind thinking 'bout money all the time, and the other done commence to talk about things I can't seem to understand in no form or fashion. What is it that's changing, Ruth?
RUTH (*soothingly, older than her years*): Now . . . you taking it all too seriously. You just got strong-willed children, and it takes a strong woman like you to keep 'em in hand.
MAMA (*looking at her plant and sprinkling a little water on it*): They spirited all right, my children. Got to admit they got spirit—Bennie and Walter. Like this little old plant that ain't never had enough sunshine or nothing —and look at it. . . .

[*She has her back to* RUTH, *who has had to stop ironing and lean against something and put the back of her hand to her forehead.*]

RUTH (*trying to keep* MAMA *from noticing*): You . . . sure . . . loves that little old thing, don't you? . . .

MAMA: Well, I always wanted me a garden like I used to see sometimes at the back of the houses down home. This plant is close as I ever got to having one. (*She looks out of the window as she replaces the plant.*) Lord, ain't nothing as dreary as the view from this window on a dreary day, is there? Why ain't you singing this morning, Ruth? Sing that "No Ways Tired." That song always lifts me up so—(*She turns at last to see that* RUTH *has slipped quietly into a chair, in a state of semiconsciousness.*) Ruth! Ruth, honey—what's the matter with you . . . Ruth!

Curtain

SCENE 2

It is the following morning; a Saturday morning, and housecleaning is in progress at the YOUNGERS'. Furniture has been shoved hither and yon, and MAMA is giving the kitchen area walls a washing down. BENEATHA, in dungarees, with a handkerchief tied around her face, is spraying insecticide into the cracks in the walls. As they work, the radio is on and a Southside disk jockey program is inappropriately filling the house with a rather exotic saxophone blues. TRAVIS, the sole idle one, is leaning on his arms, looking out of the window.

TRAVIS: Grandmama, that stuff Bennie is using smells awful. Can I go downstairs, please?

MAMA: Did you get all them chores done already? I ain't seen you doing much.

TRAVIS: Yes'm—finished early. Where did Mama go this morning?

MAMA (*looking at* BENEATHA): She had to go on a little errand.

TRAVIS: Where?

MAMA: To tend to her business.

TRAVIS: Can I go outside then?

MAMA: Oh, I guess so. You better stay in front of the house, though . . . and keep a good lookout for the postman.

TRAVIS: Yes'm. (*He starts out and decides to give his* AUNT BENEATHA *a good swat on the legs as he passes her.*) Leave them poor little old cockroaches alone; they ain't bothering you none.

[*He runs as she swings the spray gun at him both viciously and playfully.* WALTER *enters from the bedroom and goes to the phone.*]

MAMA: Look out there, girl, before you be spilling some of that stuff on that child!

TRAVIS (*teasing*): That's right—look out now!

[*He exits.*]

BENEATHA (*drily*): I can't imagine that it would hurt him—it has never hurt the roaches.

MAMA: Well, little boys' hides ain't as tough as Southside roaches.

WALTER (*into phone*): Hello—Let me talk to Willy Harris.

MAMA: You better get over there behind the bureau. I seen one marching out of there like Napoleon yesterday.

WALTER: Hello, Willy? It ain't come yet. It'll be here in a few minutes. Did the lawyer give you the papers?

BENEATHA: There's really only one way to get rid of them, Mama. . . .

Mama: How?

BENEATHA: Set fire to this building.

WALTER: Good. Good. I'll be right over.

BENEATHA: Where did Ruth go, Walter?

WALTER: I don't know.

[*He exits abruptly.*]

BENEATHA: Mama, where did Ruth go?

MAMA (*looking at her with meaning*): To the doctor, I think.

BENEATHA: The doctor? What's the matter? (*They exchange glances.*) You don't think. . . .

MAMA (*with her sense of drama*): Now I ain't saying what I think. But I ain't never been wrong 'bout a woman, neither.

[*The phone rings.*]

BENEATHA (*at the phone*): Hay-lo . . . (*Pause, and a moment of recognition.*) Well—when did you get back! . . . And how was it? . . . Of course I've missed you—in my way. . . . This morning? No . . . house cleaning and all that and Mama hates it if I let people come over when the house is like this. . . . You *have?* Well, that's different. . . . What is it—Oh, what the hell, come on over. . . . Right, see you then. (*She hangs up.*)

MAMA (*who has listened vigorously, as is her habit*): Who is that you inviting over here with this house looking like this? You ain't got the pride you was born with!

BENEATHA: Asagai doesn't care how houses look, Mama—he's an intellectual.

MAMA: *Who?*

BENEATHA: Asagai—Joseph Asagai. He's an African boy I met on campus. He's been studying in Canada all summer.

MAMA: What's his name?

BENEATHA: Asagai, Joseph. Ah-sah-guy. . . . He's from Nigeria.

MAMA: Oh, that's the little country that was founded by slaves way back. . . .

BENEATHA: No, Mama—that's Liberia.

MAMA: I don't think I never met no African before.

BENEATHA: Well, do me a favor and don't ask him a whole lot of ignorant questions about Africans. I mean, do they wear clothes and all that. . . .

MAMA: Well, now, I guess if you think we so ignorant round here, maybe you shouldn't bring your friends here—

BENEATHA: It's just that people ask such crazy things. All anyone seems to know about when it comes to Africa is Tarzan. . . .

MAMA (*indignantly*): Why should I know anything about Africa?

BENEATHA: Why do you give money at church for the missionary work?

MAMA: Well, that's to help save people.

BENEATHA: You mean save them from *heathenism.* . . .

MAMA (*innocently*): Yes.

BENEATHA: I'm afraid they need more salvation from the British and the French.

[RUTH *comes in forlornly and pulls off her coat with dejection. They both turn to look at her.*]

RUTH (*dispiritedly*): Well, I guess from all the happy faces—everybody knows.

BENEATHA: You pregnant?

MAMA: Lord have mercy, I sure hope it's a little old girl. Travis ought to have a sister.

[BENEATHA *and* RUTH *give her a hopeless look for this grandmotherly enthusiasm.*]

BENEATHA: How far along are you?

RUTH: Two months.

BENEATHA: Did you mean to? I mean did

you plan it or was it an accident?

MAMA: What do you know about planning or not planning?

BENEATHA: Oh, Mama.

RUTH (*wearily*): She's twenty years old, Lena.

BENEATHA: Did you plan it, Ruth?

RUTH: Mind your own business.

BENEATHA: It is my business—where is he going to live, on the *roof*?

[*There is silence following the remark as the three women react to the sense of it.*]

BENEATHA: Gee—I didn't mean that, Ruth, honest. Gee, I don't feel like that at all. I—I think it is wonderful.

RUTH (*dully*): Wonderful.

BENEATHA: Yes—really.

MAMA (*looking at* RUTH, *worried*): Doctor say everything going to be all right?

RUTH (*far away*): Yes—she says everything is going to be fine. . . .

MAMA (*immediately suspicious*): "She" —What doctor you went to?

[RUTH *folds over, near hysteria.*]

MAMA (*worriedly hovering over* RUTH): Ruth honey—what's the matter with you—you sick?

[RUTH *has her fists clenched on her thighs and is fighting hard to suppress a scream that seems to be rising in her.*]

BENEATHA: What's the matter with her, Mama?

MAMA (*working her fingers in* RUTH'S *shoulder to relax her*): She be all right. Women gets right depressed sometimes when they get her way. (*Speaking softly, expertly, rapidly.*) Now you just relax. That's right . . . just lean back; don't think 'bout nothing at all . . . nothing at all. . . .

RUTH: I'm all right. . . .

[*The glassy-eyed look melts, and then she collapses into a fit of heavy sobbing. The bell rings.*]

BENEATHA: Oh, my God—that must be Asagai.

MAMA (*to* RUTH): Come on now, honey. You need to lie down and rest awhile . . . then have some nice hot food.

[*They exit,* RUTH'S *weight on her mother-in-law.* BENEATHA, *herself profoundly disturbed, opens the door to admit a rather dramatic-looking young man with a large package.*]

ASAGAI: Hello, Alaiyo. . . .

BENEATHA (*holding the door open and regarding him with pleasure*): Hello . . .(*Long pause*) well—come in. And please excuse everything. My mother was very upset about my letting anyone come here with the place like this.

ASAGAI (*coming into the room*): You look disturbed too. . . . Is something wrong?

BENEATHA (*still at the door, absently*): Yes . . . we've all got acute ghetto-itus. (*She smiles and comes toward him, finding a cigarette and sitting.*) So— sit down! How was Canada?

ASAGAI (*a sophisticate*): Canadian.

BENEATHA (*looking at him*): I'm very glad you are back.

ASAGAI (*looking back at her in turn*): Are you really?

BENEATHA: Yes—very.

ASAGAI: Why—you were quite glad when I went away. What happened?

BENEATHA: You went away.

ASAGAI: Ahhhhhhhh.

BENEATHA: Before—you wanted to be so serious before there was time.

ASAGAI: How much time must there be

before one knows what one feels?

BENEATHA (*stalling this particular conversation. Her hands pressed together, in a deliberately childish gesture*): What did you bring me?

ASAGAI (*handing her the package*): Open it and see.

BENEATHA (*eagerly opening the package and drawing out some records and the colorful robes of a Nigerian woman*): Oh, Asagai! . . . You got them for me! . . . How beautiful . . . and the records, too! (*She lifts out the robes and runs to the mirror with them and holds the drapery up in front of herself.*)

ASAGAI (*coming to her at the mirror*): I shall have to teach you how to drape it properly. (*He flings the material about her for the moment and stands back to look at her*) Ah—Oh-pay-gay-day, oh-gbah-mu-shay. (*A Yoruba exclamation for admiration.*) You wear it well . . . very well . . . mutilated hair and all.

BENEATHA (*turning suddenly*): My hair —what's wrong with my hair?

ASAGAI (*shrugging*): Were you born with it like that?

BENEATHA (*reaching up to touch it*): No . . . of course not.

[*She looks back to the mirror, disturbed.*]

ASAGAI (*smiling*): How then?

BENEATHA: You know perfectly well how . . . as crinkly as yours . . . that's how.

ASAGAI: And it is ugly to you that way?

BENEATHA (*quickly*): Oh, no—not ugly. . . . (*More slowly, apologetically.*) But it's so hard to manage when it's, well —raw.

ASAGAI: And so to accommodate that— you mutilate it every week?

BENEATHA: It's not mutilation!

ASAGAI (*laughing aloud at her seriousness*): Oh . . . please! I am only teasing you because you are so very serious about these things. (*He stands back from her and folds his arms across his chest as he watches her pulling at her hair and frowning in the mirror.*) Do you remember the first time you met me at school? . . . (*He laughs.*) You came up to me, and you said—and I thought you were the most serious little thing I had ever seen—you said: (*He imitates her.*) "Mr. Asagai—I want very much to talk with you. About Africa. You see, Mr. Asagai, I am looking for my identity!" (*He laughs.*)

BENEATHA (*turning to him, not laughing*): Yes—(*Her face is quizzical, profoundly disturbed.*)

ASAGAI (*still teasing and reaching out and taking her face in his hands and turning her profile to him*): Well . . . it is true that this is not so much a profile of a Hollywood queen as perhaps a queen of the Nile—(*A mock dismissal of the importance of the question.*) But what does it matter? Assimilationism is so popular in your country.

BENEATHA (*wheeling, passionately, sharply*): I am not an assimilationist!

ASAGAI (*The protest hangs in the room for a moment, and* ASAGAI *studies her, his laughter fading*): Such a serious one. (*There is a pause.*) So—you like the robes? You must take excellent care of them—they are from my sister's personal wardrobe.

BENEATHA (*with incredulity*): You—you sent all the way home—for me?

ASAGAI (*with charm*): For you—I would

do much more. . . . Well, that is what I came for. I must go.

BENEATHA: Will you call me Monday?

ASAGAI: Yes. . . . We have a great deal to talk about. I mean about identity and time and all that.

BENEATHA: Time?

ASAGAI: Yes. About how much time one needs to know what one feels.

BENEATHA: You never understood that there is more than one kind of feeling which can exist between a man and a woman—or, at least, there should be.

ASAGAI (*shaking his head negatively but gently*): No. Between a man and a woman there need be only one kind of feeling. I have that for you. . . . Now even . . . right this moment. . . .

BENEATHA: I know—and by itself—it won't do. I can find that anywhere.

ASAGAI: For a woman it should be enough.

BENEATHA: I know—because that's what it says in all the novels that men write. But it isn't. Go ahead and laugh—but I'm not interested in being someone's little episode in America or—(*With feminine vengeance.*)—one of them! (ASAGAI *has burst into laughter again.*) That's funny as hell, huh!

ASAGAI: It's just that every American girl I have known has said that to me. White—black—in this you are all the same. And the same speech, too!

BENEATHA (*angrily*): Yuk, yuk, yuk!

ASAGAI: It's how you can be sure that the world's most liberated women are not liberated at all. You all talk about it too much!

[MAMA *enters and is immediately all social charm because of the presence of a guest.*]

BENEATHA: Oh—Mama—this is Mr. Asagai.

MAMA: How do you do?

ASAGAI (*total politeness to an elder*): How do you do, Mrs. Younger. Please forgive me for coming at such an outrageous hour on a Saturday.

MAMA: Well, you are quite welcome. I just hope you understand that our house don't always look like this. (*Chatterish.*) You must come again. I would love to hear all about—(*Not sure of the name.*)—your country. I think it's so sad the way our American Negroes don't know nothing about Africa 'cept Tarzan and all that. And all the money they pour into these churches when they ought to be helping you people over there drive out them French and Englishmen done taken away your land.

[*The mother flashes a slightly superior look at her daughter upon completion of the recitation.*]

ASAGAI (*taken aback by this sudden and acutely unrelated expression of sympathy*): Yes . . . yes. . . .

MAMA (*smiling at him suddenly and relaxing and looking him over*): How many miles is it from here to where you come from?

ASAGAI: Many thousands.

MAMA (*looking at him as she would* WALTER): I bet you don't half look after yourself, being away from your mama, either. I 'spec' you better come round here from time to time and get yourself some decent homecooked meals. . . .

ASAGAI (*moved*): Thank you. Thank you very much. (*They are all quiet, then*—) Well . . . I must go. I will call you Monday, Alaiyo.

MAMA: What's that he call you?

ASAGAI: Oh—"Alaiyo." I hope you don't mind. It is what you would call a nickname, I think. It is a Yoruba word. I am a Yoruba.

MAMA (*looking at* BENEATHA): I—I thought he was from—

ASAGAI (*understanding*): Nigeria is my country. Yoruba is my tribal origin—

BENEATHA: You didn't tell us what Alaiyo means . . . for all I know, you might be calling me Little Idiot or something. . . .

ASAGAI: Well . . . let me see . . . I do not know how just to explain it. . . . The sense of a thing can be so different when it changes languages.

BENEATHA: You're evading.

ASAGAI: No—really it is difficult. . . . (*Thinking*.) It means . . . it means One for Whom Bread—Food—Is Not Enough. (*He looks at her.*) Is that all right?

BENEATHA (*understanding, softly*): Thank you.

MAMA (*looking from one to the other and not understanding any of it*): Well . . . that's nice. . . . You must come see us again—Mr. . . .

ASAGAI: Ah-sah-guy. . . .

MAMA: Yes. . . . Do come again.

ASAGAI: Good-bye. (*He exits.*)

MAMA (*after him*): Lord, that's a pretty thing just went out here! (*Insinuatingly, to her daughter.*) Yes, I guess I see why we done commence to get so interested in Africa round here. Missionaries my aunt Jenny! (*She exits.*)

BENEATHA: Oh, Mama! . . .

[*She picks up the Nigerian dress and holds it up to her in front of the mirror again. She sets the headdress on haphazardly and then notices her hair again and clutches at it and then replaces the headdress and frowns at herself. Then she starts to wriggle in front of the mirror as she thinks a Nigerian woman might.* TRAVIS *enters and regards her.*]

TRAVIS: You cracking up?

BENEATHA: Shut up.

[*She pulls the headdress off and looks at herself in the mirror and clutches at her hair again and squinches her eyes as if trying to imagine something. Then, suddenly, she gets her raincoat and kerchief and hurriedly prepares for going out.*]

MAMA (*coming back into the room*): She's resting now. Travis, baby, run next door and ask Miss Johnson to please let me have a little kitchen cleanser. This here can is empty as Jacob's kettle.

TRAVIS: I just came in.

MAMA: Do as you told. (*He exits and she looks at her daughter.*) Where you going?

BENEATHA (*halting at the door*): To become a queen of the Nile!

[*She exits in a breathless blaze of glory.* RUTH *appears in the bedroom doorway.*]

MAMA: Who told you to get up?

RUTH: Ain't nothing wrong with me to be lying in no bed for. Where did Bennie go?

MAMA (*drumming her fingers*): Far as I could make out—to Egypt. (RUTH *just looks at her.*) What time is it getting to?

RUTH: Ten-twenty. And the mailman going to ring that bell this morning just like he done every morning for the last umpteen years.

[TRAVIS *comes in with the cleanser can.*]

TRAVIS: She say to tell you that she don't have much.

MAMA (*angrily*): Lord, some people I could name sure is tightfisted! (*Directing her grandson.*) Mark two cans of cleanser down on the list there. If she that hard up for kitchen cleanser, I sure don't want to forget to get her none!

RUTH: Lena—maybe the woman is just short on cleanser. . . .

MAMA (*not listening*): —Much baking powder as she done borrowed from me all these years, she could of done gone into the baking business!

[*The bell sounds suddenly and sharply and all three are stunned—serious and silent—mid-speech. In spite of all the other conversations and distractions of the morning, this is what they have been waiting for, even TRAVIS, who looks helplessly from his mother to his grandmother. RUTH is the first to come to life again.*]

RUTH (*to* TRAVIS): *Get down them steps, boy!*

[TRAVIS *snaps to life and flies out to get the mail.*]

MAMA (*her eyes wide, her hand to her breast*): You mean it done really come?

RUTH (*excited*): Oh, Miss Lena!

MAMA (*collecting herself*): Well . . . I don't know what we all so excited about round here for. We known it was coming for months.

RUTH: That's a whole lot different from having it come and being able to hold

it in your hands . . . a piece of paper worth ten thousand dollars. . . .

[TRAVIS *bursts back into the room. He holds the envelope high above his head, like a little dancer; his face is radiant and he is breathless. He moves to his grandmother with sudden slow ceremony and puts the envelope into her hands. She accepts it, and then merely holds it and looks at it.*]

RUTH: Come on! Open it. . . . Lord have mercy, I wish Walter Lee was here!

TRAVIS: Open it, Grandmama!

MAMA (*staring at it*): Now you-all be quiet. It's just a check.

RUTH: Open it. . . .

MAMA (*still staring at it*): Now don't act silly. . . . We ain't never been no people to act silly 'bout no money—

RUTH (*swiftly*): We ain't never had none before—*open it!*

[MAMA *finally makes a good strong tear and pulls out the thin blue slice of paper and inspects it closely. The boy and his mother study it raptly over* MAMA's *shoulders.*]

MAMA: *Travis!* (*She is counting off with doubt.*) Is that the right number of zeros?

TRAVIS: Yes'm . . . ten thousand dollars. Gaalee, Grandmama, you rich.

MAMA (*She holds the check away from her, still looking at it. Slowly her face sobers into a mask of unhappiness.*): Ten thousand dollars. (*She hands it to* RUTH.) Put it away somewhere, Ruth. (*She does not look at* RUTH; *her eyes seem to be seeing something somewhere very far off.*) Ten thousand dollars they give you. Ten thousand dollars.

TRAVIS (*to his mother, sincerely*): What's the matter with Grandmama —don't she want to be rich?

RUTH (*distractedly*): You go out and play now, baby.

[TRAVIS *exits.* MAMA *starts wiping dishes absently, humming intently to herself.* RUTH *turns to her, with kind exasperation.*]

RUTH: You've gone and got yourself upset.

MAMA (*not looking at her*): I 'spec' if it wasn't for you-all . . . I would just put that money away or give it to the church or something.

RUTH: Now what kind of talk is that? Mr. Younger would just be plain mad if he could hear you talking foolish like that.

MAMA (*stopping and staring off*): Yes . . . he sure would. (*Sighing.*) We got enough to do with that money, all right.

[*She halts then, and turns and looks at her daughter-in-law hard;* RUTH *avoids her eyes, and* MAMA *wipes her hands with finality and starts to speak firmly to* RUTH.]

MAMA: Where did you go today, girl?

RUTH: To the doctor.

MAMA (*impatiently*): Now, Ruth . . . you know better than that. Old Doctor Jones is strange enough in his way, but there ain't nothing 'bout him make somebody slip and call him "she"—like you done this morning.

RUTH: Well, that's what happened—my tongue slipped.

MAMA: You went to see that woman, didn't you?

RUTH (*defensively, giving herself away*): What woman you talking about?

MAMA (*angrily*): That woman who. . . .

[WALTER *enters in great excitement.*]

WALTER: Did it come?

MAMA (*quietly*): Can't you give people a Christian greeting before you start asking about money?

WALTER (*to* RUTH): Did it come?

[RUTH *unfolds the check and lays it quietly before him, watching him intently with thoughts of her own.* WALTER *sits down and grasps it close and counts off the zeros.*]

WALTER: Ten thousand dollars—(*He turns suddenly, frantically, to his mother and draws some papers out of his breast pocket.*) Mama—look. Old Willy Harris put everything on paper. . . .

MAMA: Son—I think you ought to talk to your wife. . . . I'll go on out and leave you alone if you want—

WALTER: I can talk to her later—Mama, look. . . .

MAMA: Son. . . .

WALTER: WILL SOMEBODY PLEASE LISTEN TO ME TODAY!

MAMA (*quietly*): I don't 'low no yellin' in this house, Walter Lee, and you know it—(WALTER *stares at them in frustration and starts to speak several times.*) And there ain't going to be no investing in no liquor stores. I don't aim to have to speak on that again.

[*A long pause.*]

WALTER: Oh—so you don't aim to have to speak on that again? So *you* have decided. . . . (*Crumpling his papers.*) Well, *you* tell that to my boy tonight when you put him to sleep on the living room couch. . . . (*Turning to* MAMA *and speaking directly to her.*) Yeah—and tell it to my wife, Mama, tomorrow when she has to go out of here to look after somebody else's kids. And tell it to *me*, Mama, every time we need a new pair of curtains and I have to watch *you* go out and work in somebody's kitchen. Yeah, you tell me then! (WALTER *starts out.*)

RUTH: Where you going?

WALTER: I'm going out!

RUTH: Where?

WALTER: Just out of this house somewhere. . . .

RUTH (*getting her coat*): I'll come, too.

WALTER: I don't want you to come!

RUTH: I got something to talk to you about, Walter.

WALTER: That's too bad.

MAMA (*still quietly*): Walter Lee—(*She waits and he finally turns and looks at her.*) Sit down.

WALTER: I'm a grown man, Mama.

MAMA: Ain't nobody said you wasn't grown. But you still in my house and my presence. And as long as you are —you'll talk to your wife civil. Now sit down.

RUTH (*suddenly*): Oh, let him go out and drink himself to death! He makes me sick to my stomach! (*She flings her coat against him.*)

WALTER (*violently*): And you turn mine too, baby! (RUTH *goes into their bedroom and slams the door behind her.*) That was my greatest mistake. . . .

MAMA (*still quietly*): Walter, what is the matter with you?

WALTER: Matter with me? Ain't nothing the matter with *me!*

MAMA: Yes, there is. Something eating you up like a crazy man. Something more than me not giving you this money. The past few years I been watching it happen to you. You get all nervous acting and kind of wild in the eyes—

[WALTER *jumps up impatiently at her words.*]

MAMA: I said sit there now: I'm talking to you!

WALTER: Mama—I don't need no nagging at me today.

MAMA: Seem like you getting to a place where you always tied up in some kind of knot about something. But if anybody ask you 'bout it, you just yell at 'em and bust out the house and go out and drink somewheres. Walter Lee, people can't live with that. Ruth's a good, patient girl in her way —but you getting to be too much. Boy, don't make the mistake of driving that girl away from you.

WALTER: Why—what she do for me?

MAMA: She loves you.

WALTER: Mama—I'm going out. I want to go off somewhere and be by myself for a while.

MAMA: I'm sorry 'bout your liquor store, son. It just wasn't the thing for us to do. That's what I want to tell you about. . . .

WALTER: I got to go out, Mama. . . . (*He rises.*)

MAMA: It's dangerous, son.

WALTER: What's dangerous?

MAMA: When a man goes outside his home to look for peace.

WALTER (*beseechingly*): Then why can't there never be no peace in this house, then?

MAMA: You done found it in some other house?

WALTER: No—there ain't no woman! Why do women always think there's a woman somewhere when a man gets restless. (*Coming to her.*) Mama —Mama—I want so many things. . . .

MAMA: Yes, son. . . .

WALTER: I want so many things that they are driving me kind of crazy. . . . Mama—look at me.

MAMA: I'm looking at you. You a good-looking boy. You got a job; a nice wife; a fine boy and. . . .

WALTER: A job. (*Looks at her.*) Mama, a job? I open and close car doors all day long. I drive a man around in his limousine and I say, "Yes, sir; no, sir; very good, sir; shall I take the Drive, sir?" Mama, that ain't no kind of job . . . that ain't nothing at all. (*Very quietly.*) Mama, I don't know if I can make you understand.

MAMA: Understand what, baby?

WALTER (*quietly*): Sometimes it's like I can see the future stretched out in front of me—just plain as day. The future, Mama. Hanging over there at the edge of my days. Just waiting for me—a big, looming blank space—full of *nothing*. Just waiting for *me*. (*Pause.*) Mama—sometimes when I'm downtown and I pass them cool, quiet-looking restaurants where them white boys are sitting back and talking 'bout things . . . sitting there turning deals worth millions of dollars . . . sometimes I see guys don't look much older than me—

MAMA: Son—how come you talk so much 'bout money?

WALTER (*with immense passion*): Because it is life, Mama!

MAMA (*quietly*): Oh—(*Very quietly.*) So now it's life. Money is life. Once upon a time freedom used to be life —now it's money. I guess the world really do change. . . .

WALTER: No—it was always money, Mama. We just didn't know about it.

MAMA: No . . . something has changed. (*She looks at him.*) You something new, boy. In my time we was worried about not being lynched and getting to the North if we could and how to stay alive and still have a pinch of dignity too. . . . Now here come you and Beneatha—talking 'bout things we ain't never even thought about hardly, me and your daddy. You ain't satisfied or proud of nothing we done. I mean that you had a home; that we kept you out of trouble till you was grown; that you don't have to ride to work on the back of nobody's street-car—You my children—but how different we done become.

WALTER: You just don't understand, Mama; you just don't understand.

MAMA: Son—do you know your wife is expecting another baby?

[WALTER *stands, stunned, and absorbs what his mother has said.*]

MAMA: That's what she wanted to talk to you about.

[WALTER *sinks down into a chair.*]

MAMA: This ain't for me to be telling —but you ought to know. (*She waits.*) I think Ruth is thinking 'bout getting rid of that child.

WALTER (*slowly understanding*): No— no—Ruth wouldn't do that.

MAMA: When the world gets ugly enough—a woman will do anything for her family. *The part that's already living.*

WALTER: You don't know Ruth, Mama, if you think she would do that.

Lorraine Hansberry

[RUTH *opens the bedroom door and stands there a little limp.*]

RUTH (*beaten*): Yes, I would, too, Walter. (*Pause.*) I gave her a five-dollar down payment.

[*There is total silence as the man stares at his wife and the mother stares at her son.*]

MAMA (*presently*): Well—(*Tightly.*) Well—son, I'm waiting to hear you say something . . . I'm waiting to hear how you be your father's son. Be the man he was. . . . (*Pause.*) Your wife say she going to destroy your child. And I'm waiting to hear you talk like him and say we a people who give children life, not who destroys them —(*She rises.*) I'm waiting to see you stand up and look like your daddy and say we done give up one baby to poverty and that we ain't going to give up nary another one . . . I'm waiting.

WALTER: Ruth. . . .

MAMA: If you a son of mine, tell her!

[WALTER *turns, looks at her, and can say nothing. She continues, bitterly.*]

MAMA: You . . . you are a disgrace to your father's memory. Somebody get me my hat.

Curtain

Insight
1. *Setting.* The setting of a play is the background of time and place in which the action occurs. It is important for the reader to have a clear understanding of the setting to visualize the action as it takes place. The setting provides the readers with important clues to the overall mood of the play or to a specific scene. What clues about the people living in the apartment are given by the specific details of the setting?
2. Much of the impact of the first act derives from the vivid characterizations developed through both words and deeds. How would you characterize each adult in the family? Which passages especially reveal their traits?
3. *Conflict.* Conflict is the struggle between opposing forces upon which drama depends. The conflict may be between the main character and an external force—nature, society, circumstances, other characters—or between opposing ideas which the characters are made to represent. What are some of the conflicts that appear to be developing in this play? Which, to you, seems to be evolving as the major conflict of the play?
4. "Seems like God didn't see fit to give the black man nothing but dreams." How would you describe the dreams of each of the adults as you meet them in Act I? What obstacles seem to keep those dreams from becoming reality?

ACT II
SCENE 1

TIME: Later the same day.

AT RISE: RUTH is ironing again. She has the radio going. Presently BENEATHA's bedroom door opens, and RUTH's mouth falls and she puts down the iron in fascination.

RUTH: What have we got on tonight!

BENEATHA (*emerging grandly from the doorway so that we can see her thoroughly robed in the costume Asagai brought*): You are looking at what a well-dressed Nigerian woman wears —(*She parades for* RUTH, *her hair completely hidden by the headdress; she is coquettishly fanning herself with an ornate oriental fan, mistakenly more like Butterfly than any Nigerian that ever was.*) Isn't it beautiful? (*She promenades to the radio and, with an arrogant flourish, turns off the good loud blues that is playing.*) Enough of this assimilationist junk! (RUTH *follows her with her eyes as she goes to the phonograph and puts on a record and turns and waits ceremoniously for the music to come up. Then, with a shout—*) OCOMOGOSIAY!

[RUTH *jumps. The music comes up, a lovely Nigerian melody.* BENEATHA *listens, enraptured, her eyes far away—"back to the past." She begins to dance.* RUTH *is dumfounded.*]

RUTH: What kind of dance is that?

BENEATHA: A folk dance.

RUTH (*Pearl Bailey*): What kind of folks do that, honey?

BENEATHA: It's from Nigeria. Its a dance of welcome.

RUTH: Who you welcoming?

BENEATHA: The men back to the village.

RUTH: Where they been?

BENEATHA: How should I know—out hunting or something. Anyway, they are coming back now. . . .

RUTH: Well, that's good.

BENEATHA (*with the record*):
  Alundi, alundi
  Alundi alunya
  Jop pu a jeepua
  Ang gu soooooooooo

  Ai yai yae. . . .
  Ayehaye—alundi. . . .

[WALTER *comes in during this performance; he has obviously been drinking. He leans against the door heavily and watches his sister, at first with distaste. Then his eyes look off—"back to the past"—as he lifts both his fists to the roof, screaming.*]

WALTER: YEAH . . . AND ETHIOPIA STRETCH FORTH HER HANDS AGAIN! . . .

RUTH (*drily, looking at him*): Yes—and Africa sure is claiming her own tonight. (*She gives them both up and starts ironing again.*)

WALTER (*all in a drunken, dramatic shout*): Shut up! . . . I'm digging them drums . . . them drums move me! . . . (*He makes his weaving way to his wife's face and leans in close to her.*) In my *heart of hearts*—(*He thumps his chest.*)—I am much warrior!

RUTH (*without even looking up*): In your heart of hearts you are much drunkard.

WALTER (*coming away from her and starting to wander around the room, shouting*): Me and Jomo . . . (*Intently, in his sister's face. She has stopped dancing to watch him in this unknown mood.*) That's my man, Kenyatta.[1] (*Shouting and thumping his chest.*) FLAMING SPEAR! HOT DAMN! (*He is suddenly in possession of an imaginary spear and actively spearing enemies all over the room.*) OCOMOGOSIAY . . . THE LION IS WAKING . . . OWIMO-WEH!

[*He pulls his shirt open and leaps up on a table and gestures with his spear. The bell rings.* RUTH *goes to answer.*]

BENEATHA (*to encourage* WALTER, *thoroughly caught up with this side of him*): OCOMOGOSIAY, FLAMING SPEAR!

WALTER (*on the table, very far gone, his eyes pure glass sheets. He sees what we cannot, that he is a leader of his people, a great chief, a descendant of Chaka, and that the hour to march has come.*): Listen, my black brothers. . . .

BENEATHA: OCOMOGOSIAY!

WALTER: Do you hear the waters rushing against the shores of the coastlands. . . .

BENEATHA: OCOMOGOSIAY!

WALTER: Do you hear the screeching of the cocks in yonder hills beyond where the chiefs meet in council for the coming of the mighty war. . . .

BENEATHA: OCOMOGOSIAY!

WALTER: Do you hear the beating of the wings of the birds flying low over the mountains and the low places of our land. . . .

[1] KENYATTA: African nationalist who worked for Kenya's independence and became that country's first president.

[RUTH *opens the door.* GEORGE MURCHISON *enters.*]

BENEATHA: OCOMOGOSIAY!

WALTER: Do you hear the singing of the women, singing the war songs of our fathers to the babies in the great houses . . . singing the sweet war songs? OH, DO YOU HEAR, MY BLACK BROTHERS!

BENEATHA (*completely gone*): We hear you, Flaming Spear. . . .

WALTER: Telling us to prepare for the greatness of the time—(*To* GEORGE.) Black Brother! (*He extends his hand for the fraternal clasp.*)

GEORGE: Black Brother, hell!

RUTH (*having had enough, and embarrassed for the family*): Beneatha, you got company—what's the matter with you? Walter Lee Younger, get down off that table and stop acting like a fool. . . .

[WALTER *comes down off the table suddenly and makes a quick exit to the bathroom.*]

RUTH: He's had a little to drink . . . I don't know what her excuse is.

GEORGE (*to* BENEATHA): Look honey, we're going *to* the theater—we're not going to be *in* it . . . so go change, huh?

RUTH: You expect this boy to go out with you looking like that?

BENEATHA (*looking at* GEORGE): That's up to George. If he's ashamed of his heritage. . . .

GEORGE: Oh, don't be so proud of yourself, Bennie—just because you look eccentric.

BENEATHA: How can something that's natural be eccentric?

GEORGE: That's what being eccentric means—being natural. Get dressed.

BENEATHA: I don't like that, George.

RUTH: Why must you and your brother make an argument out of everything people say?

BENEATHA: Because I hate assimilationist Negroes!

RUTH: Will somebody please tell me what assimila-whoever means!

GEORGE: Oh, it's just a college girl's way of calling people Uncle Toms—but that isn't what it means at all.

RUTH: Well, what does it mean?

BENEATHA (*cutting* GEORGE *off and staring at him as she replies to* RUTH): It means someone who is willing to give up his own culture and submerge himself completely in the dominant, and in this case, *oppressive* culture!

GEORGE: Oh, dear, dear, dear! Here we go! A lecture on the African past! On our Great West African Heritage! In one second we will hear all about the great Ashanti empires; the great Songhay civilizations; and the great sculpture of Bénin—and then some poetry in the Bantu—and the whole monologue will end with the word *heritage!* (*Nastily.*) Let's face it, baby, your heritage is nothing but a bunch of raggedy spirituals and some grass huts!

BENEATHA: *Grass huts!*

[RUTH *crosses to her and forcibly pushes her toward the bedroom.*]

BENEATHA: See there . . . you are standing there in your splendid ignorance talking about people who were the first to smelt iron on the face of the earth!

[RUTH *is pushing her through the door.*]

BENEATHA: The Ashanti were performing surgical operations when the English. . . .

[RUTH *pulls the door to, with* BENEATHA *on the other side, and smiles graciously at* GEORGE. BENEATHA *opens the door and shouts the end of the sentence defiantly at* GEORGE.]

BENEATHA: —were still tattooing themselves with the blue dragons. . . . (*She goes back inside.*)

RUTH: Have a seat, George. (*They both sit.* RUTH *folds her hands rather primly on her lap, determined to demonstrate the civilization of the family.*) Warm, ain't it? I mean for September. (*Pause.*) Just like they always say about Chicago weather. If it's too hot or cold for you, just wait a minute and it'll change. (*She smiles happily at this cliché of clichés.*) Everybody say it's got to do with them bombs and things they keep setting off. (*Pause.*) Would you like a nice cold beer?

GEORGE: No, thank you. I don't care for beer. (*He looks at his watch.*) I hope she hurries up.

RUTH: What time is the show?

GEORGE: It's an eight-thirty curtain. That's just Chicago, though. In New York standard curtain time is eight-forty. (*He is rather proud of this knowledge.*)

RUTH (*properly appreciating it*): You get to New York a lot?

GEORGE (*offhand*): Few times a year.

RUTH: Oh—that's nice. I've never been to New York.

[WALTER *enters. We feel he has relieved himself, but the edge of unreality is still with him.*]

WALTER: New York ain't nothing Chicago ain't. Just a bunch of hustling people all squeezed up together—being "Eastern." (*He turns his face into a screw of displeasure.*)

GEORGE: Oh—you've been?

WALTER: *Plenty* of times.

RUTH (*shocked at the lie*): Walter Lee Younger!

WALTER (*staring her down*): Plenty! (*Pause.*) What we got to drink in this house? Why don't you offer this man some refreshment. (*To* GEORGE.) They don't know how to entertain people in this house, man.

GEORGE: Thank you—I don't really care for anything.

WALTER (*feeling his head; sobriety coming*): Where's Mama?

RUTH: She ain't come back yet.

WALTER (*looking* MURCHISON *over from head to toe, scrutinizing his carefully casual tweed sports jacket over cashmere V-neck sweater over soft eyelet shirt and tie, and soft slacks, finished off with white buckskin shoes*): Why all you college boys wear them fairyish-looking white shoes?

RUTH: Walter Lee!

[GEORGE MURCHISON *ignores the remark.*]

WALTER (*to* RUTH): Well, they look crazy as hell—white shoes, cold as it is.

RUTH (*crushed*): You have to excuse him. . . .

WALTER: No, he don't! Excuse me for what? What you always excusing me for! I'll excuse myself when I needs to be excused! (*A pause.*) They look as funny as them black knee socks Beneatha wears out of here all the time.

RUTH: It's the college *style*, Walter.

WALTER: Style, hell. She looks like she got burnt legs or something!

RUTH: Oh, Walter. . . .

WALTER (*an irritable mimic*): Oh, Walter! Oh, Walter! (*To* MURCHISON.) How's your old man making out? I understand you-all going to buy that big hotel on the Drive? (*He finds a beer in the refrigerator, wanders over to* MURCHISON, *sipping and wiping his lips with the back of his hand, and straddling a chair backwards to talk to the other man.*) Shrewd move. Your old man is all right, man. (*Tapping his head and half winking for emphasis.*) I mean he knows how to operate. I mean he thinks *big,* you know what I mean, I mean for a *home,* you know? But I think he's kind of running out of ideas now. I'd like to talk to him. Listen, man, I got some plans that could turn this city upside down. I mean I think like he does. *Big.* Invest big, gamble big, hell, lose *big* if you have to, you know what I mean. It's hard to find a man on this whole Southside who understands my kind of thinking—you dig? (*He scrutinizes* MURCHISON *again, drinks his beer, squints his eyes, and leans in close, confidential, man-to-man.*) Me and you ought to sit down and talk sometimes, man. Man, I got me some ideas. . . .

MURCHISON (*with boredom*): Yeah—sometimes we'll have to do that, Walter.

WALTER (*understanding the indifference, and offended*): Yeah—well, when you get the time, man. I know you a busy little boy.

RUTH: Walter, please—

WALTER (*bitterly, hurt*): I know ain't nothing in this world as busy as you colored college boys with your fraternity pins and white shoes. . . .

RUTH (*covering her face with humiliation*): Oh, Walter Lee. . . .

WALTER: I see you all all the time—with the books tucked under your arms—going to your (*British a—a mimic.*) "clahsses." And for what! What the hell you learning over there? Filling up your heads—(*Counting off on his fingers.*)—with the sociology and the psychology—but they teaching you how to be a man? How to take over and run the world? They teaching you how to run a rubber plantation or a steel mill? Naw—just to talk proper and read books and wear white shoes. . . .

GEORGE (*looking at him with distaste, a little above it all*): You're all wacked up with bitterness, man.

WALTER (*intently, almost quietly, between the teeth, glaring at the boy*): And you—ain't you bitter, man? Ain't you just about had it yet? Don't you see no stars gleaming that you can't reach out and grab? You happy? —You contented . . . you happy? You got it made? Bitter? Man, I'm a volcano. Bitter? Here I am a giant—surrounded by ants! Ants who can't even understand what it is the giant is talking about.

RUTH (*passionately and suddenly*): Oh, Walter—ain't you with nobody!

WALTER (*violently*): No! 'Cause ain't nobody with me! Not even my own mother!

RUTH: Walter, that's a terrible thing to say!

[BENEATHA *enters, dressed for the evening in a cocktail dress and earrings.*]

GEORGE: Well—hey, you look great.

BENEATHA: Let's go, George. See you all later.

RUTH: Have a nice time.

GEORGE: Thanks. Good night. (*To* WALTER, *sarcastically.*) Good night, Prometheus.[1]

[BENEATHA *and* GEORGE *exit.*]

WALTER (*to* RUTH): Who is Prometheus?

RUTH: I don't know. Don't worry about it.

WALTER (*in fury, pointing after* GEORGE): See there—they get to a point where they can't insult you man to man— they got to go talk about something ain't nobody never heard of!

RUTH: How do you know it was an insult? (*To humor him.*) Maybe Prometheus is a nice fellow.

WALTER: Prometheus! I bet there ain't even no such thing! I bet that simpleminded clown. . . .

RUTH: Walter. . . . (*She stops what she is doing and looks at him.*)

WALTER (*yelling*): Don't start!

RUTH: Start what?

WALTER: Your nagging! Where was I? Who was I with? How much money did I spend?

RUTH (*plaintively*): Walter Lee—why don't we just try to talk about it. . . .

WALTER (*not listening*): I been out talking with people who understand me. People who care about the things I got on my mind.

---

[1] PROMETHEUS: Greek god who stole fire from heaven for men.

170

RUTH (*wearily*): I guess that means people like Willy Harris.

WALTER: Yes, people like Willy Harris.

RUTH (*with a sudden flash of impatience*): Why don't you all just hurry up and go into the banking business and stop talking about it!

WALTER: Why? You want to know why? 'Cause we all tied up in a race of people that don't know how to do nothing but moan, pray, and have babies! (*The line is too bitter even for him, and he looks at her and sits down.*)

RUTH: Oh, Walter.... (*Softly.*) Honey, why can't you stop fighting me?

WALTER (*without thinking*): Who's fighting you? Who even cares about you? (*This line begins the retardation of his mood.*)

RUTH: Well—(*She waits a long time, and then with resignation starts to put away her things.*) I guess I might as well go on to bed.... (*More or less to herself.*) I don't know where we lost it ... but we have.... (*Then, to him.*) I—I'm sorry about this new baby, Walter. I guess maybe I better go on and do what I started.... I guess I just didn't realize how bad things was with us.... I guess I just didn't really realize—(*She starts out to the bedroom and stops.*) You want some hot milk?

WALTER: Hot milk?

RUTH: Yes—hot milk.

WALTER: Why hot milk?

RUTH: 'Cause after all that liquor you come home with you ought to have something hot in your stomach.

WALTER: I don't want no milk.

RUTH: You want some coffee then?

WALTER: No, I don't want no coffee. I don't want nothing hot to drink. (*Almost plaintively.*) Why you always trying to give me something to eat?

RUTH (*standing and looking at him helplessly*): What else can I give you, Walter Lee Younger?

[*She stands and looks at him and presently turns to go out again. He lifts his head and watches her going away from him in a new mood which began to emerge when he asked her, "Who cares about you?"*]

WALTER: It's been rough, ain't it, baby? (*She hears and stops but does not turn around, and he continues to her back.*) I guess between two people there ain't never as much understood as folks generally think there is. I mean like between me and you—(*She turns to face him.*) How we gets to the place where we scared to talk softness to each other. (*He waits, thinking hard himself.*) Why you think it got to be like that? (*He is thoughtful, almost as a child would be.*) Ruth, what is it gets into people ought to be close?

RUTH: I don't know, honey. I think about it a lot.

WALTER: On account of you and me, you mean? The way things are with us. The way something done come down between us.

RUTH: There ain't so much between us, Walter.... Not when you come to me and try to talk to me. Try to be with me ... a little even.

WALTER (*total honesty*): Sometimes ... sometimes ... I don't even know how to try.

RUTH: Walter—

WALTER: Yes?

RUTH (*coming to him, gently and with misgiving, but coming to him*): Honey . . . life don't have to be like this. I mean sometimes people can do things so that things are better. . . . You remember how we used to talk when Travis was born . . . about the way we were going to live . . . the kind of house. . . . (*She is stroking his head.*) Well, it's all starting to slip away from us. . . .

[MAMA *enters, and* WALTER *jumps up and shouts at her.*]

WALTER: Mama, where have you been?

MAMA: My—them steps is longer than they used to be. Whew!. (*She sits down and ignores him.*) How you feeling this evening, Ruth?

[RUTH *shrugs, disturbed some at having been prematurely interrupted and watching her husband knowingly.*]

WALTER: Mama, where have you been all day?

MAMA (*still ignoring him and leaning on the table and changing to more comfortable shoes*): Where's Travis?

RUTH: I let him go out earlier and he ain't come back yet. Boy, is he going to get it!

WALTER: Mama!

MAMA (*as if she has heard him for the first time*): Yes, son?

WALTER: Where did you go this afternoon?

MAMA: I went downtown to tend to some business that I had to tend to.

WALTER: What kind of business?

MAMA: You know better than to question me like a child, Brother.

WALTER (*rising and bending over the table*): Where were you, Mama?

(*Bringing his fist down and shouting.*) Mama, you didn't go do something with that insurance money, something crazy?

[*The front door opens slowly, interrupting him, and* TRAVIS *peeks his head in, less than hopefully.*]

TRAVIS (*to his mother*): Mama, I—

RUTH: "Mama I" nothing! You're going to get it, boy! Get on in that bedroom and get yourself ready!

TRAVIS: But I—

MAMA: Why don't you-all never let the child explain hisself.

RUTH: Keep out of it now, Lena.

[MAMA *clamps her lips together, and* RUTH *advances toward her son menacingly.*]

RUTH: A thousand times I have told you not to go off like that—

MAMA (*holding out her arms to her grandson*): Well—at least let me tell him something. I want him to be the first one to hear. . . . Come here, Travis. (*The boy obeys, gladly.*) Travis—(*She takes him by the shoulder and looks into his face.*) —you know that money we got in the mail this morning?

TRAVIS: Yes'm—

MAMA: Well—what you think your grandmama gone and done with that money?

TRAVIS: I don't know, Grandmama.

MAMA (*putting her finger on his nose for emphasis*): She went out and she bought you a house! (*The explosion comes from* WALTER *at the end of the revelation, and he jumps up and turns away from all of them in a fury.* MAMA *continues, to* TRAVIS.) You glad about the house? It's going to be yours when you get to be a man.

TRAVIS: Yeah—I always wanted to live in a house.

MAMA: All right, gimme some sugar then—(TRAVIS *puts his arms around her neck as she watches her son over the boy's shoulder. Then, to* TRAVIS, *after the embrace.*) Now when you say your prayers tonight, you thank God and your grandfather—'cause it was him who give you the house—in his way.

RUTH (*taking the boy from* MAMA *and pushing him toward the bedroom*): Now you get out of here and get ready for your beating.

TRAVIS: Aw, Mama. . . .

RUTH: Get on in there—(*closing the door behind him and turning radiantly to her mother-in-law*) So you went and did it!

MAMA (*quietly, looking at her son with pain*): Yes, I did.

RUTH (*raising both arms classically*): Praise God! (*Looks at* WALTER *a moment, who says nothing. She crosses rapidly to her husband.*) Please, honey—let me be glad . . . you be glad, too. (*She has laid her hands on his shoulders, but he shakes himself free of her roughly, without turning to face her.*) Oh, Walter . . . a home . . . a home. (*She comes back to* MAMA.) Well—where is it? How big is it? How much it going to cost?

MAMA: Well—

RUTH: When we moving?

MAMA (*smiling at her*): First of the month.

RUTH (*throwing back her head with jubilance*): Praise God!

MAMA (*tentatively, still looking at her son's back turned against her and* RUTH): It's—it's a nice house too. . . . (*She cannot help speaking directly to him. An imploring quality in her voice, her manner, makes her almost like a girl now.*) Three bedrooms—nice big one for you and Ruth . . . Me and Beneatha still have to share our room, but Travis have one of his own —and (*With difficulty.*) I figure if the —new baby—is a boy, we could get one of them double-decker outfits. . . . And there's a yard with a little patch of dirt where I could maybe get to grow me a few flowers. . . . And a nice big basement. . . .

RUTH: Walter, honey, be glad—

MAMA (*still to his back, fingering things on the table*): 'Course I don't want to make it sound fancier than it is. . . . It's just a plain little old house—but it's made good and solid—and it will be *ours*. Walter Lee—it makes a difference in a man when he can walk on floors that belong to *him*. . . .

RUTH: Where is it?

MAMA (*frightened at this telling*): Well —well—it's out there in Clybourne Park—

[RUTH'S *radiance fades abruptly, and* WALTER *finally turns slowly to face his mother with incredulity and hostility.*]

RUTH: Where?

MAMA (*matter-of-factly*): Four o six Clybourne Street, Clybourne Park.

RUTH: Clybourne Park? Mama, there ain't no colored people living in Clybourne Park.

MAMA (*almost idiotically*): Well, I guess there's going to be some now.

WALTER (*bitterly*): So that's the peace and comfort you went out and bought for us today!

MAMA (*raising her eyes to meet his finally*): Son—I just tried to find the nicest place for the least amount of money for my family.

RUTH (*trying to recover from the shock*): Well—well—'course I ain't one never been 'fraid of no crackers, mind you—but—well, wasn't there no other houses nowhere?

MAMA: Them houses they put up for colored in them areas way out all seem to cost twice as much as other houses. I did the best I could.

RUTH (*Struck senseless with the news, in its various degrees of goodness and trouble, she sits a moment, her fists propping her chin in thought, and then she starts to rise, bringing her fists down with vigor, the radiance spreading from cheek to cheek again.*): Well—well!— All I can say is—if this is my time in life—my time —to say good-bye—(*And she builds with momentum as she starts to circle the room with an exuberant, almost tearfully happy release.*)—to these . . . damned cracking walls!—(*She pounds the walls.*)—and these marching roaches!—(*She wipes at an imaginary army of marching roaches.*)— and this cramped little closet which ain't now or never was no kitchen! . . . then I say it loud and good, Hallelujah! and good-bye, misery . . . I don't never want to see your ugly face again! (*She laughs joyously, having practically destroyed the apartment, and flings her arms up and lets them come down happily, slowly, reflectively, over her abdomen, aware for the first time perhaps that the life therein pulses with happiness and not despair.*) Lena?

MAMA (*moved, watching her happiness*): Yes, honey?

RUTH (*looking off*): Is there—is there a whole lot of sunlight?

MAMA (*understanding*): Yes, child, there's a whole lot of sunlight.

[*Long pause.*]

RUTH (*collecting herself and going to the door of the room* TRAVIS *is in*): Well—I guess I better see 'bout Travis. (*To* MAMA) Lord, I sure don't feel like whipping nobody today! (*She exits.*)

MAMA (*The mother and son are left alone now, and the mother waits a long time, considering deeply, before she speaks.*): Son—you—you understand what I done, don't you? (*WALTER is silent and sullen.*) I—I just seen my family falling apart today . . . just falling to pieces in front of my eyes. . . . We couldn't of gone on like we was today. We was going backwards 'stead of forwards—talking 'bout killing babies and wishing each other was dead. . . . When it gets like that in life—you just got to do something different, push on out and do something bigger. . . . (*She waits.*) I wish you say something, son. . . . I wish you'd say how deep inside you think I done the right thing—

WALTER (*crossing slowly to his bedroom door and finally turning there and speaking measuredly*): What you need me to say you done right for? *You* the head of this family. You run our lives like you want to. It was your money and you did what you wanted with it. So what you need for me to say it was all right for? (*Bitterly, to hurt her as deeply as he knows*

is possible.) So you butchered up a dream of mine—you—who always talking 'bout your children's dreams. . . .

MAMA: Walter Lee. . . .

[*He just closes the door behind him.* MAMA *sits alone, thinking heavily.*]

Curtain

SCENE 2

TIME: Friday night. A few weeks later.

AT RISE: Packing crates mark the intention of the family to move. BENEATHA and GEORGE come in, presumably from an evening out again.

GEORGE: O.K. . . . O.K., whatever you say. . . . (*They both sit on the couch. He tries to kiss her. She moves away.*) Look, we've had a nice evening; let's not spoil it, huh? . . .

[*He again turns her head and tries to nuzzle in, and she turns away from him, not with distaste but with momentary lack of interest; in a mood to pursue what they were talking about.*]

BENEATHA: I'm *trying* to talk to you.

GEORGE: We always talk.

BENEATHA: Yes—and I love to talk.

GEORGE (*exasperated; rising*): I know it and I don't mind it sometimes. . . . I want you to cut it out, see—the moody stuff, I mean. I don't like it. You're a nice-looking girl . . . all over. That's all you need; honey, forget the atmosphere. Guys aren't going to go for the atmosphere—they're going to go for what they see. Be glad for that. Drop the Garbo routine. It doesn't go with you. As for myself, I want a nice —(*Groping.*)—simple (*Thoughtfully.*)

—sophisticated girl . . . not a poet—O.K.?

[*She rebuffs him again and he starts to leave.*]

BENEATHA: Why are you angry?

GEORGE: Because this is stupid! I don't go out with you to discuss the nature of "quiet desperation" or to hear all about your thoughts—because the world will go on thinking what it thinks regardless. . . .

BENEATHA: Then why read books? Why go to school?

GEORGE (*with artificial patience, counting on his fingers*): It's simple. You read books—to learn facts—to get grades—to pass the course—to get a degree. That's all—it has nothing to do with thoughts.

[*A long pause.*]

BENEATHA: I see. (*A longer pause as she looks at him.*) Good night, George.

[GEORGE *looks at her a little oddly, and starts to exit. He meets* MAMA *coming in.*]

GEORGE: Oh—hello, Mrs. Younger.

MAMA: Hello, George; how you feeling?

GEORGE: Fine—fine, how are you?

MAMA: Oh, a little tired. You know them steps can get you after a day's work. You-all have a nice time tonight?

GEORGE: Yes—a fine time. Well, good night.

MAMA: Good night.

[*He exits.* MAMA *closes the door behind her.*]

MAMA: Hello, honey. What you sitting like that for?

BENEATHA: I'm just sitting.

MAMA: Didn't you have a nice time?

BENEATHA: No.

MAMA: No? What's the matter?

BENEATHA: Mama, George is a fool—honest. (*She rises.*)

MAMA (*hustling around unloading the packages she has entered with. She stops*): Is he, baby?

BENEATHA: Yes.

[BENEATHA *makes up* TRAVIS'S *bed as she talks.*]

MAMA: You sure?

BENEATHA: Yes.

MAMA: Well—I guess you better not waste your time with no fools.

[BENEATHA *looks up at her mother, watching her put groceries in the refrigerator. Finally she gathers up her things and starts into the bedroom. At the door she stops and looks back at her mother.*]

BENEATHA: Mama. . . .

MAMA: Yes, baby. . . .

BENEATHA: Thank you.

MAMA: For what?

BENEATHA: For understanding me this time.

[*She exits quickly and the mother stands, smiling a little, looking at the place where* BENEATHA *just stood.* RUTH *enters.*]

RUTH: Now don't you fool with any of this stuff, Lena. . . .

MAMA: Oh, I just thought I'd sort a few things out.

[*The phone rings.* RUTH *answers.*]

RUTH (*at the phone*): Hello—Just a minute. (*Goes to door.*) Walter, it's Mrs. Arnold. (*Waits. Goes back to the phone. Tense.*) Hello. Yes, this is his wife speaking. . . . He's lying down now. Yes . . . well, he'll be in tomorrow. He's been very sick. Yes—I know we should have called, but we were so sure he'd be able to come in today. Yes—yes, I'm very sorry. Yes. . . . Thank you very much. (*She hangs up.* WALTER *is standing in the doorway of the bedroom behind her.*) That was Mrs. Arnold.

WALTER (*indifferently*): Was it?

RUTH: She said if you don't come in tomorrow that they are getting a new man. . . .

WALTER: Ain't that sad—ain't that crying sad.

RUTH: She said Mr. Arnold has had to take a cab for three days. . . . Walter, you ain't been to work for three days! (*This is a revelation to her.*) Where you been, Walter Lee Younger? (WALTER *looks at her and starts to laugh.*) You're going to lose your job.

WALTER: That's right. . . .

RUTH: Oh, Walter, and with your mother working like a dog every day—

WALTER: That's sad, too—Everything is sad.

MAMA: What you been doing for these three days, son?

WALTER: Mama—you don't know all the things a man what got leisure can find to do in this city. . . . What's this —Friday night? Well—Wednesday I borrowed Willy Harris's car and I went for a drive . . . just me and myself and I drove and drove . . . way out . . . way past South Chicago, and I parked the car, and I sat and looked at the steel mills all day long. I just sat in the car and looked at them big black chimneys for hours. Then I drove back, and I went to the Green Hat. (*Pause.*) And Thursday—Thursday I borrowed the car again, and I got in it, and I pointed it the other way, and I drove the other way—for hours—way, way up to Wisconsin, and I looked at the farms. I just drove and looked at the farms. Then I drove back and I went to the Green Hat. (*Pause.*) And today—today I didn't get the car. Today I just walked. All over the Southside. And I looked at the Negroes and they looked at me and finally I just sat down on the curb at Thirty-ninth and South Parkway, and I just sat there and watched the Negroes go by. And then I went to the Green Hat. You-all sad? You-all depressed? And you know where I am going right now. . . .

[RUTH *goes out quietly.*]

MAMA: Oh, Big Walter, is this the harvest of our days?

WALTER: You know what I like about the Green Hat? (*He turns the radio on, and a steamy, deep blues pours into the room.*) I like this little cat they got there who blows a sax. . . . He blows. He talks to me. He ain't but 'bout five feet tall, and he's got a conked head, and his eyes is always closed, and he's all music. . . .

MAMA (*rising and getting some papers out of her handbag*): Walter. . . .

WALTER: And there's this other guy who plays the piano . . . and they got a sound. I mean they can work on some music. . . . They got the best little combo in the world in the Green Hat. . . . You can just sit there and drink and listen to them three men play, and you realize that don't nothing matter worth a damn, but just being there. . . .

MAMA: I've helped do it to you, haven't I, son? Walter, I been wrong.

WALTER: Naw—you ain't never been wrong about nothing, Mama.

MAMA: Listen to me, now. I say I been wrong, son. That I been doing to you what the rest of the world been doing to you. (*She stops and he looks up slowly at her and she meets his eyes pleadingly.*) Walter—what you ain't never understood is that I ain't got nothing, don't own nothing, ain't never really wanted nothing that wasn't for you. There ain't nothing as precious to me. . . . There ain't nothing worth holding on to, money, dreams, nothing else—if it means—if it means it's going to destroy my boy. (*She puts her papers in front of him, and he watches her without speaking or moving.*) I paid the man thirty-five hundred dollars down on the house. That leaves sixty-five hundred dollars. Monday morning I want you to take this money and take three thousand dollars and put it in a savings account for Beneatha's medical schooling. The rest you put in a checking account—with your name on it. And from now on any penny that come out of it or that go in it is for you to look after. For you to decide. (*She drops her hands a little helplessly.*) It ain't much, but it's all I got in the world, and I'm putting it in your hands. I'm telling you to be the head of this family from now on like you supposed to be.

WALTER (*stares at the money*): You trust me like that, Mama?

MAMA: I ain't never stop trusting you. Like I ain't never stop loving you.

[*She goes out, and* WALTER *sits looking at the money on the table as the music con-*

tinues in its idiom, pulsing in the room. Finally, in a decisive gesture, he gets up, and, in mingled joy and desperation, picks up the money. At the same moment, TRAVIS *enters for bed.*]

TRAVIS: What's the matter, Daddy? You drunk?

WALTER (*sweetly, more sweetly than we have ever known him*): No, Daddy ain't drunk. Daddy ain't going to never be drunk again. . . .

TRAVIS: Well, good night, Daddy.

[*The* FATHER *has come from behind the couch and leans over, embracing his son.*]

WALTER: Son, I feel like talking to you tonight.

TRAVIS: About what?

WALTER: Oh, about a lot of things. About you and what kind of man you going to be when you grow up. . . . Son—son, what do you want to be when you grow up?

TRAVIS: A bus driver.

WALTER (*laughing a little*): A what? Man, that ain't nothing to want to be!

TRAVIS: Why not?

WALTER: 'Cause, man—it ain't big enough—you know what I mean.

TRAVIS: I don't know, then. I can't make up my mind. Sometimes Mama asks me that, too. And sometimes when I tell you I just want to be like you— she says she don't want me to be like that, and sometimes she says she does. . . .

WALTER (*getting him up in his arms*): You know what, Travis? In seven years you going to be seventeen years old. And things is going to be very different with us in seven years, Travis. . . . One day when you are seventeen, I'll come home—home from my office downtown somewhere. . . .

TRAVIS: You don't work in no office, Daddy.

WALTER: No—but after tonight. After what your daddy gonna do tonight, there's going to be offices—a whole lot of offices. . . .

TRAVIS: What you gonna do tonight, Daddy?

WALTER: You wouldn't understand yet, son, but your daddy's gonna make a transaction . . . a business transaction that's going to change our lives. . . . That's how come one day when you 'bout seventeen years old, I'll come home and I'll be pretty tired, you know what I mean, after a day of conferences and secretaries getting things wrong the way they do . . . 'cause an executive's life is hell, man —(*The more he talks the farther away he gets.*) And I'll pull the car up on the driveway . . . just a plain black Chrysler, I think, with white walls—no—black tires. More elegant. Rich people don't have to be flashy . . . though I'll have to get something a little sportier for Ruth—maybe a Cadillac convertible to do her shopping in. . . . And I'll come up the steps to the house, and the gardener will be clipping away at the hedges, and he'll say, "Good evening, Mr. Younger." And I'll say, "Hello, Jefferson, how are you this evening?" And I'll go inside, and Ruth will come downstairs and meet me at the door, and we'll kiss each other, and she'll take my arm, and we'll go up to your room to see you sitting on the floor with the catalogues of all the great schools in

America around you. . . . All the great schools in the world! And—and I'll say, all right son—it's your seventeenth birthday, what is it you've decided? . . . Just tell me where you want to go to school and you'll go. Just tell me, what it is you want to be—and you'll *be* it. . . . Whatever you want to be—Yessir! (*He holds his arms open for* TRAVIS.) You just name it, son . . . (TRAVIS *leaps into them.*) and I hand you the world!

[WALTER'S *voice has risen in pitch and hysterical promise, and on the last line he lifts* TRAVIS *high.*]

Blackout

SCENE 3

TIME: Saturday, moving day, one week later.

AT RISE: Before the curtain rises, RUTH'S voice, a strident, dramatic church alto, cuts through the silence. It is, in the darkness, a triumphant surge, a penetrating statement of expectation: "Oh Lord, I don't feel no ways tired! Children, oh, glory hallelujah!" As the curtain rises, we see that RUTH is alone in the living room, finishing up the family's packing. It is moving day. She is nailing crates and tying cartons. BENEATHA enters, carrying a guitar case, and watches her exuberant sister-in-law.

RUTH: Hey!

BENEATHA (*putting away the case*): Hi.

RUTH (*pointing at a package*): Honey—look in that package there and see what I found on sale this morning at the South Center. (RUTH *gets up and moves to the package and draws out some curtains.*) Lookahere—hand-turned hems!

BENEATHA: How do you know the window size out there?

RUTH (*who hadn't thought of that*): Oh—Well, they bound to fit something in the whole house. Anyhow, they was too good a bargain to pass up. (RUTH *slaps her head, suddenly remembering something.*) Oh, Bennie—I meant to put a special note on that carton over there. That's your mama's good china, and she wants 'em to be very careful with it.

BENEATHA: I'll do it.

[BENEATHA *finds a piece of paper and starts to draw large letters on it.*]

RUTH: You know what I'm going to do soon as I get in that new house?

BENEATHA: What?

RUTH: Honey—I'm going to run me a tub of water up to here. . . . (*With her fingers practically up to her nostrils.*) And I'm going to get in it—and I am going to sit . . . and sit . . . and sit in that hot water, and the first person who knocks to tell *me* to hurry up and come out. . . .

BENEATHA: Gets shot at sunrise.

RUTH (*laughing happily*): You said it, sister! (*Noticing how large* BENEATHA *is absent-mindedly making the note.*) Honey, they ain't going to read that from no airplane.

BENEATHA (*laughing herself*): I guess I always think things have more emphasis if they are big, somehow.

RUTH (*looking up at her and smiling*): You and your brother seem to have that as a philosophy of life. Lord, that man—done changed so round here. You know—you know what we did last night? Me and Walter Lee?

BENEATHA: What?

RUTH (*smiling to herself*): We went to the movies. (*Looking at* BENEATHA *to see if she understands.*) We went to the movies. You know the last time me and Walter went to the movies together?

BENEATHA: No.

RUTH: Me, neither. That's how long it been. (*Smiling again.*) But we went last night. The picture wasn't much good, but that didn't seem to matter. We went—and we held hands.

BENEATHA: Oh, Lord!

RUTH: We held hands—and you know what?

BENEATHA: What?

RUTH: When we come out of the show, it was late and dark, and all the stores and things was closed up . . . and it was kind of chilly, and there wasn't many people on the streets . . . and we was still holding hands, me and Walter.

BENEATHA: You're killing me.

[WALTER *enters with a large package. His happiness is deep in him; he cannot keep still with his new-found exuberance. He is singing and wiggling and snapping his fingers. He puts his package in a corner and puts a phonograph record, which he has brought in with him, on the record player. As the music comes up, he dances over to* RUTH *and tries to get her to dance with him. She gives in at last to his raunchiness and in a fit of giggling allows herself to be drawn into his mood, and together they deliberately burlesque an old social dance of their youth.*]

BENEATHA (*regarding them a long time as they dance, then drawing in her breath for a deeply exaggerated comment which she does not particularly mean*): Talk about—olddddddddddd-fashion-eddddddd—Negroes!

WALTER (*stopping momentarily*): What kind of Negroes? (*He says this in fun. He is not angry with her today, nor with anyone. He starts to dance with his wife again.*)

BENEATHA: Old-fashioned.

WALTER (*As he dances with* RUTH): You know, when these *New Negroes* have their convention—(*Pointing at his sister.*)—that is going to be the chairman of the Committee on Unending Agitation. (*He goes on dancing, then stops.*) Race, race, race! . . . Girl, I do believe you are the first person in the history of the entire human race to successfully brainwash yourself. (BE-NEATHA *breaks up, and he goes on dancing. He stops again, enjoying his tease.*) Damn, even the N DOUBLE A C P takes a holiday sometimes!

[BENEATHA *and* RUTH *laugh. He dances with* RUTH *some more and starts to laugh and stops and pantomimes someone over an operating table.*]

WALTER: I can just see that chick someday looking down at some poor cat on an operating table before she starts to slice him, saying . . . (*Pulling his sleeves back maliciously.*) "By the way, what are your views on civil rights down there? . . ."

[*He laughs at her again and starts to dance happily. The bell sounds.*]

BENEATHA: Sticks and stones may break my bones but . . . words will never hurt me!

[BENEATHA *goes to the door and opens it as* WALTER *and* RUTH *go on with the clowning.* BENEATHA *is somewhat surprised to see a quiet-looking middle-aged white man in* a business suit holding his hat and a brief-case in his hand and consulting a small piece of paper.]

MAN: Uh—how do you do, miss. I am looking for a Mrs.—(*He looks at the slip of paper.*) Mrs. Lena Younger?

BENEATHA (*smoothing her hair with slight embarrassment*): Oh—yes, that's my mother. Excuse me. (*She closes the door and turns to quiet the other two.*) Ruth! Brother! Some-body's here. (*Then she opens the door. The man casts a curious quick glance at all of them.*) Uh—come in, please.

MAN (*coming in*): Thank you.

BENEATHA: My mother isn't here just now. Is it business?

MAN: Yes . . . well, of a sort.

WALTER (*freely, the Man of the House*) Have a seat. I'm Mrs. Younger's son. I look after most of her business mat-ters.

[RUTH *and* BENEATHA *exchange amused glances.*]

MAN (*regarding* WALTER, *and sitting*): Well—My name is Karl Lindner. . . .

WALTER (*stretching out his hand*): Wal-ter Younger. This is my wife—(RUTH *nods politely*)—and my sister.

LINDNER: How do you do.

WALTER (*amiably, as he sits himself easily on a chair, leaning with interest forward on his knees and looking ex-pectantly into the newcomer's face*): What can we do for you, Mr. Lind-ner!

LINDNER (*some minor shuffling of the hat and briefcase on his knees*): Well—I am a representative of the Clybourne Park Improvement Association. . . .

WALTER (*pointing*): Why don't you sit your things on the floor?

LINDNER: Oh—yes. Thank you. (*He slides the briefcase and hat under the chair.*) And as I was saying—I am from the Clybourne Park Improve-ment Association and we have had it brought to our attention at the last meeting that you people—or at least your mother—has bought a piece of residential property at—(*He digs for the slip of paper again.*)—four o six Clybourne Street. . . .

WALTER: That's right. Care for some-thing to drink? Ruth, get Mr. Lind-ner a beer.

LINDNER (*upset for some reason*): Oh—no, really. I mean thank you very much, but no, thank you.

RUTH (*innocently*): Some coffee?

LINDNER: Thank you, nothing at all.

[BENEATHA *is watching the man carefully.*]

LINDNER: Well, I don't know how much you folks know about our organiza-tion. (*He is a gentle man, thoughtful and somewhat labored in his man-ner.*) It is one of these community or-ganizations set up to look after—oh, you know, things like block upkeep and special projects, and we also have what we call our New Neighbors Ori-entation Committee. . . .

BENEATHA (*drily*): Yes—and what do they do?

LINDNER (*turning a little to her and then returning the main force to* WALTER): Well—it's what you might call a sort of welcoming committee, I guess. I mean they, we, I'm the chairman of the committee—go around and see the new people who move into the neighborhood and sort of give them the lowdown on the way we do things out in Clybourne Park.

BENEATHA (*with appreciation of the two meanings, which escape* RUTH *and* WALTER): Uh-huh.

LINDNER: And we also have the category of what the Association calls—(*He looks elsewhere.*)—uh—special community problems. . . .

BENEATHA: Yes—and what are some of those?

WALTER: Girl, let the man talk.

LINDNER (*with understated relief*): Thank you. I would sort of like to explain this thing in my own way. I mean I want to explain to you in a certain way.

WALTER: Go ahead.

LINDNER: Yes. Well. I'm going to try to get right to the point. I'm sure we'll all appreciate that in the long run.

BENEATHA: Yes.

WALTER: Be still now!

LINDNER: Well. . . .

RUTH (*still innocently*): Would you like another chair—you don't look comfortable.

LINDNER (*more frustrated than annoyed*): No, thank you very much. Please. Well—to get right to the point I—(*A great breath, and he is off at last.*) I am sure you people must be aware of some of the incidents which have happened in various parts of the city when colored people have moved into certain areas—

[BENEATHA *exhales heavily and starts tossing a piece of fruit up and down in the air.*]

LINDNER: Well—because we have what I think is going to be a unique type of organization in American community life—not only do we deplore that kind of thing—but we are trying to do something about it.

[BENEATHA *stops tossing and turns with a new and quizzical interest to the man.*]

LINDNER: We feel—(*Gaining confidence in his mission because of the interest in the faces of the people he is talking to.*)—we feel that most of the trouble in this world, when you come right down to it—(*He hits his knee for emphasis.*)—most of the trouble exists because people just don't sit down and talk to each other.

RUTH (*nodding as she might in church, pleased with the remark*): You can say that again, mister.

LINDNER (*more encouraged by such affirmation*): That we don't try hard enough in this world to understand the other fellow's problem. The other guy's point of view.

RUTH: Now that's right.

[BENEATHA *and* WALTER *merely watch and listen with genuine interest.*]

LINDNER: Yes—that's the way we feel out in Clybourne Park. And that's why I was elected to come here this afternoon and talk to you people. Friendly like, you know, the way people should talk to each other, and see if we couldn't find some way to work this thing out. As I say, the whole business is a matter of *caring* about the other fellow. Anybody can see that you are a nice family of folks, hard-working and honest, I'm sure.

[BENEATHA *frowns slightly, quizzically, her head tilted regarding him.*]

LINDNER: Today everybody knows what it means to be on the outside of *something*. And, of course, there is always somebody who is out to take the advantage of people who don't always understand.

WALTER: What do you mean?

LINDNER: Well—you see our community is made up of people who've worked hard as the dickens for years to build up that little community. They're not rich and fancy people; just hard-working, honest people who don't really have much but those little homes and a dream of the kind of community they want to raise their children in. Now, I don't say we are perfect, and there is a lot wrong in some of the things they want. But you've got to admit that a man, right or wrong, has the right to want to have the neighborhood he lives in a certain kind of way. And at the moment the overwhelming majority of our people out there feel that people get along better, take more of a common interest in the life of the community, when they share a common background. I want you to believe me when I tell you that race prejudice simply doesn't enter into it. It is a matter of the people of Clybourne Park believing, rightly or wrongly, as I say, that for the happiness of all concerned that our Negro families are happier when they live in their *own* communities.

BENEATHA (*with a grand and bitter gesture*): This, friends, is the Welcoming Committee!

WALTER (*dumfounded, looking at* LINDNER): Is this what you came marching all the way over here to tell us?

LINDNER: Well, now we've been having a fine conversation. I hope you'll hear me all the way through.

WALTER (*tightly*): Go ahead, man.

LINDNER: You see—in the face of all things I have said, we are prepared to make your family a very generous offer. . . .

BENEATHA: Thirty pieces and not a coin less!

WALTER: Yeah?

LINDNER (*putting on his glasses and drawing a form out of the briefcase*): Our association is prepared, through the collective effort of our people, to buy the house from you at a financial gain to your family.

RUTH: Lord have mercy; ain't this the living gall!

WALTER: All right, you through?

LINDNER: Well, I want to give you the exact terms of the financial arrangement—

WALTER: We don't want to hear no exact terms of no arrangements. I want to know if you got any more to tell us 'bout getting together?

LINDNER (*taking off his glasses*): Well— I don't suppose that you feel. . . .

WALTER: Never mind how I feel—you got any more to say 'bout how people ought to sit down and talk to each other? . . . Get out of my house, man.

[*He turns his back and walks to the door.*]

LINDNER (*looking around at the hostile faces and reaching and assembling his hat and briefcase*): Well—I don't understand why you people are reacting this way. What do you think you are going to gain by moving into a neighborhood where you just aren't wanted and where some elements—well— people can get awful worked up when they feel that their whole way of life and everything they've ever worked for is threatened.

WALTER: Get out.

LINDNER (*at the door, holding a small card*): Well—I'm sorry it went like this.

WALTER: Get out.

LINDNER (*almost sadly, regarding WALTER*): You just can't force people to change their hearts, son.

[*He turns and puts his card on a table and exits. WALTER pushes the door to with stinging hatred and stands looking at it. RUTH just sits and BENEATHA just stands. They say nothing. MAMA and TRAVIS enter.*]

MAMA: Well—this all the packing got done since I left out of here this morning. I testify before God that my children got all the energy of the dead. What time the moving men due?

BENEATHA: Four o'clock. You had a caller, Mama. (*She is smiling, teasingly.*)

MAMA: Sure enough—who?

BENEATHA (*her arms folded saucily*): The Welcoming Committee.

[WALTER *and* RUTH *giggle.*]

MAMA (*innocently*): Who?

BENEATHA: The Welcoming Committee. They said they're sure going to be glad to see you when you get there.

WALTER (*devilishly*): Yeah, they said they can't hardly wait to see your face.

[*Laughter*]

MAMA (*sensing their facetiousness*): What's the matter with you-all?

WALTER: Ain't nothing the matter with us. We just telling you 'bout the gentleman who came to see you this afternoon. From the Clybourne Park Improvement Association.

MAMA: What he want?

RUTH (*in the same mood as BENEATHA and WALTER*): To welcome you, honey.

WALTER: He said they can't hardly wait. He said the one thing they don't have, that they just *dying* to have out there is a fine family of colored people! (*To RUTH and BENEATHA.*) Ain't that right!

RUTH AND BENEATHA (*mockingly*): Yeah! He left his card in case—

[*They indicate the card, and MAMA picks it up and throws it on the floor—understanding and looking off as she draws her chair up to the table on which she has put her plant and some sticks and some cord.*]

MAMA: Father, give us strength. (*Knowingly—and without fun.*) Did he threaten us?

BENEATHA: Oh—Mama—they don't do it like that any more. He talked Brotherhood. He said everybody ought to learn how to sit down and hate each other with good Christian fellowship.

[*She and WALTER shake hands to ridicule the remark.*]

MAMA (*sadly*): Lord, protect us. . . .

RUTH: You should hear the money those folks raised to buy the house from us. All we paid and then some.

BENEATHA: What they think we going to do—eat 'em?

RUTH: No, honey, marry 'em.

MAMA (*shaking her head*): Lord, Lord, Lord. . . .

RUTH: Well—that's the way the crackers crumble. Joke.

BENEATHA (*laughingly noticing what her*

mother is doing): Mama, what are you doing?

MAMA: Fixing my plant so it won't get hurt none on the way. . . .

BENEATHA: Mama, you going to take *that* to the new house?

MAMA: Un-huh—

BENEATHA: That raggedy-looking old thing?

MAMA (*stopping and looking at her*): It expresses *me*.

RUTH (*with delight, to* BENEATHA): So there, Miss Thing!

[WALTER *comes to* MAMA *suddenly and bends down behind her and squeezes her in his arms with all his strength. She is overwhelmed by the suddenness of it, and, though delighted, her manner is like that of* RUTH *with* TRAVIS.]

MAMA: Look out now, boy! You make me mess up my thing here!

WALTER (*His face lit, he slips down on his knees beside her, his arms still about her.*): Mama . . . you know what it means to climb up in the chariot?

MAMA (*gruffly, very happy*): Get on away from me now. . . .

RUTH (*near the gift-wrapped package, trying to catch* WALTER'S *eye*): Psst—

WALTER: What the old song say, Mama. . . .

RUTH: Walter—Now? (*She is pointing at the package.*)

WALTER (*speaking the lines, sweetly, playfully, in his mother's face*):
I got wings . . . you got wings . . .
All God's children got wings. . . .

MAMA: Boy—get out of my face and do some work. . . .

WALTER:
When I get to heaven, gonna put on my wings,
Gonna fly all over God's heaven. . . .

BENEATHA (*teasingly, from across the room*): Everybody talking 'bout heaven ain't going there!

WALTER (*to* RUTH, *who is carrying the box across to them*): I don't know; you think we ought to give her that. . . . Seems to me she ain't been very appreciative around here.

MAMA (*eying the box, which is obviously a gift*): What is that?

WALTER (*taking it from* RUTH *and putting it on the table in front of* MAMA): Well—what you all think? Should we give it to her?

RUTH: Oh—she was pretty good today.

MAMA: I'll good you. . . . (*She turns her eyes to the box again.*)

BENEATHA: Open it, Mama.

[She stands up, looks at it, turns and looks at all of them, and then presses her hands together and does not open the package.]

WALTER (*sweetly*): Open it, Mama. It's for you.

[MAMA *looks into his eyes. It is the first present in her life without its being Christmas. Slowly she opens her package and lifts out, one by one, a brand-new sparkling set of gardening tools.*]

WALTER (*continues, prodding*): Ruth made up the note—read it. . . .

MAMA (*picking up the card and adjusting her glasses*): "To our own Mrs. Miniver—Love from Brother, Ruth, and Beneatha." Ain't that lovely.

TRAVIS (*tugging at his father's sleeve*): Daddy, can I give her mine now?

WALTER All right, son.

[TRAVIS *flies to get his gift.*]

WALTER: Travis didn't want to go in

with the rest of us, Mama. He got his own. (*Somewhat amused.*) We don't know what it is. . . .

TRAVIS (*racing back in the room with a large hatbox and putting it in front of his grandmother*): Here!

MAMA: Lord have mercy, baby. You done gone and bought your grandmother a hat?

TRAVIS (*very proud*): Open it!

[*She does and lifts out an elaborate, but very elaborate, wide gardening hat, and all the adults break up at the sight of it.*]

RUTH: Travis, honey, what is that?

TRAVIS (*who thinks it is beautiful and appropriate*): It's a gardening hat! Like the ladies always have on in the magazines when they work in their gardens.

BENEATHA (*giggling fiercely*): Travis—we were trying to make Mama Mrs. Miniver—not Scarlett O'Hara!

MAMA (*indignantly*): What's the matter with you-all! This here is a beautiful hat! (*Absurdly*) I always wanted me one just like it!

[*She pops it on her head to prove it to her grandson, and the hat is ludicrous and considerably oversized.*]

RUTH: Hot dog! Go, Mama!

WALTER (*doubled over with laughter*): I'm sorry, Mama—but you look like you ready to go out and chop you some cotton sure enough!

[*They all laugh except MAMA, out of deference to TRAVIS's feelings.*]

MAMA (*gathering the boy up to her*): Bless your heart—this is the prettiest hat I ever owned. . . .

[WALTER, RUTH, *and* BENEATHA *chime in—*

noisily, festively and insincerely congratulating TRAVIS on his gift.*]

MAMA: What are we all standing around here for? We ain't finished packin' yet. Bennie, you ain't packed one book.

[*The bell rings.*]

BENEATHA: That couldn't be the movers . . . it's not hardly two good yet . . .

[BENEATHA *goes into her room.* MAMA *starts for door.*]

WALTER (*turning, stiffening*): Wait—wait—I'll get it. (*He stands and looks at the door.*)

MAMA: You expecting company, son?

WALTER (*just looking at the door*): Yeah—yeah. . . .

[MAMA *looks at* RUTH, *and they exchange innocent and unfrightened glances.*]

MAMA (*not understanding*): Well, let them in, son.

BENEATHA (*from her room*): We need some more string.

MAMA: Travis—you run to the hardware and get me some string cord.

[MAMA *goes out, and* WALTER *turns and looks at* RUTH. TRAVIS *goes to a dish for money.*]

RUTH: Why don't you answer the door, man?

WALTER (*suddenly bounding across the floor to her*): 'Cause sometimes it hard to let the future begin! (*Stooping down in her face.*)
I got wings! You got wings!
All God's children got wings!

[*He crosses to the door and throws it open. Standing there is a very slight little man in a not-too-prosperous business suit and with haunted frightened eyes and a hat pulled down tightly, brim up, around his forehead. TRAVIS passes between the men and exits. WALTER leans deep in the man's face, still in his jubilance.*]

WALTER: *When I get to heaven gonna put on my wings,*
Gonna fly all over God's heaven....

[*The little man just stares at him.*]

WALTER: *Heaven....* (*Suddenly he stops and looks past the little man into the empty hallway.*) Where's Willy, man?

BOBO: He ain't with me.

WALTER (*not disturbed*): Oh—come on in. You know my wife.

BOBO (*dumbly, taking off his hat*): Yes —h'you, Miss Ruth.

RUTH (*quietly, a mood apart from her husband already, seeing BOBO*): Hello, Bobo.

WALTER: You right on time today.... Right on time. That's the way! (*He slaps BOBO on his back.*) Sit down ... lemme hear.

[*RUTH stands stiffly and quietly in back of them, as though somehow she senses death, her eyes fixed on her husband.*]

BOBO (*his frightened eyes on the floor, his hat in his hands*): Could I please get a drink of water, before I tell you about it, Walter Lee?

[*WALTER does not take his eyes off the man. RUTH goes blindly to the tap and gets a glass of water and brings it to BOBO.*]

WALTER: There ain't nothing wrong, is there?

BOBO: Lemme tell you....

WALTER: Man—didn't nothing go wrong?

BOBO: Lemme tell you—Walter Lee. (*Looking at RUTH and talking to her more than to WALTER.*) You know how it was. I got to tell you how it was. I mean first I got to tell you how it was all the way ... I mean about the money I put in, Walter Lee....

WALTER (*with taut agitation now*): What about the money you put in?

BOBO: Well—it wasn't much as we told you—me and Willy—(*He stops.*) I'm sorry, Walter. I got a bad feeling about it. I got a real bad feeling about it....

WALTER: Man, what you telling me about all this for? ... Tell me what happened in Springfield....

BOBO: Springfield.

RUTH (*like a dead woman*): What was supposed to happen in Springfield?

BOBO (*to her*): This deal that me and Walter went into with Willy—Me and Willy was going to go down to Springfield and spread some money round so's we wouldn't have to wait so long for the liquor license.... That's what we were going to do. Everybody said that was the way you had to do, you understand, Miss Ruth?

WALTER: Man—what happened down there?

BOBO (*a pitiful man, near tears*): I'm trying to tell you, Walter.

WALTER (*screaming at him suddenly*): THEN TELL ME, ... DAMMIT ... WHAT'S THE MATTER WITH YOU?

BOBO: Man ... I didn't go to no Springfield, yesterday.

WALTER (*halted, life hanging in the moment*): Why not?

BOBO (*the long way, the hard way to*

tell): 'Cause I didn't have no reasons to. . . .

WALTER: Man, what are you talking about!

BOBO: I'm talking about the fact that when I got to the train station yesterday morning—eight o'clock like we planned. . . . Man—*Willy didn't never show up.*

WALTER: Why . . . where was he . . . where is he?

BOBO: That's what I'm trying to tell you . . . I don't know . . . I waited six hours . . . I called his house . . . and I waited . . . six hours . . . I waited in that train station six hours. . . . (*Breaking into tears.*) That was all the extra money I had in the world. . . . (*Looking up at* WALTER *with the tears running down his face.*) Man, *Willy is gone.*

WALTER: Gone, what you mean Willy is gone? Gone where? You mean he went by himself. You mean he went off to Springfield by himself—to take care of getting the license—(*Turns and looks anxiously at* RUTH.) You mean maybe he didn't want too many people in on the business down there? (*Looks to* RUTH *again, as before.*) You know Willy got his own ways. (*Looks back to* BOBO.) Maybe you was late yesterday and he just went on down there without you. Maybe—maybe—he's been callin' you at home tryin' to tell you what happened or something. Maybe—maybe—he just got sick. He's somewhere—He's got to be somewhere. We just got to find him —me and you got to find him. (*Grabs* BOBO *senselessly by the collar and starts to shake him.*) We got to!

BOBO (*in sudden angry, frightened*

agony): What's the matter with you, Walter! *When a cat take off with your money, he don't leave you no maps!*

WALTER (*turning madly, as though he is looking for* WILLY *in the very room*): Willy! . . . Willy . . . don't do it. . . . Please don't do it. . . . Man, not with that money. . . . Man, please, not with that money. . . . Oh, God. . . . Don't let it be true. . . . (*He is wandering around, crying out for* WILLY *and looking for him or perhaps for help from God.*) Man . . . I trusted you. . . . Man, I put my life in your hands. . . .

[*He starts to crumple down on the floor as* RUTH *just covers her face in horror.* MAMA *opens the door and comes into the room, with* BENEATHA *behind her.*]

WALTER: Man. . . . (*He starts to pound the floor with his fists, sobbing wildly.*) That money is made out of my father's flesh. . . .

BOBO (*standing over him helplessly*): I'm sorry, Walter. . . .

[*Only* WALTER's *sobs reply.* BOBO *puts on his hat.*]

BOBO: I had my life staked on this deal, too. . . . (*He exits.*)

MAMA (*to* WALTER): Son—(*She goes to him, bends down to him, talks to his bent head.*) Son. . . . Is it gone? Son, I gave you sixty-five hundred dollars. Is it gone? All of it? Beneatha's money, too?

WALTER (*lifting his head slowly*): Mama . . . I never . . . went to the bank at all. . . .

MAMA (*not wanting to believe him*): You mean . . . your sister's school money . . . you used that too . . . Walter? . . .

WALTER: Yessss! . . . All of it. . . . It's all gone. . . .

[*There is total silence.* RUTH *stands with her face covered with her hands;* BENEATHA *leans forlornly against a wall, fingering a piece of red ribbon from the mother's gift.* MAMA *stops and looks at her son without recognition and then, quite without thinking about it, starts to beat him senselessly in the face.* BENEATHA *goes to them and stops it.*]

BENEATHA: Mama!

[MAMA *stops and looks at both of her children and rises slowly and wanders vaguely, aimlessly away from them.*]

MAMA: I seen . . . him . . . night after night . . . come in . . . and look at that rug . . . and then look at me . . . the red showing in his eyes . . . the veins moving in his head. . . . I seen him grow thin and old before he was forty . . . working and working and working like somebody's old horse . . . killing himself . . . and you—you give it all away in a day. . . .

BENEATHA: Mama. . . .

MAMA: Oh, God. . . . (*She looks up to Him.*) Look down here—and show me the strength.

BENEATHA: Mama—

MAMA (*folding over*): Strength. . . .

BENEATHA (*plaintively*): Mama. . . .

MAMA: Strength!

Curtain

Insight

1. The conflict between Ruth and Walter grows in intensity during this act. What basic disagreements appear to be at the root of their problem? Do they seem to understand each other's position? What hopeful signs for their relationship can you note?

2. On learning that Mama has used some of her money to buy a house, Walter accuses her of butchering up a "dream of mine—you—who always talking 'bout your children's dreams." To what extent do you think Walter is justified in this attack? Explain. How sympathetic do you feel toward Walter at this point?

3. Why does Mama decide to turn the remaining $6500 over to Walter? How does he react to getting the money and to Mama's words which accompany the money?

4. What message does Lindner bring to the Youngers? How does he couch his message in terms of "Brotherhood"? How does each member of the family react to what he says? In view of the cruel message that has been delivered, how do you account for the lightness that prevails in the Younger household after Lindner departs?

Lorraine Hansberry

ACT III

TIME: An hour later.

AT RISE: There is a sullen light of gloom in the living room, gray light not unlike that which began the first scene of Act I. At Left we can see WALTER within his room, alone with himself. He is stretched out on the bed, his shirt out and open, his arms under his head. He does not smoke; he does not cry out; he merely lies there, looking up at the ceiling, much as if he were alone in the world.

In the living room BENEATHA sits at the table, still surrounded by the now almost ominous packing crates. She sits looking off. We feel that this is a mood struck perhaps an hour before, and it lingers now, full of the empty sound of profound disappointment. We see on a line from her brother's bedroom the sameness of their attitudes. Presently the bell rings, and BENEATHA rises without ambition or interest in answering. It is ASAGAI, smiling broadly, striding into the room with energy and happy expectation and conversation.

ASAGAI: I came over . . . I had some free time. I thought I might help with the packing. Ah, I like the look of packing crates! A household in preparation for a journey! It depresses some people . . . but for me . . . it is another feeling. Something full of the flow of life, do you understand? Movement, progress. . . . It makes me think of Africa.

BENEATHA: Africa!

ASAGAI: What kind of a mood is this? Have I told you how deeply you move me?

BENEATHA: He gave away the money, Asagai. . . .

ASAGAI: Who gave away what money?

BENEATHA: The insurance money. My brother gave it away.

ASAGAI: Gave it away?

BENEATHA: He made an investment! With a man even Travis wouldn't have trusted.

ASAGAI: And it's gone?

BENEATHA: Gone!

ASAGAI: I'm very sorry. . . . And you, now?

BENEATHA: Me? . . . Me? . . . Me, I'm nothing. . . . Me. When I was very small . . . we used to take our sleds out in the wintertime, and the only hills we had were the ice-covered stone steps of some houses down the street. And we used to fill them in with snow and make them smooth and slide down them all day . . . and it was very dangerous, you know . . . far too steep . . . and sure enough one day a kid named Rufus came too fast and hit the sidewalk . . . and we saw his face just split open right there in front of us. . . . And I remember standing there looking at his bloody open face, thinking that was the end of Rufus. But the ambulance came, and they took him to the hospital, and they fixed the broken bones, and they sewed it all up . . . and the next time I saw Rufus, he just had a little line down the middle of his face. . . . I never got over that. . . .

[WALTER *sits up, listening on the bed. Throughout this scene it is important that we feel his reaction at all times, that he visibly respond to the words of his sister and* ASAGAI.]

ASAGAI: What?

BENEATHA: That that was what one person could do for another, fix him up —sew up the problem, make him all

191

right again. That was the most marvelous thing in the world. . . . I wanted to do that. I always thought it was the one concrete thing in the world that a human being could do. Fix up the sick, you know—and make them whole again. This was truly being God. . . .

ASAGAI: You wanted to be God?

BENEATHA: No—I wanted to cure. It used to be so important to me. I wanted to cure. It used to matter. I used to care. I mean about people and how their bodies hurt. . . .

ASAGAI: And you've stopped caring?

BENEATHA: Yes—I think so.

ASAGAI: Why?

[WALTER *rises, goes to the door of his room and is about to open it, then stops and stands listening, leaning on the door jamb.*]

BENEATHA: Because it doesn't seem deep enough, close enough to what ails mankind—I mean this thing of sewing up bodies or administering drugs. Don't you understand? It was a child's reaction to the world. I thought that doctors had the secret to all the hurts. . . . That's the way a child sees things —or an idealist.

ASAGAI: Children see things very well sometimes—and idealists even better.

BENEATHA: I know that's what you think. Because you are still where I left off—you still care. This is what you see for the world, for Africa. You with the dreams of the future will patch up all Africa—you are going to cure the Great Sore of colonialism with Independence. . . .

ASAGAI: Yes!

BENEATHA: Yes—and you think that one word is the penicillin of the human spirit: "Independence!" But then what?

ASAGAI: That will be the problem for another time. First we must get there.

BENEATHA: And where does it end?

ASAGAI: End? Who even spoke of an end? To life? To living?

BENEATHA: An end to misery!

ASAGAI (*smiling*): You sound like a French intellectual.

BENEATHA: No! I sound like a human being who just had her future taken right out of her hands! While I was sleeping in my bed in there, things were happening in this world that directly concerned me—and nobody asked me, consulted me—they just went out and did things—and changed my life. Don't you see there isn't any real progress, Asagai, there is only one large circle that we march in, around and around, each of us with our own little picture—in front of us—our own little mirage that we think is the future.

ASAGAI: That is the mistake.

BENEATHA: What?

ASAGAI: What you just said—about the circle. It isn't a circle—it is simply a long line—as in geometry, you know, one that reaches into infinity. And because we cannot see the end—we also cannot see how it changes. And it is very odd, but those who see the changes are called "idealists"—and those who cannot, or refuse to think, they are the "realists." It is very strange, and amusing too, I think.

BENEATHA: You—you are almost religious.

ASAGAI: Yes . . . I think I have the religion of doing what is necessary in the world—and of worshipping man—

because he is so marvelous, you see.

BENEATHA: Man is foul! And the human race deserves its misery!

ASAGAI: You see: *you* have become the religious one in the old sense. Already, and after such a small defeat, you are worshipping despair.

BENEATHA: From now on, I worship the truth—and the truth is that people are puny, small, and selfish. . . .

ASAGAI: Truth? Why is it that you despairing ones always think that only you have the truth? I never thought to see *you* like that. You! Your brother made a stupid, childish mistake—and you are grateful to him. So that now you can give up the ailing human race on account of it. You talk about what good is struggle; what good is anything? Where are we all going? And why are we bothering?

BENEATHA: *And you cannot answer it!* All your talk and dreams about Africa and Independence. Independence and then what? What about all the crooks and petty thieves and just plain idiots who will come into power to steal and plunder the same as before—only now they will be black and do it in the name of the new Independence —You cannot answer that.

ASAGAI (*shouting over her*): *I live the answer!* (*Pause.*) In my village at home it is the exceptional man who can even read a newspaper . . . or who ever *sees* a book at all. I will go home, and much of what I will have to say will seem strange to the people of my village. . . . But I will teach and work, and things will happen, slowly and swiftly. At times it will seem that nothing changes at all . . . and then

again . . . the sudden dramatic events which make history leap into the future. And then quiet again. Retrogression, even. Guns, murder, revolution. And I even will have moments when I wonder if the quiet was not better than all that death and hatred. But I will look about my village at the illiteracy and disease and ignorance, and I will not wonder long. And perhaps . . . perhaps I will be a great man . . . I mean perhaps I will hold on to the substance of truth and find my way always with the right course . . . and perhaps for it I will be butchered in my bed some night by the servants of empire. . . .

BENEATHA: *The martyr!*

ASAGAI: . . . or perhaps I shall live to be a very old man, respected and esteemed in my new nation. . . . And perhaps I shall hold office, and this is what I'm trying to tell you, Alaiyo; perhaps the things I believe now for my country will be wrong and outmoded, and I will not understand and do terrible things to have things my way or merely to keep my power. Don't you see that there will be young men and women, not British soldiers then, but my own black countrymen . . . to step out of the shadows some evening and slit my then useless throat? Don't you see they have always been there . . . that they always will be. And that such a thing as my own death will be an advance? They who might kill me even . . . actually replenish me!

BENEATHA: Oh, Asagai, I know all that.

ASAGAI: Good! Then stop moaning and groaning and tell me what you plan to do.

BENEATHA: Do?

ASAGAI: I have a bit of a suggestion.

BENEATHA: What?

ASAGAI (*rather quietly for him*): That when it is all over—that you come home with me. . . .

BENEATHA (*slapping herself on the forehead with exasperation born of misunderstanding*): Oh—Asagai—at this moment you decide to be romantic!

ASAGAI (*quickly understanding the misunderstanding*): My dear, young creature of the New World—I do not mean across the city—I mean across the ocean; home—to Africa.

BENEATHA (*slowly understanding and turning to him with murmured amazement*): To—to Nigeria?

ASAGAI: Yes! . . . (*Smiling and lifting his arms playfully.*) Three hundred years later the African Prince rose up out of the seas and swept the maiden back across the middle passage over which her ancestors had come—

BENEATHA (*unable to play*): Nigeria?

ASAGAI: Nigeria. Home. (*Coming to her with genuine romantic flippancy.*) I will show you our mountains and our stars and give you cool drinks from gourds and teach you the old songs and the ways of our people—and, in time, we will pretend that—(*Very softly.*)—you have only been away for a day. . . .

[*She turns her back to him, thinking. He swings her around and takes her full in his arms in a long embrace which proceeds to passion.*]

BENEATHA (*pulling away*): You're getting me all mixed up. . . .

ASAGAI: Why?

BENEATHA: Too many things—too many things have happened today. I must sit down and think. I don't know what I feel about anything right this minute. (*She promptly sits down and props her chin on her fist.*)

ASAGAI (*charmed*): All right, I shall leave you. No—don't get up. (*Touching her, gently, sweetly.*) Just sit awhile and think. . . . Never be afraid to sit awhile and think. (*He goes to door and looks at her.*) How often I have looked at you and said, "Ah—so this is what the New World hath finally wrought. . . ."

[*He exits.* BENEATHA *sits alone. Presently* WALTER *enters from his room and starts to rummage through things, feverishly looking for something. She looks up and turns in her seat.*]

BENEATHA (*hissingly*): Yes—just look at what the New World hath wrought! . . . Just look! (*She gestures with bitter disgust.*) There he is! *Monsieur le petit bourgeois noir*[1]—himself! There he is—Symbol of a Rising Class! Entrepreneur. Titan of the system!

[WALTER *ignores her completely and continues frantically and destructively looking for something and hurling things to floor and tearing things out of their place in his search.* BENEATHA *ignores the eccentricity of his actions and goes on with the monologue of insult.*]

BENEATHA: Did you dream of yachts on Lake Michigan, Brother? Did you see yourself on that Great Day sitting down at the Conference Table, surrounded by all the mighty baldheaded men in America? All halted,

---

[1] MONSIEUR LE PETIT BOURGEOIS NOIR: Mr. black lower middle-class.

waiting, breathless, waiting for your pronouncements on industry? Waiting for you—Chairman of the Board?

[WALTER *finds what he is looking for—a small piece of white paper—and pushes it in his pocket and puts on his coat and rushes out without ever having looked at her. She shouts after him.*]

BENEATHA: I look at you and I see the final triumph of stupidity in the world!

[*The door slams and she returns to just sitting again.* RUTH *comes quickly out of* MAMA's *room.*]

RUTH: Who was that?
BENEATHA: Your husband.
RUTH: Where did he go?
BENEATHA: Who knows—maybe he has an appointment at U.S. Steel.
RUTH (*anxiously, with frightened eyes*): You didn't say nothing bad to him, did you?
BENEATHA: Bad? Say anything bad to him? No—I told him he was a sweet boy and full of dreams, and everything is strictly peachy keen, as the ofay kids say!

[MAMA *enters from her bedroom. She is lost, vague, trying to catch hold, to make some sense of her former command of the world, but it still eludes her. A sense of waste overwhelms her gait; a measure of apology rides on her shoulders. She goes to her plant, which has remained on the table, looks at it, picks it up, and takes it to the window sill and sets it outside, and she stands and looks at it a long moment. Then she closes the window, straightens her body with effort, and turns around to her children.*]

MAMA: Well—ain't it a mess in here, though? (*A false cheerfulness, a beginning of something.*) I guess we all better stop moping around and get some work done. All this unpacking and everything we got to do.

[RUTH *raises her head slowly in response to the sense of the line; and* BENEATHA *in similar manner turns very slowly to look at her mother.*]

MAMA: One of you-all better call the moving people and tell 'em not to come.
RUTH: Tell 'em not to come?
MAMA: Of course, baby. Ain't no need in 'em coming all the way here and having to go back. They charges for that, too. (*She sits down, fingers to her brow, thinking.*) Lord, ever since I was a little girl, I always remembers people saying, "Lena—Lena Eggleston, you aims too high all the time. You needs to slow down and see life a little more like it is. Just slow down some." That's what they always used to say down home—"Lord, that Lena Eggleston is a high-minded thing. She'll get her due one day!"
RUTH: No, Lena. . . .
MAMA: Me and Big Walter just didn't never learn right.
RUTH: Lena, no! We gotta go. Bennie—tell her. . . . (*She rises and crosses to* BENEATHA *with her arms outstretched.* BENEATHA *doesn't respond.*) Tell her we can still move . . . the notes ain't but a hundred and twenty-five a month. We got four grown people in this house—we can work. . . .
MAMA (*to herself*): Just aimed too high all the time—
RUTH (*turning and going to* MAMA *fast —the words pouring out with ur-*

Lorraine Hansberry

gency and desperation): Lena—I'll
work.... I'll work twenty hours a
day in all the kitchens in Chicago....
I'll strap my baby on my back if I
have to and scrub all the floors in
America and wash all of the sheets in
America if I have to—but we got to
move.... We got to get out of
here....

[MAMA *reaches out absently and pats*
RUTH'*s hand*.]

MAMA: No—I sees things differently
now. Been thinking 'bout some of the
things we could do to fix this place up
some. I seen a second-hand bureau
over on Maxwell Street just the other
day that could fit right there. (*She
points to where the new furniture
might go.* RUTH *wanders away from
her.*) Would need some new handles
on it and then a little varnish and
then it look like something brand-
new. And—we can put up them new
curtains in the kitchen.... Why, this
place be looking fine. Cheer us all up
so that we forget trouble ever came.
... (*To* RUTH.) And you could get
some nice screens to put up in your
room round the baby's bassinet....
(*She looks at both of them, pleadingly.*) Sometimes you just got to
know when to give up some things
... and hold on to what you got.

[WALTER *enters from the outside, looking
spent and leaning against the door, his
coat hanging from him.*]

MAMA: Where you been, son?
WALTER (*breathing hard*): Made a call.
MAMA: To who, son?
WALTER: To The Man.
MAMA: What man, baby?
WALTER: The Man, Mama. Don't you

know who The Man is?
RUTH: Walter Lee?
WALTER: *The Man.* Like the guys in the
streets say—The Man. Captain Boss
—Mistuh Charley... Old Captain
Please Mr. Bossman....
BENEATHA (*suddenly*): Lindner!
WALTER: That's right! That's good. I
told him to come right over.
BENEATHA (*fiercely, understanding*): For
what? What do you want to see him
for!
WALTER (*looking at his sister*): We go-
ing to do business with him.
MAMA: What you talking 'bout son?
WALTER: Talking 'bout life, Mama. You-
all always telling me to see life like it
is. Well—I laid in there on my back
today ... and I figured it out. Life just
like it is. Who gets and who don't get.
(*He sits down with his coat on and
laughs.*) Mama, you know it's all divided up. Life is. Sure enough. Between the takers and the "tooken."
(*He laughs.*) I've figured it out finally.
(*He looks around at them.*) Yeah.
Some of us always getting "tooken."
(*He laughs.*) People like Willy Harris,
they don't never get "tooken." And
you know why the rest of us do?
'Cause we all mixed up. Mixed up
bad. We get to looking 'round for the
right and the wrong; and we worry
about it and cry about it and stay up
nights trying to figure out 'bout the
wrong and the right of things all the
time.... And all the time, man, them
takers is out there operating, just taking and taking. Willy Harris? Shoot
—Willy Harris don't even count. He
don't even count in the big scheme of
things. But I'll say one thing for old
Willy Harris ... he's taught me some-

thing. He's taught me to keep my eye on what counts in this world. Yeah —(*Shouting out a little.*) Thanks, Willy!

RUTH: What did you call that man for, Walter Lee?

WALTER: Called him to tell him to come on over to the show. Gonna put on a show for the man. Just what he wants to see. You see, Mama, the man came here today and he told us that them people out there where you want us to move—well, they so upset they willing to pay us not to move out there. (*He laughs again.*) And—and oh, Mama—you would of been proud of the way me and Ruth and Bennie acted. We told him to get out . . . Lord have mercy! We told the man to get out. Oh, we was some proud folks this afternoon, yeah. (*He lights a cigarette.*) We were still full of that old-time stuff. . . .

RUTH (*coming toward him slowly*): You talking 'bout taking them people's money to keep us from moving in that house?

WALTER: I ain't just talking 'bout it, baby—I'm telling you that's what's going to happen.

BENEATHA: Oh, God! Where is the bottom! Where is the real honest-to-God bottom so he can't go any farther!

WALTER: See—that's the old stuff. You and that boy that was here today. You-all want everybody to carry a flag and a spear and sing some marching songs, huh? You wanna spend your life looking into things and trying to find the right and the wrong part, huh? Yeah. You know what's going to happen to that boy someday —he'll find himself sitting in a dungeon, locked in forever—and the takers will have the key! Forget it, baby! There ain't no causes—there ain't nothing but taking in this world, and he who takes most is smartest— and it don't make a damn bit of difference *how*.

MAMA: You making something inside me cry, son. Some awful pain inside me.

WALTER: Don't cry, Mama. Understand. That white man is going to walk in that door able to write checks for more money than we ever had. It's important to him, and I'm going to help him. . . . I'm going to put on the show, Mama.

MAMA: Son—I come from five generations of people who was slaves and sharecroppers—but ain't nobody in my family never let nobody pay 'em no money that was a way of telling us we wasn't fit to walk the earth. We ain't never been that poor. (*Raising her eyes and looking at him.*) We ain't never been that dead inside.

BENEATHA: Well—we are dead now. All the talk about dreams and sunlight that goes on in this house. All dead.

WALTER: What's the matter with you all! I didn't make this world! It was give to me this way! Hell, yes, I want me some yachts someday! Yes, I want to hang some real pearls round my wife's neck. Ain't she supposed to wear no pearls? Somebody tell me— tell me, who decides which women is suppose to wear pearls in this world. I tell you I am a *man*—and I think my wife should wear some pearls in this world!

[*This last line hangs a good while, and* WALTER *begins to move about the room. The word* man *has penetrated his consciousness; he mumbles it to himself repeatedly between strange agitated pauses as he moves about.*]

MAMA: Baby, how you going to feel on the inside?

WALTER: Fine! . . . Going to feel fine . . . a man. . . .

MAMA: You won't have nothing left then, Walter Lee.

WALTER (*coming to her*): I'm going to feel fine, Mama. I'm going to look that . . . in the eyes and say—(*He falters.*)—and say, "All right, Mr. Lindner—(*He falters even more.*)—that's your neighborhood out there. You got the right to keep it like you want. You got the right to have it like you want. Just write the check and —the house is yours." And, and I am going to say—(*His voice almost breaks.*) And you—you people just put the money in my hand, and you won't have to live next to this bunch of stinking niggers! . . . (*He straightens up and moves away from his mother, walking around the room.*) Maybe—maybe I'll just get down on my black knees . . . (*He does so;* RUTH *and* BENNIE *and* MAMA *watch him in frozen horror.*) Captain, Mistuh, Bossman. (*He starts crying.*) A-hee-hee-hee! (*Wringing his hands in profoundly anguished imitation*). Yesssssuh! Great White Father, just gi' ussen de money, fo' God's sake, and we's ain't gwine come out deh and dirty up yo' white folks neighborhood. . . . (*He breaks down com-*

pletely, then gets up and goes into the bedroom.)

BENEATHA: That is not a man. That is nothing but a toothless rat.

MAMA: Yes—death done come in this here house. (*She is nodding, slowly, reflectively.*) Done come walking in my house. On the lips of my children. You what supposed to be my beginning again. You—what supposed to be my harvest. (*To* BENEATHA.) You —you mourning your brother?

BENEATHA: He's no brother of mine.

MAMA: What you say?

BENEATHA: I said that that individual in that room is no brother of mine.

MAMA: That's what I thought you said. You feeling like you better than he is today? (BENEATHA *does not answer.*) Yes? What you tell him a minute ago? That he wasn't a man? Yes? You give him up for me? You done wrote his epitaph, too—like the rest of the world? Well, who give you the privilege?

BENEATHA: Be on my side for once! You saw what he just did, Mama! You saw him—down on his knees. Wasn't it you who taught me—to despise any man who would do that. Do what he's going to do.

MAMA: Yes—I taught you that. Me and your daddy. But I thought I taught you something else, too. . . . I thought I taught you to love him.

BENEATHA: Love him? There is nothing left to love.

MAMA: There is always something left to love. And if you ain't learned that, you ain't learned nothing. (*Looking at her.*) Have you cried for that boy today? I don't mean for yourself and for the family 'cause we lost the money. I mean for him; what he been through and what it done to him. Child, when do you think is the time to love somebody the most; when they done good and made things easy for everybody? Well then, you ain't through learning—because that ain't the time at all. It's when he's at his lowest and can't believe in hisself 'cause the world done whipped him so. When you starts measuring somebody, measure him right, child, measure him right. Make sure you done taken into account what hills and valleys he come through before he got to wherever he is.

[TRAVIS *bursts into the room at the end of the speech, leaving the door open.*]

TRAVIS: Grandmama—the moving men are downstairs! The truck just pulled up.

MAMA (*turning and looking at him*): Are they, baby? They downstairs?

[*She sighs and sits.* LINDNER *appears in the doorway. He peers in and knocks lightly, to gain attention, and comes in. All turn to look at him.*]

LINDNER (*hat and briefcase in hand*): Uh —hello. . . .

[RUTH *crosses mechanically to the bedroom door and opens it and lets it swing open freely and slowly as the lights come up on* WALTER *within, still in his coat, sitting at the far corner of the room. He looks up and out through the room to* LINDNER.]

RUTH: He's here.

[*A long minute passes, and* WALTER *slowly gets up.*]

LINDNER (*coming to the table with ef-*ficiency, *putting his briefcase on the table and starting to unfold papers and unscrew fountain pens*): Well, I certainly was glad to hear from you people.

[WALTER *has begun the trek out of the room, slowly and awkwardly, rather like a small boy, passing the back of his sleeve across his mouth from time to time.*]

LINDNER: Life can really be so much simpler than people let it be most of the time. Well—with whom do I negotiate? You, Mrs. Younger, or your son here?

[MAMA *sits with her hands folded on her lap and her eyes closed as* WALTER *advances.* TRAVIS *goes close to* LINDNER *and looks at the papers curiously.*]

LINDNER: Just some official papers, sonny.

RUTH: Travis, you go downstairs.

MAMA (*opening her eyes and looking into* WALTER'S): No. Travis, you stay right here. And you make him understand what you doing, Walter Lee. You teach him good. Like Willy Harris taught you. You show where our five generations done come to. Go ahead, son. . . .

WALTER (*looks down into his boy's eyes.* TRAVIS *grins at him merrily, and* WALTER *draws him beside him with his arm lightly around his shoulders*): Well, Mr. Lindner. (BE-NEATHA *turns away.*) We called you— (*There is a profound, simple groping quality in his speech.*)—because, well, me and my family (*He looks around and shifts from one foot to the other.*) Well—we are very plain

Lorraine Hansberry

people. . . .

LINDNER: Yes—

WALTER: I mean—I have worked as a chauffeur most of my life—and my wife here, she does domestic work in people's kitchens. So does my mother. I mean—we are plain people. . . .

LINDNER: Yes, Mr. Younger—

WALTER (*really like a small boy, looking down at his shoes and then up at the man*): And—uh—well, my father, well, he was a laborer most of his life.

LINDNER (*absolutely confused*): Uh, yes—

WALTER (*looking down at his toes once again*): My father almost beat a man to death once because this man called him a bad name or something; you know what I mean?

LINDNER: No, I'm afraid I don't.

WALTER (*finally straightening up*): Well, what I mean is that we come from people who had a lot of pride. I mean—we are very proud people. And that's my sister over there and she's going to be a doctor—and we are very proud—

LINDNER: Well—I am sure that is very nice, but—

WALTER (*starting to cry and facing the man eye to eye*): What I am telling you is that we called you over here to tell you that we are very proud and that this is—this is my son, who makes the sixth generation of our family in this country, and that we have all thought about your offer, and we have decided to move into our house because my father—my father —he earned it.

[MAMA *has her eyes closed and is rocking back and forth as though she were in church, with her head nodding the amen yes.*]

WALTER: We don't want to make no trouble for nobody or fight no causes —but we will try to be good neighbors. That's all we got to say. (*He looks the man absolutely in the eyes.*) We don't want your money. (*He turns and walks away from the man.*)

LINDNER (*looking around at all of them*): I take it then that you have decided to occupy.

BENEATHA: That's what the man said.

LINDNER (*to* MAMA *in her reverie*): Then I would like to appeal to you, Mrs. Younger. You are older and wiser and understand things better, I am sure. . . . .

MAMA (*rising*): I am afraid you don't understand. My son said we was going to move and there ain't nothing left for me to say. (*Shaking her head with double meaning.*) You know how these young folks is nowadays, mister. Can't do a thing with 'em. Good-bye.

LINDNER (*folding up his materials*): Well—if you are that final about it . . . . There is nothing left for me to say. (*He finishes. He is almost ignored by the family, who are concentrating on* WALTER LEE. *At the door* LINDNER *halts and looks around.*) I sure hope you people know what you're doing. (*He shakes his head and exits.*)

RUTH (*looking around and coming to life*): Well, for God's sake—if the moving men are here—LET'S GET THE HELL OUT OF HERE!

MAMA (*into action*): Ain't it the truth! Look at all this here mess. Ruth, put Travis's good jacket on him. . . . Walter Lee, fix your tie and tuck your shirt in; you look just like somebody's hoodlum. Lord have mercy, where is my plant? (*She flies to get it amid the general bustling of the family, who are deliberately trying to ignore the nobility of the past moment.*) You-all start on down. . . . Travis, child, don't go empty-handed. . . . Ruth, where did I put that box with my skillets in it? I want to be in charge of it myself. . . . I'm going to make us the biggest dinner we ever ate to-night. . . . Beneatha, what's the matter with them stockings? Pull them things up, girl. . . .

[*The family starts to file out as two moving men appear and begin to carry out the heavier pieces of furniture, bumping into the family as they move about.*]

BENEATHA: Mama, Asagai—asked me to marry him today and go to Africa. . . .

MAMA (*in the middle of her getting-ready activity*): He did? You ain't old enough to marry nobody—(*Seeing the moving men lifting one of her chairs precariously.*) Darling, that ain't no bale of cotton; please handle it so we can sit in it again. I had that chair twenty-five years. . . .

[*The movers sigh with exasperation and go on with their work.*]

BENEATHA (*girlishly and unreasonably trying to pursue the conversation*): To go to Africa, Mama—be a doctor in Africa. . . .

MAMA (*distracted*): Yes, baby—

WALTER: Africa! What he want you to go to Africa for?

BENEATHA: To practice there. . . .

WALTER: Girl, if you don't get all them silly ideas out your head! You better marry yourself a man with some loot. . . .

BENEATHA (*angrily, precisely as in the first scene of the play*): What have you got to do with who I marry!

WALTER: Plenty. Now I think George Murchison—

[*He and* BENEATHA *go out yelling at each other vigorously;* BENEATHA *is heard saying that she would not marry* GEORGE MURCHISON *if he were Adam and she were Eve, etc. The anger is loud and real till their voices diminish.* RUTH *stands at the door and turns to* MAMA *and smiles knowingly.*]

MAMA (*fixing her hat at last*): Yeah—they something all right, my children. . . .

RUTH: Yeah—they're something. Let's go, Lena.

MAMA (*stalling, starting to look around at the house*): Yes—I'm coming. Ruth—

RUTH: Yes?

MAMA (*quietly, woman to woman*): He finally come into his manhood today, didn't he? Kind of like a rainbow after the rain. . . .

RUTH (*biting her lip lest her own pride explode in front of* MAMA): Yes, Lena.

[WALTER'S *voice calls for them raucously.*]

MAMA (*waving* RUTH *out vaguely*): All right, honey—go on down. I be down directly.

[RUTH *hesitates, then exits.* MAMA *stands,*

Lorraine Hansberry

at last alone in the living room, her plant on the table before her as the lights start to come down. She looks around at all the walls and ceilings and suddenly, despite herself, while the children call below, a great heaving thing rises in her and she puts her fist to her mouth, takes a final desperate look, pulls her coat about her, pats her hat, and goes out. The lights dim down. The door opens and she comes back in, grabs her plant, goes out for the last time.]

Curtain

Insight

1. The opening of Act III finds Beneatha a changed person. What has caused the change? What does she now appear to believe? How does Asagai react to her new outlook?

2. At the end of Act II Mama has begged for strength, strength to cope with the trials engulfing her family. Does she appear to gain strength as Act III progresses? How important is her voice in the final determination of the Younger's destiny? Cite passages to support your opinion.

3. Walter cries out, "I didn't make this world! It was give to me this way!" In what way does his consequent behavior toward Lindner belie those words? What factors contribute to the remarkable change in Walter's outlook toward Lindner and the offer he brings?

4. Mama's last action in the play is to return for her plant. What do you think the plant represents?

The Play as a Whole

1. The title of the play is taken from a line of the Langston Hughes poem "A Dream Deferred." What happens to the dreams in this play? Are they "deferred"? Do they "explode"? Do they "fester like a sore" or do they "dry up like a raisin in the sun"?

2. *A Raisin in the Sun* has been characterized as both a social protest and a human drama. Do you agree with this characterization? Explain.

3. Many characters in plays are presented to us so realistically that we tend to like or dislike them as we do real people. Other characters, however, are devised to speak for the ideas, values, or attitudes of the author. Which characters in the play were "real" for you? Which did you especially like or dislike?

4. Sometimes the theme of a play is implied or suggested in the very texture of the play. Other times one of the characters will directly state the theme in one of his or her speeches. How would you characterize the theme of this play? Is this theme implied or stated directly? Support your answer with reference to the play itself.

IN SUMMARY

Insight and Composition

1. To tell the story, develop the plot, and reveal the characters, the playwright must use spoken words. Dialogue thus becomes the most important element in the play. Examine the use of dialogue in *A Raisin in the Sun* and "Trifles." In what ways do you think the dialogue is appropriate to each play? How effective do you find it? Cite some examples of what you consider effective use of dialogue.

2. The chief character in a drama is called the protagonist. Whom do you consider the protagonist in each play? Can you note any similarity in the roles played by each protagonist?

3. *A Raisin in the Sun* and "Trifles" differ not only in their length and scope but in their purpose as well. How would you describe the purpose of each play? Which play seems more substantial to you?

4. Study one of the major characters in the two plays from an actor's point of view. Prepare a description of the costumes, make-up, vocal expressions, gestures and movements you would choose to express this character. Be certain to include a summary of the over-all effect you want your characterization to achieve.

Marisol. *The Family*, 1962

In a Role

Everyone inherits some roles, as surely as the color of
eyes. Like it or not, we all start out life as babies, so
necessarily the first role you play is as the youngest
member of some household, fulfilling, disappointing, or
embellishing the dreams of various adults. You did not
choose your parents, nor, chances are, did they choose
you. There, locked into a long intimacy, are people
who may not suit each other at all. Mary McCarthy and
her three little brothers were orphan children handed
over to an aunt and an "uncle" who was no kin to them.
The children never forgot for a moment that Uncle
Myers was not related to them. But children and parents
by "blood" may also feel strangely disconnected from
each other. Sylvia Plath, whose baby's fresh nakedness
reminds her of a statue, even feels a crazy surprise that
this is her own child. "I'm no more your mother," she
says, "than the cloud" which dissolves in the wind.
Almost every child experiences a variation on the same
feeling: "I'm a waif, a foundling. They're no relation to
me." But there we all start.

These feelings of detachment alternate with the
nudging, tugging persistence of affection. Plath, for
example, wakens and listens with wonder to the breathing of her newborn, which sounds like a "far sea" in her
ears. Now and then, every parent and every child feels a

surge of this proud love. Anne Sexton says: "My daughter, at eleven (almost twelve), is like a garden."

Some roles are not inherited, but learned. We look at the clothes, the expressions, and gestures we associate with a role, and long for them, and maybe for the substance of the role as well. The very words—"my student," "my husband," "a little Bouilloux girl," "my child"—seem invested with suggestive glamour and solace. In *that* role, we would be happy! "Seminary," a poem by Constance Carrier, describes schoolgirls in their uniforms, who only appear to be "as much alike as peas or pearls." Underneath the blur of their similarity, they are thinking, talking, judging, turning into separate people. But their distinctiveness finally is only an illusion, for they are learning and teaching each other what the roles are that they all must fill. Almost unconsciously, they change *"One should be to I am."* How much is lost when we each learn and become what "one should be"?

There are always some roles we choose deliberately to fill. For most people, choosing a person to marry seems the moment of shaping life most decisively. Here at last, I choose the person to love, the one who touches my soul, my self. Together we will grow and build a life. Or so we all think. Nothing more bewildering than to find yourself married to a stranger, or to find that being husband and wife is an oppressive bondage instead of the planned adventure. Anne Bradstreet's quiet poem to her "dear and loving husband" suggests how fulfilling marriage can be when a steady, ardent love sustains it. Phyllis McGinley's poem also suggests how much satisfaction there may be in the most conventional, American, middle-class marriage, and perhaps what it costs to achieve those joys. But in "A Domestic Dilemma," "The Farmer's Bride," and "The Yellow Wallpaper," the roles of husband and wife have gone painfully askew. In them we see the ways in which roles can imprison people. What if the role of husband or wife proves too big—or too confining? What if a man does not enjoy the role of good husband? What is a good husband? What if a woman does not want or cannot fill the role of wife? What is a good wife? What if the role of good wife conflicts with the role of good mother? What if either of these roles damages a woman's sense of self?

In these stories, poems, and reminiscences, writers examine the relations between people and the roles they play, the roles they fill. In these selections, parents look at children, children look at parents, and husbands and wives struggle to make sense of their roles. We see young people trying to figure out what they must become, the roles they must avoid, the ones they ought to fill. Here men and women try to connect their real selves to each other, through and in despite of their roles. Through all these selections, we can see the self and the roles merge, separate, blend, and break apart.

Marcia Folsom

NATURAL LAW

Babette Deutsch

If you press a stone with your finger,
Sir Isaac Newton observed,
The finger is also
Pressed by the stone.
But can a woman, pressed by memory's finger,   5
In the deep night, alone,
Of her softness move
The airy thing
That presses upon her
With the whole weight of love? This   10
Sir Isaac said nothing of.

AN ANCIENT GESTURE

Edna St. Vincent Millay

I thought, as I wiped my eyes on the corner of my apron:
Penelope did this too.
And more than once: you can't keep weaving all day
And undoing it all through the night;
Your arms get tired, and the back of your neck gets tight;   5
And along towards morning, when you think it will never be
     light,
And your husband has been gone, and you don't know where,
     for years,
Suddenly you burst into tears;
There is simply nothing else to do.

And I thought, as I wiped my eyes on the corner of my apron: 10
This is an ancient gesture, authentic, antique,
In the very best tradition, classic, Greek;
Ulysses did this too.
But only as a gesture,—a gesture which implied
To the assembled throng that he was much too moved to speak.   15
He learned it from Penelope . . .
Penelope, who really cried.

Insight

1. The speakers in each poem seem unhappy. What is the source of the unhappiness? Which speaker do you feel is more in control of her emotions? Explain.
2. How would you describe the *tone* (see page 10) of each poem? Which do you consider more bitter? Which more resigned? Explain.

i stand here ironing

Tillie Olsen

I stand here ironing, and what you asked me moves tormented back and forth with the iron.

"I wish you would manage the time to come in and talk with me about your daughter. I'm sure you can help me understand her. She's a youngster who needs help and whom I'm deeply interested in helping."

"Who needs help?" Even if I came what good would it do? You think because I am her mother I have a key, or that in some way you could use me as a key? She has lived for nineteen years. There is all that life that has happened outside of me, beyond me.

And when is there time to remember, to sift, to weigh, to estimate, to total? I will start and there will be an interruption and I will have to gather it all together again. Or I will become engulfed with all I did or did not do, with what should have been and what cannot be helped.

She was a beautiful baby. The first and only one of our five that was beautiful at birth. You do not guess how new and uneasy her tenancy in her now-loveliness. You did not know her all those years she was thought homely, or see her poring over her baby pictures, making me tell her over and over how beautiful she had been—and would be, I would tell her—and was now, to the seeing eye. But the seeing eyes were few or nonexistent. Including mine.

I nursed her. They feel that's important nowadays. I nursed all the children, but with her, with all the fierce rigidity of first motherhood, I did like the books said. Though her cries battered me to trembling and my breasts ached with swollenness, I waited till the clock decreed.

Why do I put that first? I do not even know if it matters, or if it explains anything.

She was a beautiful baby. She blew shining bubbles of sound. She loved motion, loved light, loved color and music and textures. She would lie on the floor in her blue overalls patting the surface so hard in ecstasy her hands and feet would blur. She was a miracle to me, but when she was eight months old I had to leave her daytimes with the woman downstairs to whom she was no miracle at all, for I worked or looked for work and for Emily's father, who "could no longer endure" (he wrote in his good-by note) "sharing want with us."

I was nineteen. It was the pre-relief, pre-WPA[1] world of the depression. I would start running as soon as I got off the streetcar, running up the stairs, the place smelling sour, and awake or asleep to startle awake, when she saw me she would break into a clogged weeping that could not be comforted, a weeping I can yet hear.

After a while I found a job hashing at night so I could be with her days, and it was better. But it came to where I had to bring her to his family and leave her.

It took a long time to raise the money for her fare back. Then she got chicken pox and I had to wait longer. When she finally came, I hardly knew her, walking quick and nervous like her father, looking like her father, thin, and dressed in a shoddy red that yellowed her skin and glared at the pock marks. All the baby loveliness gone.

She was two. Old enough for nursery school they said, and I did not know then what I know now—the fatigue of the long day, and the lacerations of group life in the kinds of nurseries that are only parking places for children.

Except that it would have made no difference if I had known. It was the only place there was. It was the only way we could be together, the only way I could hold a job.

And even without knowing, I knew. I knew the teacher that was evil because all these years it has curdled into my memory, the little boy hunched in the corner, her rasp, "why aren't you outside, because Alvin hits you? that's no reason, go out, scaredy." I knew Emily hated it even if she did not clutch and implore "don't go Mommy" like the other children, mornings.

She always had a reason why we should stay home. Momma, you look sick. Momma, I feel sick. Momma, the teachers aren't there today, they're sick. Momma there was a fire there last night. Momma it's a holiday today, no school, they told me.

But never a direct protest, never rebellion. I think of our others in their three-, four-year-oldness—the explosions, the tempers, the denunciations, the demands—and I feel suddenly ill. I stop the ironing. What in me demanded that goodness in her? And what was the cost, the cost to her of such goodness?

The old man living in the back once said in his gentle way: "You should smile at Emily more when you look at her." What *was* in my face when I looked at her? I loved her. There were all the acts of love.

It was only with the others I remembered what he said, so that it was the face of joy, and not of care or tightness or worry I turned to

---

[1] WPA: The Work Projects Administration was an agency established during the depression to provide jobs.

them—too late for Emily. She does not smile easily, let alone almost always as her brothers and sisters do. Her face is closed and somber, but when she wants, how fluid. You must have seen it in her pantomimes, you spoke of her rare gift for comedy on the stage that rouses a laughter out of the audience so dear they applaud and applaud and do not want to let her go.

Where does it come from, that comedy? There was none of it in her when she came back to me that second time, after I had had to send her away again. She had a new daddy now to learn to love, and I think perhaps it was a better time. Except when we left her alone nights, telling ourselves she was old enough.

"Can't you go some other time Mommy, like tomorrow?" she would ask. "Will it be just a little while you'll be gone? Do you promise?"

The time we came back, the front door open, the clock on the floor in the hall. She rigid awake. "It wasn't just a little while. I didn't cry. I called you three times, just three times, and then I ran downstairs to open the door so you could come faster. The clock talked loud, I threw it away, it scared me what it talked."

She said the clock talked loud that night I went to the hospital to have Susan. She was delirious with the fever that comes before red measles, but she was fully conscious all the week I was gone and the week after we were home when she could not come near the new baby or me.

She did not get well. She stayed skeleton thin, not wanting to eat, and night after night she had nightmares. She would call for me, and I would sleepily call back, "you're all right, darling, go to sleep, it's just a dream," and if she still called, in a sterner voice, "now go to sleep Emily, there's nothing to hurt you." Twice, only twice, when I had to get up for Susan anyhow, I went in to sit with her.

Now when it is too late (as if she would let me hold and comfort her like I do the others) I get up and go to her at her moan or restless stirring. "Are you awake? Can I get you something?" And the answer is always the same: "No, I'm all right, go back to sleep Mother."

They persuaded me at the clinic to send her away to a convalescent home in the country where "she can have the kind of food and care you can't manage for her, and you'll be free to concentrate on the new baby." They still send children to that place. I see pictures on the society page of sleek young women planning affairs to raise money for it, or dancing at the affairs, or decorating Easter eggs or filling Christmas stockings for the children.

They never have a picture of the children so I do not know if they still wear those gigantic red bows and the ravaged looks on the every other Sunday when parents can come to visit "unless otherwise notified"—as we were notified the first six weeks.

Oh it is a handsome place, green lawns and tall trees and fluted flower beds. High up on the balconies of each cottage the children stand, the girls in their red bows and white dresses, the boys in white suits and giant red ties. The parents stand below shrieking up to be heard and the children shriek down to be heard, and between them the invisible wall "Not To Be Contaminated by Parental Germs or Physical Affection."

There was a tiny girl who always stood hand in hand with Emily. Her parents never came. One visit she was gone. "They moved her to Rose Cottage," Emily shouted in explanation. "They don't like you to love anybody here."

She wrote once a week, the labored writing of a seven-year-old. "I am fine. How is the baby. If I write my leter nicly I will have a star. Love." There never was a star. We wrote every other day, letters she could never hold or keep but only hear read—once. "We simply do not have room for children to keep any personal possessions," they patiently explained when we pieced one Sunday's shrieking together to plead how much it would mean to Emily to keep her letters and cards.

Each visit she looked frailer. "She isn't eating," they told us.

(They had runny eggs for breakfast or mush with lumps, Emily said later, I'd hold it in my mouth and not swallow. Nothing ever tasted good, just when they had chicken.)

It took us eight months to get her released home, and only the fact that she gained back so little of her seven lost pounds convinced the social worker.

I used to try to hold and love her after she came back, but her body would stay stiff, and after a while she'd push away. She ate little. Food sickened her, and I think much of life too. Oh she had physical lightness and brightness, twinkling by on skates, bouncing like a ball up and down up and down over the jump rope, skimming over the hill; but these were momentary.

She fretted about her appearance, thin and dark and foreign-looking at a time when every little girl was supposed to look or thought she should look a chubby blond replica of Shirley Temple. The doorbell sometimes rang for her, but no one seemed to come and play in the house or be a best friend. Maybe because we moved so much.

There was a boy she loved painfully through two school semesters. Months later she told me how she had taken pennies from my purse to buy him candy. "Licorice was his favorite and I brought him some every day, but he still liked Jennifer better'n me. Why Mommy why?" The kind of question for which there is no answer.

School was a worry to her. She was not glib or quick in a world where glibness and quickness were easily confused with ability to learn. To her over-worked and exasperated teachers she was an overconscientious "slow learner" who kept trying to catch up and was absent entirely too often.

I let her be absent, though sometimes the illness was imaginary. How different from my now-strictness about attendance with the others. I wasn't working. We had a new baby, I was home anyhow. Sometimes, after Susan grew old enough, I would keep her home from school, too, to have them all together.

Mostly Emily had asthma, and her breathing, harsh and labored, would fill the house with a curiously tranquil sound. I would bring the two old dresser mirrors and her boxes of collections to her bed. She would select beads and single earrings, bottle tops and shells, dried flowers and pebbles, old postcards and scraps, all sorts of oddments; then she and Susan would play Kingdom, setting up landscapes and furniture, peopling them with action.

Those were the only times of peaceful companionship between her and Susan. I have edged away from it, that poisonous feeling between them, that terrible balancing of hurts and needs I had to do between the two, and did so badly, those earlier years.

Oh there are conflicts between the others too, each one human, needing, demanding, hurting, taking—but only between Emily and Susan, no, Emily toward Susan that corroding resentment. It seems so obvious on the surface, yet it is not obvious. Susan, the second child, Susan, golden and curly haired and chubby, quick and articulate and assured, everything in appearance and manner Emily was not; Susan, not able to resist Emily's precious things, losing or sometimes clumsily breaking them; Susan telling jokes and riddles to company for applause while Emily sat silent (to say to me later: that was *my* riddle, Mother, I told it to Susan); Susan, who for all the five years' difference in age was just a year behind Emily in developing physically.

I am glad for that slow physical development that widened the difference between her and her contemporaries, though she suffered over it. She was too vulnerable for that terrible world of youthful competition, of preening and parading, of constant measuring of yourself against every other, of envy: "If I had that copper hair," or "If I had that skin . . ." She tormented herself enough about not looking like the others, there was enough of the unsureness, the having to be conscious of words before you speak, the constant caring—what are they thinking of me? what kind of an impression am I making—without having it all magnified unendurably by the merciless physical drives.

Ronnie is calling. He is wet and I change him. It is rare there is such a cry now. That time of motherhood is almost behind me when the ear is not one's own but must always be racked and listening for the child cry, the child call. We sit for a while and I hold him, looking out over the city spread in charcoal with its soft aisles of light.

."*Shoogily*," he breathes and curls closer. I carry him back to bed, asleep. *Shoogily.* A funny word, a family word, inherited from Emily, invented by her to say: *comfort.*

In this and other ways she leaves her seal, I say aloud. And startle at my saying it. What do I mean? What did I start to gather together, to try and make coherent? I was at the terrible, growing years. War years. I do not remember them well. I was working again, there were four smaller ones now, there was not time for her. She had to help be a mother, and housekeeper, and shopper. She had to set her seal. Mornings of crisis and near hysteria trying to get lunches packed, hair combed, coats and shoes found, everyone to school or Child Care on time, the baby ready for transportation. And always the paper scribbled on by a smaller one, the book looked at by Susan then mislaid, the homework not done. Running out to that huge school where she was one, she was lost, she was a drop; suffering over her unpreparedness, stammering and unsure in her classes.

There was so little time left at night after the kids were bedded down. She would struggle over books, always eating (it was in those years she developed her enormous appetite that is legendary in our family) and I would be ironing, or preparing food for the next day, or writing V-mail to Bill, or tending the baby. Sometimes, to make me laugh, or out of her despair, she would imitate happenings or types at school.

I think I said once: "Why don't you do something like this in the school amateur show?" One morning she phoned me at work, hardly understandable through the weeping: "Mother, I did it. I won, I won; they gave me first prize; they clapped and clapped and wouldn't let me go."

Now suddenly she was Somebody, and as imprisoned in her difference as she had been in her anonymity.

She began to be asked to perform at other high schools, even in colleges, then at city and state-wide affairs. The first one we went to, I only recognized her that first moment when thin, shy, she almost drowned herself into the curtains. Then: Was this Emily? the control, the command, the convulsing and deadly clowning, the spell, then the roaring, stamping audience, unwilling to let this rare and precious laughter out of their lives.

Afterwards: You ought to do something about her with a gift like that—but without money or knowing how, what does one do? We have left it all to her, and the gift has as often eddied inside, clogged and clotted, as been used and growing.

She is coming. She runs up the stairs two at a time with her light graceful step, and I know she is happy tonight. Whatever it was that occasioned your call did not happen today.

"Aren't you ever going to finish the ironing, Mother? Whistler painted his mother in a rocker. I'd have to paint mine standing over an ironing board." This is one of her communicative nights and she tells me everything and nothing as she fixes herself a plate of food out of the icebox.

She is so lovely. Why did you want me to come in at all? Why were you concerned? She will find her way.

She starts up the stairs to bed. "Don't get *me* up with the rest in the morning." "But I thought you were having midterms." "Oh, those," she comes back in and says quite lightly, "in a couple of years when we'll all be atom-dead they won't matter a bit."

She has said it before. She *believes* it. But because I have been dredging the past, and all that compounds a human being is so heavy and meaningful in me, I cannot endure it tonight.

I will never total it all. I will never come in to say: She was a child seldom smiled at. Her father left me before she was a year old. I had to work away from her her first six years when there was work, or I sent her home and to his relatives. There were years she had care she hated. She was dark and thin and foreign-looking in a world where the prestige went to blondness and curly hair and dimples, she was slow where glibness was prized. She was a child of anxious, not proud, love. We were poor and could not afford for her the soil of easy growth. I was a young mother, I was a distracted mother. There were the other children pushing up, demanding. Her younger sister seemed all that she was not. There were years she did not want me to touch her. She kept too much in herself, her life was such she had to keep too much in herself. My wisdom came too late. She has much to her and probably little will come of it. She is a child of her age, of depression, of war, of fear.

Let her be. So all that is in her will not bloom—but in how many does it? There is still enough left to live by. Only help her to know —help make it so there is cause for her to know—that she is more than this dress on the ironing board, helpless before the iron.

Insight

1. "She's a youngster who needs help," states the caller from school. What help do you think Emily needs? Do you think it likely she will receive it? Explain.

2. How would you characterize the mother's feelings about Emily? Does she appear to understand her daughter? Does she seem to feel any guilt about Emily's present state of mind? Explain.

3. Why does Emily's mother find it so difficult "to remember, to sift, to weigh, to estimate, to total"? Do you think this difficulty is a common one for all people, or is it something unique to this particular situation? Explain.

4. What do you learn about the mother as a person from her comment about "becoming engulfed with all I did or did not do, with what should have been and what cannot be helped"?

5. What effect on the eventual formation of Emily's character do the other children in the family have? Why does she feel a "corroding resentment" toward Susan? What "seal" does Emily leave on her brothers and sisters?

6. How does Emily appear to view the world in which she finds herself at nineteen? Why does her mother find this attitude difficult to "endure"?

littLe giRL, MY stRing bean, MY Lovely woMAN

Anne Sexton

My daughter, at eleven
(almost twelve), is like a garden.

Oh, darling! Born in that sweet birthday suit
and having owned it and known it for so long,
now you must watch high noon enter—   5
noon, that ghost hour.
Oh, funny little girl—this one under a blueberry sky,
this one! How can I say that I've known
just what you know and just where you are?   *Cannot get into someone
                                                     else's skin*

It's not a strange place, this odd home   10
where your face sits in my hand
so full of distance,
so full of its immediate fever.
The summer has seized you,
as when, last month in Amalfi, I saw   15
lemons as large as your desk-side globe—
that miniature map of the world—   *nubile, bursting w youth*
and I could mention, too,   *(entering womanhood*
the market stalls of mushrooms
and garlic buds all engorged.   20
Or I think even of the orchard next door,
where the berries are done
and the apples are beginning to swell.
And once, with our first backyard,
I remember I planted an acre of yellow beans   25
we couldn't eat.

Oh, little girl,   *poet speaks aloud*
my stringbean,
how do you grow?
You grow this way.
You are too many to eat.   *too many facts*   30

219

I hear
as in a dream
the conversation of the old wives
speaking of *womanhood*.   35
I remember that I heard nothing myself.
I was alone.
I waited like a target.

Let high noon enter—
the hour of the ghosts.   40
Once the Romans believed
that noon was the ghost hour,
and I can believe it, too,
under that startling sun,
and someday they will come to you,   45
someday, men bare to the waist, young Romans
at noon where they belong,
with ladders and hammers
while no one sleeps.

But before they enter   50
I will have said,
Your bones are lovely,
and before their strange hands
there was always this hand that formed.

Oh, darling, let your body in,   55
let it tie you in,
in comfort.
What I want to say, Linda,
is that women are born twice.
If I could have watched you grow   60
as a magical mother might,
if I could have seen through my magical transparent belly,
there would have been such ripening within:
your embryo,
the seed taking on its own,   65
life clapping the bedpost,
bones from the pond,
thumbs and two mysterious eyes,
the awfully human head,
the heart jumping like a puppy,   70
the important lungs,
the becoming—

221

while it becomes!
as it does now,
a world of its own,   75
a delicate place.

I say hello
to such shakes and knockings and high jinks,
such music, such sprouts,
such dancing-mad-bears of music,   80
such necessary sugar,
such goings-on!

Oh, little girl,
my stringbean,
how do you grow?   85
You grow this way.
You are too many to eat.

What I want to say, Linda,
is that there is nothing in your body that lies.
All that is new is telling the truth.   90
I'm here, that somebody else,
an old tree in the background.

Darling,
stand still at your door,
sure of yourself, a white stone, a good stone—   95
as exceptional as laughter
you will strike fire,
that new thing!

222

AMUSING OUR dAUGHTERS

Carolyn Kizer

for Robert Creeley

We don't lack people here on the Northern coast,
But they are people one meets, not people one cares for.
So I bundle my daughters into the car
And with my brother poets, go to visit you, brother.

Here come your guests! A swarm of strangers and children;   5
But the strangers write verses, the children are daughters like
    yours.
We bed down on mattresses, cots, roll up on the floor:
Outside, burly old fruit trees in mist and rain;
In every room, bundles asleep like larvae.

We waken and count our daughters. Otherwise, nothing
    happens.   10
You feed them sweet rolls and melon, drive them all to the
    zoo;
Patiently, patiently, ever the father, you answer their questions.
Later we eat again, drink, listen to poems.
Nothing occurs, though we are aware you have three
    daughters
Who last year had four. But even death becomes part of our
    ease: 15
Poems, parenthood, sorrow, all we have learned
From these, of tenderness, holds us together
In the center of life, entertaining daughters
By firelight, with cake and songs.

You, my brother, are a good and violent drinker,   20
Good at reciting short-line or long-line poems.
In time we will lose all our daughters, you and I,
Be temperate, venerable, content to stay in one place,
Sending our messages over the mountains and waters.

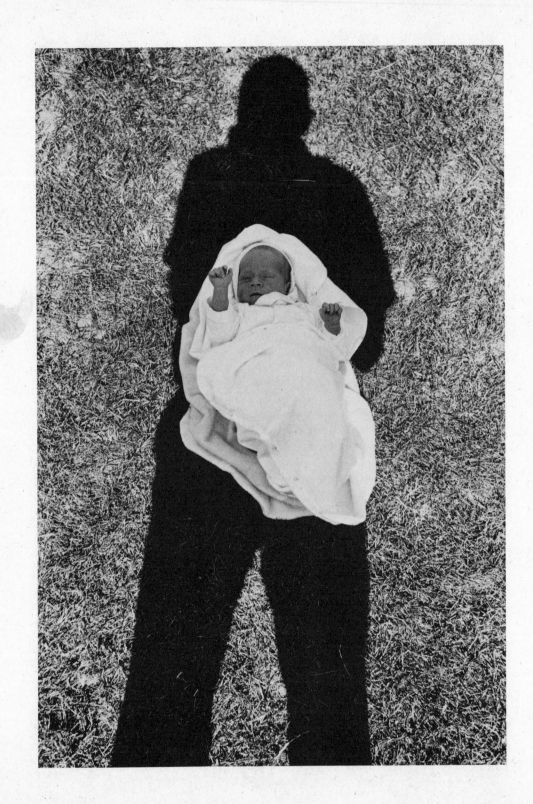

MORNING SONG

Sylvia Plath

Love set you going like a fat gold watch.
The midwife slapped your footsoles, and your bald cry
Took its place among the elements.

Our voices echo, magnifying your arrival. New statue.
In a drafty museum, your nakedness
Shadows our safety. We stand round blankly as walls.   5

I'm no more your mother
Than the cloud that distils a mirror to reflect its own slow
Effacement at the wind's hand.

All night your moth-breath   10
Flickers among the flat pink roses. I wake to listen:
A far sea moves in my ear.

One cry, and I stumble from bed, cow-heavy and floral
In my Victorian nightgown.
Your mouth opens clean as a cat's. The window square   15

Whitens and swallows its dull stars. And now you try
Your handful of notes;
The clear vowels rise like balloons.

SLEEP, DARLING

Sappho

Sleep, darling   *lullabye*

I have a small
daughter called
Cleis, who is

like a golden   *very 5 precious*
flower

    I wouldn't
take all Croesus'
kingdom with love
thrown in, for her   10

*ability return everything to sell
wealthy   whole world
wealthy key*

*How can you express how much you love a
person comparisons to equal - nothing equal
words avail enough exaggeration - nothing equal*

soft roches than any other blooming

Insight

1. The speaker of each of these poems is a mother thinking about her child. What attitudes toward the child does each speaker reveal? Which of the speakers do you feel displays a more open sense of loving? Which one is more detached?
2. The emotional atmosphere of a poem is its mood. This mood may be among others, one of joy, serenity, depression, indifference, triumph. Which of these poems reveals a joyous mood? A serene mood? What factors helped to create these moods?

EVERYThiNG ThAT RiSES MUST CONVERGE

Flannery O'Connor

Her doctor had told Julian's mother that she must lose twenty pounds on account of her blood pressure, so on Wednesday nights Julian had to take her downtown on the bus for a reducing class at the Y. The reducing class was designed for working girls over fifty, who weighed from 165 to 200 pounds. His mother was one of the slimmer ones, but she said ladies did not tell their age or weight. She would not ride the buses by herself at night since they had been integrated, and because the reducing class was one of her few pleasures, necessary for her health, and *free*, she said Julian could at least put himself out to take her, considering all she did for him. Julian did not like to consider all she did for him, but every Wednesday night he braced himself and took her.

She was almost ready to go, standing before the hall mirror, putting on her hat, while he, his hands behind him, appeared pinned to the door frame, waiting like Saint Sebastian for the arrows to begin piercing him. The hat was new and had cost her seven dollars and a half. She kept saying, "Maybe I shouldn't have paid that for it. No, I shouldn't have. I'll take it off and return it tomorrow. I shouldn't have bought it."

Julian raised his eyes to heaven. "Yes, you should have bought it," he said. "Put it on and let's go." It was a hideous hat. A purple velvet flap came down on one side of it and stood up on the other: the rest of it was green and looked like a cushion with the stuffing out. He decided it was less comical than jaunty and pathetic. Everything that gave her pleasure was small and depressed him.

She lifted the hat one more time and set it down slowly on top of her head. Two wings of gray hair protruded on either side of her florid face, but her eyes, sky-blue, were as innocent and untouched by experience as they must have been when she was ten. Were it not that she was a widow who had struggled fiercely to feed and clothe and put him through school and who was supporting him still, "until he got on his feet," she might have been a little girl that he had to take to town.

"It's all right, it's all right," he said. "Let's go." He opened the door himself and started down the walk to get her going. The sky was a dying violet and the houses stood out darkly against it, bulbous liver-colored monstrosities of a uniform ugliness though no two were alike. Since this had been a fashionable neighborhood forty years ago, his mother persisted in thinking they did well to have an apartment in it. Each house had a narrow collar of dirt around it in which sat, usually, a grubby child. Julian walked with his hands in his pockets, his head down and thrust forward and his eyes glazed with the determination to make himself completely numb during the time he would be sacrificed to her pleasure.

The door closed and he turned to find the dumpy figure, surmounted by the atrocious hat, coming toward him. "Well," she said, "you only live once and paying a little more for it, I at least won't meet myself coming and going."

"Some day I'll start making money," Julian said gloomily—he knew he never would—"and you can have one of those jokes whenever you take the fit." But first they would move. He visualized a place where the nearest neighbors would be three miles away on either side.

"I think you're doing fine," she said, drawing on her gloves. "You've only been out of school a year. Rome wasn't built in a day."

She was one of the few members of the Y reducing class who arrived in hat and gloves and who had a son who had been to college. "It takes time," she said, "and the world is in such a mess. This hat looked better on me than any of the others, though when she brought it out I said, 'Take that thing back. I wouldn't have it on my head,' and she said, 'Now wait till you see it on,' and when she put it on me, I said, 'We-ull,' and she said, 'If you ask me, that hat does something for you and you do something for the hat, and besides,' she said, 'with that hat, you won't meet yourself coming and going.' "

Julian thought he could have stood his lot better if she had been selfish, if she had been an old hag who drank and screamed at him. He walked along, saturated in depression, as if in the midst of his martyrdom he had lost his faith. Catching sight of his long, hopeless, irritated face, she stopped suddenly with a grief-stricken look, and pulled back on his arm. "Wait on me," she said. "I'm going back to the house and take this thing off and tomorrow I'm going to return it. I was out of my head. I can pay the gas bill with the seven-fifty."

He caught her arm in a vicious grip. "You are not going to take it back," he said. "I like it."

"Well," she said, "I don't think I ought . . ."

"Shut up and enjoy it," he muttered, more depressed than ever.

"With the world in the mess it's in," she said, "it's a wonder we can enjoy anything. I tell you, the bottom rail is on the top."

Julian sighed.

"Of course," she said, "if you know who you are, you can go anywhere." She said this every time he took her to the reducing class. "Most of them in it are not our kind of people," she said, "but I can be gracious to anybody. I know who I am."

"They don't give a damn for your graciousness," Julian said savagely. "Knowing who you are is good for one generation only. You haven't the foggiest idea where you stand now or who you are."

She stopped and allowed her eyes to flash at him. "I most certainly do know who I am," she said, "and if you don't know who you are, I'm ashamed of you."

"Oh hell," Julian said.

"Your great-grandfather was a former governor of this state," she said. "Your grandfather was a prosperous landowner. Your grandmother was a Godhigh."

"Will you look around you," he said tensely, "and see where you are now?" and he swept his arm jerkily out to indicate the neighborhood, which the growing darkness at least made less dingy.

"You remain what you are," she said. "Your great-grandfather had a plantation and two hundred slaves."

"There are no more slaves," he said irritably.

"They were better off when they were," she said. He groaned to see that she was off on that topic. She rolled onto it every few days like a train on an open track. He knew every stop, every junction, every swamp along the way, and knew the exact point at which her conclusion would roll majestically into the station: "It's ridiculous. It's simply not realistic. They should rise, yes, but on their own side of the fence."

"Let's skip it," Julian said.

"The ones I feel sorry for," she said, "are the ones that are half white. They're tragic."

"Will you skip it?"

"Suppose we were half white. We would certainly have mixed feelings."

"I have mixed feelings now," he groaned.

"Well let's talk about something pleasant," she said. "I remember going to Grandpa's when I was a little girl. Then the house had double stairways that went up to what was really the second floor—all the cooking was done on the first. I used to like to stay down in the kitchen on account of the way the walls smelled. I would sit with my nose pressed against the plaster and take deep breaths. Actually the place belonged to the Godhighs but your grandfather Chestny paid the mortgage and saved it for them. They were in reduced circumstances," she said, "but reduced or not, they never forgot who they were."

"Doubtless that decayed mansion reminded them," Julian muttered. He never spoke of it without contempt or thought of it without longing. He had seen it once when he was a child before it had been sold. The double stairways had rotted and been torn down. Negroes were living in it. But it remained in his mind as his mother had known it. It appeared in his dreams regularly. He would stand on the wide porch, listening to the rustle of oak leaves, then wander through the high-ceilinged hall into the parlor that opened onto it and gaze at the worn rugs and faded draperies. It occurred to him that it was he, not she, who could have appreciated it. He preferred its threadbare elegance to anything he could name and it was because of it that all the neighborhoods they had lived in had been a torment to him—whereas she had hardly known the difference. She called her insensitivity "being adjustable."

"And I remember the old darky who was my nurse, Caroline. There was no better person in the world. I've always had a great respect for my colored friends," she said. "I'd do anything in the world for them and they'd . . ."

"Will you for God's sake get off that subject?" Julian said. When he got on a bus by himself, he made it a point to sit down beside a Negro, in reparation as it were for his mother's sins.

"You're mighty touchy tonight," she said. "Do you feel all right?"

"Yes I feel all right," he said. "Now lay off."

She pursed her lips. "Well, you certainly are in a vile humor," she observed. "I just won't speak to you at all."

They had reached the bus stop. There was no bus in sight and Julian, his hands still jammed in his pockets and his head thrust forward, scowled down the empty street. The frustration of having to wait on the bus as well as ride on it began to creep up his neck like a hot hand. The presence of his mother was borne in upon him as she gave a pained sigh. He looked at her bleakly. She was holding herself very erect under the preposterous hat, wearing it like a banner of her imaginary dignity. There was in him an evil urge to break her spirit. He suddenly unloosened his tie and pulled it off and put it in his pocket.

She stiffened. "Why must you look like *that* when you take me to town?" she said. "Why must you deliberately embarrass me?"

"If you'll never learn where you are," he said, "you can at least learn where I am."

"You look like a—thug," she said.

"Then I must be one," he murmured.

"I'll just go home," she said. "I will not bother you. If you can't do a little thing like that for me . . ."

Rolling his eyes upward, he put his tie back on. "Restored to my class," he muttered. He thrust his face toward her and hissed, "True culture is in the mind, the *mind*," he said, and tapped his head, "the mind."

"It's in the heart," she said, "and in how you do things and how you do things is because of who you *are*."

"Nobody in the damn bus cares who you are."

"I care who I am," she said icily.

The lighted bus appeared on top of the next hill and as it approached, they moved out into the street to meet it. He put his hand under her elbow and hoisted her up on the creaking step. She entered with a little smile, as if she were going into a drawing room where everyone had been waiting for her. While he put in the tokens, she sat down on one of the broad front seats for three which faced the aisle. A thin woman with protruding teeth and long yellow hair was sitting on the end of it. His mother moved up beside her and left room for Julian beside herself. He sat down and looked at the floor across the aisle where a pair of thin feet in red and white canvas sandals were planted.

His mother immediately began a general conversation meant to attract anyone who felt like talking. "Can it get any hotter?" she said and removed from her purse a folding fan, black with a Japanese scene on it, which she began to flutter before her.

"I reckon it might could," the woman with the protruding teeth said, "but I know for a fact my apartment couldn't get no hotter."

"It must get the afternoon sun," his mother said. She sat forward and looked up and down the bus. It was half filled. Everybody was white. "I see we have the bus to ourselves," she said. Julian cringed.

"For a change," said the woman across the aisle, the owner of the red and white canvas sandals. "I come on one the other day and they were thick as fleas—up front and all through."

"The world is in a mess everywhere," his mother said. "I don't know how we've let it get in this fix."

"What gets my goat is all those boys from good families stealing automobile tires," the woman with the protruding teeth said. "I told my boy, I said you may not be rich but you been raised right and if I ever catch you in any such mess, they can send you on to the reformatory. Be exactly where you belong."

"Training tells," his mother said. "Is your boy in high school?"

"Ninth grade," the woman said.

"My son just finished college last year. He wants to write but he's selling typewriters until he gets started," his mother said.

The woman leaned forward and peered at Julian. He threw her such a malevolent look that she subsided against the seat. On the floor across the aisle there was an abandoned newspaper. He got up and got it and opened it out in front of him. His mother discreetly continued the conversation in a lower tone but the woman across the aisle said in a loud voice, "Well that's nice. Selling typewriters is close to writing. He can go right from one to the other."

"I tell him," his mother said, "that Rome wasn't built in a day."

Behind the newspaper Julian was withdrawing into the inner compartment of his mind where he spent most of his time. This was a kind of mental bubble in which he established himself when he could not bear to be a part of what was going on around him. From it he could see out and judge but in it he was safe from any kind of penetration from without. It was the only place where he felt free of the general idiocy of his fellows. His mother had never entered it but from it he could see her with absolute clarity.

The old lady was clever enough and he thought that if she had started from any of the right premises, more might have been expected of her. She lived according to the laws of her own fantasy world, outside of which he had never seen her set foot. The law of it was to sacrifice herself for him after she had first created the necessity to do so by making a mess of things. If he had permitted her sacrifices, it was only because her lack of foresight had made them necessary. All of her life had been a struggle to act like a Chestny without the Chestny goods, and to give him everything she thought a Chestny ought to have; but since, said she, it was fun to struggle, why complain? And when you had won, as she had won, what fun to look back on the hard times! He could not forgive her that she had enjoyed the struggle and that she thought *she* had won.

What she meant when she said she had won was that she had brought him up successfully and had sent him to college and that he had turned out so well—good looking (her teeth had gone unfilled so that his could be straightened), intelligent (he realized he was too intelligent to be a success), and with a future ahead of him (there was of course no future ahead of him). She excused his gloominess on the grounds that he was still growing up and his radical ideas on his lack of practical experience. She said he didn't yet know a thing about "life," that he hadn't even entered the real world—when already he was as disenchanted with it as a man of fifty.

The further irony of all this was that in spite of her, he had turned out so well. In spite of going to only a third-rate college, he had, on his own initiative, come out with a first-rate education; in spite of growing up dominated by a small mind, he had ended up with a large one; in spite of all her foolish views, he was free of prejudice and unafraid to face facts. Most miraculous of all, instead of being blinded by love for her as she was for him, he had cut himself emotionally free of her and could see her with complete objectivity. He was not dominated by his mother.

The bus stopped with a sudden jerk and shook him from his meditation. A woman from the back lurched forward with little steps and barely escaped falling in his newspaper as she righted herself. She got off and a large Negro got on. Julian kept his paper lowered to watch.

It gave him a certain satisfaction to see injustice in daily operation. It confirmed his view that with a few exceptions there was no one worth knowing within a radius of three hundred miles. The Negro was well dressed and carried a briefcase. He looked around and then sat down on the other end of the seat where the woman with the red and white canvas sandals was sitting. He immediately unfolded a newspaper and obscured himself behind it. Julian's mother's elbow at once prodded insistently into his ribs. "Now you see why I won't ride on these buses by myself," she whispered.

The woman with the red and white canvas sandals had risen at the same time the Negro sat down and had gone further back in the bus and taken the seat of the woman who had got off. His mother leaned forward and cast her an approving look.

Julian rose, crossed the aisle, and sat down in the place of the woman with the canvas sandals. From this position, he looked serenely across at his mother. Her face had turned an angry red. He stared at her, making his eyes the eyes of a stranger. He felt his tension suddenly lift as if he had openly declared war on her.

He would have liked to get in conversation with the Negro and to talk with him about art or politics or any subject that would be above the comprehension of those around them, but the man remained entrenched behind his paper. He was either ignoring the change of seating or had never noticed it. There was no way for Julian to convey his sympathy.

His mother kept her eyes fixed reproachfully on his face. The woman with the protruding teeth was looking at him avidly as if he were a type of monster new to her.

"Do you have a light?" he asked the Negro.

Without looking away from his paper, the man reached in his pocket and handed him a packet of matches.

"Thanks," Julian said. For a moment he held the matches foolishly. A NO SMOKING sign looked down upon him from over the door. This alone would not have deterred him; he had no cigarettes. He had quit smoking some months before because he could not afford it. "Sorry," he muttered and handed back the matches. The Negro lowered the paper and gave him an annoyed look. He took the matches and raised the paper again.

His mother continued to gaze at him but she did not take advantage of his momentary discomfort. Her eyes retained their battered look. Her face seemed to be unnaturally red, as if her blood pressure had risen. Julian allowed no glimmer of sympathy to show on his face. Having got the advantage, he wanted desperately to keep it and carry it through. He would have liked to teach her a lesson that would last her a while, but there seemed no way to continue the point. The Negro refused to come out from behind his paper.

Julian folded his arms and looked stolidly before him, facing her but as if he did not see her, as if he had ceased to recognize her existence. He visualized a scene in which, the bus having reached their stop, he would remain in his seat and when she said, "Aren't you going to get off?" he would look at her as at a stranger who had rashly addressed him. The corner they got off on was usually deserted, but it was well lighted and it would not hurt her to walk by herself the four blocks to the Y. He decided to wait until the time came and then decide whether or not he would let her get off by herself. He would have to be at the Y at ten to bring her back, but he could leave her wondering if he was going to show up. There was no reason for her to think she could always depend on him.

He retired again into the high-ceilinged room sparsely settled with large pieces of antique furniture. His soul expanded momentarily but then he became aware of his mother across from him and the vision shriveled. He studied her coldly. Her feet in little pumps dangled like a child's and did not quite reach the floor. She was training on him an exaggerated look of reproach. He felt completely detached from her. At that moment he could with pleasure have slapped her as he would have slapped a particularly obnoxious child in his charge.

He began to imagine various unlikely ways by which he could teach her a lesson. He might make friends with some distinguished Negro professor or lawyer and bring him home to spend the evening. He would be entirely justified but her blood pressure would rise to 300. He could not push her to the extent of making her have a stroke, and moreover, he had never been successful at making any Negro friends. He had tried to strike up an acquaintance on the bus with some of the better types, with ones that looked like professors or ministers or lawyers. One morning he had sat down next to a distinguished-looking dark brown man who had answered his questions with a sonorous solemnity but who had turned out to be an undertaker. Another day he had sat down beside a cigar-smoking Negro with a diamond ring on his finger, but after a few stilted pleasantries, the Negro had rung the buzzer and risen, slipping two lottery tickets into Julian's hand as he climbed over him to leave.

He imagined his mother lying desperately ill and his being able to secure only a Negro doctor for her. He toyed with that idea for a few minutes and then dropped it for a momentary vision of himself participating as a sympathizer in a sit-in demonstration. This was possible but he did not linger with it. Instead, he approached the ultimate horror. He brought home a beautiful suspiciously Negroid woman. Prepare yourself, he said. There is nothing you can do about it. This is the woman I've chosen. She's intelligent, dignified, even good, and she's suffered and she hasn't thought it *fun*. Now persecute us, go ahead and persecute us. Drive her out of here, but remember, you're driving me too. His eyes were narrowed and through the indignation he had generated, he saw his mother across the aisle, purple-faced, shrunken to the dwarflike proportions of her moral nature, sitting like a mummy beneath the ridiculous banner of her hat.

He was tilted out of his fantasy again as the bus stopped. The door opened with a sucking hiss and out of the dark a large, gaily dressed, sullen-looking colored woman got on with a little boy. The child, who might have been four, had on a short plaid suit and a Tyrolean hat with a blue feather in it. Julian hoped that he would sit down beside him and that the woman would push in beside his mother. He could think of no better arrangement.

As she waited for her tokens, the woman was surveying the seating possibilities—he hoped with the idea of sitting where she was least wanted. There was something familiar-looking about her but Julian could not place what it was. She was a giant of a woman. Her face was set not only to meet opposition but to seek it out. The downward tilt of her large lower lip was like a warning sign: DON'T TAMPER WITH ME. Her bulging figure was encased in a green crepe dress and her feet overflowed in red shoes. She had on a hideous hat. A purple velvet flap came down on one side of it and stood up on the other; the rest of it was green and looked like a cushion with the stuffing out. She carried a mammoth red pocketbook that bulged throughout as if it were stuffed with rocks.

To Julian's disappointment, the little boy climbed up on the empty seat beside his mother. His mother lumped all children, black and white, into the common category, "cute," and she thought little Negroes were on the whole cuter than little white children. She smiled at the little boy as he climbed on the seat.

Meanwhile the woman was bearing down upon the empty seat beside Julian. To his annoyance, she squeezed herself into it. He saw his mother's face change as the woman settled herself next to him and he realized with satisfaction that this was more objectionable to her than it was to him. Her face seemed almost gray and there was a look of dull recognition in her eyes, as if suddenly she had sickened at some awful confrontation. Julian saw that it was because she and the woman had, in a sense, swapped sons. Though his mother would not realize the symbolic significance of this, she would feel it. His amusement showed plainly on his face.

The woman next to him muttered something unintelligible to herself. He was conscious of a kind of bristling next to him, muted growling like that of an angry cat. He could not see anything but the red pocketbook upright on the bulging green thighs. He visualized the woman as she had stood waiting for her tokens—the ponderous

figure, rising from the red shoes upward over the solid hips, the mammoth bosom, the haughty face, to the green and purple hat.

His eyes widened.

The vision of the two hats, identical, broke upon him with the radiance of a brilliant sunrise. His face was suddenly lit with joy. He could not believe that Fate had thrust upon his mother such a lesson. He gave a loud chuckle so that she would look at him and see that he saw. She turned her eyes on him slowly. The blue in them seemed to have turned a bruised purple. For a moment he had an uncomfortable sense of her innocence, but it lasted only a second before principle rescued him. Justice entitled him to laugh. His grin hardened until it said to her as plainly as if he were saying aloud: Your punishment exactly fits your pettiness. This should teach you a permanent lesson.

Her eyes shifted to the woman. She seemed unable to bear looking at him and to find the woman preferable. He became conscious again of the bristling presence at his side. The woman was rumbling like a volcano about to become active. His mother's mouth began to twitch slightly at one corner. With a sinking heart, he saw incipient signs of recovery on her face and realized that this was going to strike her suddenly as funny and was going to be no lesson at all. She kept her eyes on the woman and an amused smile came over her face as if the woman were a monkey that had stolen her hat. The little Negro was looking up at her with large fascinated eyes. He had been trying to attract her attention for some time.

"Carver!" the woman said suddenly. "Come heah!"

When he saw that the spotlight was on him at last, Carver drew his feet up and turned himself toward Julian's mother and giggled.

"Carver!" the woman said. "You heah me? Come heah!"

Carver slid down from the seat but remained squatting with his back against the base of it, his head turned slyly around toward Julian's mother, who was smiling at him. The woman reached a hand across the aisle and snatched him to her. He righted himself and hung backwards on her knees, grinning at Julian's mother. "Isn't he cute?" Julian's mother said to the woman with the protruding teeth.

"I reckon he is," the woman said without conviction.

The Negress yanked him upright but he eased out of her grip and shot across the aisle and scrambled, giggling wildly, onto the seat beside his love.

"I think he likes me," Julian's mother said, and smiled at the woman. It was the smile she used when she was being particularly gracious to an inferior. Julian saw everything lost. The lesson had rolled off her like rain on a roof.

The woman stood up and yanked the little boy off the seat as if she were snatching him from contagion. Julian could feel the rage in her at having no weapon like his mother's smile. She gave the child a sharp slap across his leg. He howled once and then thrust his head into her stomach and kicked his feet against her shins. "Behave," she said vehemently.

The bus stopped and the Negro who had been reading the newspaper got off. The woman moved over and set the little boy down with a thump between herself and Julian. She held him firmly by the knee. In a moment he put his hands in front of his face and peeped at Julian's mother through his fingers.

"I see yoooooooo!" she said and put her hand in front of her face and peeped at him.

The woman slapped his hand down. "Quit yo' foolishness," she said, "before I knock the living Jesus out of you!"

Julian was thankful that the next stop was theirs. He reached up and pulled the cord. The woman reached up and pulled it at the same time. Oh my God, he thought. He had the terrible intuition that when they got off the bus together, his mother would open her purse and give the little boy a nickel. The gesture would be as natural to her as breathing. The bus stopped and the woman got up and lunged to the front, dragging the child, who wished to stay on, after her. Julian and his mother got up and followed. As they neared the door, Julian tried to relieve her of her pocketbook.

"No," she murmured, "I want to give the little boy a nickel."

"No!" Julian hissed. "No!"

She smiled down at the child and opened her bag. The bus door opened and the woman picked him up by the arm and descended with him, hanging at her hip. Once in the street she set him down and shook him.

Julian's mother had to close her purse while she got down the bus step but as soon as her feet were on the ground, she opened it again and began to rummage inside. "I can't find but a penny," she whispered, "but it looks like a new one."

"Don't do it!" Julian said fiercely between his teeth. There was a streetlight on the corner and she hurried to get under it so that she could better see into her pocketbook. The woman was heading off rapidly down the street with the child still hanging backward on her hand.

"Oh little boy!" Julian's mother called and took a few quick steps and caught up with them just beyond the lamppost. "Here's a bright new penny for you," and she held out the coin, which shone bronze in the dim light.

The huge woman turned and for a moment stood, her shoulders lifted and her face frozen with frustrated rage, and stared at Julian's mother. Then all at once she seemed to explode like a piece of machinery that had been given one ounce of pressure too much. Julian saw the black fist swing out with the red pocketbook. He shut his eyes and cringed as he heard the woman shout, "He don't take nobody's pennies!" When he opened his eyes, the woman was disappearing down the street with the little boy staring wide-eyed over her shoulder. Julian's mother was sitting on the sidewalk.

"I told you not to do that," Julian said angrily. "I told you not to do that!"

He stood over her for a minute, gritting his teeth. Her legs were stretched out in front of her and her hat was on her lap. He squatted down and looked her in the face. It was totally expressionless. "You got exactly what you deserved," he said. "Now get up."

He picked up her pocketbook and put what had fallen out back in it. He picked the hat up off her lap. The penny caught his eye on the sidewalk and he picked that up and let it drop before her eyes into the purse. Then he stood up and leaned over and held his hands out to pull her up. She remained immobile. He sighed. Rising above them on either side were black apartment buildings, marked with irregular rectangles of light. At the end of the block a man came out of a door and walked off in the opposite direction. "All right," he said, "suppose somebody happens by and wants to know why you're sitting on the sidewalk?"

She took the hand and, breathing hard, pulled heavily up on it and then stood for a moment, swaying slightly as if the spots of light in the darkness were circling around her. Her eyes, shadowed and confused, finally settled on his face. He did not try to conceal his irritation. "I hope this teaches you a lesson," he said. She leaned forward and her eyes raked his face. She seemed trying to determine his identity. Then, as if she found nothing familiar about him, she started off with a headlong movement in the wrong direction.

"Aren't you going on to the Y?" he asked.

"Home," she muttered.

"Well, are we walking?"

For answer she kept going. Julian followed along, his hands behind him. He saw no reason to let the lesson she had had go without backing it up with an explanation of its meaning. She might as well be made to understand what had happened to her. "Don't think that was just an uppity Negro woman," he said. "That was the whole colored race which will no longer take your condescending pennies. That was your black double. She can wear the same hat as you, and to be sure," he added gratuitously (because he thought it was funny), "it looked better on her than it did on you. What all this means," he said, "is that the old world is gone. The old manners are obsolete and your graciousness is not worth a damn." He thought bitterly of the house that had been lost for him. "You aren't who you think you are," he said.

She continued to plow ahead, paying no attention to him. Her hair had come undone on one side. She dropped her pocketbook and took no notice. He stooped and picked it up and handed it to her but she did not take it.

"You needn't act as if the world had come to an end," he said, "because it hasn't. From now on you've got to live in a new world and face a few realities for a change. Buck up," he said, "it won't kill you."

She was breathing fast.

"Let's wait on the bus," he said.

"Home," she said thickly.

"I hate to see you behave like this," he said. "Just like a child. I should be able to expect more of you." He decided to stop where he was and make her stop and wait for a bus. "I'm not going any farther," he said, stopping. "We're going on the bus."

She continued to go on as if she had not heard him. He took a few steps and caught her arm and stopped her. He looked into her face and caught his breath. He was looking into a face he had never seen before. "Tell Grandpa to come get me," she said.

He stared, stricken.

"Tell Caroline to come get me," she said.

Stunned, he let her go and she lurched forward again, walking as if one leg were shorter than the other. A tide of darkness seemed to be sweeping her from him. "Mother!" he cried. "Darling, sweetheart, wait!" Crumpling, she fell to the pavement. He dashed forward and fell at her side, crying, "Mamma, Mamma!" He turned her over. Her face was fiercely distorted. One eye, large and staring, moved slightly to the left as if it had become unmoored. The other remained fixed on him, raked his face again, found nothing and closed.

"Wait here, wait here!" he cried and jumped up and began to run for help toward a cluster of lights he saw in the distance ahead of him. "Help, help!" he shouted, but his voice was thin, scarcely a thread of sound. The lights drifted farther away the faster he ran and his feet moved numbly as if they carried him nowhere. The tide of darkness seemed to sweep him back to her, postponing from moment to moment his entry into the world of guilt and sorrow.

Insight

1. Julian's mother is described as having "eyes, sky-blue ... as innocent and untouched by experience as they must have been when she was ten." In what ways is this description appropriate to her behavior on the bus?

2. How would you characterize Julian? Would you describe him as a simple or a complex person? Explain.

3. How would you characterize the relationship between Julian and his mother? How do you account for the little cruelties they impose on each other? What basic conflicts exist between them?

4. Why does Julian think that his lot would be "better if she had been selfish, if she had been an old hag who drank and screamed at him"?

5. Throughout the bus ride, Julian seeks to teach his mother "a permanent lesson." What specifically is the lesson he seeks to teach her? Does he succeed?

6. What does the title of the story mean?

A WOMAN MOURNED
by daughters

Adrienne Rich

Now, not a tear begun,
we sit here in your kitchen,
spent, you see, already.
You are swollen till you strain
this house and the whole sky.   5
You, whom we so often
succeeded in ignoring!
You are puffed up in death
like a corpse pulled from the sea;
we groan beneath your weight.   10
And yet you were a leaf,
a straw blown on the bed,
you had long since become
crisp as a dead insect.
What is it, if not you,   15
that settles on us now
like satin you pulled down
over our bridal heads?
What rises in our throats
like food you prodded in?   20
Nothing could be enough.
You breathe upon us now
through solid assertions
of yourself: teaspoons, goblets,
seas of carpet, a forest   25
of old plants to be watered,
an old man in an adjoining
room to be touched and fed.
And all this universe
dares us to lay a finger   30
anywhere, save exactly
as you would wish it done.

Insight
1. What is the attitude of the daughters toward their dead mother?
2. The poem's effect builds through the use of images taken from
   nature. What are some of the most effective images? In what ways
   do they contribute to the poem's overall effect?

THE little
bouilloux girl

Colette

The little Bouilloux girl was so lovely that even we children noticed
it. It is unusual for small girls to recognize beauty in one of themselves and pay homage to it. But there could be no disputing such
undeniable loveliness as hers. Whenever my mother met the little
Bouilloux girl in the street, she would stop her and bend over her as
she was wont to bend over her yellow tea-rose, her red flowering
cactus or her Azure Blue butterfly trustfully asleep on the scaly bark
of the pine tree. She would stroke her curly hair, golden as a half-
ripe chestnut, and her delicately tinted cheeks, and watch the incredible lashes flutter over her great dark eyes. She would observe
the glimmer of the perfect teeth in her peerless mouth, and when, at
last, she let the child go on her way, she would look after her, murmuring, "It's prodigious!"

Several years passed, bringing yet further graces to the little Bouilloux girl. There were certain occasions recorded by our admiration: a
prize-giving at which, shyly murmuring an unintelligible recitation,
she glowed through her tears like a peach under a summer shower.
The little Bouilloux girl's first communion caused a scandal: the same
evening, after vespers, she was seen drinking a half pint at the *Café
du Commerce*, with her father, the sawyer, and that night she danced,
already feminine and flirtatious, a little unsteady in her white slippers,
at the public ball.

With an arrogance to which she had accustomed us, she informed
us later, at school, that she was to be apprenticed.

"Oh! Who to?"

"To Madame Adolphe."

"Oh! And are you to get wages at once?"

"No. I'm only thirteen, I shall start earning next year."

She left us without emotion, and coldly we let her go. Already her
beauty isolated her and she had no friends at school, where she
learned very little. Her Sundays and her Thursdays brought no intimacy with us; they were spent with a family that was considered
"unsuitable," with girl cousins of eighteen well known for their

BOUILLOUX: pronounced boo • yoo'.

brazen behavior, and with brothers, cartwright apprentices, who sported ties at fourteen and smoked when they escorted their sister to the Parisian shooting-gallery at the fair or to the cheerful bar that the widow Pimelle had made so popular.

The very next morning on my way to school I met the little Bouilloux girl setting out for the dressmaker's workrooms, and I remained motionless, thunderstruck with jealous admiration, at the corner of the Rue des Soeurs, watching Nana Bouilloux's retreating form. She had exchanged her black pinafore and short childish frock for a long skirt and a pleated blouse of pink sateen. She wore a black alpaca apron and her exuberant locks, disciplined and twisted into a "figure of eight," lay close as a helmet about the charming new shape of a round imperious head that retained nothing childish except its freshness and the not yet calculated impudence of a little village adventuress.

That morning the upper forms hummed like a hive.

"I've seen Nana Bouilloux! In a long dress, my dear, would you believe it? And her hair in a chignon! She had a pair of scissors hanging from her belt too!"

At noon I flew home to announce breathlessly:

"Mother! I met Nana Bouilloux in the street! She was passing our door. And she had on a long dress! Mother, just imagine, a long dress! And her hair in a chignon! And she had high heels and a pair of . . ."

"Eat, Minet-Chéri, eat, your cutlet will be cold."

"And an apron, mother, such a lovely alpaca apron that looked like silk! Couldn't I possibly . . ."

"No, Minet-Chéri, you certainly couldn't."

"But if Nana Bouilloux can . . ."

"Yes, Nana Bouilloux, at thirteen, can, in fact she should, wear a chignon, a short apron and a long skirt—it's the uniform of all little Bouilloux girls throughout the world, at thirteen—more's the pity."

"But . . ."

"Yes, I know you would like to wear the complete uniform of a little Bouilloux girl. It includes all that you've seen, and a bit more besides: a letter safely hidden in the apron pocket, an admirer who smells of wine and of cheap cigars; two admirers, three admirers and a little later on plenty of tears . . . and a sickly child hidden away, a child that has lain for months crushed by constricting stays. There it is, Minet-Chéri, the entire uniform of the little Bouilloux girls. Do you still want it?"

"Of course not, mother. I only wanted to see if a chignon . . ."

But my mother shook her head, mocking but serious.

"No, no! You can't have the chignon without the apron, the apron without the letter, the letter without the high-heeled slippers, or the slippers without . . . all the rest of it! It's just a matter of choice!"

My envy was soon exhausted. The resplendent little Bouilloux girl became no more than a daily passer-by whom I scarcely noticed. Bare-headed in winter and summer, her gaily colored blouses varied from week to week, and in very cold weather she swathed her elegant shoulders in a useless little scarf. Erect, radiant as a thorny rose, her eyelashes sweeping her cheeks or half revealing her dark and dewy eyes, she grew daily more worthy of queening it over crowds, of being gazed at, adorned and bedecked with jewels. The severely smoothed crinkliness of her chestnut hair could still be discerned in little waves that caught the light in the golden mist at the nape of her neck and round her ears. She always looked vaguely offended with her small, velvety nostrils reminding one of a doe.

She was fifteen or sixteen now—and so was I. Except that she laughed too freely on Sundays, in order to show her white teeth, as she hung on the arms of her brothers or her girl cousins, Nana Bouilloux was behaving fairly well.

"For a little Bouilloux girl, very well indeed!" was the public verdict.

She was seventeen, then eighteen; her complexion was like a peach on a south wall, no eyes could meet the challenge of hers and she had the bearing of a goddess. She began to take the floor at fetes and fairs, to dance with abandon, to stay out very late at night, wandering in the lanes with a man's arm round her waist. Always unkind, but full of laughter, provoking boldness in those who would have been content merely to love her.

Then came a St. John's Eve when she appeared on the dance floor that was laid down on the *Place du Grand-Jeu* under the melancholy light of malodorous oil lamps. Hobnailed boots kicked up the dust between the planks of the "floor." All the young men, as was customary, kept their hats on while dancing. Blonde girls became claret-colored in their tight bodices, while the dark ones, sunburned from their work in the fields, looked black. But there, among a band of haughty workgirls, Nana Bouilloux, in a summer dress sprigged with little flowers, was drinking lemonade laced with red wine when the Parisians arrived on the scene.

They were two Parisians such as one sees in the country in summer, friends of a neighboring landowner, and supremely bored; Parisians in tussore and white serge, come for a moment to mock at a village midsummer fete. They stopped laughing when they saw Nana Bouilloux and sat down near the bar in order to see her better. In low voices they exchanged comments which she pretended not to hear, since her pride as a beautiful creature would not let her turn her eyes in their direction and giggle like her companions. She heard the words: "A swan among geese! A Greuze! A crime to let such a wonder bury herself here. . . ." When the young man in the white suit asked the little

Bouilloux girl for a waltz she got up without surprise and danced with him gravely, in silence. From time to time her eyelashes, more beautiful than a glance, brushed against her partner's fair mustache.

After the waltz the two Parisians went away, and Nana Bouilloux sat down by the bar, fanning herself. There she was soon approached by young Leriche, by Houette, even by Honce the chemist, and even by Possy the cabinetmaker, who was ageing, but none the less a good dancer. To all of them she replied, "Thank you, but I'm tired," and she left the ball at half-past ten o'clock.

And after that, nothing more ever happened to the little Bouilloux girl. The Parisians did not return, neither they, nor others like them. Houette, Honce, young Leriche, the commercial travelers with their gold watch-chains, soldiers on leave and sheriff's clerks vainly climbed our steep street at the hours when the beautifully coiffed sempstress, on her way down it, passed them by stiffly with a distant nod. They looked out for her at dances, where she sat drinking lemonade with an air of distinction and answered their importunities with "Thank you very much, but I'm not dancing, I'm tired." Taking offense, they soon began to snigger: "Tired! Her kind of tiredness lasts for thirty-six weeks!" and they kept a sharp watch on her figure. But nothing happened to the little Bouilloux girl, neither that nor anything else. She was simply waiting, possessed by an arrogant faith, conscious of the debt owed by the hazard that had armed her too well. She was awaiting . . . not the return of the Parisian in white serge, but a stranger, a ravisher. Her proud anticipation kept her silent and pure; with a little smile of surprise, she rejected Honce, who would have raised her to the rank of chemist's lawful wife, and she would have nothing to say to the sheriff's chief clerk. With never another lapse, taking back, once and for all, the smiles, the glances, the glowing bloom of her cheeks, the red young lips, the shadowy blue cleft of her breasts which she had so prodigally lavished on mere rustics, she awaited her kingdom and the prince without a name.

Years later, when I passed through my native village, I could not find the shade of her who had so lovingly refused me what she called "The uniform of little Bouilloux girls." But as the car bore me slowly, though not slowly enough—never slowly enough—up a street where I have now no reason to stop, a woman drew back to avoid the wheel. A slender woman, her hair well dressed in a bygone fashion, dressmaker's scissors hanging from a steel "châtelaine" [1] on her black apron. Large, vindictive eyes, a tight mouth sealed by long silence, the sallow cheeks and temples of those who work by lamplight; a woman

---

[1] CHÂTELAINE: a chain worn at the waist for holding keys, purse, or watch.

of forty-five or . . . Not at all; a woman of thirty-eight, a woman of my own age, of exactly my age, there was no room for doubt. As soon as the car allowed her room to pass, "the little Bouilloux girl" went on her way down the street, erect and indifferent, after one anxious, bitter glance had told her that the car did not contain the long-awaited ravisher.

Insight

1. While the other girls at school envy Nana Bouilloux for her beauty, even then "her beauty isolated her and she had no friends at school." In what ways does her beauty continue to contribute to her unsatisfied life?

2. What attitude does the Bouilloux girl appear to present to the world as she reaches her late teens? How would you account for this attitude?

3. Describe Nana Bouilloux physically and psychologically as she is last seen by the narrator in the story. What future do you think she has before her? Explain.

A Tin buTTeRfly

Mary McCarthy

The man we had to call Uncle Myers was no relation to us. This was
a point on which we four orphan children were very firm. He had
married our great-aunt Margaret shortly before the death of our
parents and so became our guardian while still a benedict—not perhaps a very nice eventuality for a fat man of forty-two who has just
married an old maid with a little income to find himself summoned
overnight from his home in Indiana to be the hired parent of four
children, all under seven years old.

When Myers and Margaret got us, my three brothers and me, we
were a handful; on this there were no two opinions in the McCarthy
branch of the family. The famous flu epidemic of 1918, which had
stricken our little household en route from Seattle to Minneapolis and
carried off our parents within a day of each other, had, like all God's
devices, a meritorious aspect, soon discovered by my grandmother
McCarthy: a merciful end had been put to a regimen of spoiling and
coddling, to Japanese houseboys, iced cakes, picnics, upset stomachs,
diamond rings (imagine!), an ermine muff and neckpiece, furred hats
and coats. My grandmother thanked her stars that Myers and her
sister Margaret were available to step into the breach. Otherwise, we
might have had to be separated, an idea that moistened her hooded
gray eyes, or been taken over by "the Protestants"—thus she grimly
designated my grandfather Preston, a respectable Seattle lawyer of
New England antecedents who, she many times declared with awful
emphasis, had refused to receive a Catholic priest in his house! But
our Seattle grandparents, coming on to Minneapolis for the funeral,
were too broken up, she perceived, by our young mother's death to
protest the McCarthy arrangements. Weeping, my Jewish grandmother (Preston, born Morganstern), still a beauty, like her lost
daughter, acquiesced in the wisdom of keeping us together in the religion my mother had espoused. In my sickbed, recovering from the
flu in my grandmother McCarthy's Minneapolis house, I, the eldest
and the only girl, sat up and watched the other grandmother cry,
dampening her exquisite black veil. I did not know that our parents
were dead or that my sobbing grandmother—whose green Seattle terraces I remembered as delightful to roll down on Sundays—had just
now, downstairs in my grandmother McCarthy's well-heated sun parlor, met the middle-aged pair who had come on from Indiana to undo

MISS MARY
M'CARTHY

The granddaughter
of Mr. and Mrs.
Harold Preston,
who left last
week for the
East to enter
Vassar Col-
lege.
—Walker's
Studio.

her daughter's mistakes. I was only six years old and had just started school in a Sacred Heart convent on a leafy boulevard in Seattle before the fatal November trek back east, but I was sharp enough to see that Grandmother Preston did not belong here, in this dour sickroom, and vain enough to pride myself on drawing the inference that something had gone awry.

We four children and our keepers were soon installed in the yellow house at 2427 Blaisdell Avenue that had been bought for us by my grandfather McCarthy. It was situated two blocks away from his own prosperous dwelling, with its grandfather clock, tapestries, and Italian paintings, in a block that some time before had begun to "run down." Flanked by two-family houses, it was simply a crude box in which to stow furniture, and lives, like a warehouse; the rooms were small and brownish and for some reason dark, though I cannot think why, since the house was graced by no ornamental planting; a straight cement driveway ran up one side; in the back, there was an alley. Downstairs, there were a living room, a "den," a dining room, a kitchen, and a lavatory; upstairs, there were four bedrooms and a bathroom. The dingy wallpaper of the rooms in which we children slept was promptly defaced by us; bored without our usual toys, we amused ourselves by making figures on the walls with our wet tongues. This was our first crime, and I remember it because the violence of the whipping we got surprised us; we had not known we were doing wrong. The splotches on the walls remained through the years to fix this first whipping and the idea of badness in our minds; they stared at us in the evenings when, still bored but mute and tamed, we learned to make shadow figures on the wall—the swan, the rabbit with its ears wiggling—to while away the time.

It was this first crime, perhaps, that set Myers in his punitive mold. He saw that it was no sinecure he had slipped into. Childless, middle-aged, he may have felt in his slow-turning mind that his inexperience had been taken advantage of by his wife's grandiloquent sister, that the vexations outweighed the perquisites; in short, that he had been sold. This, no doubt, was how it must have really looked from where he sat—in a brown leather armchair in the den, wearing a blue work shirt, stained with sweat, open at the neck to show an undershirt and lion-blond, glinting hair on his chest. Below this were workmen's trousers of a brownish-gray material, straining at the buttons and always gaping slightly, just below the belt, to show another glimpse of underwear, of a yellowish white. On his fat head, frequently, with its crest of bronze curly hair, were the earphones of a crystal radio set, which he sometimes, briefly, in a generous mood, fitted over the grateful ears of one of my little brothers.

A second excuse for Myers' behavior is manifest in this description. He had to contend with Irish social snobbery, which looked upon him dispassionately from four sets of green eyes and set him down as "not a gentleman." "My father was a gentleman and you're not"—what I meant by these categorical words I no longer know precisely, except that my father had had a romantic temperament and was a spendthrift; but I suppose there was also included some notion of courtesy. Our family, like many Irish Catholic new-rich families, was filled with aristocratic delusions; we children were always being told that we were descended from the kings of Ireland and that we were related to General "Phil" Sheridan, a dream of my great-aunt's. More precisely, my great-grandfather on this side had been a streetcar conductor in Chicago.

But at any rate Myers (or Meyers) Shriver (or Schreiber—the name had apparently been Americanized) was felt to be beneath us socially. Another count against him in our childish score was that he was a German, or, rather, of German descent, which made us glance at him fearfully in 1918, just after the armistice. In Minneapolis at that time, there was great prejudice among the Irish Catholics, not only against the Protestant Germans, but against all the northern bloods and their hateful Lutheran heresy. Lutheranism to us children was, first of all, a religion for servant girls and, secondly, a sort of yellow corruption associated with original sin and with Martin Luther's tongue rotting in his mouth as God's punishment. Bavarian Catholics, on the other hand, were singled out for a special regard; we saw them in an Early Christian light, brunette and ringleted, like the Apostles. This was due in part to the fame of Oberammergau and the Passion Play,[1] and in part to the fact that many of the clergy in our diocese were Bavarians; all through this period I confided my sins of disobedience to a handsome, dark, young Father Elderbush. Uncle Myers, however, was a Protestant, although, being too indolent, he did not go to church; he was not one of us. And the discovery that we could take refuge from him at school, with the nuns, at church, in the sacraments, seemed to verify the ban that was on him; he was truly outside grace. Having been impressed with the idea that our religion was a sort of logical contagion, spread by holy books and good example, I could never understand why Uncle Myers, bad as he was, had not caught it; and his obduracy in remaining at home in his den on Sundays, like a somnolent brute in its lair, seemed to me to go against nature.

Indeed, in the whole situation there was something unnatural and inexplicable. His marriage to Margaret, in the first place: he was younger than his wife by three years, and much was made of this

---

[1] OBERAMMERGAU . . . PASSION PLAY: Oberammergau is a village in Germany famous for presenting the Passion Play in which the suffering and death of Christ is depicted.

difference by my grandmother McCarthy, his wealthy sister-in-law, as though it explained everything in a slightly obscene way. Aunt Margaret, née Sheridan, was a well-aged quince of forty-five, with iron-gray hair shading into black, a stiff carriage, high-necked dresses, unfashionable hats, a copy of *Our Sunday Visitor* always under her arm—folded, like a flail—a tough dry skin with soft colorless hairs on it, like dust, and furrowed and corrugated, like the prunes we ate every day for breakfast. It could be said of her that she meant well, and she meant especially well by Myers, all two hundred and five pounds, dimpled double chin, and small, glinting, gross blue eyes of him. She called him "Honeybunch," pursued him with attentions, special foods, kisses, to which he responded with tolerance, as though his swollen passivity had the character of a male thrust or assertion. It was clear that he did not dislike her, and that poor Margaret, as her sister said, was head over heels in love with him. To us children, this honeymoon rankness was incomprehensible; we could not see it on either side for, quite apart from everything else, both parties seemed to us very old, as indeed they were, compared to our parents, who had been young and handsome. That he had married her for her money occurred to us inevitably, though it may not have been so; very likely it was his power over her that he loved, and the power he had to make her punish us was perhaps her strongest appeal to him. They slept in a bare, ugly bedroom with a tall, cheap pine chiffonier on which Myers' black wallet and his nickels and dimes lay spread out when he was at home—did he think to arouse our cupidity or did he suppose that this stronghold of his virility was impregnable to our weak desires? Yet, as it happened, we did steal from him, my brother Kevin and I —rightfully, as we felt, for we were allowed no pocket money (two pennies were given us on Sunday morning to put into the collection plate) and we guessed that the money paid by our grandfather for the household found its way into Myers' wallet.

And here was another strange thing about Myers. He not only did nothing for a living but he appeared to have no history. He came from Elkhart, Indiana, but beyond this fact nobody seemed to know anything about him—not even how he had met my aunt Margaret. Reconstructed from his conversation, a picture of Elkhart emerged for us that showed it as a flat place consisting chiefly of ball parks, poolrooms, and hardware stores. Aunt Margaret came from Chicago, which consisted of the Loop, Marshall Field's, assorted priests and monsignors, and the black-and-white problem. How had these two worlds impinged? Where our family spoke freely of its relations, real and imaginary, Myers spoke of no one, not even a parent. At the very beginning, when my father's old touring car, which had been shipped on, still remained in our garage, Myers had certain seedy cronies whom he took riding in it or who simply sat in it in our drive-way, as if anchored in a houseboat; but when the car went, they went or were banished. Uncle Myers and Aunt Margaret had no friends, no couples with whom they exchanged visits—only a middle-aged, black haired, small, emaciated woman with a German name and a yellowed skin whom we were taken to see one afternoon because she was dying of cancer. This protracted death had the aspect of a public execution, which was doubtless why Myers took us to it; that is, it was a spectacle and it was free, and it inspired restlessness and de-pression. Myers was the perfect type of rootless municipalized man who finds his pleasures in the handouts or overflow of an industrial civilization. He enjoyed standing on a curbstone, watching parades, the more nondescript the better, the Labor Day parade being his favorite, and next to that a military parade, followed by the com-mercial parades with floats and girls dressed in costumes; he would even go to Lake Calhoun or Lake Harriet for doll-carriage parades and competitions of children dressed as Indians. He liked bandstands, band concerts, public parks devoid of grass; skywriting attracted him; he was quick to hear of a department-store demonstration where colored bubbles were blown, advertising a soap, to the tune of "I'm

Forever Blowing Bubbles," sung by a mellifluous soprano. He collected coupons and tinfoil, bundles of newspaper for the old rag-and-bone man (thus interfering seriously with our school paper drives), free samples of cheese at Donaldson's, free tickets given out by a neighborhood movie house to the first installment of a serial—in all the years we lived with him, we never saw a full-length movie but only those truncated beginnings. He was also fond of streetcar rides (could the system have been municipally owned?), soldiers' monuments, cemeteries, big, coarse flowers like cannas and cockscombs set in beds by city gardeners. Museums did not appeal to him, though we did go one night with a large crowd to see Marshal Foch on the steps of the Art Institute. He was always weighing himself on penny weighing machines. He seldom left the house except on one of these purposeless errands, or else to go to a ball game, by himself. In the winter, he spent the days at home in the den, or in the kitchen, making candy. He often had enormous tin trays of decorated fondants cooling in the cellar, which leads my brother Kevin to think today that at one time in Myers' life he must have been a pastry cook or a confectioner. He also liked to fashion those little figures made of pipe cleaners that were just then coming in as favors in the better candy shops, but Myers used *old* pipe cleaners, stained yellow and brown. The bonbons, with their pecan or almond topping, that he laid out in such perfect rows were for his own use; we were permitted to watch him set them out, but never—and my brother Kevin confirms this—did we taste a single one.

In the five years we spent with Myers, the only candy I ever had was bought with stolen money and then hidden in the bottom layer of my paper-doll set; the idea of stealing to buy candy and the hiding place were both lifted from Kevin. Opening my paper-doll box one day, I found it full of pink and white soft-sugar candies, which it seemed to me God or the fairies had sent me in response to my wishes and prayers, until I realized that Kevin was stealing, and using my paper-doll box for a cache; we had so few possessions that he had no place of his own to hide things in. Underneath the mattress was too chancy, as I myself found when I tried to secrete magazines of Catholic fiction there; my aunt, I learned, was always tearing up the bed and turning the mattress to find out whether you had wet it and attempted to hide your crime by turning it over. Reading was forbidden us, except for schoolbooks and, for some reason, the funny papers and magazine section of the Sunday Hearst papers, where one read about leprosy, the affairs of Count Boni de Castellane, and a strange disease that turned people to stone creepingly from the feet up.

This prohibition against reading was a source of scandal to the nuns who taught me in the parochial school, and I think it was due to their intervention with my grandmother that finally, toward the end, I was allowed to read openly the Camp Fire Girls series, *Fabiola,* and other books I have forgotten. Myers did not read; before the days of the crystal set, he passed his evenings listening to the phonograph in the living room: Caruso, Harry Lauder, "Keep the Home Fires Burning," "There's a Sweet Little Nest," and "Listen to the Mocking Bird." It was his pleasure to make the four of us stand up in a line and sing to him the same tunes he had just heard on the phonograph, while he laughed at my performance, for I tried to reproduce the staccato phrasing of the sopranos, very loudly and off key. Also, he hated long words, or, rather, words that he regarded as long. One summer day, in the kitchen, when I had been ordered to swat flies, I said, "They disappear so strangely," a remark that he mimicked, for years whenever he wished to humiliate me, and the worst of this torture was that I could not understand what was peculiar about the sentence, which seemed to me plain ordinary English, and, not understanding, I knew that I was in perpetual danger of exposing myself to him again.

So far as we knew, he had never been in any army, but he liked to keep smart military discipline. We had frequently to stand in line, facing him, and shout answers to his questions in chorus. "Forward *march!*" he barked after every order he gave us. The Fourth of July was the only holiday he threw himself into with geniality. Anything that smacked to him of affectation or being "stuck-up" was subject to the harshest reprisals from him, and I, being the oldest, and the one who remembered my parents and the old life best, was the chief sinner, sometimes on purpose, sometimes unintentionally.

When I was eight, I began writing poetry in school: "Father Gaughan is our dear parish priest/And he is loved from west to east." And "Alas, Pope Benedict is dead,/The sorrowing people said." Pope Benedict at that time was living, and, as far as I know, in good health; I had written this opening couplet for the rhyme and the sad idea; but then, very conveniently for me, about a year later he died, which gave me a feeling of fearsome power, stronger than a priest's power of loosing and binding. I came forward with my poem and it was beautifully copied out by our teacher and served as the school's elegy at a memorial service for the Pontiff. I dared not tell that I had had it ready in my desk. Not long afterward, when I was ten, I wrote an essay for a children's contest on "The Irish in American History," which won first the city and then the state prize. Most of my facts I had cribbed from a series on Catholics in American history that was running in *Our Sunday Visitor.* I worked on the assumption that anybody who was Catholic must be Irish, and then, for good measure, I went over the signers of the Declaration of Independence and added any name that sounded Irish to my ears. All this was clothed in rhetoric invoking "the lilies of France"—God knows why, except that I was in love with France and somehow, through Marshal MacMahon, had made Lafayette out an Irishman. I believe that even Kosciusko figured as an Irishman *de coeur*.[1] At any rate, there was a school ceremony, at which I was presented with the city prize (twenty-five dollars, I think, or perhaps that was the state prize); my aunt was in the audience in her best mallard-feathered hat, looking, for once, proud and happy. She spoke kindly to me as we walked home, but when we came to our ugly house, my uncle silently rose from his chair, led me into the dark downstairs lavatory, which always smelled of shaving cream, and furiously beat me with the razor strop—to teach me a lesson, he said, lest I become stuck-up. Aunt Margaret did not intervene. After her first look of discomfiture, her face settled into folds of approval; she had been too soft. This was the usual tribute she paid Myers' greater discernment—she was afraid of losing his love by weakness. The money was taken, "to keep for me," and that, of course, was the end of it. Such was the fate of anything considered "much too good for her," a category that was rivaled only by its pendant, "plenty good enough."

We were beaten all the time, as a matter of course, with the hairbrush across the bare legs for ordinary occasions, and with the razor strop across the bare bottom for special occasions, like the prize-winning. It was as though these ignorant people, at sea with four frightened children, had taken a Dickens novel—*Oliver Twist*, perhaps, or *Nicholas Nickleby*—for a navigation chart. Sometimes our punishments were earned, sometimes not; they were administered gratuitously, often, as preventive medicine. I was whipped more frequently than my brothers, simply by virtue of seniority; that is, every time one of them was whipped, I was whipped also, for not having set a better example, and this was true for all four of us in a descending line. Kevin was whipped for Preston's misdeeds and for Sheridan's, and Preston was whipped for Sheridan's, while Sheridan, the baby and the favorite, was whipped only for his own. This naturally made us fear and distrust each other, and only between Kevin and myself was there a kind of uneasy alliance. When Kevin ran away, as he did on one famous occasion, I had a feeling of joy and defiance, mixed with the fear of punishment for myself, mixed with something worse, a vengeful anticipation of the whipping *he* would surely get. I suppose that the two times I ran away, his feelings were much the same—envy, awe, fear, admiration, and a certain evil thrill, collusive with my uncle, at the thought of the strop ahead. Yet, strange to say, nobody was beaten on these historic days. The culprit, when found, took refuge

[1] DE COEUR: at heart.

at my grandmother's, and a fearful hush lay over the house on Blaisdell Avenue at the thought of the monstrous daring and deceitfulness of the runaway; Uncle Myers, doubtless, was shaking in his boots at the prospect of explanations to the McCarthy family council. The three who remained at home were sentenced to spend the day upstairs, in strict silence. But if my uncle's impartial application of punishment served to make us each other's enemies very often, it did nothing to establish discipline, since we had no incentive to behave well, not knowing when we might be punished for something we had not done or even for something that by ordinary standards would be considered good. We knew not when we would offend, and what I learned from this, in the main, was a policy of lying and concealment; for several years after we were finally liberated, I was a problem liar.

Despite Myers' quite justified hatred of the intellect, of reading and education (for he was right—it *was* an escape from him), my uncle, like all dictators, had one book that he enjoyed. It was *Uncle Remus*, in a red cover—a book I detested—which he read aloud to us in his den over and over again in the evenings. It seemed to me that this reduction of human life to the level of talking animals and this corruption of language to dialect gave my uncle some very personal relish. He knew I hated it and he rubbed it in, trotting my brother Sheridan on his knee as he dwelt on some exploit of Br'er Fox's with many chuckles and repetitions. In *Uncle Remus*, he had his hour, and to this day I cannot read anything in dialect or any fable without some degree of repugnance.

A distinction must be made between my uncle's capricious brutality and my aunt's punishments and repressions, which seem to have been dictated to her by her conscience. My aunt was not a bad woman; she was only a believer in method. Since it was the family theory that we had been spoiled, she undertook energetically to remedy this by quasi-scientific means. Everything we did proceeded according to schedule and in line with an over-all plan. She was very strong, naturally, on toilet-training, and everything in our life was directed toward the after-breakfast session on "the throne." Our whole diet—not to speak of the morning orange juice with castor oil in it that was brought to us on the slightest pretext of "paleness"—was centered around this levee. We had prunes every day for breakfast, and cornmeal mush, Wheatena, or farina, which I had to eat plain, since by some medical whim it had been decided that milk was bad for me. The rest of our day's menu consisted of parsnips, turnips, rutabagas, carrots, boiled potatoes, boiled cabbage, onions, Swiss chard, kale, and so on; most green vegetables, apparently, were too dear to be appropriate for us, though I think that, beyond this, the family had a sort of moral affinity for the root vegetable, stemming, perhaps, from everything fibrous, tenacious, watery, and knobby in the Irish peasant stock. Our desserts were rice pudding, farina pudding, overcooked custard with little air holes in it, prunes, stewed red plums, rhubarb, stewed pears, stewed dried peaches. We must have had meat, but I have only the most indistinct recollection of pale lamb stews in which the carrots outnumbered the pieces of white, fatty meat and bone and gristle; certainly we did not have steak or roasts or turkey or fried chicken, but perhaps an occasional boiled fowl was served to us with its vegetables (for I do remember the neck, shrunken in its collar of puckered skin, coming to me as my portion, and the fact that if you sucked on it, you could draw out an edible white cord), and doubtless there was meat loaf and beef stew. There was no ice cream, cake, pie, or butter, but on rare mornings we had johnnycake or large woolly pancakes with Karo syrup.

We were not allowed to leave the table until every morsel was finished, and I used to sit through half a dark winter afternoon staring at the cold carrots on my plate, until, during one short snowy period,

I found that I could throw them out the back window if I raised it very quietly. (Unfortunately, they landed on the tar roofing of a sort of shed next to the back porch, and when the snow finally melted, I met a terrible punishment.) From time to time, we had a maid, but the food was so wretched that we could not keep "girls," and my aunt took over the cooking, with sour enthusiasm, assisted by her sister, Aunt Mary, an arthritic, white-haired, wan, devout old lady who had silently joined our household and earned her keep by helping with the sewing and dusting and who tried to stay out of Myers' way. With her gentle help, Aunt Margaret managed to approximate, on a small scale, the conditions prevailing in the orphan asylums we four children were always dreaming of being let into.

Myers did not share our diet. He sat at the head of the table, with a napkin around his neck, eating the special dishes that Aunt Margaret prepared for him and sometimes putting a spoonful on the plate of my youngest brother, who sat next to him in a high chair. At breakfast, he had corn flakes or shredded wheat with bananas or fresh sliced peaches, thought by us to be a Lucullan treat. At dinner, he had pigs' feet and other delicacies I cannot remember. I only know that he shared them with Sheridan, who was called Herdie, as my middle brother was called Pomps, or Pompsie—childish affectionate nicknames inherited from our dead parents that sounded damp as grave-mold in my aunt Margaret's flannelly voice, which reminded one of a chest rag dipped in asafetida to ward off winter throat ailments.

In addition to such poultices, and mustard plasters, and iron pills to fortify our already redoubtable diet, we were subject to other health fads of the period and of my great-aunt's youth. I have told elsewhere of how we were put to bed at night with our mouths sealed with adhesive tape to prevent mouth-breathing; ether, which made me sick, was used to help pull the tape off in the morning, but a grimy, gray, rubbery remainder was usually left on our upper lips and in the indentations of our pointed chins when we set off for school in our heavy outer clothes, long underwear, black stockings, and high shoes. Our pillows were taken away from us; we were given a sulphur-and-molasses spring tonic, and in the winter, on Saturdays and Sundays, we were made to stay out three hours in the morning and three in the afternoon, regardless of the temperature. We had come from a mild climate, in Seattle, and at fifteen, twenty, or twenty-four below zero we could not play, even if we had had something to play with, and used simply to stand in the snow, crying, and beating sometimes on the window with our frozen mittens, till my aunt's angry face would appear there and drive us away.

No attempt was made to teach us a sport, winter or summer; we were forbidden to slide in Fairoaks Park nearby, where in winter the poorer children made a track of ice down a hill, which they flashed down sitting or standing, but I loved this daring sport and did it anyway, on the way home from school, until one day I tore my shabby coat on the ice and was afraid to go home. A kind woman named Mrs. Corkerey, who kept a neighborhood candy store across from our school, mended it for me, very skillfully, so that my aunt never knew; nevertheless, sliding lost its lure for me, for I could not risk a second rip.

The neighbors were often kind, surreptitiously, and sometimes they "spoke" to the sisters at the parochial school, but everyone, I think, was afraid of offending my grandparents, who diffused an air of wealth and pomp when they entered their pew at St. Stephen's Church on Sunday. Mrs. Corkerey, in fact, got herself and me in trouble by feeding me in the mornings in her kitchen above the candy store when I stopped to pick up her daughter, Clarazita, who was in my class. I used to lie to Mrs. Corkerey and say that I had had no breakfast (when the truth was that I was merely hungry), and she went to the nuns finally in a state of indignation. The story was checked with my aunt, and I was obliged to admit that I had lied and that they did feed me, which must have disillusioned Mrs. Corkerey forever with the pathos of orphaned childhood. It was impossible for me to explain to her then that what I needed was her pity and her fierce choleric heart. Another neighbor, Mr. Harrison, a well-to-do old bachelor or widower who lived in the corner house, used sometimes to take us bathing, and it was thanks to his lessons that I learned to swim—a strange antiquated breast stroke—copied from an old man with a high-necked bathing suit and a beard. In general, we were not supposed to have anything to do with the neighbors or with other children. It was a rule that other children were not allowed to come into our yard or we to go into theirs, nor were we permitted to walk to school with another boy or girl. But since we were in school most of the day, five days a week, our guardians could not prevent us from making friends despite them; other children were, in fact, very much attracted to us, pitying us for our woebegone condition and respecting us because we were thought to be rich. Our grandmother's chauffeur, Frank, in her winter Pierce-Arrow and summer Locomobile, was well known in the neighborhood, waiting outside church on Sunday to take her home from Mass. Sometimes we were taken, too, and thus our miserable clothes and underfed bodies were associated with high financial status and became a sort of dubious privilege in the eyes of our classmates.

We both had enviable possessions and did not have them. In the closet in my bedroom, high on the top shelf, beyond my reach even standing on a chair, was a stack of cardboard doll boxes, containing wonderful French dolls, dressed by my Seattle grandmother in silks, laces, and satins, with crepe-de-Chine underwear and shoes with high heels. These and other things were sent us every year at Christmas-time, but my aunt had decreed that they were all too good for us, so they remained in their boxes and wrappings, *verboten*,[1] except on the rare afternoon, perhaps once in a twelvemonth or so, when a relation or a friend of the family would come through from the West, and then down would come the dolls, out would come the baseball gloves and catchers' masks and the watches and the shiny cars and the doll houses, and we would be set to playing with these things on the floor of the living room while the visitor tenderly looked on. As soon as the visitor left, bearing a good report of our household, the dolls and watches and cars would be whisked away, to come out again for the next emergency. If we had been clever, we would have refused this bait and paraded our misery, but we were too simple to do anything but seize the moment and play out a whole year's playtime in this gala hour and a half. Such techniques, of course, are common in concentration camps and penal institutions, where the same sound calculation of human nature is made. The prisoners snatch at their holiday; they trust their guards and the motto *"Carpe diem"* [2] more than they do the strangers who have come to make the inspection. Like all people who have been mistreated, we were wary of being taken in; we felt uneasy about these visitors—Protestants from Seattle—who might be much worse than our uncle and aunt. The latter's faults, at any rate, we knew. Moreover, we had been subjected to propaganda: we had been threatened with the Seattle faction, time and again, by our uncle, who used to jeer and say to us, *"They'd* make you toe the chalk line."

The basis, I think, of my aunt's program for us was in truth totalitarian: she was idealistically bent on destroying our privacy. She imagined herself as enlightened in comparison with our parents, and a super-ideal of health, cleanliness, and discipline softened in her own eyes the measures she applied to attain it. A nature not unkindly was warped by bureaucratic zeal and by her subservience to her husband, whose masterful autocratic hand cut through our nonsense like a cleaver. The fact that our way of life resembled that of an orphan asylum was not a mere coincidence; Aunt Margaret strove purposefully toward a corporate goal. Like most heads of institutions, she longed for the eyes of Argus.[3] To the best of her ability, she saw to it that nothing was hidden from her. Even her health measures had this purpose. The aperients we were continually dosed with guaranteed

---

[1] VERBOTEN: forbidden.
[2] CARPE DIEM: seize the day.
[3] ARGUS: in Greek mythology a giant with a hundred eyes.

that our daily processes were open to her inspection, and the monthly medical checkup assured her, by means of stethoscope and searchlight and tongue depressor, that nothing was happening inside us to which she was not privy. Our letters to Seattle were written under her eye, and she scrutinized our homework sharply, though her arithmetic, spelling, and grammar were all very imperfect. We prayed, under supervision, for a prescribed list of people. And if we were forbidden companions, candy, most toys, pocket money, sports, reading, entertainment, the aim was not to make us suffer but to achieve efficiency. It was simpler to interdict other children than to inspect all the children with whom we might want to play. From the standpoint of efficiency, our lives, in order to be open, had to be empty; the books we might perhaps read, the toys we might play with figured in my aunt's mind, no doubt, as what the housewife calls "dust catchers"— around these distractions, dirt might accumulate. The inmost folds of consciousness, like the belly button, were regarded by her as unsanitary. Thus, in her spiritual outlook, my aunt was an early functionalist.

Like all systems, my aunt's was, of course, imperfect. Forbidden to read, we told stories, and if we were kept apart, we told them to ourselves in bed. We made romances out of our schoolbooks, even out of the dictionary, and read digests of novels in the *Book of Knowledge* at school. My uncle's partiality for my youngest brother was a weakness in him, as was my aunt Mary's partiality for me. She was supposed to keep me in her room, sewing on squares of cheap cotton, making handkerchiefs with big, crude, ugly hems, and ripping them out and making them over again, but though she had no feeling for art or visual beauty (she would not even teach me to darn, which is an art, or to do embroidery, as the nuns did later on, in the convent), she liked to talk of the old days in Chicago and to read sensational religious fiction in a magazine called the *Extension*, which sometimes she let me take to my room, with a caution against being caught. And on the Sunday walks that my uncle headed, at the end of an interminable streetcar ride, during which my bigger brothers had to scrunch down to pass for under six, there were occasions on which he took us (in military order) along a wooded path, high above the Mississippi River, and we saw late-spring harebells and, once, a coral-pink snake. In Minnehaha Park, a favorite resort, we were allowed to play on the swings and to examine the other children riding on the ponies or on a little scenic railway. Uncle Myers always bought himself a box of Cracker Jack, which we watched him eat and delve into, to find the little favor at the bottom—a ritual we deeply envied, for, though we sometimes had popcorn at home (Myers enjoyed popping it) and even, once or twice, homemade popcorn balls with molasses, we had never had more than a taste of this commercial

Cracker Jack, with peanuts in it, which seemed to us the more valuable because *he* valued it and would often come home eating a box he had bought at a ball game. But one Sunday, Uncle Myers, in full, midsummer mood, wearing his new pedometer, bought my brother Sheridan a whole box for himself.

Naturally, we envied Sheridan—the only blond among us, with fair red-gold curls, while the rest of us were all pronounced brunets, with thick black brows and lashes—as we watched him, the lucky one, munch the sticky stuff and fish out a painted tin butterfly with a little pin on it at the bottom. My brothers clamored around him, but I was too proud to show my feelings. Sheridan was then about six years old, and this butterfly immediately became his most cherished possession—indeed, one of the few he had. He carried it about the house with him all the next week, clutched in his hand or pinned to his shirt, and my two other brothers followed him, begging him to be allowed to play with it, which slightly disgusted me, at the age of ten, for I knew that I was too sophisticated to care for tin butterflies and I felt in this whole affair the instigation of my uncle. He was relishing my brothers' performance and saw to it, strictly, that Sheridan clung to his rights in the butterfly and did not permit anybody to touch it. The point about this painted tin butterfly was not its intrinsic value; it was the fact that it was virtually the only toy in the house that had not been, so to speak, socialized, but belonged privately to one individual. Our other playthings—a broken-down wooden swing, an old wagon, a dirty sandbox, and perhaps a fire engine or so and some defaced blocks and twisted second-hand train tracks in the attic— were held by us all in common, the velocipedes we had brought with us from Seattle having long ago foundered, and the skipping rope, the jacks, the few marbles, and the pair of rusty roller skates that were given us being decreed to be the property of all. Hence, for a full week this butterfly excited passionate emotions, from which I held myself stubbornly apart, refusing even to notice it, until one afternoon, at about four o'clock, while I was doing my weekly chore of dusting the woodwork, my white-haired aunt Mary hurried softly into my room and, closing the door behind her, asked whether I had seen Sheridan's butterfly.

The topic wearied me so much that I scarcely lifted my head, answering no, shortly, and going on with my dusting. But Aunt Mary was gently persistent: Did I know that he had lost it? Would I help her look for it? This project did not appeal to me but in response to some faint agitation in her manner, something almost pleading, I put down my dustcloth and helped her. We went all over the house, raising carpets, looking behind curtains, in the kitchen cupboards, in the Victrola, everywhere but in the den, which was closed, and in my aunt's and uncle's bedroom. Somehow—I do not know why—I did not expect to find the butterfly, partly, I imagine, because I was indifferent to it and partly out of the fatalism that all children have toward lost objects, regarding them as irretrievable, vanished into the flux of things. At any rate I was right: we did not find it and I went back to my dusting, vindicated. Why should *I* have to look for Sheridan's stupid butterfly, which he ought to have taken better care of? "Myers is upset," said Aunt Mary, still hovering, uneasy and diffident, in the doorway. I made a slight face, and she went out, plaintive, remonstrant, and sighing, in her pale, high necked, tight-buttoned dress.

It did not occur to me that I was suspected of stealing this toy, even when Aunt Margaret, five minutes later, burst into my room and ordered me to come and look for Sheridan's butterfly. I protested that I had already done so, but she paid my objections no heed and seized me roughly by the arm. "Then do it again, Miss, and mind that you find it." Her voice was rather hoarse and her whole furrowed iron-gray aspect somewhat tense and disarrayed, yet I had the impression that she was not angry with me but with something in outer reality— what one would now call fate or contingency. When I had searched again, lackadaisically, and again found nothing, she joined in with

vigor, turning everything upside down. We even went into the den, where Myers was sitting, and searched all around him, while he watched us with an ironical expression, filling his pipe from a Bull Durham sack. We found nothing, and Aunt Margaret led me upstairs to my room, which I ransacked while she stood and watched me. All at once, when we had finished with my bureau drawers and my closet, she appeared to give up. She sighed and bit her lips. The door cautiously opened and Aunt Mary came in. The two sisters looked at each other and at me. Margaret shrugged her shoulders. "She hasn't got it, I do believe," she said.

She regarded me then with a certain relaxing of her thick wrinkles, and her heavy-skinned hand, with its wedding ring, came down on my shoulder. "Uncle Myers thinks you took it," she said in a rusty whisper, like a spy or a scout. The consciousness of my own innocence, combined with a sense of being let into the confederacy of the two sisters, filled me with excitement and self-importance. "But I didn't, Aunt Margaret," I began proclaiming, making the most of my moment. "What would I want with his silly old butterfly?" The two sisters exchanged a look. "That's what I said, Margaret!" exclaimed old Aunt Mary sententiously. Aunt Margaret frowned; she adjusted a bone hairpin in the coiled rings of her unbecoming coiffure. "Mary Therese," she said to me, solemnly, "if you know anything about the butterfly, if one of your brothers took it, tell me now. If we don't find it, I'm afraid Uncle Myers will have to punish you." "He *can't* punish me, Aunt Margaret," I insisted, full of righteousness. "Not if I didn't do it and *you* don't think I did it." I looked up at her, stagily trustful, resting gingerly on this solidarity that had suddenly appeared between us. Aunt Mary's pale old eyes watered. "You mustn't let Myers punish her, Margaret, if you don't think she's done wrong." They both glanced up at the Murillo Madonna that was hanging on my stained wall. Intelligence passed between them and I was sure that, thanks to our Holy Mother, Aunt Margaret would save me. "Go along, Mary Therese," she said hoarsely. "Get yourself ready for dinner. And don't you say a word of this to your uncle when you come downstairs."

When I went down to dinner, I was exultant, but I tried to hide it. Throughout the meal, everyone was restrained; Herdie was in the dumps about his butterfly, and Preston and Kevin were silent, casting covert looks at me. My brothers, apparently, were wondering how I had avoided punishment, as the eldest, if for no other reason. Aunt Margaret was rather flushed, which improved her appearance slightly. Uncle Myers had a cunning look, as though events would prove him right. He patted Sheridan's golden head from time to time and urged him to eat. After dinner, the boys filed into the den behind Uncle Myers, and I helped Aunt Margaret clear the table. We did not have to do the dishes, for at this time there was a "girl" in the kitchen. As we were lifting the white tablecloth and the silence pad, we found the butterfly—pinned to the silence pad, right by my place.

My hash was settled then, though I did not know it. I did not catch the significance of its being found at *my* place. To Margaret, however, this was grimly conclusive. She had been too "easy," said her expression; once again Myers had been right. Myers went through the formality of interrogating each of the boys in turn ("No, sir," "No, sir," "No, sir") and even, at my insistence, of calling in the Swedish girl from the kitchen. Nobody knew how the butterfly had got there. It had not been there before dinner, when the girl set the table. My judges therefore concluded that I had had it hidden on my person and had slipped it under the tablecloth at dinner, when nobody was looking. This unanimous verdict maddened me, at first simply as an indication of stupidity—how could they be so dense as to imagine that I would hide it by my own place, where it was sure to be discovered? I did not really believe that I was going to be punished on such ridiculous evidence, yet even I could form no theory of how the butterfly had come there. My first base impulse to accuse the maid was scoffed out of my head by reason. What would a grownup want with a silly six-year-old's toy? And the very unfairness of the condemnation that rested on me made me reluctant to transfer it to one of my brothers. I kept supposing that the truth somehow would out, but the interrogation suddenly ended and every eye avoided mine.

Aunt Mary's dragging step went up the stairs, the boys were ordered to bed, and then, in the lavatory, the whipping began. Myers beat me with the strop, until his lazy arm tired; whipping is hard work for a fat man, out of condition, with a screaming, kicking, wriggling ten-year-old in his grasp. He went out and heaved himself, panting, into his favorite chair and I presumed that the whipping was over. But Aunt Margaret took his place, striking harder than he, with a hairbrush, in a businesslike, joyless way, repeating, "Say you did it, Mary Therese, say you did it." As the blows fell and I did not give in, this formula took on an intercessory note, like a prayer. It was clear to me that she was begging me to surrender and give Myers his satisfaction, for my own sake, so that the whipping could stop. When I finally cried out "All right!" she dropped the hairbrush with a sigh of relief; a new doubt of my guilt must have been visiting her, and my confession set everything square. She led me in to my uncle, and we both stood facing him, as Aunt Margaret, with a firm but not ungentle hand on my shoulder, whispered, "Just tell him, 'Uncle Myers, I did it,' and you can go to bed." But the sight of him, sprawling in his leather chair, complacently waiting for this, was too much for me. The words froze on my tongue. I could not utter them to *him*. Aunt Margaret urged me on, reproachfully, as though I were breaking our compact, but as I looked straight at him and assessed his ugly nature, I burst into yells. "I didn't! I didn't!" I gasped, between screams. Uncle Myers shot a vindictive look at his wife, as though he well understood that there had been collusion between us. He ordered me back to the dark lavatory and symbolically rolled up his sleeve. He laid on the strop decisively, but this time I was beside myself, and when Aunt Margaret hurried in and tried to reason with me, I could only answer with wild cries as Uncle Myers, gasping also, put the strop back on its hook. "You take her," he articulated, but Aunt Margaret's hairbrush this time was perfunctory, after the first few angry blows that punished me for having disobeyed her. Myers did not take up the strop again; the whipping ended, whether from fear of the neighbors or of Aunt Mary's frail presence upstairs or sudden guilty terror, I do not know; perhaps simply because it was past my bedtime.

I finally limped up to bed, with a crazy sense of inner victory, like a saint's, for I had not recanted, despite all they had done or could do to me. It did not occur to me that I had been unchristian in refusing to answer a plea from Aunt Margaret's heart and conscience. Indeed, I rejoiced in the knowledge that I had *made* her continue to beat me long after she must have known that I was innocent; this was her punishment for her condonation of Myers. The next morning, when I opened my eyes on the Murillo Madonna and the Baby Stuart, my feeling of triumph abated; I was afraid of what I had done. But throughout that day and the next, they did not touch me. I walked on air, increduously and, no doubt, somewhat pompously, seeing myself as a figure from legend: my strength was *as* the strength of ten because my *heart* was pure! Afterward, I was beaten, in the normal routine way, but the question of the butterfly was closed forever in that house.

In my mind, there was, and still is, a connection between the butterfly and our rescue, by our Protestant grandfather, which took place the following year, in the fall or early winter. Already defeated, in their own view, or having ceased to care what became of us, our guardians, for the first time, permitted two of us, my brother Kevin and me, to be alone with this strict, kindly lawyer, as we walked the two blocks between our house and our grandfather McCarthy's. In the course of our walk, between the walls of an early snow, we told Grandpa Preston everything, overcoming our fears and fixing our minds on the dolls, the baseball gloves, and the watches. Yet, as it happened, curiously enough, albeit with a certain aptness, it was not the tale of the butterfly or the other atrocities that chiefly impressed him as he followed our narration with precise legal eyes but the fact that I was not wearing my glasses. I was being punished for breaking them in a fall on the school playground by having to go without; and

I could not see why my account of this should make him flush up with anger—to me it was a great relief to be free of those disfiguring things. But he shifted his long, lantern jaw and, settling our hands in his, went straight as a writ up my grandfather McCarthy's front walk. Hence it was on a question of health that this good American's alarms finally alighted; the rest of what we poured out to him he either did not believe or feared to think of, lest he have to deal with the problem of evil.

On health grounds, then, we were separated from Uncle Myers, who disappeared back into Elkhart with his wife and Aunt Mary. My brothers were sent off to the sisters in a Catholic boarding school, with the exception of Sheridan, whom Myers was permitted to bear away with him, like a golden trophy. Sheridan's stay, however, was of short duration. Very soon, Aunt Mary died, followed by Aunt Margaret, followed by Uncle Myers; within five years, still in the prime of life, they were all gone, one, two, three, like ninepins. For me, a new life began, under a happier star. Within a few weeks after my Protestant grandfather's visit, I was sitting in a compartment with him on the train, watching the Missouri River go westward to its source, wearing my white-gold wrist watch and a garish new red hat, a highly nervous child, fanatical against Protestants, who, I explained to Grandpa Preston, all deserved to be burned at the stake. In the dining car, I ordered greedily, lamb chops, pancakes, sausages, and then sat, unable to eat them. "Her eyes," observed the waiter, "are bigger than her stomach."

Six or seven years later, on one of my trips east to college, I stopped in Minneapolis to see my brothers, who were all together now, under the roof of a new and more indulgent guardian, my uncle Louis, the handsomest and youngest of the McCarthy uncles. All the old people were dead; my grandmother McCarthy, but recently passed away, had left a fund to erect a chapel in her name in Texas, a state with which she had no known connection. Sitting in the twilight of my uncle Louis' screened porch, we sought a common ground for our reunion and found it in Uncle Myers. It was then that my brother Preston told me that on the famous night of the butterfly, he had seen Uncle Myers steal into the dining room from the den and lift the tablecloth, with the tin butterfly in his hand.

Mary McCarthy

1. How would you describe the way Mary McCarthy was brought up for the first six years of her life? What memories does she have of her parents?

2. Mary McCarthy clearly describes Uncle Myers physically and psychologically. How do you picture him? How would you assess his personality and character? Are there any factors which might tend to excuse some of his actions? Explain.

3. The five years Mary McCarthy spends with Myers and Margaret change her life in many ways. What characteristics does she believe resulted from her treatment during those years?

4. Although clearly disliking Myers, Mary reveals mixed feelings toward Margaret. How do you account for these mixed feelings? Does she seem fair in her appraisal of her aunt? What is your reaction to Margaret?

5. Sometimes one incident can serve to symbolize an entire pattern of behavior. How does the tin butterfly serve this purpose in establishing Myers' character? What exactly does this incident reveal about him?

MORE OF A CORPSE
THAN A WOMAN

Muriel Rukeyser

Give them my regards when you go to the school reunion;
and at the marriage-supper, say that I'm thinking about them.
They'll remember my name;   I went to the movies with that one;
feeling the weight of their death where she sat at my elbow;
       she never said a word   5
       but all of them were heard.

All of them alike, expensive girls, the leaden friends:
one used to play the piano, one of them once wrote a sonnet,
one even seemed awakened enough to photograph wheatfields—
the dull girls with the educated minds and technical passions—   10
       pure love was their employment,
       they tried it for enjoyment.

Meet them at the boat   :   they've brought the souvenirs of
    boredom
a seashell from the faltering monarchy;
the nose of a marble saint;   and from the battlefield,   15
an empty shell divulged from a flower-bed.
       The lady's wealthy breath
       perfumes the air with death.

The leaden lady faces the fine, voluptuous woman,
faces a rising world bearing its gifts in its hands.   20
Kisses her casual dreams upon the lips she kisses,
risen, she moves away;   takes others;   moves away.
       Inadequate to love,
       supposes she's enough.

Give my regards to the well-protected woman,   25
I knew the ice-cream girl, we went to school together.
There's something to bury, people, when you begin to bury.
When your women are ready and rich in their wish for the world,
       destroy the leaden heart,
       we've a new race to start.   30

SEMINARY

Constance Carrier

They go along the graveled walks,
a straggle of academy girls
with notebooks and with hockey sticks—
from blue berets to ankle socks
as much alike as peas or pearls.   5

Their uniform is their defense
against a too-large world, their claim
to be both separate and the same—
at once distinguished and at once
group-blurred to any casual glance.   10

Unmindful of the rule's intent,
of what their pious elders meant—
that all mutations of the breed
are equal in the sight of God
and cause for neither shame nor pride—   15

they do not question such a rule:
it, or its letter, they betray
in the belief that they obey.
They are not rebels, not at all—
only intensely practical.   20

They recognize their own elect,
discriminate, appraise, condemn,
and, with no hint of disrespect,
almost unconsciously they come
to change *One should be* to *I am.*   25

Insight
1. What attitude is conveyed toward the women described in each
   poem? Which lines do you find most revealing in determining the
   attitude?
2. Study the behavior of the women in each poem. In what ways are
   they similar? In what ways are they different?
3. To what extent is conformity a factor in each poem? To what do
   each set of women conform? To what extent do you think they
   recognize their own conformity?

A domestic dilemma

Carson McCullers

On Thursday Martin Meadows left the office early enough to make
the first express bus home. It was the hour when the evening lilac
glow was fading in the slushy streets, but by the time the bus had
left the mid-town terminal the bright city night had come. On Thursdays the maid had a half-day off and Martin liked to get home as
soon as possible, since for the past year his wife had not been—well.
This Thursday he was very tired and, hoping that no regular com-
muter would single him out for conversation, he fastened his attention to the newspaper until the bus had crossed the George Washington Bridge. Once on 9-W Highway Martin always felt that the trip
was halfway done; he breathed deeply, even in cold weather when
only ribbons of draught cut through the smoky air of the bus, con-
fident that he was breathing country air. It used to be that at this
point he would relax and begin to think with pleasure of his home.
But in the last year nearness brought only a sense of tension and he
did not anticipate the journey's end. This evening Martin kept his
face close to the window and watched the barren fields and lonely
lights of passing townships. There was a moon, pale on the dark
earth and areas of late, porous snow; to Martin the countryside
seemed vast and somehow desolate that evening. He took his hat
from the rack and put his folded newspaper in the pocket of his overcoat a few minutes before time to pull the cord.

The cottage was a block from the bus stop, near the river but not
directly on the shore; from the living-room window you could look
across the street and opposite yard and see the Hudson. The cottage
was modern, almost too white and new on the narrow plot of yard.
In summer the grass was soft and bright and Martin carefully tended
a flower border and a rose trellis. But during the cold, fallow months
the yard was bleak and the cottage seemed naked. Lights were on
that evening in all the rooms in the little house and Martin hurried
up the front walk. Before the steps he stopped to move a wagon out
of the way.

The children were in the living room, so intent on play that the
opening of the front door was at first unnoticed. Martin stood looking at his safe, lovely children. They had opened the bottom drawer
of the secretary and taken out the Christmas decorations. Andy had
managed to plug in the Christmas tree lights and the green and red
bulbs glowed with out-of-season festivity on the rug of the living

room. At the moment he was trying to trail the bright cord over Marianne's rocking horse. Marianne sat on the floor pulling off an angel's wings. The children wailed a startling welcome. Martin swung the fat little baby girl up to his shoulder and Andy threw himself against his father's legs.

"Daddy, Daddy, Daddy!"

Martin set down the little girl carefully and swung Andy a few times like a pendulum. Then he picked up the Christmas tree cord.

"What's all this stuff doing out? Help me put it back in the drawer. You're not to fool with the light socket. Remember I told you that before. I mean it, Andy."

The six-year-old child nodded and shut the secretary drawer. Martin stroked his fair soft hair and his hand lingered tenderly on the nape of the child's frail neck.

"Had supper yet, Bumpkin?"

"It hurt. The toast was hot."

The baby girl stumbled on the rug and, after the first surprise of the fall, began to cry; Martin picked her up and carried her in his arms back to the kitchen.

"See, Daddy," said Andy. "The toast—"

Emily had laid the children's supper on the uncovered porcelain table. There were two plates with the remains of cream-of-wheat and eggs and silver mugs that had held milk. There was also a platter of cinnamon toast, untouched except for one tooth-marked bite. Martin sniffed the bitten piece and nibbled gingerly. Then he put the toast into the garbage pail. "Hoo-phui—What on earth!"

Emily had mistaken the tin of cayenne for the cinnamon.

"I like to have burnt up," Andy said. "Drank water and ran out-doors and opened my mouth. Marianne didn't eat none."

"Any," corrected Martin. He stood helpless, looking around the walls of the kitchen. "Well, that's that, I guess," he said finally. "Where is your mother now?"

"She's up in you alls' room."

Martin left the children in the kitchen and went up to his wife. Outside the door he waited for a moment to still his anger. He did not knock and once inside the room he closed the door behind him. Emily sat in the rocking chair by the window of the pleasant room. She had been drinking something from a tumbler and as he entered she put the glass hurriedly on the floor behind the chair. In her attitude there was confusion and guilt which she tried to hide by a show of spurious vivacity. *not genuine*

"Oh, Marty! You home already? The time slipped up on me. I was just going down——" She lurched to him and her kiss was strong with sherry. When he stood unresponsive she stepped back a pace and giggled nervously.

"What's the matter with you? Standing there like a barber pole. Is anything wrong with you?"

"Wrong with *me?*" Martin bent over the rocking chair and picked up the tumbler from the floor. "If you could only realize how sick I am—how bad it is for all of us."

Emily spoke in a false, airy voice that had become too familiar to him. Often at such times she affected a slight English accent, copying perhaps some actress she admired. "I haven't the vaguest idea what you mean. Unless you are referring to the glass I used for a spot of sherry. I had a finger of sherry—maybe two. But what is the crime in that, pray tell me? I'm quite all right. Quite all right."

"So anyone can see."

As she went into the bathroom Emily walked with careful gravity. She turned on the cold water and dashed some on her face with her cupped hands, then patted herself dry with the corner of a bath towel. Her face was delicately featured and young, unblemished.

"I was just going down to make dinner." She tottered and balanced herself by holding to the door frame.

"I'll take care of dinner. You stay up here. I'll bring it up."

"I'll do nothing of the sort. Why, whoever heard of such a thing?"

"Please," Martin said.

"Leave me alone. I'm quite all right. I was just on the way down——"

"Mind what I say."

"Mind your grandmother."

She lurched toward the door, but Martin caught her by the arm. "I don't want the children to see you in this condition. Be reasonable."

"Condition!" Emily jerked her arm. Her voice rose angrily. "Why, because I drink a couple of sherries in the afternoon you're trying to make me out a drunkard. Condition! Why, I don't even touch whiskey. As well you know. *I* don't swill liquor at bars. And that's more than you can say. I don't even have a cocktail at dinnertime. I only sometimes have a glass of sherry. What, I ask you, is the disgrace of that? Condition!"

Martin sought words to calm his wife. "We'll have a quiet supper by ourselves up here. That's a good girl." Emily sat on the side of the bed and he opened the door for a quick departure. "I'll be back in a jiffy."

As he busied himself with the dinner downstairs he was lost in the familiar question as to how this problem had come upon his home. He himself had always enjoyed a good drink. When they were still living in Alabama they had served long drinks or cocktails as a matter of course. For years they had drunk one or two—possibly three—drinks before dinner, and at bedtime a long nightcap. Evenings before holidays they might get a buzz on, might even become a little tight. But

275

alcohol had never seemed a problem to him, only a bothersome expense that with the increase in the family they could scarcely afford. It was only after his company had transferred him to New York that Martin was aware that certainly his wife was drinking too much. She was tippling, he noticed, during the day.

The problem acknowledged, he tried to analyze the source. The change from Alabama to New York had somehow disturbed her; accustomed to the idle warmth of a small Southern town, the matrix of the family and cousinship and childhood friends, she had failed to accommodate herself to the stricter, lonelier mores of the North. The duties of motherhood and housekeeping were onerous to her. Homesick for Paris City, she had made no friends in the suburban town. She read only magazines and murder books. Her interior life was insufficient without the artifice of alcohol. The revelations of incontinence insidiously undermined his previous conceptions of his wife. There were times of unexplainable malevolence, times when the alcoholic fuse caused an explosion of unseemly anger. He encountered a latent coarseness in Emily, inconsistent with her natural simplicity. She lied about drinking and deceived him with unsuspected stratagems.

Then there was an accident. Coming home from work one evening about a year ago, he was greeted with screams from the children's room. He had found Emily holding the baby, wet and naked from her bath. The baby had been dropped, her frail, frail skull striking the table edge, so that a thread of blood was soaking into the gossamer hair. Emily was sobbing and intoxicated. As Martin cradled the hurt child, so infinitely precious at that moment, he had an affrightened vision of the future.

The next day Marianne was all right. Emily vowed that never again would she touch liquor, and for a few weeks she was sober, cold and downcast. Then gradually she began—not whisky or gin—but quantities of beer, or sherry, or outlandish liqueurs; once he had come across a hatbox of empty crème de menthe bottles. Martin found a dependable maid who managed the household competently. Virgie was also from Alabama and Martin had never dared tell Emily the wage scale customary in New York. Emily's drinking was entirely secret now, done before he reached the house. Usually the effects were almost imperceptible—a looseness of movement or the heavy-lidded eyes. The times of irresponsibilities, such as the cayenne-pepper toast, were rare, and Martin could dismiss his worries when Virgie was at the house. But, nevertheless, anxiety was always latent, a threat of indefined disaster that underlay his days.

"Marianne!" Martin called, for even the recollection of that time brought the need for reassurance. The baby girl, no longer hurt, but no less precious to her father, came into the kitchen with her brother.

Martin went on with the preparations for the meal. He opened a can of soup and put two chops in the frying pan. Then he sat down by the table and took his Marianne on his knees for a pony ride. Andy watched them, his fingers wobbling the tooth that had been loose all that week.

"Andy-the-candyman!" Martin said. "Is that old critter still in your mouth? Come closer, let Daddy have a look."

"I got a string to pull it with." The child brought from his pocket a tangled thread. "Virgie said to tie it to the tooth and tie the other end of the doorknob and shut the door real suddenly."

Martin took out a clean handkerchief and felt the loose tooth carefully. "That tooth is coming out of my Andy's mouth tonight. Otherwise I'm awfully afraid we'll have a tooth tree in the family."

"A what?"

"A tooth tree," Martin said. "You'll bite into something and swallow that tooth. And the tooth will take root in poor Andy's stomach and grow into a tooth tree with sharp little teeth instead of leaves."

"Shoo, Daddy," Andy said. But he held the tooth firmly between his grimy little thumb and forefinger. "There ain't any tree like that. I never seen one."

"There *isn't* any tree like that and I never *saw* one."

Martin tensed suddenly. Emily was coming down the stairs. He listened to her fumbling footsteps, his arm embracing the little boy with dread. When Emily came into the room he saw from her movements and her sullen face that she had again been at the sherry bottle. She began to yank open drawers and set the table.

"Condition!" she said in furry voice. "You talk to me like that. Don't think I'll forget. I remember every dirty lie you say to me. Don't you think for a minute that I forget."

"Emily!" he begged. "The children——"

"The children—yes! Don't think I don't see through your dirty plots and schemes. Down here trying to turn my own children against me. Don't think I don't see and understand."

"Emily! I beg you—please go upstairs."

"So you can turn my children—my very own children——" Two large tears coursed rapidly down her cheeks. "Trying to turn my little boy, my Andy, against his own mother."

With drunken impulsiveness Emily knelt on the floor before the startled child. Her hands on his shoulders balanced her. "Listen, my Andy—you wouldn't listen to any lies your father tells you? You wouldn't believe what he says? Listen. Andy, what was your father telling you before I came downstairs?" Uncertain, the child sought his father's face. "Tell me. Mama wants to know."

"About the tooth tree."

"What?"

The child repeated the words and she echoed them with unbelieving terror. "The tooth tree!" She swayed and renewed her grasp on the child's shoulder. "I don't know what you're talking about. But listen, Andy, Mama is all right, isn't she?" The tears were spilling down her face and Andy drew back from her, for he was afraid. Grasping the table edge, Emily stood up.

"See! You have turned my child against me."

Marianne began to cry, and Martin took her in his arms.

"That's all right, you can take *your* child. You have always shown partiality from the very first. I don't mind, but at least you can leave me my little boy."

Andy edged close to his father and touched his leg. "Daddy," he wailed.

Martin took the children to the foot of the stairs. "Andy, you take up Marianne and Daddy will follow you in a minute."

"But Mama?" the child asked, whispering.

"Mama will be all right. Don't worry."

Emily was sobbing at the kitchen table, her face buried in the crook of her arm. Martin poured a cup of soup and set it before her. Her rasping sobs unnerved him; the vehemence of her emotion, irrespective of the source, touched in him a strain of tenderness. Unwillingly he laid his hand on her dark hair. "Sit up and drink the soup." Her face as she looked up at him was chastened and imploring. The boy's withdrawal or the touch of Martin's hand had turned the tenor of her mood.

"Ma-Martin," she sobbed. "I'm so ashamed."

"Drink the soup."

Obeying him, she drank between gasping breaths. After a second cup she allowed him to lead her up to their room. She was docile now and more restrained. He laid her nightgown on the bed and was about to leave the room when a fresh round of grief, the alcoholic tumult, came again.

"He turned away. My Andy looked at me and turned away."

Impatience and fatigue hardened his voice, but he spoke warily. "You forget that Andy is still a little child—he can't comprehend the meaning of such scenes."

"Did I make a scene? Oh, Martin, did I make a scene before the children?"

Her horrified face touched and amused him against his will. "Forget it. Put on your nightgown and go to sleep."

"My child turned away from me. Andy looked at his mother and turned away. The children——"

She was caught in the rhythmic sorrow of alcohol. Martin withdrew from the room saying: "For God's sake go to sleep. The children will forget by tomorrow."

As he said this he wondered if it was true. Would the scene glide so easily from memory—or would it root in the unconscious to fester in the after-years? Martin did not know, and the last alternative sickened him. He thought of Emily, foresaw the morning-after humiliation: the shards of memory, the lucidities that glared from the obliterating darkness of shame. She would call the New York office twice—possibly three or four times. Martin anticipated his own embarrassment, wondering if the others at the office could possibly suspect. He felt that his secretary had divined the trouble long ago and that she pitied him. He suffered a moment of rebellion against his fate; he hated his wife.

Once in the children's room he closed the door and felt secure for the first time that evening. Marianne fell down on the floor, picked herself up and calling: "Daddy, watch me," fell again, got up and continued the falling-calling routine. Andy sat in the child's low chair, wobbling the tooth. Martin ran the water in the tub, washed his own hands in the lavatory, and called the boy into the bathroom.

"Let's have another look at that tooth." Martin sat on the toilet, holding Andy between his knees. The child's mouth gaped and Martin grasped the tooth. A wobble, a quick twist and the nacreous milk tooth was free. Andy's face was for the first moment split between terror, astonishment, and delight. He mouthed a swallow of water and spat into the lavatory. "Look, Daddy! It's blood. Marianne!"

Martin loved to bathe his children, loved inexpressibly the tender, naked bodies as they stood in the water so exposed. It was not fair of Emily to say that he showed partiality. As Martin soaped the delicate boy-body of his son he felt that further love would be impossible. Yet he admitted the difference in the quality of his emotions for the two children. His love for his daughter was graver, touched with a strain of melancholy, a gentleness that was akin to pain. His pet names for the little boy were the absurdities of daily inspiration—he called the little girl always Marianne, and his voice as he spoke it was a caress. Martin patted dry the fat baby stomach. The washed child faces were radiant as flower petals, equally loved.

"I'm putting the tooth under my pillow. I'm supposed to get a quarter."

"What for?"

"You know, Daddy. Johnny got a quarter for his tooth."

"Who puts the quarter there?" asked Martin. "I used to think the fairies left it in the night. It was a dime in my day, though."

"That's what they say in kindergarten."

"Who does put it there?"

"Your parents," Andy said. "You!"

Martin was pinning the cover on Marianne's bed. His daughter was already asleep. Scarcely breathing. Martin bent over and kissed her forehead, kissed again the tiny hand that lay palm-upward, flung in slumber beside her head.

"Good night, Andy-man."

The answer was only a drowsy murmur. After a minute Martin took out his change and slid a quarter underneath the pillow. He left a night light in the room.

As Martin prowled about the kitchen making a late meal, it occurred to him that the children had not once mentioned their mother or the scene that must have seemed to them incomprehensible. Absorbed in the instant—the tooth, the bath, the quarter—the fluid passage of child-time had borne these weightless episodes like leaves in the swift current of a shallow stream while the adult enigma was beached and forgotten on the shore. Martin thanked the Lord for that.

But his own anger, repressed and lurking, arose again. His youth was being frittered by a drunkard's waste, his very manhood subtly undermined. And the children, once the immunity of incomprehension passed—what would it be like in a year or so? With his elbows on the table he ate his food brutishly, untasting. There was no hiding the truth—soon there would be gossip in the office and in the town; his wife was a dissolute woman. Dissolute. And he and his children were bound to a future of degradation and slow ruin.

Martin pushed away from the table and stalked into the living room. He followed the lines of a book with his eyes but his mind conjured miserable images: he saw his children drowned in the river, his wife a disgrace on the public street. By bedtime the dull, hard anger was like a weight upon his chest and his feet dragged as he climbed the stairs.

The room was dark except for the shafting light from the half-opened bathroom door. Martin undressed quietly. Little by little, mysteriously, there came in him a change. His wife was asleep, her peaceful respiration sounding gently in the room. Her high-heeled shoes with the carelessly dropped stockings made to him a mute appeal. Her underclothes were flung in disorder on the chair. Martin picked up the girdle and the soft, silk brassière and stood for a moment with them in his hands. For the first time that evening he looked at his wife. His eyes rested on the sweet forehead, the arch of the fine brow. The brow had descended to Marianne, and the tilt at the end of the delicate nose. In his son he could trace the high cheekbones and pointed chin. Her body was full-bosomed, slender and undulant. As Martin watched the tranquil slumber of his wife the ghost of the old anger vanished. All thoughts of blame or blemish were distant from him now. Martin put out the bathroom light and raised the window. Careful not to awaken Emily he slid into the bed. By moonlight he watched his wife for the last time. His hand sought the adjacent flesh and sorrow paralleled desire in the immense complexity of love.

Carson McCullers

Insight

1. A dilemma is defined as a choice between equally unsatisfactory alternatives. What exactly is the dilemma faced by Martin Meadows? Which alternative do you think Martin will eventually choose? Explain.

2. What reasons does Martin feel are at the "source" of his wife's drinking too much? Are any other reasons hinted at in the story?

3. Martin displays a deeply protective attitude toward his children. What reasons can you cite for the intensity of his attitude? Emily accuses him of favoring Marianne. Does he appear to do so? What "difference in the quality of his emotions for the two children" does he admit to?

4. Ambivalence is a simultaneous feeling of attraction toward and repulsion from a person or situation. What lines can you cite which reveal the ambivalence Martin feels toward his wife?

THE FARMER'S BRIDE

Charlotte Mew

Three summers since I chose a maid,
Too young maybe—but more's to do
At harvest-time than bide and woo.
   When us was wed she turned afraid
Of love and me and all things human;   5
Like the shut of a winter's day.
Her smile went out, and 'twasn't a woman—
   More like a little frightened fay.
      One night, in the Fall, she runned away.

"Out 'mong the sheep, her be," they said,   10
"Should properly have been abed;"
But sure enough she wasn't there
Lying awake with her wide brown stare.
So over seven-acre field and up-along across the down
We chased her, flying like a hare   15
Before our lanterns. To Church-Town
   All in a shiver and a scare
We caught her, fetched her home at last
   And turned the key upon her, fast.

She does the work about the house   20
As well as most, but like a mouse:
   Happy enough to chat and play
   With birds and rabbits and such as they,
   So long as men-folk keep away.
"Not near, not near!" her eyes beseech   25
When one of us comes within reach.
   The women say that beasts in stall
   Look round like children at her call.
   I've hardly heard her speak at all.

Shy as a leveret*, swift as he,   30
Straight and slight as a young larch tree,
Sweet as the first wild violets, she
To her wild self. But what to me?

   [30] LEVERET: a young hare.

The short days shorten and the oaks are brown,
    The blue smoke rises to the low gray sky,   35
One leaf in the still air falls slowly down,
    A magpie's spotted feathers lie
On the black earth spread white with rime*,
The berries redden up to Christmas-time.
    What's Christmas-time without there be   40
    Some other in the house than we!

    She sleeps up in the attic there
    Alone, poor maid. 'Tis but a stair
Betwixt us. Oh! my God! the down,
    The soft young down of her, the brown,   45
The brown of her—her eyes, her hair, her hair . . .

³⁸ RIME: frost or granular ice coating, as on grass and trees.

THE 5:32

Phyllis McGinley

3rd person   She said, If tomorrow my world were torn in two,
Blacked out, dissolved, I think I would remember
(As if transfixed in unsurrendering amber)
This hour best of all the hours I knew:
When cars came backing into the shabby station,   5
Children scuffing the seats, and the women driving
With ribbons around their hair, and the trains arriving,
And the men getting off with tired but practiced motion.   *daily reunion*

Yes, I would remember my life like this, she said:
Autumn, the platform red with Virginia creeper,   *autumn* 10
And a man coming toward me, smiling, the evening paper
Under his arm, and his hat pushed back on his head;
And wood smoke lying like haze on the quiet town,
And dinner waiting, and the sun not yet gone down.

TO MY dEAR ANd loving HusbANd

17th Cent Colonial America

Anne Bradstreet

1st American woman poet

not a sonnet

underscore

If ever two were one, then surely we.   a
If ever man were lov'd by wife, then thee;   a
If ever wife was happy in a man,   b
Compare with me ye women if you can.   b
I prize thy love more than whole mines of gold,   c 5
Or all the riches that the East doth hold.   c
My love is such that rivers cannot quench,   d
Nor aught but love from thee give recompence.   d
Thy love is such I can no way repay,   e
The heavens reward thee manifold I pray.   e 10
Then while we live, in love let's so persevere,   f
That when we live no more, we may live ever.   f

love's universality

Insight

1. Contrast the degrees of happiness and warmth described in the marriages in these three poems. Which relationship appears closest? Which, most distant? What reasons do you have for your choices?

2. What different roles do each of the three wives appear to play in relation to their husbands?

3. How do the fleeting thoughts of death in "The 5:32" and "To My Dear and Loving Husband" contribute to the quality of the love expressed by each woman?

THE yellow wallpaper

Charlotte Perkins Gilman

It is very seldom that mere ordinary people like John and myself secure ancestral halls for the summer.

A colonial mansion, a hereditary estate, I would say a haunted house, and reach the height of romantic felicity—but that would be asking too much of fate!

Still I will proudly declare that there is something queer about it.

Else, why should it be let so cheaply? And why have stood so long untenanted?

John laughs at me, of course, but one expects that in marriage.

John is practical in the extreme. He has no patience with faith, an intense horror of superstition, and he scoffs openly at any talk of things not to be felt and seen and put down in figures.

John is a physician, and *perhaps*—(I would not say it to a living soul, of course, but this is dead paper and a great relief to my mind) —*perhaps* that is one reason I do not get well faster.

You see he does not believe I am sick!

And what can one do?

If a physician of high standing, and one's own husband, assures friends and relatives that there is really nothing the matter with one but temporary nervous depression—a slight hysterical tendency— what is one to do?

My brother is also a physician, and also of high standing, and he says the same thing.

So I take phosphates or phosphites—whichever it is, and tonics, and journeys, and air, and exercise, and am absolutely forbidden to "work" until I am well again.

Personally, I disagree with their ideas.

Personally, I believe that congenial work, with excitement and change, would do me good.

But what is one to do?

I did write for a while in spite of them; but it *does* exhaust me a good deal—having to be so sly about it, or else meet with heavy opposition.

I sometimes fancy that in my condition if I had less opposition and more society and stimulus—but John says the very worst thing I can do is to think about my condition, and I confess it always makes me feel bad.

So I will let it alone and talk about the house.

The most beautiful place! It is quite alone, standing well back from the road, quite three miles from the village. It makes me think of English places that you read about, for there are hedges and walls and gates that lock, and lots of separate little houses for the gardeners and people.

There is a *delicious* garden! I never saw such a garden—large and shady, full of box-bordered paths, and lined with long grape-covered arbors with seats under them.

There were greenhouses, too, but they are all broken now.

There was some legal trouble, I believe, something about the heirs and coheirs; anyhow, the place has been empty for years.

That spoils my ghostliness, I am afraid, but I don't care—there is something strange about the house—I can feel it.

I even said so to John one moonlight evening, but he said what I felt was a *draught*, and shut the window.

I get unreasonably angry with John sometimes. I'm sure I never used to be so sensitive. I think it is due to this nervous condition.

But John says if I feel so, I shall neglect proper self-control; so I take pains to control myself—before him, at least, and that makes me very tired.

I don't like our room a bit. I wanted one downstairs that opened on the piazza and had roses all over the window, and such pretty old-fashioned chintz hangings! but John would not hear of it.

He said there was only one window and not room for two beds, and no near room for him if he took another.

He is very careful and loving, and hardly lets me stir without special direction.

I have a schedule prescription for each hour in the day; he takes all care from me, and so I feel basely ungrateful not to value it more.

He said we came here solely on my account, that I was to have perfect rest and all the air I could get. "Your exercise depends on your strength, my dear," said he, "and your food somewhat on your appetite; but air you can absorb all the time." So we took the nursery at the top of the house.

It is a big, airy room, the whole floor nearly, with windows that look all ways, and air and sunshine galore. It was nursery first and then playroom and gymnasium, I should judge; for the windows are barred for little children, and there are rings and things in the walls.

The paint and paper look as if a boys' school had used it. It is stripped off—the paper—in great patches all around the head of my bed, about as far as I can reach, and in a great place on the other side of the room low down. I never saw a worse paper in my life.

One of those sprawling flamboyant patterns committing every artistic sin.

It is dull enough to confuse the eye in following, pronounced enough to constantly irritate and provoke study, and when you follow the lame uncertain curves for a little distance they suddenly commit suicide—plunge off at outrageous angles, destroy themselves in unheard of contradictions.

The color is repellent, almost revolting; a smouldering unclean yellow, strangely faded by the slow-turning sunlight.

It is a dull yet lurid orange in some places, a sickly sulphur tint in others.

No wonder the children hated it! I should hate it myself if I had to live in this room long.

There comes John, and I must put this away,—he hates to have me write a word.

We have been here two weeks, and I haven't felt like writing before, since that first day.

I am sitting by the window now, up in this atrocious nursery, and there is nothing to hinder my writing as much as I please, save lack of strength.

John is away all day, and even some nights when his cases are serious.

I am glad my case is not serious!

But these nervous troubles are dreadfully depressing.

John does not know how much I really suffer. He knows there is no *reason* to suffer, and that satisfies him.

Of course it is only nervousness. It does weigh on me so not to do my duty in any way!

I meant to be such a help to John, such a real rest and comfort, and here I am a comparative burden already!

Nobody would believe what an effort it is to do what little I am able,—to dress and entertain, and order things.

It is fortunate Mary is so good with the baby. Such a dear baby!

And yet I *cannot* be with him, it make me so nervous.

I suppose John never was nervous in his life. He laughs at me so about this wallpaper!

At first he meant to repaper the room, but afterwards he said that I was letting it get the better of me, and that nothing was worse for a nervous patient than to give way to such fancies.

He said that after the wallpaper was changed it would be the heavy bedstead, and then the barred windows, and then that gate at the head of the stairs, and so on.

"You know the place is doing you good," he said, "and really, dear, I don't care to renovate the house just for a three months' rental."

"Then do let us go downstairs," I said, "there are such pretty rooms there."

Then he took me in his arms and called me a blessed little goose, and said he would go down to the cellar, if I wished, and have it whitewashed into the bargain.

But he is right enough about the beds and windows and things.

It is an airy and comfortable room as any one need wish, and, of course, I would not be so silly as to make him uncomfortable just for a whim.

I'm really getting quite fond of the big room, all but that horrid paper.

Out of one window I can see the garden, those mysterious deep-shaded arbors, the riotous old-fashioned flowers, and bushes and gnarly trees.

Out of another I get a lovely view of the bay and a little private wharf belonging to the estate. There is a beautiful shaded lane that runs down there from the house. I always fancy I see people walking in these numerous paths and arbors, but John has cautioned me not to give way to fancy in the least. He says that with my imaginative power and habit of story making, a nervous weakness like mine is sure to lead to all manner of excited fancies, and that I ought to use my will and good sense to check the tendency. So I try.

I think sometimes that if I were only well enough to write a little it would relieve the press of ideas and rest me.

But I find I get pretty tired when I try.

It is so discouraging not to have any advice and companionship about my work. When I get really well, John says we will ask Cousin Henry and Julia down for a long visit; but he says he would as soon put fireworks in my pillowcase as to let me have those stimulating people about now.

I wish I could get well faster.

But I must not think about that. This paper looks to me as if it *knew* what a vicious influence it had!

There is a recurrent spot where the pattern lolls like a broken neck and two bulbous eyes stare at you upside down.

I get positively angry with the impertinence of it and the everlastingness. Up and down and sideways they crawl, and those absurd, unblinking eyes are everywhere. There is one place where two breadths didn't match, and the eyes go all up and down the line, one a little higher than the other.

I never saw so much expression in an inanimate thing before, and we all know how much expression they have! I used to lie awake as a child and get more entertainment and terror out of blank walls and plain furniture than most children could find in a toy store.

I remember what a kindly wink the knobs of our big, old bureau used to have, and there was one chair that always seemed like a strong friend.

I used to feel that if any of the other things looked too fierce I could always hop into that chair and be safe.

The furniture in this room is no worse than inharmonious, however, for we had to bring it all from downstairs. I suppose when this was used as a playroom they had to take the nursery things out, and no wonder! I never saw such ravages as the children have made here.

The wallpaper, as I said before, is torn off in spots, and it sticketh closer than a brother—they must have had perseverance as well as hatred.

Then the floor is scratched and gouged and splintered, the plaster itself is dug out here and there, and this great heavy bed which is all we found in the room, looks as if it had been through the wars.

But I don't mind it a bit—only the paper.

There comes John's sister. Such a dear girl as she is, and so careful of me! I must not let her find me writing.

She is a perfect and enthusiastic housekeeper, and hopes for no better profession. I verily belief she thinks it is the writing which made me sick!

But I can write when she is out, and see her a long way off from these windows.

There is one that commands the road, a lovely shaded winding road, and one that just looks off over the country. A lovely country, too, full of great elms and velvet meadows.

This wallpaper has a kind of subpattern in a different shade, a particularly irritating one, for you can only see it in certain lights, and not clearly then.

But in the places where it isn't faded and where the sun is just so —I can see a strange, provoking, formless sort of figure, that seems to skulk about behind that silly and conspicuous front design.

There's sister on the stairs!

Well, the Fourth of July is over! The people are all gone and I am tired out. John thought it might do me good to see a little company, so we just had mother and Nellie and the children down for a week.

Of course I didn't do a thing. Jennie sees to everything now.

But it tired me all the same.

John says if I don't pick up faster he shall send me to Weir Mitchell in the fall.

But I don't want to go there at all. I had a friend who was in his hands once, and she says he is just like John and my brother, only more so!

Besides, it is such an undertaking to go so far.

I don't feel as if it was worth while to turn my hand over for anything, and I'm getting dreadfully fretful and querulous.

I cry at nothing, and cry most of the time.

Of course I don't when John is here, or anybody else, but when I am alone.

And I am alone a good deal just now. John is kept in town very often by serious cases, and Jennie is good and lets me alone when I want her to.

So I walk a little in the garden or down that lovely lane, sit on the porch under the roses, and lie down up here a good deal.

I'm getting really fond of the room in spite of the wallpaper. Perhaps *because* of the wallpaper.

It dwells in my mind so!

I lie here on this great immovable bed—it is nailed down, I believe —and follow that pattern about by the hour. It is as good as gymnastics, I assure you. I start, we'll say, at the bottom, down in the corner over there where it has not been touched, and I determine for the thousandth time that I *will* follow that pointless pattern to some sort of a conclusion.

I know a little of the principle of design, and I know this thing was not arranged on any laws of radiation, or alternation, or reptition, or symmetry, or anything else that I ever heard of.

It is repeated, of course, by the breadths, but not otherwise.

Looked at in one way each breadth stands alone, the bloated curves and flourishes—a kind of "debased Romanesque" with *delirium tremens*[1]—go waddling up and down in isolated columns of fatuity.

But, on the other hand, they connect diagonally, and the sprawling outlines run off in great slanting waves of optic horror, like a lot of wallowing seaweeds in full chase.

The whole thing goes horizontally, too, at least it seems so, and I exhaust myself in trying to distinguish the order of its going in that direction.

They have used a horizontal breadth for a frieze, and that adds wonderfully to the confusion.

There is one end of the room where it is almost intact, and there, when the crosslights fade and the low sun shines directly upon it, I can almost fancy radiation after all,—the interminable grotesques seem to form around a common centre and rush off in headlong plunges of equal distraction.

It makes me tired to follow it. I will take a nap I guess.

I don't know why I should write this.

I don't want to.

I don't feel able.

And I know John would think it absurd. But I *must* say what I feel and think in some way—it is such a relief!

---

[1] DELIRIUM TREMENS: an acute case of mental confusion caused by alcohol poisoning.

But the effort is getting to be greater than the relief.

Half the time now I am awfully lazy, and lie down ever so much.

John says I mustn't lose my strength, and has me take cod liver oil and lots of tonics and things, to say nothing of ale and wine and rare meat.

Dear John! He loves me very dearly, and hates to have me sick. I tried to have a real earnest reasonable talk with him the other day, and tell him how I wish he would let me go and make a visit to Cousin Henry and Julia.

But he said I wasn't able to go, nor able to stand it after I got there; and I did not make out a very good case for myself, for I was crying before I had finished.

It is getting to be a great effort for me to think straight. Just this nervous weakness I suppose.

And dear John gathered me up in his arms, and just carried me upstairs and laid me on the bed, and sat by me and read to me till it tired my head.

He said I was his darling and his comfort and all he had, and that I must take care of myself for his sake, and keep well.

He says no one but myself can help me out of it, that I must use my will and self-control and not let any silly fancies run away with me.

There's one comfort, the baby is well and happy, and does not have to occupy this nursery with the horrid wallpaper.

If we had not used it, that blessed child would have! What a fortunate escape! Why, I wouldn't have a child of mine, an impressionable little thing, live in such a room for worlds.

I never thought of it before, but it is lucky that John kept me here after all, I can stand it so much easier than a baby, you see.

Of course I never mention it to them any more—I am too wise,—but I keep watch of it all the same.

There are things in that paper that nobody knows but me, or ever will.

Behind that outside pattern the dim shapes get clearer every day.

It is always the same shape, only very numerous.

And it is like a woman stooping down and creeping about behind that pattern. I don't like it a bit. I wonder—I begin to think—I wish John would take me away from here!

It is so hard to talk with John about my case, because he is so wise, and because he loves me so.

But I tried it last night.

It was moonlight. The moon shines in all around just as the sun does.

I hate to see it sometimes, it creeps so slowly, and always comes in by one window or another.

John was asleep and I hated to waken him, so I kept still and watched the moonlight on that undulating wallpaper till I felt creepy.

The faint figure behind seemed to shake the pattern, just as if she wanted to get out.

I got up softly and went to feel and see if the paper *did* move, and when I came back John was awake.

"What is it, little girl?" he said. "Don't go walking about like that —you'll get cold."

I thought it was a good time to talk, so I told him that I really was not gaining here, and that I wished he would take me away.

"Why darling!" said he, "our lease will be up in three weeks, and I can't see how to leave before.

"The repairs are not done at home, and I cannot possibly leave town just now. Of course if you were in any danger, I could and would, but you really are better, dear, whether you can see it or not. I am a doctor, dear, and I know. You are gaining flesh and color, your appetite is better, I feel really much easier about you."

"I don't weigh a bit more," said I, "nor as much; and my appetite my be better in the evening when you are here, but it is worse in the morning when you are away!"

"Bless her little heart!" said he with a big hug, "she shall be as sick as she pleases! But now let's improve the shining hours by going to sleep, and talk about it in the morning!"

"And you won't go away?" I asked gloomily.

"Why, how can I, dear? It is only three weeks more and then we will take a nice little trip of a few days while Jennie is getting the house ready. Really dear you are better!"

"Better in body perhaps—" I began, and stopped short, for he sat up straight and looked at me with such a stern, reproachful look that I could not say another word.

"My darling," said he, "I beg of you, for my sake and for our child's sake, as well as for your own, that you will never for one instant let that idea enter your mind! There is nothing so dangerous, so fascinating, to a temperament like yours. It is a false and foolish fancy. Can you not trust me as a physician when I tell you so?"

So of course I said no more on that score, and we went to sleep before long. He thought I was asleep first, but I wasn't, and lay there for hours trying to decide whether that front pattern and the back pattern really did move together or separately.

On a pattern like this, by daylight, there is a lack of sequence, a defiance of law, that is a constant irritant to a normal mind.

The color is hideous enough, and unreliable enough, and infuriating enough, but the pattern is torturing.

You think you have mastered it, but just as you get well underway in following, it turns a back-somersault and there you are. It slaps you in the face, knocks you down, and tramples upon you. It is like a bad dream.

The outside pattern is a florid arabesque, reminding one of a fungus. If you can imagine a toadstool in joints, an interminable string of toadstools, budding and sprouting in endless convolutions—why, that is something like it.

That is, sometimes!

There is one marked peculiarity about this paper, a thing nobody seems to notice but myself, and that is that it changes as the light changes.

When the sun shoots in through the east window—I always watch for that first long, straight ray—it changes so quickly that I never can quite believe it.

That is why I watch it always.

By moonlight—the moon shines in all night when there is a moon —I wouldn't know it was the same paper.

At night in any kind of light, in twilight, candle light, lamplight, and worst of all by moonlight, it becomes bars! The outside pattern I mean, and the woman behind it is as plain as can be.

I didn't realize for a long time what the thing was that showed behind, that dim subpattern, but now I am quite sure it is a woman.

By daylight she is subdued, quiet. I fancy it is the pattern that keeps her so still. It is so puzzling. It keeps me quiet by the hour.

I lie down ever so much now. John says it is good for me, and to sleep all I can.

Indeed he started the habit by making me lie down for an hour after each meal.

It is a very bad habit I am convinced, for you see I don't sleep.

And that cultivates deceit, for I don't tell them I'm awake—O no!

The fact is I am getting a little afraid of John.

He seems very queer sometimes, and even Jennie has an inexplicable look.

It strikes me occasionally, just as a scientific hypothesis,—that perhaps it is the paper!

I have watched John when he did not know I was looking, and come into the room suddenly on the most innocent excuses, and I've caught him several times *looking at the paper!* And Jennie too. I caught Jennie with her hand on it once.

She didn't know I was in the room, and when I asked her in a quiet, a very quiet voice, with the most restrained manner possible, what she was doing with the paper—she turned around as if she had been caught stealing, and looked quite angry—asked me why I should frighten her so!

Then she said that the paper stained everything it touched, that she had found yellow smooches on all my clothes and John's, and she wished we would be more careful!

Did not that sound innocent? But I know she was studying that pattern, and I am determined that noboby shall find it out but myself!

Life is very much more exciting now than it used to be. You see I have something more to expect, to look forward to, to watch. I really do eat better, and am more quiet than I was.

John is so pleased to see me improve! He laughed a little the other day, and said I seemed to be flourishing in spite of my wallpaper.

I turned it off with a laugh. I had no intention of telling him it was *because* of the wallpaper—he would make fun of me. He might even want to take me away.

I don't want to leave now until I have found it out. There is a week more, and I think that will be enough.

I'm feeling ever so much better! I don't sleep much at night, for it is so interesting to watch developments; but I sleep a good deal in the daytime.

In the daytime it is tiresome and perplexing.

There are always new shoots on the fungus, and new shades of yellow all over it. I cannot keep count of them, though I have tried conscientiously.

It is the strangest yellow, that wallpaper! It makes me think of all the yellow things I ever saw—not beautiful ones like buttercups, but old foul, bad yellow things.

But there is something else about that paper—the smell! I noticed it the moment we came into the room, but with so much air and sun it was not bad. Now we have had a week of fog and rain, and whether the windows are open or not, the smell is here.

It creeps all over the house.

I find it hovering in the dining room, skulking in the parlor, hiding in the hall, lying in wait for me on the stairs.

It gets into my hair.

Even when I go to ride, if I turn my head suddenly and surprise it—there is that smell!

Such a peculiar odor, too! I have spent hours in trying to analyze it, to find what it smelled like.

It is not bad—at first, and very gentle, but quite the subtlest, most enduring odor I ever met.

In this damp weather it is awful, I wake up in the night and find it hanging over me.

It used to disturb me at first. I thought seriously of burning the house—to reach the smell.

But now I am used to it. The only thing I can think of that it is like is the *color* of the paper! A yellow smell.

There is a very funny mark on this wall, low down, near the mop-board. A streak that runs round the room. It goes behind every piece of furniture, except the bed, a long, straight, even *smooch,* as if it had been rubbed over and over.

I wonder how it was done and who did it, and what they did it for. Round and round and round—round and round and round—it makes me dizzy!

I really have discovered something at last.

Through watching so much at night, when it changes so, I have finally found out.

The front pattern *does* move—and no wonder! The woman behind shakes it!

Sometimes I think there are a great many women behind, and sometimes only one, and she crawls around fast, and her crawling shakes it all over.

Then in the very bright spots she keeps still, and in the very shady spots she just takes hold of the bars and shakes them hard.

And she is all the time trying to climb through. But nobody could climb through that pattern—it strangles so; I think that is why it has so many heads.

They get through, and then the pattern strangles them off and turns them upside down, and makes their eyes white!

If those heads were covered or taken off it would not be half so bad.

I think that woman gets out in the daytime!

And I'll tell you why—privately—I've seen her!

I can see her out of every one of my windows!

It is the same woman, I know, for she is always creeping, and most women do not creep by daylight.

I see her on that long road under the trees, creeping along, and when a carriage comes she hides under the blackberry vines.

I don't blame her a bit. It must be very humiliating to be caught creeping by daylight!

I always lock the door when I creep by daylight. I can't do it at night, for I know John would suspect something at once.

And John is so queer now, that I don't want to irritate him. I wish he would take another room! Besides, I don't want anybody to get that woman out at night but myself.

I often wonder if I could see her out of all the windows at once.

But, turn as fast as I can, I can only see out of one at one time.

And though I always see her, she *may* be able to creep faster than I can turn!

I have watched her sometimes away off in the open country, creeping as fast as a cloud shadow in a high wind.

If only that top pattern could be gotten off from the under one! I mean to try it, little by little.

I have found out another funny thing, but I shan't tell it this time! It does not do to trust people too much.

There are only two more days to get this paper off, and I believe John is beginning to notice. I don't like the look in his eyes.

And I heard him ask Jennie a lot of professional questions about me. She had a very good report to give.

She said I slept a good deal in the daytime.

John knows I don't sleep very well at night, for all I'm so quiet!

He asked me all sorts of questions, too, and pretended to be very loving and kind.

As if I couldn't see through him!

Still, I don't wonder he acts so, sleeping under this paper for three months.

It only interests me, but I feel sure John and Jennie are secretly affected by it.

Hurrah! This is the last day, but it is enough. John to stay in town over night, and won't be out until this evening.

Jennie wanted to sleep with me—the sly thing! but I told her I should undoubtedly rest better for a night all alone.

That was clever, for really I wasn't alone a bit! As soon as it was moonlight and that poor thing began to crawl and shake the pattern, I got up and ran to help her.

I pulled and she shook, I shook and she pulled, and before morning we had peeled off yards of that paper.

A strip about as high as my head and half around the room.

And then when the sun came and that awful pattern began to laugh at me, I declared I would finish it today!

We go away tomorrow, and they are moving all my furniture down again to leave things as they were before.

Jennie looked at the wall in amazement, but I told her merrily that I did it out of pure spite at the vicious thing.

She laughed and said she wouldn't mind doing it herself, but I must not get tired.

How she betrayed herself that time!

But I am here, and no person touches this paper but me,—not *alive!*

She tried to get me out of the room—it was too patent! But I said it was so quiet and empty and clean now that I believed I would lie down again and sleep all I could; and not to wake me even for dinner—I would call when I woke.

So now she is gone, and the servants are gone, and the things are gone, and there is nothing left but that great bedstead nailed down, with the canvas mattress we found on it.

We shall sleep downstairs tonight, and take the boat home tomorrow.

I quite enjoy the room, now it is bare again.

How those children did tear about here!

This bedstead is fairly gnawed!

But I must get to work.

I have locked the door and thrown the key down into the front path.

I don't want to go out, and I don't want to have anybody come in, till John comes.

I want to astonish him.

I've got a rope up here that even Jennie did not find. If that woman does get out, and tries to get away, I can tie her!

But I forgot I could not reach far without anything to stand on!

This bed will *not* move!

I tried to lift and push it until I was lame, and then I got so angry I bit off a little piece at one corner—but it hurt my teeth.

Then I peeled off all the paper I could reach standing on the floor. It sticks horribly and the pattern just enjoys it! All those strangled heads and bulbous eyes and waddling fungus growths just shriek with derision!

I am getting angry enough to do something desperate. To jump out of the window would be admirable exercise, but the bars are too strong even to try.

Besides I wouldn't do it. Of course not. I know well enough that a step like that is improper and might be misconstrued.

I don't like to *look* out of the windows even—there are so many of those creeping women, and they creep so fast.

I wonder if they all come out of that wallpaper as I did?

But I am securely fastened now by my well-hidden rope—you don't get *me* out in the road there!

I suppose I shall have to get back behind the pattern when it comes night, and that is hard!

It is so pleasant to be out in this great room and creep around as I please!

I don't want to go outside. I won't, even if Jennie asks me to.

For outside you have to creep on the ground, and everything is green instead of yellow.

But here I can creep smoothly on the floor, and my shoulder just fits in that long smooch around the wall, so I cannot lose my way.

Why there's John at the door!

It is no use, young man, you can't open it!

How he does call and pound!

Now he's crying for an axe.

It would be a shame to break down that beautiful door!

"John dear!" said I in the gentlest voice, "the key is down by the front steps, under a plantain leaf!"

That silenced him for a few moments.

Then he said—very quietly indeed, "Open the door, my darling!"

"I can't," said I. "The key is down by the front door under a plantain leaf!"

And then I said it again, several times, very gently and slowly, and said it so often that he had to go and see, and he got it of course, and came in. He stopped short by the door.

"What is the matter?" he cried. "For God's sake, what are you doing!"

I kept on creeping just the same, but I looked at him over my shoulder.

"I've got out at last," said I, "in spite of you and Jane. And I've pulled off most of the paper, so you can't put me back!"

Now why should that man have fainted? But he did, and right across my path by the wall, so that I had to creep over him every time!

Insight

1. The relationship between John and his wife is critical to the story. How would you describe their relationship at the start of the story? In what ways does the wife's attitude toward her husband change as the story progresses? What reasons can you cite for this change?

2. Early in the story the narrator asks, "And what can one do?" She quickly follows this question with "What is one to do?" and finally with "But what is one to do?" What do these three rapid questions reveal about her feeling about herself and her situation?

3. How would you evaluate the husband's personal and professional treatment of his wife? To what degree is his treatment of her responsible for her situation? Explain.

PATTERNS

Amy Lowell

I walk down the garden paths,
And all the daffodils
Are blowing, and the bright blue squills.*

I walk down the patterned garden paths
In my stiff, brocaded gown.   5
With my powdered hair and jeweled fan,
I too am a rare
Pattern. As I wander down
The garden paths.

My dress is richly figured,   10
And the train
Makes a pink and silver stain
On the gravel, and the thrift*

Of the borders.
Just a plate of current fashion,   15
Tripping by in high-heeled, ribboned shoes.
Not a softness anywhere about me,
Only whalebone and brocade.
And I sink on a seat in the shade
Of a lime tree. For my passion   20
Wars against the stiff brocade.
The daffodils and squills
Flutter in the breeze
As they please.
And I weep;   25
For the lime tree is in blossom
And one small flower has dropped upon my bosom.

And the plashing of waterdrops
In the marble fountain
Comes down the garden paths.   30
The dripping never stops.

---

³ SQUILLS: narrow leaved plants bearing bell shaped flowers.   ¹³ THRIFT: pink or
white flowers.

Underneath my stiffened gown
Is the softness of a woman bathing in a marble basin,
A basin in the midst of hedges grown
So thick, she cannot see her lover hiding,   35
But she guesses he is near,
And the sliding of the water
Seems the stroking of a dear
Hand upon her.
What is Summer in a fine brocaded gown!   40
I should like to see it lying in a heap upon the ground.
All the pink and silver crumpled up on the ground.

I would be the pink and silver as I ran along the paths,
And he would stumble after,
Bewildered by my laughter.   45
I should see the sun flashing from his sword hilt and the buckles
    on his shoes.
I would choose
To lead him in a maze along the patterned paths,
A bright and laughing maze for my heavy-booted lover.
Till he caught me in the shade,   50
And the buttons of his waistcoat bruised my body as he
    clasped me,
Aching, melting, unafraid.
With the shadows of the leaves and the sundrops,
And the plopping of the waterdrops,
All about us in the open afternoon—   55
I am very like to swoon
With the weight of this brocade,
For the sun sifts through the shade.

Underneath the fallen blossom
In my bosom,   60
Is a letter I have hid.
It was brought to me this morning by a rider from the Duke.
"Madam, we regret to inform you that Lord Hartwell
Died in action Thursday se'nnight." *
As I read it in the white, morning sunlight,   65
The letters squirmed like snakes.
"Any answer, Madam," said my footman.
"No," I told him.
"See that the messenger takes some refreshment.

303   ⁶⁴ SE'NNIGHT: a period of seven days and nights.

No, no answer."   70
And I walked into the garden,
Up and down the patterned paths,
In my stiff, correct brocade.
The blue and yellow flowers stood up proudly in the sun,
Each one.   75
I stood upright too,
Held rigid to the pattern
By the stiffness of my gown.
Up and down I walked,
Up and down.   80

In a month he would have been my husband.
In a month, here, underneath this lime,
We would have broke the pattern;
He for me, and I for him,
He as Colonel, I as Lady,   85
On this shady seat.
He had a whim
That sunlight carried blessing.
And I answered, "It shall be as you have said."
Now he is dead.   90

In Summer and in Winter I shall walk
Up and down
The patterned garden paths
In my stiff, brocaded gown.
The squills and daffodils   95
Will give place to pillared roses, and to asters, and to snow.
I shall go
Up and down
In my gown.

Gorgeously arrayed,   100
Boned and stayed.
And the softness of my body will be guarded from embrace
By each button, hook, and lace.
For the man who should loose me is dead,
Fighting with the Duke in Flanders,   105
In a pattern called a war.
Christ! What are patterns for?

flowers, lilies, people, brocades were all are pattern up by

Insight

1. The setting of a poem often contributes to an understanding of its emotional tone, its mood, and its theme. Where does this poem take place? In what century? In what season of the year? How do these details of setting help to clarify the poem as a whole?

2. What is the event that has caused the speaker's reflections? What is the mood of the speaker? How would you describe the speaker and her reaction to this event?

3. The speaker refers to five particular patterns that concern her. What are these five individual patterns? What is their significance to the speaker?

IN SUMMARY

Insight and Composition

1. Over a hundred years ago Thoreau observed that most people "lead lives of quiet desperation." Which of the major characters in this unit reflect Thoreau's description? Explain.

2. At best the parent-child relationship is a difficult one. Feelings of inadequacy and guilt often cloud a relationship that should be open and loving. Examine the parent-child relationships in this unit. Which relationships seem to you most tenuous? Which, most satisfying? Explain.

3. With the possible exception of motherhood, the role of woman as wife is the most often examined in literature. What are your impressions of this role after reading the selections in this unit? Which selection made the greatest impression upon you? Why?

4. To be an individual in theory is easy; to be one in practice, often difficult. Subtle and sometimes not so subtle factors of time, place, or circumstance frequently frustrate our desires or control our destinies. Still, in every generation some people fulfill their individualism in spite of all obstacles. Which of the characters in this unit do you feel most successfully accomplished this end? What obstacles had to be overcome?

5. The poet speaks directly to the reader. She voices her anxieties, her frustrations, her joys, her sorrows. Many of the poets in this unit react to finding themselves in a given role. Which poets seem most outspoken in their protests? Which seem most accepting?

POETRY

"This is my letter to the World/That never wrote to me."
In this way Emily Dickinson describes her poetry.
Writing is risky—no one asks for the poet's letter.
Dickinson's letter contains, she says, the "simple
News" told her by Nature, and she realizes that she
commits Nature's message "To hands I cannot see."
She does not know who will read her letter. Some of
those who will read it have not yet been born. They
may be critical, they may judge harshly the poet's
unsolicited communication. But for the sake of Nature,
she quietly asks, "Judge tenderly—of Me." The message is so important, she says, that for its sake never
mind how impertinent, how bold, how surprising you
may find me for writing to you.

All poetry is a kind of letter to the world. A poem may
be a public statement or a private confession, it may
narrate a story or teach a moral idea, or sing about
experience, or describe a place or an object or a feeling. But it is meant to be received—to be read. Most
people have been in touch with poetry since childhood.
Nursery rhymes, jump rope ditties, ballads, songs without music, rhyming riddles, scary verses, and metrical
magic spells weave their way into the lives of children
in every culture. The pleasures of spoken poetry are the
deeply rooted basis of the later, richer pleasures of

written poetry. We have a feeling of how to read poetry because we have had the experience of hearing it; sounding it, remembering it, making it up and saying it, before we even learned to read.

We have gathered here some thirty poems written by women. The Greek poet Sappho, who was probably born in the seventh century B.C., is first. She was greatly admired as a poet in her day, and now, more than 2500 years later, her tender, deft, witty and passionate poetry reminds women of their venerable poetic tradition. Virginia Woolf said, "we think back through our mothers if we are women." For women poets, Sappho is the great mother.

We have included poems by some of the most famous women poets: Elizabeth Barrett Browning, Emily Brontë, Christina Rossetti, and Emily Dickinson, all from the nineteenth century, may be the most familiar names. We have also included several sixteenth and seventeenth century poets whose carefully constructed and toughminded poetry deserves to be better known. Within this unit we have included some poets writing in this century, and elsewhere in the book appear poems by other major twentieth century poets. In this section, however, we have brought together poems which give some idea of the riches available in poetry by women, and poems which fit together thematically in suggestive ways.

The main themes linking these poems are childhood, love, and death. The scenes from childhood range from the magical time recalled in May Swenson's poem "Centaur," to the "dark streets of fear" which dominated Marya Zaturenska's youth. There are poems here which celebrate the wonder and joy of love, others which explore the longing, pain, deceptions, loss, frustrations, and danger of love. The poems about death reveal a remarkable variety of attitude and experience. One poem expresses quiet Christian confidence about the soul's new life, another follows a long-dead ghost who has come back to haunt a beloved cottage. One poem describes mourning for someone who has been dead for fifteen Decembers, another cynically rejects suicide through a rejection of all available methods of killing oneself. Possibly the strangest poem here about death is the one where the speaker describes the moment just before her own death, when the stumbling buzz of a fly slips distractingly into her consciousness.

Why do people read poetry? Why do poets write it? One answer is a passion for authentic, raw experience. Emily Dickinson says, "I like a look of Agony,/Because I know it's true." It is not that she is indifferent to suffering, that she enjoys seeing a convulsion, a fit, a death. It is that so much human exchange is fake, half-real, simulated, that a genuine expression of extreme pain—or extreme anything—cuts through all artifice down to the marrow.

Marcia Folsom

POEMS

Sappho

So short
couldnt shorter

Tell everyone

Now, today, I shall
sing beautifully for
my friends' pleasure

immediate *just as alive as 27, cent. ago.*
about something tragic or happy

communicenty   *all friends*

gift of song   *a poet explains being a poet.*

Can be separate

We shall enjoy it   *could be anything*

As for him who finds
fault, may silliness
and sorrow take him!

single   *% of those who enjoy to those*
who dont, many to me

gender inclusive language

his misfortune

309

if, lord, thy love for me is strong

Teresa of Avila

If, Lord, thy love for me is strong
As this which binds me unto thee,
What holds me from thee, Lord, so long,
What holds thee, Lord, so long from me?

O soul, what then desirest thou?   5
—Lord, I would see thee, who thus choose thee.
What fears can yet assail thee now?
—All that I fear is but to lose thee.

Love's whole possession I entreat,
Lord, make my soul thine own abode,   10
And I will build a nest so sweet
It may not be too poor for God.

O soul in God hidden from sin,
What more desires for thee remain,
Save but to love, and love again,   15
And, all on flame with love within,
Love on, and turn to love again?

tHe soul's garment

Margaret Cavendish,

Duchess of Newcastle

Great Nature clothes the soul, which is but thin,
With fleshly garments, which the Fates do spin,
And when these garments are grown old and bare,
With sickness torn, Death takes them off with care,
And folds them up in peace and quiet rest,
And lays them safe within an earthly chest:
Then scours them well and makes them sweet and clean,
Fit for the soul to wear those clothes again.

Insight
1. Which speaker seems more uncertain about her relationship with God? What is the source of that uncertainty?
2. Which speaker appears to have worked out a more reassuring approach to life? What basic ideas constitute this approach?
3. *Apostrophe.* Apostrophe is a poetic device in which someone or something inhuman is addressed as if it were present and able to reply to what the speaker is saying. For example in the line, "Oh Romeo, Romeo! Wherefore art thou Romeo?" the absent lover is being addressed as if he were present. What is the apostrophe in the first poem? What does the use of this poetic device have upon the effectiveness of the poem?

SONG

Aphra Behn

Love in fantastic triumph sat,
Whilst bleeding hearts around him flowed,
For whom fresh pains he did create,
And strange tyrannic power he showed;
From thy bright eyes he took his fire,   5
Which round about, in sport he hurled;
But 'twas from mine, he took desire,
Enough to undo the amorous world.

From me he took his sighs and tears,
From thee his pride and cruelty;   10
From me his languishments and fears,
And every killing dart from thee;
Thus thou and I, the God have armed,
And set him up a deity;
But my poor heart alone is harmed,   15
Whilst thine the victor is, and free.

i can't hold you and i can't leave you

Sister Juana Inés de la Cruz

I can't hold you and I can't leave you,
and sorting the reasons to leave you or hold you,
I find an intangible one to love you,
and many tangible ones to forgo you.

As you won't change, nor let me forgo you,   5
I shall give my heart a defense against you,
so that half shall always be armed to abhor you,
though the other half be ready to adore you.

Then, if our love, by loving flourish,
let it not in endless feuding perish;   10
let us speak no more in jealousy and suspicion.

He offers not part, who would all receive—
so know that when it is your intention,
mine shall be to make believe.

Translated by Judith Thurman

A SONG

Anne Finch,

Countess of Winchilsea

'Tis strange, this Heart within my breast,
　　Reason opposing, and her Pow'rs,
Cannot one gentle Moment rest,
　　Unless it knows what's done in Yours.

In vain I ask it of your Eyes,　　　　　　　5
　　Which subt'ly wou'd my Fears controul;
For Art has taught them to disguise,
　　Which Nature made t' explain the Soul.

In vain that Sound, your Voice affords,
　　Flatters sometimes my easy Mind;　　　10
But of too vast Extent are Words
　　In them the Jewel Truth to find.

Then let my fond Enquiries cease,
　　And so let all my Troubles end:
For, sure, that Heart shall ne'er know Peace,　15
　　Which on Anothers do's depend.

Insight
1. How is love portrayed in each poem?
2. *Personification.* Personification is a figure of speech in which animals, objects, places, or ideas are given attributes of human beings. In other words, things are made to resemble persons. A child, for example, will often play with a doll and pretend that it is a baby with actual emotions and needs. As a result, that doll becomes more real to the child. In the Behn poem the emotion of love is personified as it takes on various human characteristics. What are these characteristics? What is the effect of the use of personification in this poem?

ON bEiNG bROUGHT FROM AFRICA TO AMERICA

Phillis Wheatley

'Twas mercy brought me from my *Pagan* land,
Taught my benighted soul to understand
That there's a God, that there's a *Saviour* too;
Once I redemption neither sought nor knew.
Some view our sable race with scornful eye,
"Their color is a diabolic die."
Remember, *Christians*, *Negroes*, black as *Cain*,
May be refined, and join th' angelic train.

Insight
1. Characterize the speaker of the poem.
2. How would you describe the "redemption" that the speaker "neither sought nor knew"?
3. *Allusion.* The literary device known as allusion is a reference to a place or a person which the poet assumes will be familiar to the reader. What are the allusions in this poem?

SONNETS FROM THE PORTUGUESE

Elizabeth Barrett Browning

Italian

XIV

*How much I
want you to
love me*

If thou must love me, let it be for nought   a
Except for love's sake only. Do not say   b
I love her for her smile—her look—her way   b
Of speaking gently,—for a trick of thought   a   *octave*
That falls in well with mine, and certes brought   5   a   *8*
A sense of pleasant ease on such a day'—   b
For these things in themselves, Belovèd, may   b
Be changed, or change for thee,—and love, so wrought,   a

changeable   May be unwrought so. Neither love me for   c
Thine own dear pity's wiping my cheeks dry,—   d   10
A creature might forget to weep, who bore   c
Thy comfort long, and lose thy love thereby!   d   *sestet*
But love me for love's sake, that evermore   c   *6*
Thou mayst love on, through love's eternity.   d

*for whats
unchanging
for* 'eternity' — *unknowable*

---

autobiographical

XXXV 35

mrs

If I leave all for thee, wilt thou exchange
And be all to me? Shall I never miss
Home-talk and blessing and the common kiss   *same*
That comes to each in turn, nor count it strange,
When I look up, to drop on a new range   5
Of walls and floors, another home than this?
Nay, wilt thou fill that place by me which is
*eyes tired from
weeping?*   Filled by dead eyes too tender to know change?   *parents, those left
behind*
That's hardest. If to conquer love, has tried,
*grief can only be
felt when one loves*   To conquer grief, tries more, as all things prove;   10
For grief indeed is love and grief beside.
Alas, I have grieved so I am hard to love.
Yet love me—wilt thou? Open thine heart wide,
And fold within the wet wings of thy dove.

*grief to be overcome
by love*

*conflict between love & grief
I've given up all & grief must be replaced by st. love*

Elizabeth Barrett Browning

XLIII

How do I love thee? Let me count the ways.
I love thee to the depth and breadth and height
My soul can reach, when feeling out of sight
For the ends of Being and ideal Grace.
I love thee to the level of everyday's   5
Most quiet need, by sun and candle-light.
I love thee freely, as men strive for Right;
I love thee purely, as they turn from Praise.
I love thee with the passion put to use
In my old griefs, and with my childhood's faith.   10
I love thee with a love I seemed to lose
With my lost saints,—I love thee with the breath,
Smiles, tears, of all my life!—and, if God choose,
I shall but love thee better after death.

Insight

1. *Sonnet.* A sonnet is a fourteen line lyric poem written in iambic
   pentameter usually employing a rhyme scheme of abba abba (octave) cd cd cd (sestet) as in the Petrarchan or Italian sonnet or
   ababcdcdefef (three quatrains) gg (one couplet) as in the Shakes-
   pearean or English sonnet. The first division of a sonnet (the octave
   or quatrains) will often ask a question or state an idea or situation.
   The last lines (the sestet or couplet) often reveal a change in
   thought or summarize or answer the original question asked. Examine the rhyme scheme of each of Browning's sonnets. Are these
   Italian or English sonnets? What is the general situation or question
   with which each opens? With what comment or answer does each
   close?

2. In Sonnet XIV the speaker asks that she be loved "for love's sake
   only". Why is this important to her? For what does she not care to
   be loved?

3. In Sonnet XXXV the speaker states what she will be leaving behind
   should she go with her lover. What will she be leaving? What does
   she wish from her lover?

4. "How do I love thee? Let me count the ways" is probably one of
   the most famous lines in English literature. Yet, "the ways" the
   speaker loves are not as well known. What are "the ways" she
   enumerates?

319

REMEMBRANCE

Emily Brontë

Cold in the earth, and the deep snow piled above thee!
Far, far removed, cold in the dreary grave!
Have I forgot, my only Love, to love thee,
Severed at last by Time's all-wearing wave?

Now, when alone, do my thoughts no longer hover   5
Over the mountains, on Angora's shore,
Resting their wings where heath and fern-leaves cover
That noble heart for ever, ever more?

Emily Brontë

Cold in the earth, and fifteen wild Decembers
From those brown hills, have melted into spring: 10
Faithful, indeed, is the spirit that remembers
After such years of change and suffering!

Sweet Love of youth, forgive, if I forget thee,
While the world's tide is bearing me along;
Sterner desires and darker hopes beset me,   15
Hopes which obscure, but cannot do thee wrong!

No other sun has lightened up my heaven,
No other star has ever shone for me;
All my life's bliss from thy dear life was given,
All my life's bliss is in the grave with thee.   20

But, when the days of golden dreams had perished,
And even Despair was powerless to destroy,
Then did I learn how existence could be cherished,
Strengthened, and fed without the aid of joy.

Then did I check the tears of useless passion—   25
Weaned my young soul from yearning after thine;
Sternly denied its burning wish to hasten
Down to that tomb already more than mine.

And, even yet, I dare not let it languish,
Dare not indulge in memory's rapturous pain;   30
Once drinking deep of that divinest anguish,
How could I seek the empty world again?

Insight

1. To whom is the poem addressed?
2. Why is it that the speaker feels she "dare not indulge in memory's rapturous pain"?
3. What has the speaker learned over the years?
4. *End rhymes.* The poetic device in which the end of one line repeats the stressed sound from the end of another line is known as an end rhyme. What are the end rhymes in the first three stanzas?

A birthday

Christina Rossetti

My heart is like a singing bird
    Whose nest is in a watered shoot:
My heart is like an apple-tree
    Whose boughs are bent with thickset fruit;
My heart is like a rainbow shell   5
    That paddles in a halcyon* sea;
My heart is gladder than all these
    Because my love is come to me.

Raise me a dais of silk and down;
    Hang it with vair* and purple dyes;   10
Carve it in doves and pomegranates,
    And peacocks with a hundred eyes;
Work it in gold and silver grapes,
    In leaves and silver fleur-de-lys;
Because the birthday of my life   15
    Is come, my love is come to me.

⁶ HALCYON: peaceful, calm.   ¹⁰ VAIR: a fur, used in medieval times to trim robes.

Insight
1. *Simile.* A simile is a figure of speech in which a comparison of unlike objects is expressed. The comparison is indicated by the words "like" or "as." To what has the speaker compared her heart in the first stanza? What effect does the use of simile have?
2. What event has caused the speaker's joy? How does she propose to celebrate the event?

emily dickinson

this is my letter to the world

This is my letter to the World
That never wrote to Me—
The simple News that Nature told—
With tender Majesty

Her Message is committed
To Hands I cannot see—
For love of Her—Sweet—countrymen—
Judge tenderly—of Me

i like a look of agony

I like a look of Agony,
Because I know it's true—
Men do not sham Convulsion,
Nor simulate, a Throe—*

The Eyes glaze once—and that is Death—
Impossible to feign
The Beads upon the Forehead
By homely Anguish strung.

* THROE: a violent pang or spasm of pain.

THERE'S BEEN A DEATH, IN THE OPPOSITE HOUSE

There's been a Death, in the Opposite House,
As lately as Today—
I know it, by the numb look
Such Houses have—alway—

The Neighbors rustle in and out—   5
The Doctor—drives away—
A Window opens like a Pod—
Abrupt—mechanically—

Somebody flings a Mattrass out—
The Children hurry by—   10
They wonder if it died—on that—
I used to—when a Boy—

The Minister—goes stiffly in—
As if the House were His—
And He owned all the Mourners—now—   15
And little Boys—besides—

And then the Milliner—and the Man
Of the Appalling Trade—
To take the measure of the House—

There'll be that Dark Parade—   20

Of Tassels—and of Coaches—soon—
Its easy as a Sign—
The Intuition of the News—
In just a Country Town—

i Heard a fly buzz

I heard a Fly buzz—when I died—
The Stillness in the Room
Was like the Stillness in the Air—
Between the Heaves of Storm—

The Eyes around—had wrung them dry—   5
And Breaths were gathering firm
For that last Onset—when the King
Be witnessed—in the Room—

I willed my Keepsakes—Signed away
What portion of me be   10
Assignable—and then it was
There interposed a Fly—

With Blue—uncertain stumbling Buzz—
Between the light—and me—
And then the Windows failed—and then   15
I could not see to see—

Insight

1. To what does "This" in "This Is My Letter to the World" refer? What subject matter will her letter contain? What relationship toward the world does the speaker imply? *vulnerable*

2. In "I Like a Look of Agony" what specific reasons does the speaker note for liking a "look of agony"? By implication, what is she implying about other emotions?

3. In "There's Been a Death" what specific observations cause the speaker to "know it"? Does she, in fact, "know it" or does she sense "the intuition of the news"? Who is "the Man/Of the Appalling Trade"? Why does the speaker say he takes "the measure of the House"?

4. In "I Heard a Fly Buzz" what ironic contrasts does the fly present to the events of the poem? What attitudes does the speaker imply about the fly's presence? What has happened to the speaker in the last two lines?

PURITAN SONNET

Elinor Wylie

Down to the Puritan marrow of my bones   a
There's something in this richness that I hate. b
I love the look, austere, immaculate,   b *dark*   *octet 8*
Of landscapes drawn in pearly monotones. a *gray*
There's something in my very blood that owns a   5
Bare hills, cold silver on a sky of slate,   b
A thread of water, churned to milky spate   b *rapid flow*
Streaming through slanted pastures fenced with stones. a

I love those skies, thin blue or snowy gray,   *thin cover of clouds*
Those fields sparse-planted, rendering meager sheaves; 10 d
That spring, briefer than apple-blossom's breath,   e   *sestet 6*
Summer, so much too beautiful to stay, *too rich* c *doesn't last*
Swift autumn, like a bonfire of leaves,   *cycles nature* d
And sleepy winter, like the sleep of death. *seems* e *frozen*

327

in tune w. her point → *she's never in tune*

a winter person

cold fear

Elizabeth Madox Roberts

As I came home through Drury's woods,
My face stung in the hard sleet.
The rough ground kept its frozen tracks;
They stumbled my feet.

The trees shook off the blowing frost.   5
The wind found out my coat was thin.
It tried to tear my clothes away.
And the cold came in.

The ice drops rattled where there was ice.
Each tree pushed back the other ones.   10
I did not pass a single bird,
Or anything that crawls or runs.

I saw a moth wing that was dry
And thin; it hung against a burr.
A few black leaves turned in a bush;   15
The grass was like cold, dead fur.

As I climbed over Howard's fence,
The wind came there with a sudden rush.
My teeth made a chattering sound,
And a bush said, "Hush!"   20

When I was in our house again,
With people there and fire and light,
A thought kept coming back to say,
"It will be cold out there tonight."

The clods are cold and the stones are cold,   25
The stiff trees shake and the hard air, . . .
And something said again to me,
"It will be cold out there."

And even when I talked myself,
And all the talk made a happy sound,   30
I kept remembering the wind
And the cold ground.

THE PEAR TREE

H.D. *Hilda Doolittle* *poet speaking to tree*

Silver dust
lifted from the earth,
higher than my arms reach,
you have mounted.
O silver, 5
higher than my arms reach
you front us with great mass;
no flower ever opened
so staunch a white leaf,
no flower ever parted silver 10
from such rare silver;

O white pear,
your flower-tufts
thick on the branch
bring summer and ripe fruits 15
in their purple hearts.

Insight
1. What is the setting (see page 25) of each poem? In each case
   what is the speaker's relationship to that setting?
2. Which poem presents the most terrifying picture of nature? Which
   speaker seems most appreciative of nature? Which poem offers
   the most vivid contrast?
3. *Imagery.* Imagery creates through words a representation of sense
   impressions as pictures do through color and line. Visual imagery, a
   picture seen in the mind, is the most common type of imagery in
   poetry. But poetic images may also portray other sense experiences
   as well—sound, touch, taste, smell. What images in these poems
   did you find most effective?

still falls the rain

Edith Sitwell

The Raids, 1940. Night and Dawn

Still falls the Rain—
Dark as the world of man, black as our loss—
Blind as the nineteen hundred and forty nails
Upon the cross.

Still falls the Rain   5
With a sound like the pulse of the heart that is changed to the
      hammer-beat
In the Potter's Field, and the sound of the impious feet

On the Tomb:
           Still falls the Rain
In the Field of Blood where the small hopes breed and the human
      brain   10
Nurtures its greed, that worm with the brow of Cain.

Still falls the Rain
At the feet of the Starved Man hung upon the Cross.

Christ that each day, each night, nails there, have mercy on us—
On Dives and on Lazarus: 15
Under the rain the sore and the gold are as one.

Still falls the Rain—
Still falls the blood from the Starved Man's wounded Side:
He bears in His Heart all wounds,—those of the light that died,
The last faint spark   20
In the self-murdered heart, the wounds of the sad uncompre-
      hending dark,

The wounds of the baited bear,—
The blind and weeping bear whom the keepers beat
On his helpless flesh . . . the tears of the hunted hare.

Still falls the Rain—   25
Then—O Ile leape up to my God: who pulles me doune—
See, see where Christ's blood streames in the firmament:
It flows from the Brow we nailed upon the tree
Deep to the dying, to the thirsting heart
That holds the fires of the world,—dark-smirched with pain   30
As Caesar's laurel crown.

Then sounds the voice of One who like the heart of man
Was once a child who among beasts has lain—
"Still do I love, still shed my innocent light, my Blood, for thee."

Insight
1. Sitwell portrays a modern event through references to an historical event. What are the two events? What does the poem say about each?
2. *Symbol.* When a word, an action, or an object stands for something larger than itself it can be considered a symbol. A heart, for example, has long been considered a symbol of love while a snake has long symbolized evil. In this poem what could the rain symbolize? Explain.

iN ThE EVENiNG

Anna Akhmatova

On the terrace, violins played
the most heartbreaking songs.
A sharp, fresh smell of the sea
came from oysters on a dish of ice.

He said: *I'm a faithful friend,*   5
touching my dress.
How far from a caress,
the touch of that hand!

The way you stroke a cat, a bird,
the look you give a shapely bareback rider.   10
In his calm eyes, only laughter
under the light-gold lashes.

And the violins mourn on
behind drifting smoke:
Thank your stars, you're at last alone   15
with the man you love.

Adapted by Adrienne Rich

INTIMATE

Gabriela Mistral

Squeeze not my hands
for eternity will come,
time to rest amid the dust
and shade with fingers
all entwined.   5

And you may say: "I cannot
love her, for already are her
fingers falling off like grains
from ears of corn."

Kiss not my lips,   10
for there will come the time
of diffused light in which I shall be
lipless, lifeless,
and lie on the damp earth.

And you may say,   15
"I loved her, but I cannot
love her now for she cannot breathe
the clean sweetness of my kiss."

And what anguish to hear this
and you would talk on blind and crazily,   20
for when my fingers fall
my hand shall strike your brow
and my breath shall blow
upon your anxious face.

Touch me not.   25
I should lie telling you
that I confer my love within these
extended arms, my mouth, my neck
and you, believing you have drunk me down,
will deceive yourself like a blinded child.   30

For my love is not alone this frail shell,
the tired, dried corn-husk of my frame
which trembles at the rushing wind
and holds me down when I would fly.

For it is the kiss' meaning, not the lip,   35
what the voice says, not the chest.
A wind from God cutting through
and all the frailty of my flesh, away.

Insight

1. How does each speaker characterize her lover?
2. Compare the tone (see page 10) of the two poems. Which words or lines are particularly effective in conveying the tone?

siLENCE

Marianne Moore

My father used to say,
"Superior people never make long visits,
have to be shown Longfellow's grave
or the glass flowers at Harvard.
Self-reliant like the cat—   5
that takes its prey to privacy,
the mouse's limp tail hanging like a shoelace from its mouth—
they sometimes enjoy solitude,
and can be robbed of speech
by speech which has delighted them.   10
The deepest feeling always shows itself in silence;
not in silence, but restraint."
Nor was he insincere in saying, "Make my house your inn."
Inns are not residences.

Insight
1. How, according to the speaker's father, do "superior people" act?
2. The last two lines perfectly illustrate the values that are important
   to the speaker's father. What is the irony (see page 5) of these
   two lines?

A LETTER

Marina Tsvetayeva

So they don't expect
letters. So they wait for—
a letter.

A ragged scrap
circled   5
by sticky tape. Inside—

a scribble,
and happiness.
And that's all.

So, they don't expect   10
happiness. So they expect—
the end.

A soldierly
salute, and
three slugs of lead in the breast.   15

They see a flash
of red. And
that's all.

It's not happiness, old girl!
The wildflower color—   20
the wind blew it away.

A square courtyard
and black gun-muzzles.
A square letter,

ink, sorcery.   25
When it comes to
death, the

last dream, no one's
old.
A square letter.   30

Adapted by Denise Levertov

Elizabeth

Sylvia Townsend Warner

"Elizabeth the Beloved"—
So much says the stone
That is all with weather defaced,
With moss overgrown.

But if to husband or child,   5
Brother or sire, most dear
Is past deciphering;
This only is clear:

That once she was beloved,
Was Elizabeth,   10
And is now beloved no longer,
If it be not of Death.

RÉSUMÉ

Dorothy Parker

Razors pain you;
Rivers are damp;
Acids stain you;
And drugs cause cramp.
Guns aren't lawful;
Nooses give;
Gas smells awful;
You might as well live.

Insight
1. *Paradox.* Paradox is an apparent contradiction which, on the surface, seems contradictory, yet if interpreted figuratively involves an
   element of truth. Wordsworth's line, "The child is father of the
   man," is a contradiction, but does indeed reveal some truth. What
   apparent contradictions appear in "A Letter"? What effect does the
   use of paradox have in this poem?
2. What is the situation presented in "Elizabeth"?
3. Parker in "Résumé," Warner in "Elizabeth," and Tsvetayeva in
   "A Letter" all speak of death. What attitude toward death does
   each poem reveal?

THE MEETING

Louise Bogan

For years I thought I knew, at the bottom of the dream,
Who spoke but to say farewell,
Whose smile dissolved, after his first words
Gentle and plausible.

Each time I found him, it was always the same: 5
Recognition and surprise,
And then the silence, after the first words,
And the shifting of the eyes.

Then the moment when he had nothing to say
And only smiled again,   10
But this time toward a place beyond me, where I could not stay—
No world of men.

Now I am not sure. Who are you? Who have you been?
Why do our paths cross?
At the deepest bottom of the dream you are let in,   15
A symbol of loss.

Eye to eye we look, and we greet each other.
Like friends from the same land.
Bitter compliance! Like a faithless brother
You take and drop my hand.   20

Insight

1. Describe the relationship between the speaker and the man in this poem.

2. How would you describe the tone (see page 10) of the poem? Which lines were particularly effective in establishing the tone?

to the dark god

Paula Ludwig

Who told you where I am
have I then a name
was I not well hidden in the brush
cloaked in the brown of fallen leaf
green boughs hanging over me   5
were my eyes not sunk into the damp forest floor
my toes not entwined in the roots of the sweetwood?

How did you nonetheless trace me
with the scent of a hunter
without trap or dagger   10
you drew near on the darkest path
With the eye that no one sees
you looked at me

Because I betrayed myself there in the dim
no leaf moved   15
no drop fell
But in the stillness could be heard
my hands growing toward you.

Translated by Candice L. McRee

Insight
1. From whom has the speaker been hiding? How is it that she has
   been found?
2. What is the significance of the speaker's statement, "I betrayed
   myself"?

SONG

Marya Zaturenska

Life with her weary eyes,
Smiles, and lifts high her horn
Of plenty and surprise,
Not so where I was born

In the dark streets of fear,   5
In the damp houses where greed
Grew sharper every year
Through hunger and through need.

Lest the harsh atmosphere
Corrode, defeat, destroy   10
I built a world too clear,
Too luminous for joy.

Unnatural day on night
I built—tall tower on tower,
Bright on supernal light   15
Transfixed the too-bright flower.

But see how it has grown!
The cold dream melts, the frost
Dissolves,—the dream has sown
A harvest never lost.   20

Blood runs into the veins,
The wild hair in the wind
Waves in the natural rains;
The harsh world and unkind

Smiles, and its eye grown mild   25
Surveys this nothingness
Like an indifferent child
Too sleepy to undress.

RiDE

Josephine Miles

It's not my world, I grant, but I made it.
It's not my ranch, lean oak, buzzard crow,
Not my fryers, mixmaster, well-garden.
And now it's down the road and I made it.

It's not your rackety car but you drive it.
It's not your four-door, top-speed, white-wall tires,
Not our state, not even, I guess, our nation,
But now it's down the road, and we're in it.

Insight
1. The speaker in "Song" mentions two different worlds with which she is familiar. What are the differences in these two worlds? What has the speaker done to protect herself from the conditions under which she was born? What eventually happens to this protection?
2. How does the speaker in "Song" finally view the world around her? What might have been the "surprise" in the horn of plenty?
3. Compare the way the speaker has dealt with her world in the Miles poem as contrasted with the speaker in the Zaturenska poem.

iN TiME liKE AiR

May Sarton

Consider the mysterious salt:
In water it must disappear.
It has no self. It knows no fault.
Not even sight may apprehend it.
No one may gather it or spend it.   5
It is dissolved and everywhere.

May Sarton

But out of water into air
It must resolve into a presence,
Precise, and tangible, and here.
Faultlessly pure, faultlessly white,   10
It crystallizes in our sight
And has defined itself to essence.

What element dissolves the soul
So it may be both found and lost,
In what suspended as a whole?   15
What is the element so blest
In which identity can rest
As salt in the clear water cast?

Love in its early transformation,
And only love, may so design it   20
That the self flows in pure sensation,
Is all dissolved and found at last
Without a future or a past,
And a whole life suspended in it.

The faultless crystal of detachment   25
Comes after, cannot be created
Without the first intense attachment.
Even the saints achieve this slowly;
For us, more human and less holy,
In time like air is essence stated.   30

Insight
1. "Consider the mysterious salt" the poem begins. What does the
   speaker feel is so mysterious about salt?
2. How are the first two stanzas a preparation for the question posed
   in the third stanza?
3. What is the element that "dissolves," "defines," and "transforms"
   the soul? What are the stages this element goes through?
4. *Metaphor.* An implied comparison between unlike objects is known
   as a metaphor. What is the metaphor with which the poet deals
   here?

347

beverly hills, chicago

Gwendolyn Brooks

("and the people live till they have white hair")
                                        E. M. Price

The dry brown coughing beneath their feet,
(Only a while, for the handyman is on his way)
These people walk their golden gardens.
We say ourselves fortunate to be driving by today.

That we may look at them, in their gardens where   5
The summer ripeness rots. But not raggedly.
Even the leaves fall down in lovelier patterns here.
And the refuse, the refuse is a neat brilliancy.

When they flow sweetly into their houses
With softness and slowness touched by that everlasting gold,   10
We know what they go to. To tea. But that does not mean
They will throw some little black dots into some water and add
        sugar and the juice of the cheapest lemons that are sold,

While downstairs that woman's vague phonograph bleats,
        "Knock me a kiss."   15
And the living all to be made again in the sweatingest physical
        manner
Tomorrow. . . . Not that anybody is saying that these people have
        no trouble.
Merely that it is trouble with a gold-flecked beautiful banner.   20

Nobody is saying that these people do not ultimately cease to be.
        And
Sometimes their passings are even more painful than ours.
It is just that so often they live till their hair is white.
They make excellent corpses, among the expensive flowers. . . .   25

Nobody is furious. Nobody hates these people.
At least, nobody driving by in this car.
It is only natural, however, that it should occur to us
How much more fortunate they are than we are.

It is only natural that we should look and look   30
At their wood and brick and stone
And think, while a breath of pine blows,
How different these are from our own.

We do not want them to have less.
But it is only natural that we should think we have not enough.   35
We drive on, we drive on.
When we speak to each other our voices are a little gruff.

Insight

1. Who is the speaker in this poem? Where is she going?
2. Contrast the two neighborhoods that are described by Brooks.
3. Does the speaker covet the Beverly Hills neighborhood? What is it that she wants?
4. *Alliteration.* The repetition of consonant sounds in words close together is called alliteration. For example, "golden gardens" is an alliterative phrase in the first stanza. What other examples of alliteration can you find in this poem?

THE CENTAUR

May Swenson

Both horse & rider

The summer that I was ten—
Can it be there was only one
summer that I was ten? It must

have been a long one then—
each day I'd go out to choose   5
a fresh horse from my stable

which was a willow grove
down by the old canal.
I'd go on my two bare feet.

But when, with my brother's jack-knife,   10
I had cut me a long limber horse
with a good thick knob for a head,

and peeled him slick and clean
except a few leaves for the tail,
and cinched my brother's belt   15

around his head for a rein,
I'd straddle and canter him fast
up the grass bank to the path,

trot along in the lovely dust
that talcumed over his hoofs,   20
hiding my toes, and turning

his feet to swift half-moons.
The willow knob with the strap
jouncing between my thighs   *uplifted protruding part of saddle*

was the pommel and yet the poll *   *also*   25
of my nickering pony's head.
My head and my neck were mine,

[25] POLL: the top of the head where hair grows.

yet they were shaped like a horse.
My hair flopped to the side
like the mane of a horse in the wind.   30

My forelock swung in my eyes,
my neck arched and I snorted.
I shied and skittered and reared,

stopped and raised my knees,
pawed at the ground and quivered.   35
My teeth bared as we wheeled

and swished through the dust again.
I was the horse and the rider,
and the leather I slapped to his rump

spanked my own behind.   40
Doubled, my two hoofs beat
a gallop along the bank,

the wind twanged in my mane,
my mouth squared to the bit.
And yet I sat on my steed   45

quiet, negligent riding,
my toes standing the stirrups,
my thighs hugging his ribs.

At a walk we drew up to the porch.
I tethered him to a paling.   50
Dismounting, I smoothed my skirt

and entered the dusky hall.
My feet on the clean linoleum
left ghostly toes in the hall.

Where have you been? said my mother.   55
Been riding, I said from the sink,
and filled me a glass of water.

What's that in your pocket? she said.
Just my knife. It weighted my pocket
and stretched my dress awry.   60

Go tie back your hair, said my mother,
and *Why is your mouth all green?*
Rob Roy, he pulled some clover   ~~sweet grass~~
as we crossed the field, I told her.

Insight

1. What is it about the speaker's tenth summer that was so memorable to her? What does she imply in the first two lines of the poem?
2. What is significant about the mother's comments when the speaker returns home from her game?
3. *Onomatopoeia.* When the sound of a word suggests its meaning it is said to be onomatopoetic. Slush, murmur, gurgle are examples of onomatopoetic words. This device is used to express sense through sound. What examples can you find in "The Centaur"?

tHE AlARM clock

Mari Evans

Alarm clock
sure sound
loud
this mornin' . . .
remind me of the time   5
I sat down
in a drug store
with my
mind
away far off . . .   10
until the girl
and she was small
it seems to me
with yellow hair
a hangin'   15
smiled up and said
"I'm sorry but
we don't serve
you people
here"   20
and I woke up
quick
like I did this mornin
when the
alarm   25
went off . . .
It don't do
to wake up
quick . . .

Insight
1. Why does the morning alarm clock remind the speaker of the incident in the drug store? What similarities exist between the two
   wakings?
2. To what did the speaker awaken in the drug store? What details in
   the poem contribute to the shock of the awakening?

353

THE GARDENER TO HIS GOD

Mona Van Duyn

"Amazing research proves simple
prayer makes flowers grow many times
faster, stronger, larger."
—*Advertisement in* The Flower Grower

I pray that the great world's flowering stay as it is,
that larkspur and snapdragon keep to their ordinary size,
and bleedingheart hang in its old way, and Judas tree
stand well below oak, and old oaks color the fall sky.
For the myrtle to keep underfoot, and no rose   5
to send up a swollen face, I pray simply.

There is no disorder but the heart's. But if love goes leaking
outward, if shrubs take up its monstrous stalking,
all greenery is spurred, the snapping lips are overgrown,
and over oaks red hearts hang like the sun.   10
Deliver us from its giant gardening, from walking
all over the earth with no rest from its disproportion.

Let all flowers turn to stone before ever they begin to share
love's spaciousness, and faster, stronger, larger
grow from a sweet thought, before any daisy   15
turns, under love's gibberellic* wish, to the day's eye.
Let all blooms take shape from cold laws, down from a cold air
let come their small grace or measurable majesty.

For in every place but love the imagination lies
in its limits. Even poems draw back from images   20
of that one country, on top of whose lunatic stemming
whoever finds himself there must sway and cling
until the high cold God takes pity, and it all dies
down, down into the great world's flowering.

354   16 GIBBERELLIC: gibberellic acid is used to promote stem growth of plants.

MAY 10TH

Maxine Kumin

I mean
the fiddleheads have forced their babies,
blind topknots first, up from the thinking rhizomes,
and the shrew's children, twenty to a teaspoon,
breathe to their own astonishment   5
in the peephole burrow.

I mean
a new bat hangs upside down in the privy;
its eyes are stuck tight, its wrinkled pink mouth twitches,
and in the pond, itself an invented puddle,   10
tadpoles quake from the jello
and come into being.

I mean walk softly.
The maple's little used-up bells are dropping
and the new leaves are now unpacking,   15
still wearing their dime-store lacquer,
still cramped and wet from the journey.

Insight
1. Why does the speaker in the Van Duyn poem "pray that the great
    world's flowering stay as it is"? What has brought this prayer upon
    her?
2. What aspects of nature does the speaker of the Kumin poem talk
    about? How would you define her attitude toward nature?
3. Nature has always been an inspiration for poetry. While clouds,
    skylarks, spring rain, and autumn colors have never ceased to
    amaze all sensitive persons, they have particularly inspired poets
    to expressions of appreciation. In which of these poems do the
    more typical images of nature appear? With what kind of images
    are these two poets concerned? In which poem do you feel the
    imagery is most successful?

fuRTHER NOTES foR THE aluMNi bulleTiN

Patricia Cumming

We thought—we thought
we could,
like everyone,
marry, have children, work, give

dinner parties for our friends;   5
at the end
of each day the wedding silver
would shine on the table,

the candles would be
lit, everything in   10
order. We thought we could banish
the faceless

dark, the sticky
cobwebs in the hall:
we thought the   15
hollowness would go away.

Then we'd be free to make
beds and salad dressing, get our watches
fixed, and the car, like
everyone. But   20

look.
The ashtrays are overflowing,
we cannot get up
to empty them; the candles are

burned out; the silver's   25
tarnished, useless; the bottles have been
empty for weeks. We
sit, frozen, trying

to live, murdering each other
for ourselves, for the darkness love   30
could not lighten—and the children,
the children wait,

silent now, and, in the morning,
go to school.

Insight
1. What were the speaker's expectations of life when she got married? In what way has she been disappointed?
2. What attitude toward children is expressed in the fourth line of the
   poem? Is a different attitude expressed about children at the end
   of the poem?

ON SEEING MY GREAT-AUNT
IN A FUNERAL PARLOR

Diana Chang

She died away from home
Moved to floral rooms
Hotels of death are near

My aunt lies quiet here
The smiling winter bride   5
Her wedding bed the earth

My aunt receives the spade
Her stony flesh is frail
Her bones light as at birth

The trees are human veins   10
The sunset cries anew
Her blood was used in love

The old are girlish now
Going to their grooms
They marry mysteries   15

She travels past the light
She leaves us listening
Her speech is young somewhere

We are the sleeping guests
Talking in our night   20
On her happy dawn

The heart does leap in love
Though the growing spirit hurts
The pain of joy is life.

Insight
1. What two ceremonial events are mentioned in the poem? What
   similarities exist between these events?
2. What basic paradox (see page 340) about life and death exists in
   the poem? What basic attitude toward death is implied?

A dREAM

Bella Akhmadulina

It's all familiar,
the fall air, clear and sober,
the little house, the door half open,
the salty taste of our apples,

but a stranger is raking the garden.   5
He says he is the rightful owner now,
and asks me in. The brick floor, the blank
where the clock stood, that slant of light,

my rushed, uncertain steps,
my eyes that saw, and saw nothing,   10
your tender voices . . . but the gardener's wife
is standing there waiting.

"It's so foggy here! I lived here too, once,
a hundred years ago . . .
it's all the same, that same   15
smoky smell over the garden,

the dog's fur still wet on my fingers . . ."
"You don't say," the gardener answers,
cocking his head, coming closer.
Then he smiles, and asks,   20

"Isn't it you, though, that picture
up in the attic? Isn't it her,
with the long, old-fashioned curls?
But your eyes have changed

since those terrible old days   25
a hundred years ago,
when you died, alone in the house here,
poor, without work or friends."

Adapted by Jean Valentine

Insight
1. What dream does the speaker have?
2. What present fears does the speaker reveal through the dream?

361

EdEN iS A ZOO

Margaret Atwood

I keep my parents in a garden
among lumpy trees, green sponges
on popsickle sticks. I give them a lopsided
sun which drops its heat
in spokes the colour of yellow crayon.   5

They have thick elephant legs,
quills for hair and tiny heads;
they clump about under the trees
dressed in the clothes of thirty years
ago, on them innocent as plain skin.   10

Are they bewildered when they come across
corners of rooms in the forest,
a tin cup shining like pearl,
a frayed pink blanket, a rusted shovel?

Does it bother them to perform   15
the same actions over and over,
hands gathering white flowers
by the lake or tracing designs in the sand,
a word repeated till it hangs carved

forever in the blue air?   20

Are they content?

Do they want to get out?

Do they see me looking at them
from across the hedge of spikes
and cardboard fire painted red   25
I built with so much time
and pain, but
they don't know is there?

Insight

1. "I keep my parents in a garden" states the speaker. What kind of garden does she describe? Why are her parents there?
2. Beginning with the third stanza, the speaker asks several questions which go unanswered. What are these questions? Are any answers implied?
3. "Eden Is a Zoo" abounds in unique images that stand for an idea in the poet's mind. Which images are particularly effective?

iN SUMMARY

Insight and Composition

1. As stated in the introduction to this unit, "A poem may be a public statement or a private confession, it may narrate a story or teach a moral idea, or sing about experience, or describe a place or an object or a feeling." Select poems from this unit that you feel fit into each of these categories. Which categories do you find most prevalent?
2. Poetry is a special kind of language, a language less literal and more figurative than prose. The use, for example, of metaphor, simile, and imagery enhances meaning and feeling. Which poems in the unit did you find most striking in their use of figurative language?
3. Sometimes poets appear to speak directly to the reader as, for example, in the Wheatley or Dickinson poems. At other times poets create a speaker to convey the poem's idea and emotion. In either case, however, a human voice is heard. Which voices did you find most compelling? What quality in each voice most impressed you?
4. All poetry is concerned with experience. A poet seeks to allow a reader to share in an experience, whether the experience be a physical or a mental one. Which poems allowed you most vividly to share in the poet's experience?
5. The poems in this unit are thematically linked primarily around childhood, love, and death. What are some of the poems that fall into each theme? What similarities do you find within each theme? Can you note any other themes that recur in these poems?

BREAKING FREE

Have you ever felt like opening all the windows and letting the wind blow through your room? From some buried region of the psyche comes a need to empty drawers, to sweep under the bed, to throw away all your tired old scraps of paper, worn-out clothes, unfinished letters. Did you ever suddenly want to rearrange furniture, change the pictures, make everything fresh and simple and clean? When you break free of old forms, old failures, old rubbish, suddenly you feel like a new person.

In the final section of this book are gathered works of literature which explore the problems and the rewards of different ways of breaking free. Two of the stories examine what happens when someone misses her chance to break free. A teacher longs to be a painter. From every word she says describing color, light and shadow, the mood of a landscape, the arrangement of a postcard on a table, we know that she should be a painter and not a teacher. But she loses her nerve. In Jessamyn West's strong, vengeful story, we discover the malignant effects of personal cowardice. The story by Ursula Mac-Dougall begins with a woman's death. Her sister seems at last to be liberated from her role as "the quiet one." But there are tremendous pressures on her to go on fulfilling that outgrown role.

Doris Lessing's story, "An Old Woman and Her Cat," is about a success in breaking free. Hetty, a woman who does not want to be respectable and to grow older in a tame, boring rest home, manages to escape her children, the law, all of society in fact, and lives a gypsy life at the edge of conventional London. But at what a cost! On the other hand, in "A New England Nun," a woman lives the most respectable and tame existence imaginable: in her spotless, orderly household, Louisa seems utterly unlike Hetty. But she too treasures her solitude, and breaking free for her—as for Hetty—means preserving her independence rather than fulfilling even her own conventional expectations. Sara Teasdale's "Advice to a Girl" is to remember that: "No one worth possessing can be quite possessed."

Breaking free may be simple, personal, and physical—like finding the strength to quit smoking, or lose twenty pounds, or learning a sport which makes you proud of your new, strong body. And sometimes breaking free is a major emotional upheaval—involving other people as well as yourself. Leaving parents for the first time—whether you plan it together in goodwill or run away in a fit of rage—means a new start and maybe old longings for everyone. Ending a marriage, breaking free of old fantasies, leaving a town you have hated or loved, all may be moments when you determine your own psychic health.

Margaret Walker's poem, "For My People," makes clear that one way for individuals to break free of poverty, drudgery, and confusion is for groups of people to break free together. Edna St. Vincent Millay reflects that understanding in her poem to Inez Milholland, a fighter for women's rights. And in the first chapter of Virginia Woolf's great essay, *A Room of One's Own,* we can see how intertwined are personal and political freedom. Somehow, she says, there is a connection between leisure and creativity, between everyday life and immortal fiction, between good food and good feelings, between economics and art, between time to work and the chance for expression. Breaking free for women means not having thirteen children, not having to grub and struggle for privacy, means at least a little solitary time (interruptions there will always be), and hopefully, a room of one's own, for reflection, and perhaps, for writing.

Marcia Folsom

A NEW ENGLAND NUN

Mary Wilkins Freeman

It was late in the afternoon, and the light was waning. There was a difference in the look of the tree shadows out in the yard. Somewhere in the distance, cows were lowing and a little bell was tinkling; now and then a farm wagon tilted by, and the dust flew; some blue-shirted laborers with shovels over their shoulders plodded past; little swarms of flies were dancing up and down before the people's faces in the soft air. There seemed to be a gentle stir arising over every-thing for the mere sake of subsidence—a very premonition of rest and hush and night.

This soft diurnal commotion was over Louisa Ellis also. She had been peacefully sewing at her sitting-room window all the afternoon. Now she quilted her needle carefully into her work, which she folded precisely, and laid in a basket with her thimble and thread and scissors. Louisa Ellis could not remember that ever in her life she had mis-laid one of these little feminine appurtenances, which had become, from long use and constant association, a very part of her personality.

Louisa tied a green apron round her waist, and got out a flat straw hat with a green ribbon. Then she went into the garden with a little blue crockery bowl, to pick some currants for her tea. After the cur-rants were picked she sat on the back doorstep and stemmed them, collecting the stems carefully in her apron and afterward throwing them into the hencoop. She looked sharply at the grass beside the step to see if any had fallen there. *fastidious*

Louisa was slow and still in her movements; it took her a long time to prepare her tea; but when ready it was set forth with as much grace as if she had been a veritable guest to her own self. The little square table stood exactly in the center of the kitchen, and was covered with a starched linen cloth whose border pattern of flowers glistened. Louisa had a damask napkin on her tea tray, where were arranged a cut-glass tumbler full of teaspoons, a silver cream pitcher, a china sugar bowl, and one pink china cup and saucer. Louisa used china every day—something which none of her neighbors did. They whis-pered about it among themselves. Their daily tables were laid with common crockery, their sets of best china stayed in the parlor closet, and Louisa Ellis was no richer nor better bred than they. Still she would use the china. She had for her supper a glass dish full of sugared currants, a plate of little cakes, and one of light white biscuits.

Also a leaf or two of lettuce, which she cut up daintily. Louisa was very fond of lettuce, which she raised to perfection in her little garden. She ate quite heartily, though in a delicate, pecking way; it seemed almost surprising that any considerable bulk of the food should vanish.

After tea she filled a plate with nicely baked thin corn cakes, and carried them out into the back yard.

"Caesar!" she called. "Caesar! Caesar!"

There was a little rush, and the clank of a chain, and a large yellow-and-white dog appeared at the door of his tiny hut, which was half hidden among the tall grasses and flowers. Louisa patted him and gave him the corn cakes. Then she returned to the house and washed the tea things, polishing the china carefully. The twilight had deepened; the chorus of the frogs floated in at the open window wonderfully loud and shrill, and once in a while a long sharp drone from a tree toad pierced it. Louisa took off her green gingham apron, disclosing a shorter one of pink-and-white print. She lighted her lamp, and sat down again with her sewing.

In about half an hour Joe Dagget came. She heard his heavy step on the walk, and rose and took off her pink-and-white apron. Under that was still another—white linen with a little cambric edging on the bottom; that was Louisa's company apron. She never wore it without her calico sewing apron over it unless she had a guest. She had barely folded the pink-and-white one with methodical haste and laid it in a table drawer when the door opened and Joe Dagget entered.

He seemed to fill up the whole room. A little yellow canary that had been asleep in his green cage at the south window woke up and fluttered wildly, beating his little yellow wings against the wires. He always did so when Joe Dagget came into the room.

"Good evening," said Louisa. She extended her hand with a kind of solemn cordiality.

"Good evening, Louisa," returned the man, in a loud voice.

She placed a chair for him, and they sat facing each other, with the table between them. He sat bolt upright, toeing out his heavy feet squarely, glancing with a good-humored uneasiness around the room. She sat gently erect, folding her slender hands in her white-linen lap.

"Been a pleasant day," remarked Dagget.

"Real pleasant," Louisa assented, softly. "Have you been haying?" she asked, after a little while.

"Yes, I've been haying all day, down in the ten-acre lot. Pretty hot work."

"It must be."

"Yes, it's pretty hot work in the sun."

"Is your mother well today?"

"Yes, Mother's pretty well."

"I suppose Lily Dyer's with her now?"

Dagget colored. "Yes, she's with her," he answered, slowly.

He was not very young, but there was a boyish look about his large face. Louisa was not quite so old as he, her face was fairer and smoother, but she gave people the impression of being older.

"I suppose she's a good deal of help to your mother," she said, further.

"I guess she is; I don't know how mother'd get along without her," said Dagget, with a sort of embarrassed warmth.

"She looks like a real capable girl. She's pretty-looking too," remarked Louisa.

"Yes, she is pretty fair looking."

Presently Dagget began fingering the books on the table. There was a square red autograph album, and a Young Lady's Gift Book which had belonged to Louisa's mother. He took them up one after the other and opened them; then laid them down again, the album on the Gift Book.

Louisa kept eyeing them with mild uneasiness. Finally she rose and changed the position of the books, putting the album underneath. That was the way they had been arranged in the first place.

Dagget gave an awkward little laugh. "Now what difference did it make which book was on top?" said he.

Louisa looked at him with a deprecating smile. "I always keep them that way," murmured she.

"You do beat everything," said Dagget, trying to laugh again. His large face was flushed.

He remained about an hour longer, then rose to take leave. Going out, he stumbled over a rug, and trying to recover himself, hit Louisa's work basket on the table, and knocked it on the floor.

He looked at Louisa, then at the rolling spools; he ducked himself awkwardly toward them, but she stopped him. "Never mind," said she; "I'll pick them up after you're gone."

She spoke with a mild stiffness. Either she was a little disturbed, or his nervousness affected her and made her seem constrained in her effort to reassure him.

When Joe Dagget was outside he drew in the sweet evening air with a sigh, and felt much as an innocent and perfectly well-intentioned bear might after his exit from a china shop.

Louisa, on her part, felt much as the kind-hearted, long-suffering owner of the china shop might have done after the exit of the bear.

She tied on the pink, then the green apron, picked up all the scattered treasures and replaced them in her work basket, and straightened the rug. Then she set the lamp on the floor and began sharply examining the carpet. She even rubbed her fingers over it, and looked at them.

"He's tracked in a good deal of dust," she murmured. "I thought he must have."

Louisa got a dustpan and brush, and swept Joe Dagget's track carefully.

If he could have known it, it would have increased his perplexity and uneasiness, although it would not have disturbed his loyalty in the least. He came twice a week to see Louisa Ellis, and every time, sitting there in her delicately sweet room, he felt as if surrounded by a hedge of lace. He was afraid to stir lest he should put a clumsy foot or hand through the fairy web, and he had always the consciousness that Louisa was watching fearfully lest he should.

Still the lace and Louisa commanded perforce his perfect respect and patience and loyalty. They were to be married in a month, after a singular courtship which had lasted for a matter of fifteen years. For fourteen out of the fifteen years the two had not once seen each other, and they had seldom exchanged letters. Joe had been all those years in Australia, where he had gone to make his fortune, and where he had stayed until he made it. He would have stayed fifty years if it had taken so long, and come home feeble and tottering, or never come home at all, to marry Louisa.

But the fortune had been made in the fourteen years, and he had come home now to marry the woman who had been patiently and unquestioningly waiting for him all that time.

Shortly after they were engaged he had announced to Louisa his determination to strike out into new fields and secure a competency before they should be married. She had listened and assented with the sweet serenity which never failed her, not even when her lover set forth on that long and uncertain journey. Joe, buoyed up as he was by his steady determination, broke down a little at the last, but Louisa kissed him with a mild blush, and said good-by.

"It won't be for long," poor Joe had said, huskily; but it was for fourteen years.

In that length of time much had happened. Louisa's mother and brother had died, and she was all alone in the world. But greatest happening of all—a subtle happening which both were too simple to understand—Louisa's feet had turned into a path, smooth maybe under a calm, serene sky, but so straight and unswerving that it could only meet a check at her grave, and so narrow that there was no room for anyone at her side.

Louisa's first emotion when Joe Dagget came home (he had not apprised her of his coming) was consternation, although she would not admit it to herself, and he never dreamed of it. Fifteen years ago she had been in love with him—at least she considered herself to be. Just at that time, gently acquiescing with and falling into the natural drift of girlhood, she had seen marriage ahead as a reasonable feature and a probable desirability of life. She had listened with calm docility to her mother's views upon the subject. Her mother was remarkable for her cool sense and sweet, even temperament. She talked wisely to her daughter when Joe Dagget presented himself, and Louisa accepted him with no hesitation. He was the first lover she had ever had.

She had been faithful to him all these years. She had never dreamed of the possibility of marrying anyone else. Her life, especially for the last seven years, had been full of a pleasant peace; she had never felt discontented nor impatient over her lover's absence; still, she had always looked forward to his return and their marriage as the inevitable conclusion of things. However, she had fallen into a way of placing it so far in the future that it was almost equal to placing it over the boundaries of another life.

When Joe came she had been expecting him, and expecting to be married for fourteen years, but she was as much surprised and taken aback as if she had never thought of it.

Joe's consternation came later. He eyed Louisa with an instant confirmation of his old admiration. She had changed but little. She still kept her pretty manner and soft grace, and was, he considered, every whit as attractive as ever. As for himself, his stent was done; he had turned his face away from fortune seeking, and the old winds of romance whistled as loud and sweet as ever through his ears. All the song which he had been wont to hear in them was Louisa; he had for a long time a loyal belief that he heard it still, but finally it seemed to him that although the winds sang always that one song, it had another name. But for Louisa the wind had never more than murmured; now it had gone down, and everything was still. She listened for a little while with half-wistful attention; then she turned quietly away and went to work on her wedding clothes.

Joe had made some extensive and quite magnificent alterations in his house. It was the old homestead; the newly-married couple would live there, for Joe could not desert his mother, who refused to leave her old home. So Louisa must leave hers. Every morning, rising and going about among her neat maidenly possessions, she felt as one looking her last upon the faces of dear friends. It was true that in a measure she could take them with her, but, robbed of their old environments, they would appear in such new guises that they would almost cease to be themselves.

Then there were some peculiar features of her happy solitary life which she would probably be obliged to relinquish altogether. Sterner tasks than these graceful but half-needless ones would probably devolve upon her. There would be a large house to care for; there would be company to entertain; there would be Joe's rigorous and feeble old mother to wait upon; and it would be contrary to all thrifty village traditions for her to keep more than one servant.

Louisa had a little still, and she used to occupy herself pleasantly in summer weather with distilling the sweet and aromatic essences from roses and peppermint and spearmint. By-and-by her still must be laid away. Her store of essences was already considerable, and there would be no time for her to distill for the mere pleasure of it. Then Joe's mother would think it foolishness; she had already hinted her opinion in the matter.

Louisa dearly loved to sew a linen seam, not always for use, but for the simple, mild pleasure which she took in it. She would have been loathe to confess how more than once she had ripped a seam for the mere delight of sewing it together again. Sitting at her window during long sweet afternoons, drawing her needle gently through the dainty fabric, she was peace itself. But there was small chance of such foolish comfort in the future. Joe's mother, domineering, shrewd old matron that she was even in her old age, and very likely even Joe himself, with his honest masculine rudeness, would laugh and frown down all these pretty but senseless old maiden ways.

Louisa had almost the enthusiasm of an artist over the mere order and cleanliness of her solitary home. She had throbs of genuine triumph at the sight of the windowpanes which she had polished until they shone like jewels. She gloated gently over her orderly bureau drawers, with their exquisitely folded contents redolent with lavender and sweet clover and very purity. Could she be sure of the endurance of even this? She had visions, so startling that she half repudiated them as indelicate, of coarse masculine belongings strewn about in endless litter; of dust and disorder arising necessarily from a coarse masculine presence in the midst of all this delicate harmony.

Among her forebodings of disturbance, not the least was with regard to Caesar. Caesar was a veritable hermit of a dog. For the greater part of his life he had dwelt in his secluded hut, shut out from the society of his kind and all innocent canine joys. Never had Caesar since his early youth watched at a woodchuck's hole; never had he known the delights of a stray bone at a neighbor's kitchen door. And it was all on account of a sin committed when hardly out of his puppyhood. No one knew the possible depth of remorse of which this mild-visaged, altogether innocent-looking old dog might be capable; but whether or not he had encountered remorse, he had encountered a full measure of righteous retribution. Old Caesar seldom lifted up his voice in a growl or a bark; he was fat and sleepy; there were yellow rings which looked like spectacles around his dim old eyes; but there was a neighbor who bore on his hand the imprint of several of Caesar's sharp white youthful teeth, and for that he had lived at the end of a chain, all alone in a little hut, for fourteen years. The neighbor, who was choleric and smarting with the pain of his wound, had demanded either Caesar's death or complete ostracism. So Louisa's brother, to whom the dog had belonged, had built him his little kennel and tied him up. It was now fourteen years since, in a flood of youthful spirits, he had inflicted that memorable bite, and with the exception of short excursions, always at the end of the chain, under the strict guardianship of his master or Louisa, the old dog had remained a close prisoner. It is doubtful if, with his limited ambition, he took much pride in the fact, but it is certain that he was possessed of considerable cheap fame. He was regarded by all the children in the village and by many adults as a very monster of ferocity. St. George's dragon could hardly have surpassed in evil repute Louisa Ellis's old yellow dog. Mothers charged their children with solemn emphasis not to go too near to him, and the children listened and believed greedily, with a fascinated appetite for terror, and ran by Louisa's house stealthily, with many sidelong and backward glances at the terrible dog. If perchance he sounded a hoarse bark, there was a panic. Wayfarers chancing into Louisa's yard eyed him with respect, and inquired if the chain were stout. Caesar at large might have seemed a very ordinary dog and excited no comment whatever; chained, his reputation overshadowed him, so that he lost his own proper outlines and looked darkly vague and enormous. Joe Dagget, however, with his good-humored sense and shrewdness, saw him as he was. He strode valiantly up to him and patted him on the head, in spite of Louisa's soft clamor of warning, and even attempted to set him loose. Louisa grew so alarmed that he desisted, but kept announcing his opinion in the matter quite forcibly at intervals. "There ain't a better-natured dog in town," he would say, "and it's downright cruel to keep him tied up there. Some day I'm going to take him out."

Louisa had very little hope that he would not, one of these days, when their interests and possessions should be more completely fused in one. She pictured to herself Caesar on the rampage through the quiet and unguarded village. She saw innocent children bleeding in his path. She was herself very fond of the old dog, because he had belonged to her dead brother, and he was always very gentle with her; still she had great faith in his ferocity. She always warned people not to go too near him. She fed him on ascetic fare of corn mush and cakes, and never fired his dangerous temper with heating and sanguinary diet of flesh and bones. Louisa looked at the old dog munching his simple fare, and thought of her approaching marriage and trembled. Still no anticipation of disorder and confusion in lieu of sweet peace and harmony, no forebodings of Caesar on the rampage, no wild fluttering of her little yellow canary, were sufficient to turn her a hair's-breadth. Joe Dagget had been fond of her and working for

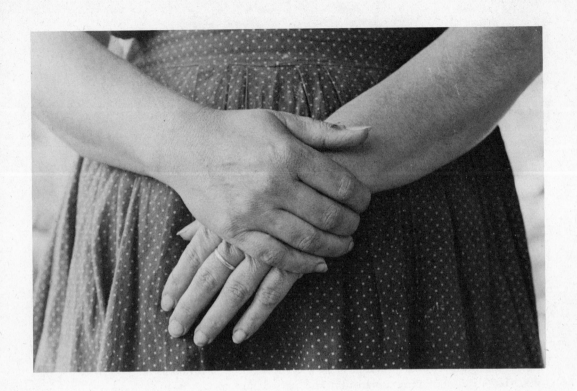

her all these years. It was not for her, whatever came to pass, to prove untrue and break his heart. She put the exquisite little stitches into her wedding garments, and the time went on until it was only a week before her wedding day. It was a Tuesday evening, and the wedding was to be a week from Wednesday.

There was a full moon that night. About nine o'clock Louisa strolled down the road a little way. There were harvest fields on either hand, bordered by low stone walls. Luxuriant clumps of bushes grew beside the wall, and trees—wild cherry and old apple trees—at intervals. Presently Louisa sat down on the wall and looked about her with mildly sorrowful reflectiveness. Tall shrubs of blueberry and meadowsweet, all woven together and tangled with blackberry vines and horsebriers, shut her in on either side. She had a little clear space between them. Opposite her, on the other side of the road, was a spreading tree; the moon shone between its boughs, and the leaves twinkled like silver. The road was bespread with a beautiful shifting dapple of silver and shadow; the air was full of a mysterious sweetness. "I wonder if it's wild grapes?" murmured Louisa. She sat there some time. She was just thinking of rising, when she heard footsteps and low voices, and remained quiet. It was a lonely place, and she felt a little timid. She thought she would keep still in the shadow and let the persons, whoever they might be, pass her.

But just before they reached her the voices ceased, and the footsteps. She understood that their owners had also found seats upon the stone wall. She was wondering if she could not steal away unobserved, when the voice broke the stillness. It was Joe Dagget's. She sat still and listened.

The voice was announced by a loud sigh, which was as familiar as itself. "Well," said Dagget, "you've made up your mind, then, I suppose?"

"Yes," returned another voice; "I'm going day after tomorrow."

"That's Lily Dyer," thought Louisa to herself. The voice embodied itself in her mind. She saw a girl tall and full-figured, with a firm, fair face, looking fairer and firmer in the moonlight, her strong yellow hair braided in a close knot. A girl full of a calm rustic strength and bloom, with a masterful way which might have beseemed a princess. Lily Dyer was a favorite with the village folk; she had just the qualities to arouse the admiration. She was good and handsome and smart. Louisa had often heard her praises sounded.

"Well," said Joe Dagget, "I ain't got a word to say."

"I don't know what you could say," returned Lily Dyer.

"Not a word to say," repeated Joe, drawing out the words heavily. Then there was a silence. "I ain't sorry," he began at last, "that that happened yesterday—that we kind of let on how we felt to each other. I guess it's just as well we knew. Of course I can't do anything any different. I'm going right on an' get married next week. I ain't going back on a woman that's waited for me fourteen years, an' break her heart."

"If you should jilt her tomorrow, I wouldn't have you," spoke up the girl, with sudden vehemence.

"Well, I ain't going to give you the chance," said he; "but I don't believe you would, either."

"You'd see I wouldn't. Honor's honor, an' right's right. An' I'd never think anything of any man that went against 'em for me or any other girl; you'd find that out, Joe Dagget."

"Well, you'll find out fast enough that I ain't going against 'em for you or any other girl," returned he. Their voices sounded almost as if they were angry with each other. Louisa was listening eagerly.

"I'm sorry you feel as if you must go away," said Joe, "but I don't know but it's best."

"Of course it's best. I hope you and I have got common sense."

"Well, I suppose you're right." Suddenly Joe's voice got an undertone of tenderness. "Say, Lily," said he, "I'll get along well enough myself, but I can't bear to think—You don't suppose you're going to fret much over it?"

"I guess you'll find out I shan't fret much over a married man."

"Well, I hope you won't—I hope you won't, Lily. God knows I do. And—I hope—one of these days—you'll—come across somebody else—"

"I don't see any reason why I shouldn't." Suddenly her tone changed. She spoke in a sweet, clear voice, so loud that she could have been heard across the street. "No, Joe Dagget," said she, "I'll never marry any other man as long as I live. I've got good sense, an' I ain't going to break my heart nor make a fool of myself; but I'm never going to be married, you can be sure of that. I ain't that sort of a girl to feel this way twice."

Louisa heard an exclamation and a soft commotion behind the bushes; then Lily spoke again—the voice sounded as if she had risen. "This must be put a stop to," said she. "We've stayed here long enough. I'm going home."

Louisa sat there in a daze, listening to their retreating steps. After a while she got up and slunk softly home herself. The next day she did her housework methodically; that was as much a matter of course as breathing; but she did not sew on her wedding clothes. She sat at her window and meditated. In the evening Joe came. Louisa Ellis had never known that she had any diplomacy in her, but when she came to look for it that night she found it, although meek of its kind, among her little feminine weapons. Even now she could hardly believe that she had heard right, and that she would not do Joe a terrible injury should she break her troth plight. She wanted to sound him out without betraying too soon her own inclinations in the matter. She did it successfully, and they finally came to an understanding; but it was a difficult thing, for he was as afraid of betraying himself as she.

She never mentioned Lily Dyer. She simply said that while she had no cause of complaint against him, she had lived so long in one way that she shrank from making a change.

"Well, I never shrank, Louisa," said Dagget. "I'm going to be honest enough to say that I think maybe it's better this way; but if you'd wanted to keep on, I'd have stuck to you till my dying day. I hope you know that."

"Yes, I do," said she.

That night she and Joe parted more tenderly than they had done for a long time. Standing in the door, holding each other's hands, a last great wave of regretful memory swept over them.

"Well, this ain't the way we've thought it was all going to end, is it, Louisa?" said Joe.

She shook her head. There was a little quiver on her placid face.

"You let me know it there's ever anything I can do for you," said he. "I ain't ever going to forget you, Louisa." Then he kissed her, and went down the path.

Louisa, all alone by herself that night, wept a little, she hardly knew why; but the next morning, on waking, she felt like a queen who, after fearing lest her domain be wrested away from her, sees it firmly insured in her possession.

Now the tall weeds and grasses might cluster around Caesar's little hermit hut, the snow might fall on its roof year in and year out, but he never would go on a rampage through the unguarded village. Now the little canary might turn itself into a peaceful yellow ball night after night, and have no need to wake and flutter with wild terror against its bars. Louisa could sew linen seams, and distill roses, and dust and polish and fold away in lavender, as long as she listed. That afternoon she sat with her needlework at the window, and felt fairly steeped in peace. Lily Dyer, tall and erect and blooming, went past; but she felt no qualm. If Louisa Ellis had sold her birthright she did not know it; the taste of the pottage was so delicious, and had been her sole satisfaction for so long. Serenity and placid narrowness had become to her as the birthright itself. She gazed ahead through a long reach of future days strung together like pearls in a rosary, every one like the others, and all smooth and flawless and innocent, and her heart went up in thankfulness. Outside was the fervid summer afternoon; the air was filled with the sounds of the busy harvest of men and birds and bees; there were halloos, metallic clatterings, sweet calls, and long hummings. Louisa sat, prayerfully numbering her days, like an uncloistered nun.

Insight

1. How would you characterize the life Louisa Ellis has led for the past fourteen years? What satisfactions have those years brought her?
2. How does Joe view Louisa upon his return? What causes him to change that view?
3. In what respects does Louisa come to see Joe as almost a kind of intruder into her life? How aware of this feeling does Joe appear to be?
4. Given the misgivings Joe and Louisa feel about their impending marriage, why is each willing to go through with it? What does their willingness reveal about them as human beings?
5. Discuss the appropriateness of the title to the story as a whole. In this connection, note especially the significance of the last sentence of the story.

THE SOLiTARY

Sara Teasdale

My heart has grown rich with the passing of years,
　　I have less need now than when I was young
To share myself with every comer
　　Or shape my thoughts into words with my tongue.

It is one to me that they come or go　　　　　　　　5
　　If I have myself and the drive of my will,
And strength to climb on a summer night
　　And watch the stars swarm over the hill.

Let them think I love them more than I do,
　　Let them think I care, though I go alone;　　　　10
If it lifts their pride, what is it to me
　　Who am self-complete as a flower or a stone.

Insight

1. How does the speaker of the poem feel about herself? How does
   she feel about other people? Has she always felt this way?
2. "Lonely," "desolate," "forsaken" are words that might describe a
   solitary life. Are these words appropriate to the speaker's life in
   this poem? Explain.

Titty's dead and Tatty weeps

Ursula MacDougall

That noise must have been Ella's door banging shut. I shouldn't have thought I could hear it across the street, but on a clear cold night like this you can hear every sound. There go her heavy overshoes clumping down her front steps. Funny how all the spring goes out of your feet when you're past sixty. I've noticed that about my own—hardly worth picking them up and putting them down plunk so many times in a day. I'll just stand here and listen through the door until I'm sure that Ella's coming here. Oh, I know very well she'll be over here in a minute, filling all my living-room, overflowing into every corner of my house, and my life, telling me what to do now that Sally's gone. Don't you walk across that street, Ella. I can't have you in my house tonight, not even for an hour. Now that Sally's dead I don't need advice from anybody—you, Ella, or Martha Yates either. *Titty's dead and Tatty weeps and the stool hops and the broom sweeps.* What's that story popping into my head for all day long, over and over? First thing in the morning and when I wake up in the night. I hadn't thought of it for years and now I can't get away from it. It's worse since I got back two days ago—the first time I've been alone in the house. I'm glad I dismissed Mary, though. No matter what I wanted, she would have kept on doing things the way Sally liked them done.

I don't believe Ella crossed the street after all. There's no use my waiting here in the hall for her. She must have gone to Martha Yates's house. She'll bring her here. They'll both think I was terribly heartless to let Mary go, after so many years in my family. It was heartless of me, too, and I'll never forget her face when I told her, and right after the funeral. I might have waited a day. "I'm going to Bermuda, Mary," I said, "and when I get back I shall want someone younger and stronger for the housework." I wanted to cry, but how could I have kept her? She turned the Delft vases on the mantel flower side out again when I had changed them to the windmill side the very hour Sally was brought home. It was too plain a sign of how things would be, the house not a bit my house with Mary here remembering Sally's ways, and how I used to give in to her. *Titty mouse and Tatty mouse both lived in a house, Titty mouse went a-leasing and Tatty mouse went a-leasing, so they both went a-leasing.* I've got to stop saying those silly words. I can remember exactly how that English Fairy Tales book looked—gray with lavender letters. It was third from the right, second shelf from the bottom in the nursery bookcase. Nana read it to us so often we knew it by heart. *Titty mouse leased an ear of corn and Tatty mouse leased an ear of corn, so they both leased an ear of corn.* No, I oughtn't to have dismissed Mary, if for no other reason than that she was Nana's daughter. And all she said was, "Miss Susan, I don't understand. I've been with you and your sister thirty-two years." Ella and Martha Yates will have something to say about that when they get here—and they're sure to come because Ella told me this morning in the post office that they'd be over tonight. So they could help me arrange things, she said. If I'd been the one killed they'd have known better than to try to arrange things for Sally!

It's been like that all along. I'm the "quiet Winslow girl." I can remember in our high-school days how both the boys who came Sunday evenings really came to see Sally. I could have laughed and made jokes, too, if Sally's laugh hadn't been so loud and jolly and her jokes such funny ones. "Oh, Susan's always been solemn," she'd say to them. "Haven't you, Susie?" "*Then,*" *said the door, "I'll jar," so the door jarred.* I never was sure what that meant—did it mean stay ajar? "The Three Sillies" was in that book, and "Nimmy Nimmy Not, your name's Tom Tit Tot," and "Master of All Masters." That was the funniest. We used to laugh till our stomachs ached over White-faced Siminy. Sally always hoped for a white-faced kitten to name that.

They'll be here any minute now. I don't suppose I have to stand here any longer waiting for them. Only I'd like to decide what I'm going to say to them. Oh, I don't want them to come. They'll spoil it. I've been a different person since Sally died. I think I've been myself and Sally too. All the time in Bermuda and on the boat I felt like Sally. Nobody knew I was supposed to be shy, so for once I could use my tongue and talk when I wanted to. I played shuffleboard to make a fourth one day just because no one expected me to hang back and refuse. And at the hotel they said I was a friendly person. That was the way I felt inside too. I still do. I want to stay this way, like Sally, and not be afraid. I believe I changed the very minute I knew that Sally was dead. I didn't have time to plan how I'd feel. When they brought her home and laid her on the bed, I felt strong suddenly. It may have been her strength that went into me. Even at the funeral I wasn't unhappy. I seemed new all over to myself—like a butterfly just out of its chrysalis. *Now there was an old form outside the house and when the window creaked the form said, "Window, why do you creak?" "Oh," said the window, "Titty's dead and Tatty weeps and the stool hops and the broom sweeps, the door jars and so I creak." "Then," said the old form, "I'll run round the house." So the old form ran around the house.*

Now that's what my going to Bermuda was like—like the old form running around the house. It's what Sally would have done if I'd been the one to die and nobody would have been surprised. But "So unlike *you*, Susan," they said. Anyway, I've learned now what sort of person I might have been. I'm like Sally, but only when people like Sally aren't around. There's only room for one really free person in any family, I suppose, and Sally chose that role for herself. What happened to me didn't matter. Of course I loved her. She was your older sister, Susan Winslow, you and she were inseparable. You were like a cup and saucer or a hook and eye. But I didn't cry at the cemetery—I didn't feel like crying even. Instead, those foolish words kept saying themselves over and over to me, interrupting my grieving over Sally. *Titty mouse made a pudding and Tatty mouse made a pudding. So they both made a pudding. And Tatty mouse put her pudding into the pot to boil but when Titty went to put hers in, the pot tumbled over and scalded her to death.*

If I should get Mary back she'd listen and say nothing when I ordered buttered carrots with the lamb, but when she served the dinner there'd be peas, the way Sally always planned it. Thirty-two years she said she'd been with us. But suppose she had heard me yesterday singing those negro spirituals at the top of my voice—she knew that Sally was the one who sang and that it was Sally that had bursts of noisiness like that—"Miss Susan's the quiet one." Oh, I'd never have dared to open my mouth to sing a note with Mary in the house. And then what if she had caught me this morning eating tomato soup for breakfast and a sardine sandwich? "Miss Susan was never one for changes," she liked to say about me. "Always a three-minute egg and two pieces of light brown toast for her." *Then Tatty sat down and wept; then a three-legged stool said, "Tatty, why do you weep?" "Titty's dead," said Tatty, "and so I weep." Then said the stool, "I'll hop," so the stool hopped.* But Ella will think I should have kept Mary —she'll say so, too. She won't know I have to have someone new here who won't know I'm different now from the person I used to be. And Martha Yates will back Ella up and they'll scold me, too, just the way they're used to hearing Sally do. Perhaps they won't say anything tonight about the living room furniture's being all changed around, but I'll see them looking.

I think that's Martha's door shutting. I'll open this one a little and listen. Yes, they're on their way here now. Ella said they would have a plan to suggest. They don't know I have a plan, too. If Bob hadn't died of pneumonia that winter when we were young, Sally would have married, and I wouldn't have lived with her all these years. In that case I'd really be like her, now. Joe Hendricks said to me this morning outside the chain store, "Why, the trip did you good, Susan! I've never seen you looking so hearty—more like your sister than yourself." It was after I met Ella at the post office that I saw Joe. He kept me talking—didn't seem to want to go on. After all, we're the only people left in town he calls by their first names, Sally and me. Poor fellow! He said he didn't have much to live for any more except his walk to the post office and the chance of a word with an old friend like me now and then. He almost cried telling me how they're going to tear down the Carter House and put a block of stores there. "I've lived in that hotel for twenty years," he said, "in the same room all that time." It was the way he said Sally and I have always been able to cheer him up more than anybody ("You two always knew how to get some fun out of life," he said) that put the notion into my head. He thinks I'm just like Sally, because she always did the talking and I never opened my mouth except to agree with her.

I thought it all out on my way home from the marketing. Ella would drop dead if she knew the letter's all written and in my pocket. After they go tonight, I'll walk to the corner and mail it so that I won't change my mind. I've made it very clear to him that it's a favor to me, not to him. I couldn't say that, with him in my house so old and mournful and set in his ways, I'd be able to keep the new self that's grown out of the me Sally left behind her. I told him in the letter, "You mustn't be afraid of what they'll say about us, Joe. The whole town will laugh, of course, but they'll all know we're both past the age for foolishness." That ought to make it seem all right to him—not as if I had any ideas in my head. It will upset the church people to have me marry so soon after Sally's death—but with him to look after and plan for and with a new maid who won't stand there with her mouth open if I tell him a funny joke—well, Sally won't be so dead as people think she is. I'll hold the letter tight like this all the time they are here. Perhaps I'll say, toss it off as Sally would, "I'm thinking of getting married. My plans are made, so don't trouble yourselves about me." But I'd better not mention Joe's name to them, until he's had time to answer.

They're turning into the gate now. Overshoes make a queer squeek on hard-packed snow. I wish I hadn't changed the furniture around just yet, they are sure to notice. Oh, don't come in. Please go away, don't ring my doorbell. They know me so well—the way Sally and Mary knew me. I needn't open the door—I don't have to. I can call to them through this panel and say I have a sore throat and can't see them tonight. What was that story with the name we couldn't ever remember? It was in the same book—something about The Laidly Worm. That picture always gave me the shivers, but I didn't have to hurry past it fast so as not to see—the way I did with The Golden Arm. His wife stood there in her grave clothes, wanting her arm. He was half sitting up in bed, just catching sight of her in the doorway.

William Shew, "Mother and Daughter" 1845–1850

There was another story named the Golden something—it came just after Titty Mouse and Tatty Mouse—*So the walnut tree shed all its leaves and the little bird moulted all its feathers.*

Up the steps now, overshoes stamping off the snow on the porch. Their voices are too loud. "Come in, Ella. It's nice to see you, Martha. I'm glad you could both come over tonight." I've said those words. Now they'll say words, too, but I'll be holding on to the letter, stamped and ready in my pocket. I'll listen to what they say, but I'll mail it when they've gone. Martha's eyes are on the furniture. Now she's saying, "Quite a few changes here, I see, Susan." I don't need to answer anything. Ella's saying that I ought to try to get more rest, I look worn out and no wonder, she's saying. She's glad I'm back so she can look after me and chirk me up a bit, she says. She's saying she has a perfectly marvellous plan to tell me. She says I'm to wait— just wait till she tells me. Now we're sitting down—it's nice to be sitting. The Delft vases are still windmill-side-out, the way I put them again when Mary left. I wonder if Ella knows what I did about Mary —she won't like it, when she knows. Ella's voice is laughing—it sounds so sure. It shrivels me up so that it's hard to listen. She's saying that she's all alone and that I'm all alone now, too, and that I'm to rent this house and move over to her house with her and that I'm to bring Mary with me. She says I won't have any worries any more and wouldn't Sally be pleased? Ella's excited, she's quite out of breath.

Now I must say something to her. I'll say, "What a kind idea! We must talk it over."

That's what I meant to say, but I think I heard my voice saying something quite different. I think I said, *"Then," said the old man, "I'll tumble off the ladder and break my neck."* I must have spoken quite softly because they didn't seem to understand. "What?" That was Martha Yates asking me, crossly, too. "What on earth are you muttering, Susan?" That was Ella.

"I said that I thought we ought to think it over and not be hasty." That was my voice, so I said that.

Now I think Ella is getting angry at me. Her voice sounds louder. "Nonsense," she is saying. "I tell you there's no need to think it over or even discuss it. It's much the best arrangement for you. Everything's settled. All you have to do, Susan, is to agree."

Ella is telling me a lot more about how it will be living in her house. Martha Yates is saying Yes and Yes. I don't know just when I crumpled up my letter, but I can feel it all wrinkled now in my pocket. Well, I suppose it doesn't matter, much. I can't seem to listen to Ella when her voice goes on and on so without ever stopping. If she would speak more softly I would know what she's saying. She and Martha

Yates seem to be feeling very pleased about something. While they're talking I'll just finish up—the words keep crowding down on me, faster. There's no need to go on shoving them out of my mind. *So he tumbled off the ladder and broke his neck. And when the old man broke his neck, the great walnut tree fell down with a crash and upset the old form and the house, and the house falling knocked the window out and the window knocked the door down and the door upset the broom, and the broom upset the stool and poor little Tatty mouse was buried beneath the ruins.*

Insight

1. How do people view Susan before the death of her sister? How accurate has their perception of her been? How does their view differ from Susan's view of herself?

2. Characterize the relationship between Susan and Sally. Has it been a healthy one for Susan? How affected by her sister's death does Susan appear to be? How would you account for her feelings?

3. What changes in personality and behavior occur in Susan after Sally's death? What factors are responsible for these changes? How deep and lasting do they appear to be?

4. "Anyway I've learned now what sort of person I might have been," says Susan. How would you describe that person? Why has she never become what she "might have been"?

5. What change in feelings overcomes Susan as she hears Ella and Martha "turning into the gate"? In view of the many changes Susan has brought to her life since Sally's death, why do you suppose her nerve fails her now?

SONNET 67

Edna St. Vincent Millay

To Inez Milholland

Read in Washington, November eighteenth,
1923, at the unveiling of a statue of three
leaders in the cause of Equal Rights for
Women

Upon this marble bust that is not I
Lay the round, formal wreath that is not fame;
But in the forum of my silenced cry
Root ye the living tree whose sap is flame.
I, that was proud and valiant, am no more;—   5
Save as a dream that wanders wide and late,
Save as a wind that rattles the stout door,
Troubling the ashes in the sheltered grate.
The stone will perish; I shall be twice dust.
Only my standard on a taken hill   10
Can cheat the mildew and the red-brown rust
And make immortal my adventurous will.
Even now the silk is tugging at the staff:
Take up the song; forget the epitaph.

A Wish

Fanny Kemble

Let me not die for ever, when I'm gone
   To the cold earth! but let my memory
Live like the gorgeous western light that shone
   Over the clouds where sank day's majesty.
Let me not be forgotten; though the grave   5
   Has clasped its hideous arms around my brow.
Let me not be forgotten! though the wave
   Of time's dark current rolls above me now.
Yet not in tears remembered be my name;
   Weep over those ye loved; for me, for me,   10
Give me the wreath of glory, and let fame
   Over my tomb spread immortality!

Insight
1. Describe the speaker in the two preceding poems. What kinds of people do they appear to be? In what ways are they similar? Different?
2. Both speakers are concerned with the world's view of them after they have died. What are the hopes of each? Which, do you feel, is more likely of having her hopes fulfilled?

THE CONDEMNED LIBRARIAN

Jessamyn West

Louise McKay, M.D., the librarian at Beaumont High School, sent me another card today. It was on the wickerwork table, where Mother puts my snack, when I got home from teaching. This afternoon the snack was orange juice and graham crackers, the orange juice in a plain glass, so that the deepness, the thickness of the color was almost like a flame inside a hurricane lamp. The graham crackers were on a blue willowware plate, and it just so happened that Dr. McKay's card was Van Gogh's "Sunflowers." It was a perfect still life, the colors increasing in intensity through the pale sand of the wickerwork table to the great bong (I want to say), for I swear I could hear it, of Van Gogh's flaming sunflowers. I looked at the picture Mother had composed for me (I don't doubt) for some time before I read Dr. McKay's card.

Dr. McKay sends me about four cards a year—not at any particular season, Christmas, Easter, or the like. Her sentiments are not suited to such festivals. Usually her message is only a line or two: "Why did you do it?" or "Condemned, condemned, condemned." Something very dramatic and always on a post card, so that the world at large can read it if it chooses. Mother shows her perfect tact by saying nothing if she does read. Perhaps she doesn't; though a single sentence in a big masculine hand is hard to miss. Except for her choice of the Van Gogh print, which showed her malice, Dr. McKay's message this afternoon was very mild—for her. "I am still here, which will no doubt make you happy."

Apart from the fact that anyone interested in the welfare of human beings generally would want her there (or at least not practicing in a hospital), it does make me happy. This evening when I pulled down the flag, I was somehow reassured, standing there in the schoolyard with the cold north wind blowing the dust in my face, to think that over there on the other side of the mountains Louise McKay was ending her day, too. Take away the mountains and fields and we might be gazing into each other's eyes.

I sat down in my room with the juice my mother had squeezed— we hate substitutes—and looked at the card and remembered when I had first seen that marching handwriting. Everything else about her has changed, but not that. I saw it first on the card she gave me telling me of my next date with her. From the moment I arrived at Oakland State, I started hearing about Dr. Louise McKay. She was a real campus

389

heroine, though for no real reason. Except that at a teachers college, with no football heroes, no faculty members with off-campus reputations, the craving for superiority must satisfy itself on the material at hand, however skimpy. And for a student body made up of kids and middle-aged teachers come to Oakland from the lost little towns of mountain and desert, I suppose it was easy to think of Dr. McKay as heroic or fascinating or accomplished.

I was different, though. I was neither middle-aged nor a kid. I was twenty-six years old and I had come to Oakland expecting something. I had had choices. I had made sacrifices to get there, sacrifices for which no "heroic" lady doctor, however "fascinating," "well dressed" (I can remember all the phrases used about her now), could be a substitute.

I had a very difficult time deciding to go to Oakland State. I had taught at Liberty School for six years and I loved that place. It was "beautiful for situation," as the Bible says, located ten miles out of town in the rolling semi-dry upland country where the crop was grain, not apricots and peaches. It was a one-room school, and I was its only teacher. It stood in the midst of this sea of barley and oats like an island. In winter and spring this big green sea of ripening grain rolled and tossed about us—all but crested and broke—all but, though never quite. In a way, this was irritating.

For half the year at Liberty there were no barley waves to watch, only the close-cut stubble of reaped fields and the enormous upthrust of the San Jacinto Mountains beyond. Color was my delight then. I used to sit out in the schoolyard at noon or recess and paint. A former teacher had discarded an old sleigh-back sofa, had it put out in the yard halfway between the school and the woodshed. It stood amidst the volunteer oats and mustard like a larger growth. It seemed planted in earth. In the fall when Santa Anas blew, tumbleweeds piled up about it. I don't know how long it had been there when I arrived, but it had taken well to its life in the fields; its legs balanced, its springs stayed inside the upholstery, and the upholstery itself still kept some of its original cherry tones. There I sat—when I wasn't playing ball with the kids—like a hunter, hidden in a game blind; only my game wasn't lions and tigers, it was the whole world, so to speak: the mountains, the grain fields, the kids, the schoolhouse itself. I sat there and painted.

Oh, not well. I've never said that, ever. Never claimed that for a minute. And it's easy to impress children and country people who think it's uncanny if you can draw an apple that looks like an apple. And I could do much more than that. I could make mountains that looked like mountains, children who looked like children. How that impressed the parents! So I had gotten in the habit of being praised, though from no one who counted, no one who knew. I had been sensibly brought up by my mother, taught to evaluate these plaudits rightly. I understood that my schoolyard talent didn't make me a Bonheur or Cassatt.[1] Even so, there was nothing else I had ever wanted to do. This schoolteaching was just a way of making money, of helping my mother, who was a widow.

So, because of the time I had for painting and because of the gifts Liberty School had for my eyes, I had six happy years. I sat like a queen on that sofa in the grass while the meadowlarks sang and the butcherbirds first caught their lunches, then impaled their suppers, still kicking, on the barbed-wire fence. I didn't paint all the time, of course. Kids learned to read there. At the end of the sixth year there was only one eighth grader who could beat me in mental arithmetic. I was the acknowledged champion at skin-the-cat and could play adequately any position on the softball team.

There was not much left to learn at Liberty, and I began, I don't know how, to feel that learning, not teaching, was my business.

In the middle of my sixth year I had to put a tarpaulin over the sofa. A spring broke through the upholstery, a leg crumbled. After that I had to prop it on a piece of stove wood. That spring I noticed for the first time that the babies of age six I had taught my first year were developing Adam's apples or busts. Girls who had been thirteen and fourteen my first year came back to visit Liberty School, married and with babies in their arms.

"You haven't changed," they would tell me. "Oh, it's a real anchor to find you here, just the same."

Their husbands, who were often boys my own age, twenty-four or twenty-five, treated me like an older woman. I might have been their mother, or mother-in-law. I was the woman who had taught their wives. I don't think I looked so much old then as ageless. I've taken out some of the snaps of that year, pictures taken at school. My face, in a way, looks as young as my pupils; in other ways, as old as Mt. Tahquitz. It looks back at me with the real stony innocence of a face in a coffin—or cradle.

At Thanksgiving time I was to be out of school three days before the holiday, so that I could have a minor operation. When I left school on Friday, Mary Elizabeth Ross, one of my fourth graders, clasped me fondly and said, "May I be the first to hold your baby when you get back from the hospital?"

She wouldn't believe it when I told her I was going to the hospital because I was sick, not to get a baby, and she cried when I came back to school empty-armed.

---

[1] BONHEUR ... CASSATT: Rosa Bonheur, French painter and sculptor. Mary Cassatt, American painter and printmaker.

That I noticed these things showed my restlessness. It might have passed, I might have settled into a lifetime on that island, except that at Christmas I hung some of my paintings with my pupils' pictures at the annual Teachers' Institute exhibit. They caused a stir, and I began foolishly to dream of painting full time, of going to a big city, Los Angeles or San Francisco, where I would take a studio and have lessons. I didn't mention the idea to anyone, scarcely to myself. When anyone else suggested such a thing to me, I pooh-poohed it. "Me, paint? Don't be funny."

But I dreamed of it; the less I said, the more I dreamed; and the more I dreamed, the less possible talking became. I didn't paint much that winter, but I moved through those months with the feel of a paintbrush in my hand. I could feel, way up in my arm, the strokes I would need to make to put Tahquitz, dead white against the green winter sky, on canvas, put it there so people could see how it really floated, that great peak, was hung aloft there like a giant ship against the sky. But I didn't say a word to anyone about my plans, not even to the School Board when I handed in my resignation at Easter. I hadn't lost my head entirely. I told them I was going to "study." I didn't say what. They thought education, of course.

The minute I had resigned, I was filled with fear. I sat on my three-legged sofa amidst the waves of grain that never crested and shivered until school was out. I had undoubtedly been a fool; not only was I without money, but where would I find anything as good as what I had? Everything began to say "stay." I would enter my room at night (the one in which I now write), which my mother kept so exquisitely, books ranged according to size and color, the white bedspread at once taut and velvety, the blue iris in a fan-shaped arc in a brown bowl—and I was a part of that composition. If I walked out, the composition collapsed. And outside, I, too, was a fragment. I would stand there asking myself, "Where will you find anything better?"

There was never any answer.

I could only find something different, and possibly worse. So why go? I had seen myself as a lady Sherwood Anderson, locking the factory door behind me and walking down the tracks toward freedom and self-expression. I could dream that dream but I was afraid to act it. I would stand in my perfectly neat bedroom and frighten myself with pictures of my next room, far away, sordid, with strangers on each side. Fear was in my chest like a stone that whole spring. I had no talent, I was gambling everything on an egotistical attention-seeking whim. It was perfectly natural to have done so, but my misery finally drove me to talking with my mother. It was perfectly natural, she assured me, to want a change of scene and occupation. Who didn't occasionally? But why run away to big cities and studios? Why wouldn't the perfectly natural, perfectly logical thing (since I'd already resigned) be to go to Oakland State and study for my Secondary Credential? The minute I, or Mother—I don't remember which of us—thought of this way out, I was filled with bliss, real bliss. I would get away, go to a real city, be surrounded with people devoted to learning, but not risk everything.

I heard about Dr. Louise McKay from the minute I arrived on the campus. She was, as I've said, a kind of college heroine, though it was hard to understand why. What had she done that was so remarkable? She had been a high-school librarian, and had become a doctor. What's so extraordinary about that? The girls, and by that I mean the women students—for many of them were teachers themselves, well along in their thirties and forties, or even fifties—the girls always spoke about Louise McKay's change of profession as if it were a Lazaruslike feat; as if she had practically risen from the dead. People are always so romantic about doctors, and it's understandable, I suppose, dealing as they do with life and death. But Louise McKay! The girls talked about her as if what she'd done had been not only romantic, but also heroic.

In the first place, they emphasized her age. Forty-two! To me at twenty-six that didn't, of course, seem young. Still, it was silly to go on about her as if she were a Grandma Moses of medicine—and as if medicine itself were not, quite simply, anything more than doctoring people; saying, "This ails you" and "I think this pill will help you." They spoke of doctoring as if it were as hazardous as piloting a jet plane. And they spoke of Louise McKay's size, "that tiny, tiny thing," as if she'd been a six-year-old, praising her for her age and her youth at one and the same time. Her size, they said, made it seem as if the child-examining-doll game were reversed; as if doll took out stethoscope and examined child. She was that tiny and dainty, they said, that long-lashed and pink-cheeked. They exclaimed over her clothes, too. They were delightful in themselves, but particularly so because they emphasized the contrast between her profession and her person. She was a scientist and might have been expected to wear something manly and practical—or something dowdy. She did neither. They'd all been to her for their physical examinations—somehow I'd never been scheduled for that—and could give a complete inventory of her chic wardrobe. I saw her only once before I called on her professionally in December. I didn't see many people, as a matter of fact, at Oakland State, in any capacity, except professional.

True, I was studying. Not that the work was difficult—or interesting either. History of Education, Principles of Secondary Education, Classroom Management, Curriculum Development. But the books were better than the people. Had I lived out there on my three-legged sofa with children and nature too long? Or was there something really wrong with the people in teachers colleges? Anyway, I had no friends, and the nearer I got to a Secondary Credential, the less I wanted it. But I wanted something—miserably, achingly, wretchedly. I wanted something. Whether or not this longing, this sense of something lost, had anything to do with the illness that came upon me toward the end of December, I don't know. I attributed this illness at first to the raw damp bay weather after my lifetime in the warmth and dryness of the inland foothills; I thought that my lack of routine, after days of orderly teaching, might be responsible, and, finally, after I had adopted a routine and had stayed indoors out of the mists and fogs and the discomfort persisted, I told myself that everyone as he grew older lost some of his early exuberant health. I was no longer in my first youth, and thus, "when my health began to fail"—I thought of it in that way rather than as having any specific ailment—accounted for my miseries. I had always been impatient with the shufflings and snuffings, the caution on stairs and at the table of the no-longer-young. I thought they could do better if they tried. Now I began to understand that they couldn't do better and that they probably were trying. I was trying. I couldn't do better. I panted on the hills and puffed on the library steps. I leaned against handrails, I hawked and spat and harrumphed like any oldster past his prime. I did what I could to regain the well-being of my youth. I took long walks to get back my lost wind, ate sparingly, plunged under tingling showers.

By the end of December I felt so miserable I decided to see Dr. McKay at the infirmary. So many new things had been discovered about glands and vitamins, about toxins and antitoxins, that one pill a day was possibly all that stood between me and perfect health. I had the feeling, as people do who have always been well, that a doctor commands a kind of magic—can heal with a glance. Even Dr. McKay, this little ex-librarian, a doll of a woman, with her big splashy ear-rings and high-heeled shoes and expensive perfumes, could cast a spell of health upon me.

That was the first time I'd ever seen Louise McKay close. My first thought was, She looks every inch her age. She had dark hair con-siderably grayed, there were lines about her eyes, and her throat muscles were somewhat slack. My second thought was, Why doesn't she admit it? I was dressed more like a middle-aged woman than she. Of course, since she had on a white surgeon's coat, all that could be seen of her "personal attire" was the three or four inches of brown tweed skirt beneath it. But she wore red, very high-heeled shell pumps. Her hair was set in a modified page boy, ends turned under in a soft roll, with a thick, rather tangly fringe across her forehead. It was a somewhat advanced hair style for that year—certainly for a middle-aged doctor. Her eyebrows, which were thick and dark, had been obviously shaped by plucking, and her fingernails were painted coral. She was smiling when I came in. She had considerable color in her face for a dark-haired woman, and she sat at a desk with flowers and pictures on it—not family pictures, but little prints of famous paintings.

She said, looking at her appointment calendar, which had my name on it, "Miss McCullars?"

I said, "Yes."

Then she said, "I see we have something in common." She meant our Scotch names of course, but out of some contrariness which I find hard to explain now, I pretended not to understand, so that she had to explain her little joke to me. But then, it wasn't very funny. She discovered, in looking through her files, that I hadn't had the usual physical examination on entering college.

"Why not?" she asked.

"I didn't get a notice to come," I said, "so I just skipped it."

"It would've helped," she told me, "to have that record now to check against. Just what seems to be the trouble?"

"It's probably nothing. I'm probably just the campus hypochondriac."

"That role's already filled."

I didn't feel well even then, though the stimulation of the talk and of seeing the famous Dr. McKay did make me forget some of my miseries. So I began that afternoon what I always continued in her office—an impersonation of high-spirited, head-tossing health. I don't know why. It wasn't a planned or analyzed action. It just happened that the minute I opened her office door I began to act the part of a person bursting with vitality and health. There I was, practically dying on my feet, as it was later proved, but hiding the fact by every device I could command. What did I think I was doing? The truth is, I wasn't thinking at all.

"I must say you don't look sick," she admitted. Then she began to ask me about my medical history.

"I don't have any medical history. Except measles at fifteen."

"Was there some specific question you wanted to ask me? Some problem?"

So she thought I was one of those girls? Or one of her worshipers just come in to marvel.

"I don't feel well."

"What specifically?"

"Oh—aches and pains."

"Where?"

"Oh—here, there, and everywhere."

"We'll run a few tests, and I'll examine you. The nurse will help you get undressed."

When it was over, she said, "Is your temperature ordinarily a little high?"

"I don't know. I never take it."

"You have a couple of degrees now."

"Above or below normal?"

A little of her school-librarian manner came out. "Are you trying to be funny?"

I wasn't in the least.

"A fever is always above normal."

"What does it mean to have a fever?"

"An infection of some sort."

"It could be a tooth? A tonsil?"

"Yes, it could be. I want to see you tomorrow at ten."

I remember my visit next morning very well. The acacia trees were in bloom, and Dr. McKay's office was filled with their dusty honeybee scent. Dr. McKay was still in street clothes—a blouse, white, high-necked, but frothy with lace and semitransparent, so that you saw more lace beneath. As if she were determined to have everything, I thought: age and youth, practicality and ornamentation, science and femininity. You hero of the campus, I thought, ironically. But she rebuked us schoolteachers by the way she dressed and held herself—and lived, I expected; she really did. And I, I rebuked her in turn, for our hurt honor.

"How do you feel this morning?" she asked.

What did she think to uncover in me? A crybaby and complainer, she standing there in her lovely clothes and I in my dress sun-faded from the Liberty schoolyard?

"Fine," I told her, "I feel fine."

How I felt was her business to discover, wasn't it, not mine to tell? If I knew exactly how I felt, and why, what would've been the use of seeing a doctor? Besides, once again in her office I was stimulated by her presence so that my miseries when not there seemed quite possibly something I had imagined.

"I wanted to check your temperature this morning," she told me.

She sat me down on a white stool, put a thermometer in my mouth, then, while we waited, asked me questions which she thought I could answer with a nod of the head.

"You like teaching? You want to go on with it? You have made friends here?"

She was surprised when she took the thermometer from my mouth. After looking at it thoughtfully, she shook it down and said, "Morning temperature, too."

"You didn't expect that?"

"No, frankly, I didn't."

"Why not?"

"In the kind of infection I suspected you had, a morning temperature isn't usual."

I didn't ask what infection she suspected. I had come to her office willing to be thumped, X-rayed, tested in any way she thought best. I was willing to give her samples of sputum or urine, to cough when told to cough, say ahhh or hold my breath while she counted ten. Whatever she told me to do I would do. But she had turned doctor, not I. If she was a doctor, not a librarian, now was her chance to prove it. Here I was with my fever, come willingly to her office. Let her tell me its cause.

For the next month, Dr. McKay lived, so far as I was concerned, the life of a medical detective, trying to find the villain behind the temperature. The trouble was that the villain's habits differed from day to day. It was as if a murderer had a half-dozen different thumbprints, and left now one, now another, behind him. One day much temperature, the next day none. Dr. McKay eliminated villain after villain: malaria, tonsillitis, rheumatic fever, infected teeth. And while she found disease after disease which I did not have, I grew steadily worse. By May about the only time I ever felt well was while I was in Dr. McKay's office. Entering it was like going onto a stage. However near I might have been to collapse before that oak door opened, once inside it I was to play with perfect ease my role of health. I was unable, actually, to do anything else. I assumed health when I entered her office, as they say Dickens, unable to stand without support, assumed health when he walked out before an audience.

It was nothing I planned. I couldn't by an act of will have feigned exuberance and well-being, gone to her office day after day consciously to play the role of Miss Good Health of 1940, could I? No, something unconscious happened the minute I crossed that threshold, something electric—and ironic. I stood, sat, stooped, reclined, breathed soft, breathed hard, answered questions, flexed my muscles, exposed my reflexes for Dr. McKay with vigor and pleasure—and irony. Especially irony. I was sick, sick, falling apart, crumbling dying on my feet, and I knew it. And this woman, this campus hero whose province it was to know it, was ignorant of the fact. I didn't know what ailed me and wasn't supposed to. She was. It was her business to know.

In the beginning, tuberculosis had been included among the other suspected diseases. But the nontubercular fever pattern, the absence of positive sputum, the identical sounds of the lungs when percussed all had persuaded Dr. McKay that the trouble lay elsewhere. I did not speculate at all about my sickness. I had never been sick before, or even, for that matter, known a sick person. For all I knew, I might have elephantiasis or leprosy, and when Dr. McKay began once again to suspect tuberculosis, I was co-operative and untroubled. She was going to give me what she called a "patch test." Whether this is still used, I don't know. The test then consisted of the introduction of a small number of tubercle bacilli to a patch of scraped skin. If, after a day or two, there was no "positive" reaction, no inflammation of the skin, one was thought to have no tubercular infection.

On the day Dr. McKay began this test she used the word "tuberculosis" for the first time. I had experienced when I entered her office that afternoon my usual heightening of well-being, what amounted to a real gaiety.

"So you still don't give up?" I asked when she announced her plan for the new test. "Still won't admit that what you have on your hands is a hypochondriac?"

It was a beautiful afternoon in late May. School was almost over for the year. Students drifted past the window walking slowly homeward, relishing the sunshine and the blossoming hawthorn, their faces lifted to the light. Cubberly and Thorndyke and Dewey given the go-by for an hour or two. Some of this end-of-the-year, lovely-day quiet came into my interview with Dr. McKay. Though it had started with my usual high-spirited banter, I stopped that. It seemed inappropriate. I experienced my usual unusual well-being, but there was added to it that strange, quiet, listening tenderness which marks the attainment of a pinnacle of some kind.

Dr. McKay stood before her window, her surgeon's jacket off—I was her last patient for the day—in her usual frothy blouse, very snow-white against the rose-red of the hawthorn trees.

She turned away from the window and said to me, "You aren't a hypochondriac."

She shook her head. "I don't know." Then she explained the patch test to me.

"Tuberculosis?" I asked. "And no hectic flush, no graveyard cough, no skin and bones?"

The words were still bantering, possibly, but the tone had changed, tender, tender, humorous, and fondling; the battle—if there had been one—over; and the issue, whatever it was, settled. "In spite of all that, this test?"

"In spite of all that," she said.

She did the scraping deftly. I watched her hands, and while I doubt that there is any such thing as a "surgeon's hands," Dr. McKay's didn't look like a librarian's either, marked by fifteen years of mucilage pots, library stamps, and ten-cent fines. I could smell her perfume and note at close range the degree to which she defied time and the expected categories.

"Come back Monday at the same time," she told me when she had finished.

"What do you expect Monday?" I asked.

"I'm not a prophet," she answered. "If I were . . ." She didn't finish her sentence.

We parted like comrades who have been together on a long and dangerous expedition. I don't know what she felt or thought—that she had really discovered, at last, the cause of my illness, perhaps. What I felt is difficult to describe. Certainly my feelings were not those of the usual patient threatened with tuberculosis. Instead, I experienced a tranquility I hadn't known for a long time. I felt like a lover and a winner, triumphant but tranquil. I knew there would be no positive reaction to the skin test. Beyond that I didn't think.

I was quite right about the reaction. Dr. McKay was completely professional Monday afternoon; buttoned up in her jacket, stethoscope hanging about her neck. I entered her office feeling well, but strange. My veins seemed bursting with blood or triumph. I looked out the window and remembered where I had been a year ago. Breathing was difficult, but in the past months I had learned to live without breathing. I wore a special dress that afternoon because I thought the occasion special. I wouldn't be seeing Dr. McKay again. It was made of white men's-shirting Madras and had a deep scooped neckline, bordered with a ruffle.

"How do you feel?" Dr. McKay asked, as she always did, when I entered.

"Out of this world," I told her.

"Don't joke," she said.

"I wasn't. It's the truth. I feel wonderful."

"Let's have a look at the arm."

"You won't find anything."

"How do you know? Did you peek?"

"No, I didn't, but you won't find anything."

"I'll have a look anyway."

There was nothing, just as I'd known. Not a streak of pink even. Nothing but the marks of the adhesive tape to distinguish one arm from the other. Dr. McKay looked and looked. She touched the skin and pinched it.

"Okay," she said, "you win."

"What do you mean I win? You didn't want me to be infected, did you?"

"Of course not."

"I told you all along I was a hypochondriac."

"Okay, Miss McCullars," she said again, "you win." She sat down at her desk and wrote something on my record sheet.

"What's the final verdict?" I asked.

She handed the sheet to me. What she had written was "TB patch test negative. Fluctuating temperature due to neurotic causes."

"So I won't need to come back?"

"No."

"Nor worry about my lungs?"

"No."

Then with precise timing, as if that were the cue for which for almost six months I had been waiting, I had, there in Dr. McKay's office, my first hemorrhage. A hemorrhage from the lungs is always frightening, and this was a very bad one and my first. They got me to the infirmary at once, but there behind me in Dr. McKay's office was the card stained with my blood and saying that nothing ailed me. I was not allowed to speak for twenty-four hours, and my thought, once the hemorrhage had stopped, was contained in two words, which ran through my mind, over and over again. "I've won. I've won." What had I won? Well, for one thing, I'd won my release from going on with my work for that Secondary Credential. All that could be forgotten, and forgotten also the need to leave Liberty at all. I could go back there, back to my stranded sofa and the school library and the mountains, blue over the green barley.

When at the end of twenty-four hours I was permitted to whisper, Dr. Stegner, the head physician at Oakland State, came to see me.

"When did you first see Dr. McKay?" he asked.

"In December."

"What course of treatment did she prescribe?"

"Not any. She didn't know what was wrong with me."

"Did she ever X-ray you?"

"No."

This, I began to learn, was the crux of the case against Dr. McKay. For there was one. She should have X-rayed me. She should have known that in cases of far advanced tuberculosis, and that was what I had, the already deeply infected system pays no attention to the introduction of one or two more bacilli. All of its forces are massed elsewhere—there are no guards left to repulse border attacks of unimportant skirmishers. But by this time my mother had arrived, alert, knowledgeable, and energetic.

"My poor little girl," she said, "this woman doctor has killed you."

I wasn't dead yet, but as I heard the talk around me I began to understand that in another year or two I might very well be so. And listening to my mother's talk, I began to agree with her. Dr. McKay had robbed me not only of health, but also of a promising career—I had been poised upon the edge of something unusual. I was training myself for service. I had remarkable talents. And now all was denied me, and for this denial I could blame Dr. McKay. I did. She had cut me down in mid-career through her ignorance. What did the campus think of its hero now? For the campus had heard of Dr. McKay's mistake. And the Board of Regents! My mother said it was her duty; that she owed the steps she was taking to some other poor girl who might suffer as I had through Dr. McKay's medical incompetence. I thought it was a matter for her to decide, and besides, I was far too ill to have or want any say in such decisions. I was sent, as soon as I was able to be moved, to a sanatorium near my home in Southern California.

I had been there four months when I saw Dr. McKay again. At the beginning of the visiting hour on the first Saturday in October, the nurse on duty came to my room.

"Dr. McKay to see you," she said.

I had no chance to refuse to see her—though I don't know that I would have refused if I'd had the chance—for Dr. McKay followed the nurse into the room and sat down by my bed.

She had changed a good deal; she appeared little, nondescript, and mousy. She had stopped shaping her eyebrows and painting her nails. I suppose I had changed, too. With the loss of my fever, I had lost also all my show of exuberance and life. I lay there in the hospital bed looking, I knew, as sick as I really was. We stared at each other without words for a time.

Then I said, to say something, for she continued silent, "How are things at Oakland State this year?"

"I'm not at Oakland State. I was fired."

I hadn't known it. I was surprised and dismayed, but for a heart-beat—in a heartbeat—I experienced a flash of that old outrageous exultation I had known in her office. I was, in spite of everything, for a second, well and strong and tender in victory. Though what my victory was, I sick and she fired, I couldn't have told.

"I'm sorry," I said. I was. It is a pitiful thing to be out of work.

"Don't lie," she said.

"I am not lying," I told her.

She didn't contradict me. "Why did you do it?" she asked me.

"Do what?" I said, at first really puzzled. Then I remembered my mother's threats. "I had nothing to do with it. Even if I'd wanted to, I was too sick. You know that. I had no idea you weren't in Oakland this year.

"I don't mean my firing—directly. I mean that long masquerade. I mean that willingness to kill yourself, if necessary, to punish me. I tell you a doctor of fifty years' experience would've been fooled by you. Why? I'd never seen you before. I wanted nothing but good for you. Why did you do it? Why?"

"I don't know what you mean."

"What had I ever done to you? Lost there in that dark library, dreaming of being a doctor, saving my money and finally escaping. How had I harmed or threatened you that you should be willing to risk your life to punish me?"

Dr. McKay had risen and was walking about the room, her voice, for one so small, surprisingly loud and commanding. I was afraid a nurse would come to ask her to be quiet. Yet I hesitated myself to remind her to speak more quietly.

"Well," she said, "you have put yourself in a prison, a fine narrow prison. Elected it of your own free will. And that's all right for you, if you wanted a prison. But you had no right to elect it for me, too. That was murderous. Really murderous." I began to fear that she was losing control of herself, and tried to ask questions that would divert her mind from the past.

"Where are you practicing, now?" I asked.

She stopped her pacing and stood over me. "I am no longer in medicine," she said. "I'm the librarian in the high school at Beaumont."

"That's not where you were before?"

"No, it's much smaller and hotter."

"It's only thirty miles—as the crow flies—from Liberty, where I used to teach. I'm going back there as soon as I'm well. It was a mistake to leave it." She said nothing.

"I really love Liberty," I said, "and teaching. The big fields of barley, the mountains. There was an old sofa in the schoolyard, where I used to sit. It was like a throne. I thought for a while I wanted to get away from there and try something else. But that was all a crazy dream. All I want to do now is get back."

"I wish you could have discovered that before you came to Oakland."

I ignored this. "Don't you love books?"

"I had better love books," she said, and left the room.

As it happened, I've never seen her again, though I get these cards. I didn't go back to Liberty four years later—when I was able again to teach. I got this other school, but somehow the magic I had felt earlier with the children, I felt no longer. An outdated little schoolroom with the windows placed high so that neither teacher nor pupils could see out; a dusty schoolyard; and brackish water. The children I teach now look so much like their predecessors that I have the illusion of living in a dream, of being on a treadmill teaching the same child the same lesson through eternity. Outside on the school grounds, my erstwhile throne, the sofa, does not exist. The mountains, of course, are still there—a great barrier at the end of the valley.

Just across the mountains are Beaumont and Dr. McKay; and I am sometimes heartened, standing on the packed earth of the schoolyard in the winter dusk, as she suggested, to think of her reshelving her

books, closing the drawer of her fine-till, at the same hour. We can't all escape; some of us must stay home and do the homely tasks, however much we may have dreamed of painting or doctoring. "You have company," I tell myself, looking toward her across the mountains. Then I get into my car to drive into town, where my mother has all this loveliness waiting for me; a composition, once again, that really includes me.

Insight

1. Describe the six years Miss McCullars spent at the Liberty School. What were the major satisfactions the position provided? What are the reasons she decides to leave?

2. Why is Miss McCullars "filled with fear" upon resigning? How would you account for her uncertainties at this point? What effect does her mother have on resolving these uncertainties?

3. Describe the developing relationship between the doctor and her patient. Why does Miss McCullars choose to be a difficult patient? How do you account for her "exuberance and well-being" when in the doctor's office?

4. "Okay, you win," Dr. McKay finally admits to her patient who feels "like a lover and a winner." How would you describe the battle between these two women? Has there, indeed, been a winner? Explain.

5. How is Dr. McKay changed at the last meeting with the narrator? Of what does she accuse her former patient? Do you think her accusation has any validity? Explain.

Advice to a Girl

Sara Teasdale

No one worth possessing
Can be quite possessed;
Lay that on your heart,
My young angry dear;
This truth, this hard and precious stone,   5
Lay it on your hot cheek,
Let it hide your tear.
Hold it like a crystal
When you are alone
And gaze in the depths of the icy stone.   10
Long, look long and you will be blessed:
No one worth possessing
Can be quite possessed.

Insight
1. The first two lines and the last two lines constitute the advice given
   the young girl. How would you explain the "truth" of this advice?
   Do you think it is good advice? Explain.
2. Who is the speaker addressing? What, do you suppose, is the occasion for this advice?

THE RING

Isak Dinesen

On a summer morning a hundred and fifty years ago a young Danish squire and his wife went out for a walk on their land. They had been married a week. It had not been easy for them to get married, for the wife's family was higher in rank and wealthier than the husband's. But the two young people, now twenty-four and nineteen years old, had been set on their purpose for ten years; in the end her haughty parents had had to give in to them.

They were wonderfully happy. The stolen meeting and secret, tearful love letters were now things of the past. To God and man they were one; they could walk arm in arm in broad daylight and drive in the same carriage, and they would walk and drive so till the end of their days. Their distant paradise had descended to earth and had proved, surprisingly, to be filled with the things of everyday life: with jesting and railleries, with breakfasts and suppers, with dogs, haymaking and sheep. Sigismund, the young husband, had promised himself that from now there should be no stone in his bride's path, nor should any shadow fall across it. Lovisa, the wife, felt that now, every day and for the first time in her young life, she moved and breathed in perfect freedom because she could never have any secret from her husband.

To Lovisa—whom her husband called Lise—the rustic atmosphere of her new life was a matter of wonder and delight. Her husband's fear that the existence he could offer her might not be good enough for her filled her heart with laughter. It was not a long time since she had played with dolls; as now she dressed her own hair, looked over her linen press and arranged her flowers she again lived through an enchanting and cherished experience: one was doing everything gravely and solicitously, and all the time one knew one was playing.

It was a lovely July morning. Little woolly clouds drifted high up in the sky, the air was full of sweet scents. Lise had on a white muslin frock and a large Italian straw hat. She and her husband took a path through the park; it wound on across the meadows, between small groves and groups of trees, to the sheep field. Sigismund was going to show his wife his sheep. For this reason she had not brought her small white dog, Bijou, with her, for he would yap at the lambs and frighten them, or he would annoy the sheep dogs. Sigismund prided himself on his sheep; he had studied sheep-breeding in Mecklenburg and England, and had brought back with him Cotswold rams by which to improve his Danish stock. While they walked he explained to Lise the great possibilities and difficulties of the plan.

She thought: "How clever he is, what a lot of things he knows!" and at the same time: "What an absurd person he is, with his sheep! What a baby he is! I am a hundred years older than he."

But when they arrived at the sheepfold the old sheepmaster Mathias met them with the sad news that one of the English lambs was dead and two were sick. Lise saw that her husband was grieved by the tidings; while he questioned Mathias on the matter she kept silent and only gently pressed his arm. A couple of boys were sent off to fetch the sick lambs, while the master and servant went into the details of the case. It took some time.

Lise began to gaze about her and to think of other things. Twice her own thoughts made her blush deeply and happily, like a red rose, then slowly her blush died away, and the two men were still talking about sheep. A little while after their conversation caught her attention. It had turned to a sheep thief.

This thief during the last months had broken into the sheepfolds of the neighborhood like a wolf, had killed and dragged away his prey like a wolf and like a wolf had left no trace after him. Three nights ago the shepherd and his son on an estate ten miles away had caught him in the act. The thief had killed the man and knocked the boy senseless, and had managed to escape. There were men sent out to all sides to catch him, but nobody had seen him.

Lise wanted to hear more about the horrible event, and for her benefit old Mathias went through it once more. There had been a long fight in the sheep house, in many places the earthen floor was soaked with blood. In the fight the thief's left arm was broken; all the same, he had climbed a tall fence with a lamb on his back. Mathias added that he would like to string up the murderer with these two hands of his, and Lise nodded her head at him gravely in approval. She remembered Red Ridinghood's wolf, and felt a pleasant little thrill running down her spine.

Sigismund had his own lambs in his mind, but he was too happy in himself to wish anything in the universe ill. After a minute he said: "Poor devil."

Lise said: "How can you pity such a terrible man? Indeed Grandmamma was right when she said that you were a revolutionary and a danger to society!" The thought of Grandmamma, and of the tears of past days, again turned her mind away from the gruesome tale she had just heard.

The boys brought the sick lambs and the men began to examine them carefully, lifting them up and trying to set them on their legs; they squeezed them here and there and made the little creatures whimper. Lise shrank from the show and her husband noticed her distress.

"You go home, my darling," he said, "this will take some time. But just walk ahead slowly, and I shall catch up with you."

So she was turned away by an impatient husband to whom his sheep meant more than his wife. If any experience could be sweeter than to be dragged out by him to look at those same sheep, it would be this. She dropped her large summer hat with its blue ribbons on the grass and told him to carry it back for her, for she wanted to feel the summer air on her forehead and in her hair. She walked on very slowly, as he had told her to do, for she wished to obey him in everything. As she walked she felt a great new happiness in being altogether alone, even without Bijou. She could not remember that she had ever before in all her life been altogether alone. The landscape around her was still, as if full of promise, and it was hers. Even the swallows cruising in the air were hers, for they belonged to him, and he was hers.

She followed the curving edge of the grove and after a minute or two found that she was out of sight to the men by the sheep house. What could now, she wondered, be sweeter than to walk along the path in the long flowering meadow grass, slowly, slowly, and to let her husband overtake her there? It would be sweeter still, she reflected, to steal into the grove and to be gone, to have vanished from the surface of the earth from him when, tired of the sheep and longing for her company, he should turn the bend of the path to catch up with her.

An idea struck her; she stood still to think it over.

A few days ago her husband had gone for a ride and she had not wanted to go with him, but had strolled about with Bijou in order to explore her domain. Bijou then, gamboling, had led her straight into the grove. As she had followed him, gently forcing her way into the shrubbery, she had suddenly come upon a glade in the midst of it, a narrow space like a small alcove with hangings of thick green and golden brocade, big enough to hold two or three people in it. She had felt at that moment that she had come into the very heart of her new home. If today she could find the spot again she would stand perfectly still there, hidden from all the world. Sigismund would look for her in all directions; he would be unable to understand what had become of her and for a minute, for a short minute—or, perhaps, if she was firm and cruel enough, for five—he would realize what a void, what an unendurably sad and horrible place the universe would be when she was no longer in it. She gravely scrutinized the grove to find the right entrance to her hiding-place, then went in.

She took great care to make no noise at all, therefore advanced exceedingly slowly. When a twig caught the flounces of her ample skirt she loosened it softly from the muslin, so as not to crack it.

Once a branch took hold of one of her long golden curls; she stood still, with her arms lifted, to free it. A little way into the grove the soil became moist; her light steps no longer made any sound upon it. With one hand she held her small handkerchief to her lips, as if to emphasize the secretness of her course. She found the spot she sought and bent down to divide the foliage and make a door to her sylvan closet. At this the hem of her dress caught her foot and she stopped to loosen it. As she rose she looked into the face of a man who was already in the shelter.

He stood up erect, two steps off. He must have watched her as she made her way straight toward him.

She took him in in one single glance. His face was bruised and scratched, his hands and wrists stained with dark filth. He was dressed in rags, barefooted, with tatters wound round his naked ankles. His arms hung down to his sides, his right hand clasped the hilt of a knife. He was about her own age. The man and the woman looked at each other.

This meeting in the wood from beginning to end passed without a word; what happened could only be rendered by pantomime. To the two actors in the pantomime it was timeless; according to a clock it lasted four minutes.

She had never in her life been exposed to danger. It did not occur to her to sum up her position, or to work out the length of time it would take to call her husband or Mathias, whom at this moment she could hear shouting to his dogs. She beheld the man before her as she would have beheld a forest ghost: the apparition itself, not the sequels of it, changes the world to the human who faces it.

Although she did not take her eyes off the face before her she sensed that the alcove had been turned into a covert. On the ground a couple of sacks formed a couch; there were some gnawed bones by it. A fire must have been made here in the night, for there were cinders strewn on the forest floor.

After a while she realized that he was observing her just as she was observing him. He was no longer just run to earth and crouching for a spring, but he was wondering, trying to know. At that she seemed to see herself with the eyes of the wild animal at bay in his dark hiding-place: her silently approaching white figure, which might mean death.

He moved his right arm till it hung down straight before him between his legs. Without lifting the hand he bent the wrist and slowly raised the point of the knife till it pointed at her throat. The gesture was mad, unbelievable. He did not smile as he made it, but his nostrils distended, the corners of his mouth quivered a little. Then slowly he put the knife back in the sheath by his belt.

She had no object of value about her, only the wedding ring which her husband had set on her finger in church, a week ago. She drew it off, and in this movement dropped her handkerchief. She reached out her hand with the ring toward him. She did not bargain for her life. She was fearless by nature, and the horror with which he inspired her was not fear of what he might do to her. She commanded him, she besought him to vanish as he had come, to take a dreadful figure out of her life, so that it should never have been there. In the dumb movement her young form had the grave authoritativeness of a priestess conjuring down some monstrous being by a sacred sign.

He slowly reached out his hand to hers, his finger touched hers, and her hand was steady at the touch. But he did not take the ring. As she let it go it dropped to the ground as her handkerchief had done.

For a second the eyes of both followed it. It rolled a few inches toward him and stopped before his bare foot. In a hardly perceivable movement he kicked it away and again looked into her face. They remained like that, she knew not how long, but she felt that during that time something happened, things were changed.

He bent down and picked up her handkerchief. All the time gazing at her, he again drew his knife and wrapped the tiny bit of cambric round the blade. This was difficult for him to do because his left arm was broken. While he did it his face under the dirt and sun-tan slowly grew whiter till it was almost phosphorescent. Fumbling with both hands, he once more stuck the knife into the sheath. Either the sheath was too big and had never fitted the knife, or the blade was much worn—it went in. For two or three more seconds his gaze rested on her face; then he lifted his own face a little, the strange radiance still upon it, and closed his eyes.

The movement was definitive and unconditional. In this one motion he did what she had begged him to do: he vanished and was gone. She was free.

She took a step backward, the immovable, blind face before her, then bent as she had done to enter the hiding-place, and glided away as noiselessly as she had come. Once outside the grove she stood still and looked round for the meadow path, found it and began to walk home.

Her husband had not yet rounded the edge of the grove. Now he saw her and helloed to her gaily; he came up quickly and joined her.

The path here was so narrow that he kept half behind her and did not touch her. He began to explain to her what had been the matter with the lambs. She walked a step before him and thought: All is over.

After a while he noticed her silence, came up beside her to look at her face and asked, "What is the matter?"

She searched her mind for something to say, and at last said: "I have lost my ring."

"What ring?" he asked her.

She answered, "My wedding ring."

As she heard her own voice pronounce the words she conceived their meaning.

Her wedding ring. "With this ring"—dropped by one and kicked away by another—"with this ring I thee wed." With this lost ring she had wedded herself to something. To what? To poverty, persecution, total loneliness. To the sorrows and the sinfulness of this earth. "And what therefore God has joined together let man not put asunder."

"I will find you another ring," her husband said. "You and I are the same as we were on our wedding day; it will do as well. We are husband and wife today too, as much as yesterday, I suppose."

Her face was so still that he did not know if she had heard what he said. It touched him that she should take the loss of his ring so to heart. He took her hand and kissed it. It was cold, not quite the same hand as he had last kissed. He stopped to make her stop with him.

"Do you remember where you had the ring on last?" he asked.

"No," she answered.

"Have you any idea," he asked, "where you may have lost it?"

"No," she answered. "I have no idea at all."

Insight

1. In what ways has the marriage between Sigismund and Lise fallen short of the "distant paradise" they had anticipated? To what extent have their respective backgrounds contributed to the nature of their relationship before Lise's encounter with the thief?

2. How would you explain Lise's desire "to hear more about the horrible event"? Why do you suppose she remembers the story of "Little Red Riding Hood" and feels a "pleasant little thrill running down her spine"?

3. What motivates Lise to wish "to steal into the grove and to be gone, to have vanished from the surface of the earth from him . . ."?

4. What victory has Lise won over the thief? What victory has she won over herself?

for my people

Margaret Walker

For my people everywhere singing their slave songs repeatedly: their dirges and their ditties and their blues and
 jubilees, praying their prayers nightly to an unknown
 god, bending their knees humbly to an unseen power;

For my people lending their strength to the years, to the gone 5
 years and the now years and the maybe years, washing
 ironing cooking scrubbing sewing mending hoeing
 plowing digging planting pruning patching dragging
 along never gaining never reaping never knowing and
 never understanding; 10

For my playmates in the clay and dust and sand of Alabama
 backyards playing baptizing and preaching and doctor and jail and soldier and school and mama and
 cooking and playhouse and concert and store and hair
 and Miss Choomby and company; 15

For the cramped bewildered years we went to school to learn
 to know the reasons why and the answers to and the
 people who and the places where and the days when,
 in memory of the bitter hours when we discovered we
 were black and poor and small and different and 20
 nobody cared and nobody wondered and nobody
 understood;

For the boys and girls who grew in spite of these things to be
 man and woman, to laugh and dance and sing and
 play and drink their wine and religion and success, to 25
 marry their playmates and bear children and then die
 of consumption and anemia and lynching;

For my people thronging 47th Street in Chicago and Lenox
 Avenue in New York and Rampart Street in New
 Orleans, lost disinherited dispossessed and happy 30
 people filling the cabarets and taverns and other
 people's pockets needing bread and shoes and milk
 and land and money and something—something all
 our own;

For my people walking blindly spreading joy, losing time   35
being lazy, sleeping when hungry, shouting when
burdened, drinking when hopeless, tied and shackled
and tangled among ourselves by the unseen creatures
who tower over us omnisciently and laugh;

For my people blundering and groping and floundering in   40
the dark of churches and schools and clubs and
societies, associations and councils and committees
and conventions, distressed and disturbed and deceived and devoured by money-hungry glory-craving
leeches, preyed on by facile force of state and fad and   45
novelty, by false prophet and holy believer;

For my people standing staring trying to fashion a better
way from confusion, from hypocrisy and misunderstanding, trying to fashion a world that will hold all
the people, all the faces, all the adams and eves and   50
their countless generations;

Let a new earth rise. Let another world be born. Let a bloody
peace be written in the sky. Let a second generation
full of courage issue forth; let a people loving freedom come to growth. Let a beauty full of healing   55
and a strength of final clenching be the pulsing in
our spirits and our blood. Let the martial songs be
written, let the dirges disappear. Let a race of men
now rise and take control.

Insight

1. The speaker is seeking a new world for black people. Why does she say this new world is necessary? What conditions have warranted this need?
2. The poet concludes by saying "For my people ... Let a new earth rise." What will this new earth symbolize for her people? What will this new world have that the old one did not? How does the speaker imply that the new earth will come about?

WHAT ARE YEARS?

Marianne Moore

What is our innocence,
what is our guilt? All are
    naked, none is safe. And whence
is courage: the unanswered question,
the resolute doubt—   5
dumbly calling, deafly listening—that
in misfortune, even death,
    encourages others
    and in its defeat, stirs

    the soul to be strong? He   10
sees deep and is glad, who
    accedes to mortality
and in his imprisonment, rises
upon himself as
the sea in a chasm, struggling to be   15
free and unable to be,
    in its surrendering
    finds its continuing.

    So he who strongly feels,
behaves. The very bird,   20
    grown taller as he sings, steels
his form straight up. Though he is captive,
his mighty singing
says, satisfaction is a lowly
thing, how pure a thing is joy.   25
    This is mortality,
    this is eternity.

Insight

1. "What is our innocence,/what is our guilt?" What is the meaning of this question? What answer does the poet give? What other question is asked in this first stanza, and how is this question related to the first question?

2. In the second stanza, the speaker elaborates upon her position. How does she describe courage in this stanza?

3. The last stanza develops the metaphor of a bird. Where is this bird? What is its meaning?

4. What is the answer to the question raised by the title of the poem?

AN old WOMAN
ANd HER CAT

Doris Lessing

Her name was Hetty, and she was born with the twentieth century. She was seventy when she died of cold and malnutrition. She had been alone for a long time, since her husband had died of pneumonia in a bad winter soon after the Second World War. He had not been more than middleaged. Her four children were now middleaged, with grown children. Of these descendants one daughter sent her Christmas cards, but otherwise she did not exist for them. For they were all respectable people, with homes and good jobs and cars. And Hetty was not respectable. She had always been a bit strange, these people said, when mentioning her at all.

When Fred Pennefather, her husband, was alive and the children just growing up, they all lived much too close and uncomfortable in a council flat in that part of London which is like an estuary, with tides of people flooding in and out: they were not half a mile from the great stations of Euston, St. Pancras, and King's Cross. The blocks of flats were pioneers in that area, standing up grim, grey, hideous, among many acres of little houses and gardens, all soon to be demolished so that they could be replaced by more tall grey blocks. The Pennefathers were good tenants, paying their rent, keeping out of debt; he was a building worker, "steady," and proud of it. There was no evidence then of Hetty's future dislocation from the normal, unless it was that she very often slipped down for an hour or so to the platforms where the locomotives drew in and ground out again. She liked the smell of it all, she said. She liked to see people moving about, "coming and going from all those foreign places." She meant Scotland, Ireland, the North of England. These visits into the din, the smoke, the massed swirling people were for her a drug, like other people's drinking or gambling. Her husband teased her, calling her a gypsy. She was in fact part-gypsy, for her mother had been one, but had chosen to leave her people and marry a man who lived in a house. Fred Pennefather liked his wife for being different from the run of the women he knew, and had married her because of it, but her children were fearful that her gypsy blood might show itself in worse ways than haunting railway stations. She was a tall woman with a lot of glossy black hair, a skin that tanned easily, and dark strong eyes. She wore bright colours, and enjoyed quick tempers and sudden reconciliations. In her prime she attracted attention, was proud and handsome. All this made it inevitable that the people in those streets should refer to her as "that gypsy woman." When she heard them, she shouted back that she was none the worse for that.

After her husband died and the children married and left, the Council moved her to a small flat in the same building. She got a job selling food in a local store, but found it boring. There seem to be traditional occupations for middleaged women living alone, the busy and responsible part of their lives being over. Drink. Gambling. Looking for another husband. A wistful affair or two. That's about it. Hetty went through a period of, as it were, testing out all these, like hobbies, but tired of them. While still earning her small wage as a saleswoman, she began a trade in buying and selling secondhand clothes. She did not have a shop of her own, but bought or begged clothes from householders, and sold these to stalls and the second-hand shops. She adored doing this. It was a passion. She gave up her respectable job and forgot all about her love of trains and travellers. Her room was always full of bright bits of cloth, a dress that had a pattern she fancied and did not want to sell, strips of beading, old furs, embroidery, lace. There were street traders among the people in the flats, but there was something in the way Hetty went about it that lost her friends. Neighbours of twenty or thirty years' standing said she had gone queer, and wished to know her no longer. But she did not mind. She was enjoying herself too much, particularly the moving about the streets with her old perambulator, in which she crammed what she was buying or selling. She liked the gossiping, the bargaining, the wheedling from householders. It was this last which —and she knew this quite well of course—the neighbours objected to. It was the thin edge of the wedge. It was begging. Decent people did not beg. She was no longer decent.

Lonely in her tiny flat, she was there as little as possible, always preferring the lively streets. But she had after all to spend some time in her room, and one day she saw a kitten lost and trembling in a dirty corner, and brought it home to the block of flats. She was on a fifth floor. While the kitten was growing into a large strong tom, he ranged about that conglomeration of staircases and lifts and many dozens of flats, as if the building were a town. Pets were not actively persecuted by the authorities, only forbidden and then tolerated. Hetty's life from the coming of the cat became more sociable, for the beast was always making friends with somebody in the cliff that was the block of flats across the court, or not coming home for nights at a time so that she had to go and look for him and knock on doors and ask, or returning home kicked and limping, or bleeding after a fight with his kind. She made scenes with the kickers, or the owners of the enemy cats, exchanged cat lore with cat lovers, was always having to bandage and nurse her poor Tibby. The cat was soon a scarred warrior with fleas, a torn ear, and a ragged look to him. He was a multicoloured cat and his eyes were small and yellow. He was a long way down the scale from the delicately coloured, elegantly shaped pedigree cats. But he was independent, and often caught himself pigeons when he could no longer stand the tinned cat food, or the bread and packet gravy Hetty fed him, and he purred and nestled when she grabbed him to her bosom at those times she suffered loneliness. This happened less and less. Once she had realised that her children were hoping that she would leave them alone because the old rag trader was an embarrassment to them, she accepted it, and a bitterness that always had wild humour in it, only welled up at times like Christmas. She sang or chanted to the cat: "You nasty old beast, filthy old cat, nobody wants you, do they Tibby, no, you're just an alley tom, just an old stealing cat, hey Tibs, Tibs, Tibs."

The building teemed with cats. There were even a couple of dogs. They all fought up and down the grey cement corridors. There were sometimes dog and cat messes which someone had to clear up, but which might be left for days and weeks as part of neighbourly wars and feuds. There were many complaints. Finally an official came from the Council to say that the ruling about keeping animals was going to be enforced. Hetty, like others, would have to have her cat destroyed. This crisis coincided with a time of bad luck for her. She had had 'flu; had not been able to earn money, had found it hard to get out for her pension, had run into debt. She owed a lot of back rent, too. A television set she had hired and was not paying for attracted the visits of a television representative. The neighbours were gossiping that Hetty had "gone savage." This was because the cat had brought up the stairs and along the passageways a pigeon he had caught, shedding feathers and blood all the way; a woman coming in to complain found Hetty plucking the pigeon to stew it, as she had done with others, sharing the meal with Tibby.

"You're filthy," she would say to him, setting the stew down to cool in his dish. "Filthy old thing. Eating that dirty old pigeon. What do you think you are, a wild cat? Decent cats don't eat dirty birds. Only those old gypsies eat wild birds."

One night she begged help from a neighbour who had a car, and put into the car herself, the television set, the cat, bundles of clothes, and the pram. She was driven across London to a room in a street that was a slum because it was waiting to be done up. The neighbour made a second trip to bring her bed and her mattress, which were tied to the roof of the car, a chest of drawers, an old trunk, saucepans. It was in this way that she left the street in which she had lived for thirty years, nearly half her life.

She set up house again in one room. She was frightened to go near "them" to re-establish pension rights and her identity, because of the arrears of rent she had left behind, and because of the stolen television set. She started trading again, and the little room was soon spread, like her last, with a rainbow of colours and textures and lace and sequins. She cooked on a single gas ring and washed in the sink. There was no hot water unless it was boiled in saucepans. There were several old ladies and a family of five children in the house, which was condemned.

She was in the ground floor back, with a window which opened onto a derelict garden, and her cat was happy in a hunting ground that was a mile around this house where his mistress was so splendidly living. A canal ran close by, and in the dirty city-water were islands which a cat could reach by leaping from moored boat to boat. On the islands were rats and birds. There were pavements full of fat London pigeons. The cat was a fine hunter. He soon had his place in the hierarchies of the local cat population and did not have to fight much to keep it. He was a strong male cat, and fathered many litters of kittens.

In that place Hetty and he lived five happy years. She was trading well, for there were rich people close by to shed what the poor needed to buy cheaply. She was not lonely, for she made a quarrelling but satisfying friendship with a woman on the top floor, a widow like herself who did not see her children either. Hetty was sharp with the five children, complaining about their noise and mess, but she slipped them bits of money and sweets after telling their mother that "she was a fool to put herself out for them, because they wouldn't appreciate it." She was living well, even without her pension. She sold the television set and gave herself and her friend upstairs some day-trips to the coast, and bought a small radio. She never read books or magazines. The truth was that she could not write or read, or only so badly it was no pleasure to her. Her cat was all reward and no cost, for he fed himself, and continued to bring in pigeons for her to cook and eat, for which in return he claimed milk.

"Greedy Tibby, you greedy *thing*, don't think I don't know, oh yes I do, you'll get sick eating those old pigeons, I do keep telling you that, don't I?"

At last the street was being done up. No longer a uniform, long, disgraceful slum, houses were being bought by the middle-class people. While this meant more good warm clothes for trading—or begging, for she still could not resist the attraction of getting something for nothing by the use of her plaintive inventive tongue, her still flashing handsome eyes—Hetty knew, like her neighbours, that soon this house with its cargo of poor people would be bought for improvement.

In the week Hetty was seventy years old, came the notice that was the end of this little community. They had four weeks to find somewhere else to live.

Usually, the shortage of housing being what it is in London—and everywhere else in the world, of course—these people would have had to scatter, fending for themselves. But the fate of this particular street was attracting attention, because a municipal election was pending. Homelessness among the poor was finding a focus in this street which was a perfect symbol of the whole area, and indeed the whole city, half of it being fine converted tasteful houses, full of people who spent a lot of money, and half being dying houses tenanted by people like Hetty.

As a result of speeches by councillors and churchmen, local authorities found themselves unable to ignore the victims of this redevelopment. The people in the house Hetty was in were visited by a team consisting of an unemployment officer, a social worker, and a rehousing officer. Hetty, a strong gaunt old woman wearing a scarlet wool suit she had found among her castoffs that week, a black knitted teacosy on her head, and black buttoned Edwardian boots too big for her, so that she had to shuffle, invited them into her room. But although all were well used to the extremes of poverty, none wished to enter the place, but stood in the doorway and made her this offer: that she should be aided to get her pension—why had she not claimed it long ago? and that she, together with the four other old ladies in the house should move to a Home run by the Council out in the northern suburbs. All these women were used to, and enjoyed, lively London, and while they had no alternative but to agree, they fell into a saddened and sullen state. Hetty agreed too. The last two winters had set her bones aching badly, and a cough was never far away. And while perhaps she was more of an urban soul even than the others, since she had walked up and down so many streets with her old perambulator loaded with rags and laces, and since she knew so intimately London's texture and taste, she minded least of all the idea of a new home "among green fields." There were, in fact, no fields near the promised Home, but for some reason all the old ladies had chosen to bring out this old song of a phrase, as if it belonged to their situation, that of old women not far off death. "It will be nice to be near green fields again," they said to each other over cups of tea.

The housing officer came to make final arrangements. Hetty Pennefather was to move with the others in two weeks' time. The young man, sitting on the very edge of the only chair in the crammed room, because it was greasy and he suspected it had fleas or worse in it, breathed as lightly as he could because of the appalling stink: there was a lavatory in the house, but it had been out of order for three days, and it was just the other side of a thin wall. The whole house smelled.

The young man, who knew only too well the extent of the misery due to lack of housing, who knew how many old people abandoned by their children did not get the offer to spend their days being looked after by the authorities, could not help feeling that this wreck of a human being could count herself lucky to get a place in this "Home," even if it was—and he knew and deplored the fact—an institution in which the old were treated like naughty and dimwitted children until they had the good fortune to die.

But just as he was telling Hetty that a van would be coming to take her effects and those of the other four old ladies, and that she need not take anything more with her than her clothes "and perhaps a few photographs," he saw what he had thought was a heap of multi-coloured rags get up and put its ragged gingery-black paws on the old woman's skirt. Which today was a cretonne curtain covered with pink and red roses that Hetty had pinned around her because she liked the pattern.

"You can't take that cat with you," he said automatically. It was something he had to say often, and knowing what misery the statement caused, he usually softened it down. But he had been taken by surprise.

Tibby now looked like a mass of old wool that has been matting together in dust and rain. One eye was permanently half-closed, because a muscle had been ripped in a fight. One ear was vestigial. And down a flank was a hairless slope with a thick scar on it. A cat-hating man had treated Tibby as he treated all cats, to a pellet from his air-gun. The resulting wound had taken two years to heal. And Tibby smelled.

No worse, however, than his mistress, who sat stiffly still, bright-eyed with suspicion, hostile, watching the wellbrushed tidy young man from the Council.

"How old is that beast?"

"Ten years, no, only eight years, he's a young cat about five years old," said Hetty, desperate.

"It looks as if you'd do him a favour to put him out of his misery," said the young man.

When the official left, Hetty had agreed to everything. She was the only one of the old women with a cat. The others had budgerigars or nothing. Budgies were allowed in the Home.

She made her plans, confided in the others, and when the van came for them and their clothes and photographs and budgies, she was not there, and they told lies for her. "Oh, we don't know where she can have gone, dear," the old women repeated again and again to the indifferent van driver. "She was here last night, but she did say something about going to her daughter in Manchester." And off they went to die in the Home.

Hetty knew that when houses have been emptied for redevelopment they may stay empty for months, even years. She intended to go on living in this one until the builders moved in.

It was a warm autumn. For the first time in her life she lived like her gypsy forbears, and did not go to bed in a room in a house like respectable people. She spent several nights, with Tibby, sitting crouched in a doorway of an empty house two doors from her own. She knew exactly when the police would come around, and where to hide herself in the bushes of the overgrown shrubby garden.

As she had expected, nothing happened in the house, and she moved back in. She smashed a back windowpane so that Tibby could move in and out without her having to unlock the front door for him, and without leaving a window suspiciously open. She moved to the top back room and left it every morning early, to spend the day in the streets with her pram and her rags. At night she kept a candle glimmering low down on the floor. The lavatory was still out of order, so she used a pail on the first floor, instead, and secretly emptied it at night into the canal which in the day was full of pleasure boats and people fishing.

Tibby brought her several pigeons during that time.

"Oh you are a clever puss, Tibby, Tibby! Oh you're clever, you are. You know how things are, don't you, you know how to get around and about."

The weather turned very cold; Christmas came and went. Hetty's cough came back, and she spent most of her time under piles of blankets and old clothes, dozing. At night she watched the shadows of the candle flame on floor and ceiling—the windowframes fitted badly, and there was a draught. Twice tramps spent the night in the bottom of the house and she heard them being moved on by the police. She had to go down to make sure the police had not blocked up the broken window the cat used, but they had not. A blackbird had flown in and had battered itself to death trying to get out. She plucked it, and roasted it over a fire made with bits of floorboard in a baking pan: the gas of course had been cut off. She had never eaten very much, and was not frightened that some dry bread and a bit of cheese was all that she had eaten during her sojourn under the heap of clothes. She was cold, but did not think about that much. Outside there was slushy brown snow everywhere. She went back to her nest thinking that soon the cold spell would be over and she could get back to her trading. Tibby sometimes got into the pile with her, and she clutched the warmth of him to her. "Oh you clever cat, you clever old thing, looking after yourself, aren't you? That's right my ducky, that's right my lovely."

And then, just as she was moving about again, with snow gone off the ground for a time but winter only just begun, in January, she saw a builder's van draw up outside, a couple of men unloading their gear. They did not come into the house: they were to start work next day. By then Hetty, her cat, her pram piled with clothes and her two blankets, were gone. She also took a box of matches, a candle, an old saucepan and a fork and spoon, a tinopener, a candle and a rat-trap. She had a horror of rats.

About two miles away, among the homes and gardens of amiable Hampstead, where live so many of the rich, the intelligent and the famous, stood three empty, very large houses. She had seen them on an occasion, a couple of years before, when she had taken a bus. This was a rare thing for her, because of the remarks and curious looks provoked by her mad clothes, and by her being able to appear at the same time such a tough battling old thing, and a naughty child. For the older she got, this disreputable tramp, the more there strengthened in her a quality of fierce, demanding childishness. It was all too much of a mixture; she was uncomfortable to have near.

She was afraid that "they" might have rebuilt the houses, but there they still stood, too tumbledown and dangerous to be of much use to tramps, let alone the armies of London's homeless. There was no glass left anywhere. The flooring at ground level was mostly gone, leaving small platforms and juts of planking over basements full of water. The ceilings were crumbling. The roofs were going. The houses were like bombed buildings.

But on the cold dark of a late afternoon she pulled the pram up the broken stairs and moved cautiously around the frail boards of a second floor room that had a great hole in it right down to the bottom of the house. Looking into it was like looking into a well. She held a candle to examine the state of the walls, here more or less whole, and saw that rain and wind blowing in from the window would leave one corner dry. Here she made her home. A sycamore tree screened the gaping window from the main road twenty yards away. Tibby, who was cramped after making the journey under the clothes piled in the pram, bounded down and out and vanished into neglected undergrowth to catch his supper. He returned fed and pleased, and seemed happy to stay clutched in her hard thin old arms. She had come to watch for his return after hunting trips, because the warm purring bundle of bones and fur did seem to allay, for a while, the permanent ache of cold in her bones.

Next day she sold her Edwardian boots for a few shillings—they were fashionable again—and bought a loaf and some bacon scraps. In a corner of the ruins well away from the one she had made her own, she pulled up some floor boards, built a fire, and toasted bread and the bacon scraps. Tibby had brought in a pigeon, and she roasted that, but not very efficiently. She was afraid of the fire catching and the whole mass going up in flames; she was afraid too of the smoke showing and attracting the police. She had to keep damping down the fire, and so the bird was bloody and unappetising, and in the end Tibby got most of it. She felt confused, and discouraged, but thought it was because of the long stretch of winter still ahead of her before spring could come. In fact, she was ill. She made a couple of attempts to trade and earn money to feed herself before she acknowledged she was ill. She knew she was not yet dangerously ill, for she had been that in her life, and would have been able to recognise the cold listless indifference of a real last-ditch illness. But all her bones ached, and her head ached, and she coughed more than she ever had. Yet she still did not think of herself as suffering particularly from the cold, even in that sleety January weather. She had never, in all her life, lived in a properly heated place, had never known a really warm home, not even when she lived in the Council flats. Those flats had electric fires, and the family had never used them, for the sake of economy, except in very bad spells of cold. They piled clothes onto themselves, or when to bed early. But she did know that to keep herself from dying now she could not treat the cold with her usual indifference. She knew she must eat. In the comparatively dry corner of the windy room, away from the gaping window through which snow and sleet were drifting, she made another nest—her last. She had found a piece of plastic sheeting in the rubble, and she laid that down first, so that the damp would not strike up. Then she spread her two blankets over that. Over them were heaped the mass of old clothes. She wished she had another piece of plastic to put on top, but she used sheets of newspaper instead. She heaved herself into the middle of this, with a loaf of bread near to her hand. She dozed, and waited, and nibbled bits of bread, and watched the snow drifting softly in. Tibby sat close to the old blue face that poked out of the pile and put up a paw to touch it. He miaowed and was restless, and then went out into the frosty morning and brought in a pigeon. This the cat put, still struggling and fluttering a little, close to the old woman. But she was afraid to get out of the pile in which the heat was being made and kept with such difficulty. She really could not climb out long enough to pull up more splinters of plank from the floors, to make a fire, to pluck the pigeon, to roast it. She put out a cold hand to stroke the cat.

"Tibby you old thing, you brought it for me then did you? You did, did you? Come here, come in here . . ." But he did not want to get in with her. He miaowed again, pushed the bird closer to her. It was now limp and dead.

"You have it then. You eat it. I'm not hungry, thank you Tibby."

But the carcase did not interest him. He had eaten a pigeon before bringing this one up to Hetty. He fed himself well. In spite of his matted fur, and his scars and his half-closed yellow eye, he was a strong healthy cat.

At about four the next morning there were steps and voices downstairs. Hetty shot out of the pile and crouched behind a fallen heap of plaster and beams, now covered with snow, at the end of the room near the window. She could see through the hole in the floorboards down to the first floor, which had collapsed entirely, and through it to the ground floor. She saw a man in a thick overcoat and muffler and leather gloves holding a strong torch to illuminate a thin bundle of clothes lying on the floor. She saw this bundle was a sleeping man or woman. She was indignant—*her* home was being trespassed upon. And she was afraid because she had not been aware of this other tenant of the ruin. Had he, or she, heard her talking to the cat? And where was the cat? If he wasn't careful he would be caught, and that would be the end of him. The man with a torch went off and came back with a second man. In the thick dark far below Hetty, was a small cave of strong light, which was the torchlight. In this space of light two men bent to lift the bundle, which was the corpse of a man or a woman like Hetty. They carried it out across the dangertraps of fallen and rotting boards that made gangplanks over the waterfilled basements. One man was holding the torch in the hand that supported the dead person's feet, and the light jogged and lurched over trees and grasses: the corpse was being taken through the shrubberies to a car.

There are men in London who, between the hours of two and five in the morning, when the real citizens are asleep, who should not be disturbed by such unpleasantness as the corpses of the poor, make the rounds of all the empty, rotting houses they know about, to collect the dead, and to warn the living that they ought not to be there at all, inviting them to one of the official Homes or lodgings for the homeless.

Hetty was too frightened to get back into her warm heap. She sat with the blankets pulled around her, and looked through gaps in the fabric of the house, making out shapes and boundaries and holes and puddles and mounds of rubble, as her eyes, like her cat's, became accustomed to the dark.

She heard scuffling sounds and knew they were rats. She had meant to set the trap, but the thought of her friend Tibby, who might catch his paw, had stopped her. She sat up until the morning light came in grey and cold, after nine. Now she did know herself to be very ill and in danger, for she had lost all the warmth she had huddled into her bones under the rags. She shivered violently. She was shaking herself apart with shivering. In between spasms she drooped limp and exhausted. Through the ceiling above her—but it was not a ceiling, only a cobweb of slats and planks, she could see into a dark cave which had been a garret, and through the roof above that, the grey sky, teeming with incipient rain. The cat came back from where he had been hiding, and sat crouched on her knees, keeping her stomach warm, while she thought out her position. These were her last clear thoughts. She told herself that she would not last out until spring unless she allowed "them" to find her, and take her to hospital. After that, she would be taken to a "Home."

But what would happen to Tibby, her poor cat? She rubbed the old beast's scruffy head with the ball of her thumb and muttered: "Tibby, Tibby, they won't get you, no, you'll be all right, yes, I'll look after you."

Towards midday, the sun oozed yellow through miles of greasy grey cloud, and she staggered down the rotting stairs, to the shops. Even in those London streets, where the extraordinary has become usual, people turned to stare at a tall gaunt woman, with a white face that had flaming red patches on it, and blue compressed lips, and restless black eyes. She wore a tightly buttoned man's overcoat, torn brown woollen mittens, and an old fur hood. She pushed a pram loaded with old dresses and scraps of embroidery and torn jerseys and shoes, all stirred into a tight tangle, and she kept pushing this pram up against people as they stood in queues, or gossiped, or stared into windows, and she muttered: "Give me your old clothes darling, give me your old pretties, give Hetty something, poor Hetty's hungry." A woman gave her a handful of small change, and Hetty bought a roll filled with tomato and lettuce. She did not dare go into a cafe, for even in her confused state she knew she would offend, and would probably be asked to leave. But she begged a cup of tea at a street stall, and when the hot sweet liquid flooded through her she felt she might survive the winter. She bought a carton of milk and pushed the pram back through the slushy snowy street to the ruins.

Tibby was not there. She urinated down through the gap in the boards, muttering "A nuisance, that old tea," and wrapped herself in a blanket and waited for the dark to come.

Tibby came in later. He had blood on his foreleg. She had heard scuffling and she knew that he had fought a rat, or several, and had been bitten. She poured the milk into the tilted saucepan and Tibby drank it all.

She spent the night with the animal held against her chilly bosom. They did not sleep, but dozed off and on. Tibby would normally be hunting, the night was his time, but he had stayed with the old woman now for three nights.

Early next morning they again heard the corpse removers among the rubble on the ground floor, and saw the beams of the torch moving on wet walls and collapsed beams. For a moment the torch light was almost straight on Hetty, but no one came up: who could believe that a person could be desperate enough to climb those dangerous stairs, to trust those crumbling splintery floors, and in the middle of winter?

Hetty had now stopped thinking of herself as ill, of the degrees of her illness, of her danger—of the impossibility of her surviving. She had cancelled out in her mind the presence of winter and its lethal weather, and it was as if spring was nearly here. She knew that if it had been spring when she had had to leave the other house, she and the cat could have lived here for months and months, quite safely and comfortably. Because it seemed to her an impossible and even a silly thing that her life, or rather, her death, could depend on something so arbitrary as builders starting work on a house in January rather than in April, she could not believe it: the fact would not stay in her mind. The day before she had been quite clearheaded. But today her thoughts were cloudy, and she talked and laughed aloud. Once she scrambled up and rummaged in her rags for an old Christmas card she had got four years before from her good daughter.

In a hard harsh angry grumbling voice she said to her four children that she needed a room of her own now that she was getting on. "I've been a good mother to you," she shouted to them before invisible witnesses—former neighbours, welfare workers, a doctor. "I never let you want for anything, never! When you were little you always had the best of everything! You can ask anybody, go on, ask them then!"

She was restless and made such a noise that Tibby left her and bounded onto the pram and crouched watching her. He was limping, and his foreleg was rusty with blood. The rat had bitten deep. When the daylight came, he left Hetty in a kind of a sleep, and went down into the garden where he saw a pigeon feeding on the edge of the pavement. The cat pounced on the bird, dragged it into the bushes, and ate it all, without taking it up to his mistress. After he had finished eating, he stayed hidden, watching the passing people. He stared at them intently with his blazing yellow eye, as if he were thinking, or planning. He did not go into the old ruin and up the crumbling wet stairs until late—it was as if he knew it was not worth going at all.

He found Hetty, apparently asleep, wrapped loosely in a blanket, propped sitting in a corner. Her head had fallen on her chest, and her quantities of white hair had escaped from a scarlet woollen cap, and concealed a face that was flushed a deceptive pink—the flush of coma from cold. She was not yet dead, but she died that night. The rats came up the walls and along the planks and the cat fled down and away from them, limping still, into the bushes.

Hetty was not found for a couple of weeks. The weather changed to warm, and the man whose job it was to look for corpses was led up the dangerous stairs by the smell. There was something left of her, but not much.

As for the cat, he lingered for two or three days in the thick shrubberies, watching the passing people and beyond them, the thundering traffic of the main road. Once a couple stopped to talk on the pavement, and the cat, seeing two pairs of legs, moved out and rubbed himself against one of the legs. A hand came down and he was stroked and patted for a little. Then the people went away.

The cat saw he would not find another home, and he moved off, nosing and feeling his way from one garden to another, through empty houses, finally into an old churchyard. This graveyard already had a couple of stray cats in it, and he joined them. It was the beginning of a community of stray cats going wild. They killed birds, and the field mice that lived among the grasses, and they drank from puddles. Before winter had ended the cats had had a hard time of it from thirst, during the two long spells when the ground froze and there was snow and no puddles and the birds were hard to catch because the cats were so easy to see against the clean white. But on the whole they managed quite well. One of the cats was female, and soon there were a swarm of wild cats, as wild as if they did not live in the middle of a city surrounded by streets and houses. This was just one of half a dozen communities of wild cats living in that square mile of London.

Then an official came to trap the cats and take them away. Some of them escaped, hiding till it was safe to come back again. But Tibby was caught. He was not only getting old and stiff—he still limped from the rat's bite—but he was friendly, and did not run away from the man, who had only to pick him up in his arms.

"You're an old soldier, aren't you?" said the man. "A real tough one, a real old tramp."

It is possible that the cat even thought that he might be finding another human friend and a home.

But it was not so. The haul of wild cats that week numbered hundreds, and while if Tibby had been younger a home might have been found for him, since he was amiable, and wished to be liked by the human race, he was really too old, and smelly and battered. So they gave him an injection and, as we say, "put him to sleep."

Insight

1. In her novel *The Golden Notebook*, Doris Lessing speaks of "free women" who lead "what is known as free lives, that is, lives like men." In what ways is Hetty a free woman? Has she voluntarily chosen her way of life or has it been thrust upon her? How strong a person is she? What examples of her strength can you note?

2. Tibby, the cat, is as much a central character to this story as Hetty, the old woman. What similarities do you see between these two characters? What role does the cat play in Hetty's life? In the development of the story? In the outcome of the story?

3. To what extent does Hetty appear to understand herself? Does she at any time seem to deceive herself?

THANKING MY MOTHER
FOR PIANO LESSONS

Diane Wakoski

The relief of putting your fingers on the keyboard,
as if you were walking on the beach
and found a diamond
as big as a shoe;

as if   5
you had just built a wooden table
and the smell of sawdust was in the air,
your hands dry and woody;

as if
you had eluded   10
the man in the dark hat who had been following you
all week;

the relief
of putting your fingers on the keyboard,
playing the chords of   15
Beethoven,
Bach,
Chopin
      in an afternoon when I had no one to talk to,
      when the magazine advertisement forms of soft sweaters   20
      and clean shining Republican middle-class hair
      walked into carpeted houses
      and left me alone
      with bare floors and a few books

I want to thank my mother   25
for working every day
in a drab office
in garages and water companies
cutting the cream out of her coffee at 40
to lose weight, her heavy body   30
writing its delicate bookkeeper's ledgers

alone, with no man to look at her face,
her body, her prematurely white hair
in love
        I want to thank   35
my mother for working and always paying for
my piano lessons
before she paid the Bank of America loan
or bought the groceries
or had our old rattling Ford repaired.   40

I was a quiet child,
afraid of walking into a store alone,
afraid of the water,
the sun,
the dirty weeds in back yards,   45
afraid of my mother's bad breath,
and afraid of my father's occasional visits home,
knowing he would leave again;
afraid of not having any money,
afraid of my clumsy body,   50
that I knew
        no one would ever love

But I played my way
on the old upright piano
obtained for $10,   55
played my way through fear,
through ugliness,
through growing up in a world of dime-store purchases,
and a desire to love
a loveless world.   60

I played my way through an ugly face
and lonely afternoons, days, evenings, nights,
mornings even, empty
as a rusty coffee can,
played my way through the rustles of spring   65
and wanted everything around me to shimmer like the narrow tide
on a flat beach at sunset in Southern California,
I played my way through
an empty father's hat in my mother's closet
and a bed she slept on only one side of,   70
never wrinkling an inch of

the other side,
waiting,
waiting,

I played my way through honors in school,   75
the only place I could
talk
    the classroom,
    or at my piano lessons, Mrs. Hillhouse's canary always
    singing the most for my talents,   80
    as if I had thrown some part of my body away upon entering
    her house
    and was now searching every ivory case
    of the keyboard, slipping my fingers over black
    ridges and around smooth rocks,   85
    wondering where I had lost my bloody organs,
    or my mouth which sometimes opened
    like a California poppy, wide and with contrasts
    beautiful in sweeping fields,
    entirely closed morning and night,   90

I played my way from age to age,
but they all seemed ageless
or perhaps always
old and lonely,
wanting only one thing, surrounded by the dusty bitter-smelling   95
leaves of orange trees,
wanting only to be touched by a man who loved me,
who would be there every night
to put his large strong hand over my shoulder,
whose hips I would wake up against in the morning,   100
whose mustaches might brush a face asleep,
dreaming of pianos that made the sound of Mozart
and Schubert without demanding
that life suck everything
out of you each day,   105
without demanding the emptiness
of a timid little life.

I want to thank my mother
for letting me wake her up sometimes at 6 in the morning
when I practiced my lessons   110
and for making sure I had a piano
to lay my school books down on, every afternoon.
I haven't touched the piano in 10 years,

perhaps in fear that what little love I've been able to
pick, like lint, out of the corners of pockets,   115
will get lost,
slide away,
into the terribly empty cavern of me
if I ever open it all the way up again.
Love is a man   120
with a mustache
gently holding me every night,
always being there when I need to touch him;
he could not know the painfully loud
music from the past that   125
his loving stops from pounding, banging,
battering through my brain,
which does its best to destroy the precarious gray matter when I
am alone;
he does not hear Mrs. Hillhouse's canary singing for me,   130
liking the sound of my lesson this week,
telling me,
confirming what my teacher says,
that I have a gift for the piano
few of her other pupils had.   135

When I touch the man
I love,
I want to thank my mother for giving me
piano lessons
all those years,   140
keeping the memory of Beethoven,
a deaf tortured man,
in mind;
            of the beauty that can come
from even an ugly   145
past.

Insight
1. How would you characterize the speaker of the poem? To what
   extent does she appear to understand herself?
2. What had the piano meant to the speaker when she was a young
   girl? What satisfactions did it provide her? What does the piano
   now mean to the speaker? Why does she no longer play it?

from A ROOM Of ONE'S OWN

Virginia Woolf

But, you may say, we asked you to speak about women and fiction—what has that got to do with a room of one's own? I will try to explain. When you asked me to speak about women and fiction I sat down on the banks of a river and began to wonder what the words meant. They might mean simply a few remarks about Fanny Burney; a few more about Jane Austen; a tribute to the Brontës and a sketch of Haworth Parsonage under snow; some witticisms if possible about Miss Mitford; a respectful allusion to George Eliot; a reference to Mrs. Gaskell and one would have done. But at second sight the words seemed not so simple. The title women and fiction might mean, and you may have meant it to mean, women and what they are like; or it might mean women and the fiction that they write; or it might mean women and the fiction that is written about them; or it might mean that somehow all three are inextricably mixed together and you want me to consider them in that light. But when I began to consider the subject in this last way, which seemed the most interesting, I soon saw that it had one fatal drawback. I should never be able to come to a conclusion. I should never be able to fulfil what is, I understand, the first duty of a lecturer—to hand you after an hour's discourse a nugget of pure truth to wrap up between the pages of your notebooks and keep on the mantelpiece for ever. All I could do was to offer you an opinion upon one minor point—a woman must have money and a room of her own if she is to write fiction; and that, as you will see, leaves the great problem of the true nature of woman and the true nature of fiction unsolved. I have shirked the duty of coming to a conclusion upon these two questions—women and fiction remain, so far as I am concerned, unsolved problems. But in order to make some amends I am going to do what I can to show you how I arrived at this opinion about the room and the money. I am going to develop in your presence as fully and freely as I can the train of thought which led me to think this. Perhaps if I lay bare the ideas, the prejudices, that lie behind this statement you will find that they have some bearing upon women and some upon fiction. At any rate, when a subject is highly controversial—and any question about sex is that—one cannot hope to tell the truth. One can only show how one came to hold whatever opinion one does hold. One can only give one's audience the chance of drawing their own conclusions as they observe the limitations, the prejudices, the idiosyncrasies of the speaker. Fiction here is likely to contain more truth than fact. Therefore I propose, making use of all the liberties and licences of a novelist, to tell you the story of the two days that preceded my coming here—how, bowed down by the weight of the subject which you have laid upon my shoulders, I pondered it, and made it work in and out of my daily life. I need not say that what I am about to describe has no existence; Oxbridge is an invention; so is Fernham; "I" is only a convenient term for somebody who has no real being. Lies will flow from my lips, but there may perhaps be some truth mixed up with them; it is for you to seek out this truth and to decide whether any part of it is worth keeping. If not, you will of course throw the whole of it into the wastepaper basket and forget all about it.

Here then was I (call me Mary Beton, Mary Seton, Mary Carmichael or by any name you please—it is not a matter of any importance) sitting on the banks of a river a week or two ago in fine October weather, lost in thought. That collar I have spoken of, women and fiction, the need of coming to some conclusion on a subject that raises all sorts of prejudices and passions, bowed my head to the ground. To the right and left bushes of some sort, golden and crimson, glowed with the colour, even it seemed burnt with heat, of fire. On the further bank the willows wept in perpetual lamentation, their hair about their shoulders. The river reflected whatever it chose of sky and bridge and burning tree, and when the undergraduate had oared his boat through the reflections they closed again, completely, as if he had never been. There one might have sat the clock round lost in thought. Thought—to call it by a prouder name than it deserved—had let its line down into the stream. It swayed, minute after minute, hither and thither among the reflections and the weeds, letting the water lift it and sink it, until—you know the little tug—the sudden conglomeration of an idea at the end of one's line: and then the cautious hauling of it in, and the careful laying of it out? Alas, laid on the grass how small, how insignificant this thought of mine looked; the sort of fish that a good fisherman puts back into the water so that it may grow fatter and be one day worth cooking and eating. I will not trouble you with that thought now, though if you look carefully you may find it for yourselves in the course of what I am going to say.

But however small it was, it had, nevertheless, the mysterious property of its kind—put back into the mind, it became at once very exciting, and important; and as it darted and sank, and flashed hither and thither, set up such a wash and tumult of ideas that it was impossible to sit still. It was thus that I found myself walking with extreme rapidity across a grass plot. Instantly a man's figure rose to intercept me. Nor did I at first understand that the gesticulations of a curious-looking object, in a cut-away coat and evening shirt, were aimed at me. His face expressed horror and indignation. Instinct rather than reason came to my help; he was a Beadle;[1] I was a woman. This was the turf; there was the path. Only the Fellows and Scholars are allowed here; the gravel is the place for me. Such thoughts were the work of a moment. As I regained the path the arms of the Beadle sank, his face assumed its usual repose, and though turf is better walking than gravel, no very great harm was done. The only charge I could bring against the Fellows and Scholars of whatever the college might happen to be was that in protection of their turf, which has been rolled for 300 years in succession, they had sent my little fish into hiding.

What idea it had been that had sent me so audaciously trespassing I could not now remember. The spirit of peace descended like a cloud from heaven, for if the spirit of peace dwells anywhere, it is in the courts and quadrangles of Oxbridge on a fine October morning. Strolling through those colleges past those ancient halls the roughness of the present seemed smoothed away; the body seemed contained in a miraculous glass cabinet through which no sound could penetrate, and the mind, freed from any contact with facts (unless one trespassed on the turf again), was at liberty to settle down upon whatever meditation was in harmony with the moment. As chance would have it, some stray memory of some old essay about revisiting Oxbridge in the long vacation brought Charles Lamb to mind—Saint Charles, said Thackeray, putting a letter of Lamb's to his forehead. Indeed, among all the dead (I give you my thoughts as they came to me), Lamb is one of the most congenial; one to whom one would have liked to say, Tell me then how you wrote your essays? For his essays are superior even to Max Beerbohm's, I thought, with all their perfection, because of that wild flash of imagination, that lightning crack of genius in the middle of them which leaves them flawed and imperfect, but starred with poetry. Lamb then came to Oxbridge perhaps a hundred years ago. Certainly he wrote an essay—the name escapes me—about the manuscript of one of Milton's poems which he saw here. It was *Lycidas* perhaps, and Lamb wrote how it shocked him to think it possible that any word in *Lycidas* could have been different from what it is. To think of Milton changing the words in that poem seemed to him a sort of sacrilege. This led me to remember what I could of *Lycidas* and to amuse myself with guessing which word it could have been that Milton had altered, and why. It then occurred to me that the very manuscript itself which Lamb had looked at was only a few hundred yards away, so that one could follow Lamb's footsteps across the quadrangle to that famous library where

[1] BEADLE: an official at an English university who supervises and walks before processions.

the treasure is kept. Moreover, I recollected, as I put this plan into execution, it is in this famous library that the manuscript of Thackeray's *Esmond* is also preserved. The critics often say that *Esmond* is Thackeray's most perfect novel. But the affectation of the style, with its imitation of the eighteenth century, hampers one, so far as I remember; unless indeed the eighteenth-century style was natural to Thackeray—a fact that one might prove by looking at the manuscript and seeing whether the alterations were for the benefit of the style or of the sense. But then one would have to decide what is style and what is meaning, a question which—but here I was actually at the door which leads into the library itself. I must have opened it, for instantly there issued, like a guardian angel barring the way with a flutter of black gown instead of white wings, a deprecating, silvery, kindly gentleman, who regretted in a low voice as he waved me back that ladies are only admitted to the library if accompanied by a Fellow of the College or furnished with a letter of introduction.

That a famous library has been cursed by a woman is a matter of complete indifference to a famous library. Venerable and calm, with all its treasures safe locked within its breast, it sleeps complacently and will, so far as I am concerned, so sleep for ever. Never will I wake those echoes, never will I ask for that hospitality again, I vowed as I descended the steps in anger. Still an hour remained before luncheon, and what was one to do? Stroll on the meadows? sit by the river? Certainly it was a lovely autumn morning; the leaves were fluttering red to the ground; there was no great hardship in doing either. But the sound of music reached my ear. Some service or celebration was going forward. The organ complained magnificently as I passed the chapel door. Even the sorrow of Christianity sounded in that serene air more like the recollection of sorrow than sorrow itself; even the groanings of the ancient organ seemed lapped in peace. I had no wish to enter had I the right, and this time the verger[1] might have stopped me, demanding perhaps my baptismal certificate, or a letter of introduction from the Dean. But the outside of these magnificent buildings is often as beautiful as the inside. Moreover, it was amusing enough to watch the congregation assembling, coming in and going out again, busying themselves at the door of the chapel like bees at the mouth of a hive. Many were in cap and gown; some had tufts of fur on their shoulders; others were wheeled in bath-chairs; others, though not past middle age, seemed creased and crushed into shapes so singular that one was reminded of those giant crabs and crayfish who heave with difficulty across the sand of an aquarium. As I leant against the wall the University indeed seemed a sanctuary in which are preserved rare types which would soon be obsolete if left to fight

[1] VERGER: a person who has charge of the interior of a church.

for existence on the pavement of the Strand. Old stories of old deans and old dons came back to mind, but before I had summoned up courage to whistle—it used to be said that at the sound of a whistle old Professor —— instantly broke into a gallop—the venerable congregation had gone inside. The outside of the chapel remained. As you know, its high domes and pinnacles can be seen, like a sailing-ship always voyaging never arriving, lit up at night and visible for miles, far away across the hills. Once, presumably, this quadrangle with its smooth lawns, its massive buildings, and the chapel itself was marsh too, where the grasses waved and the swine rootled. Teams of horses and oxen, I thought, must have hauled the stone in wagons from far countries, and then with infinite labour the grey blocks in whose shade I was now standing were poised in order one on top of another, and then the painters brought their glass for the windows, and the masons were busy for centuries up on that roof with putty and cement, spade and trowel. Every Saturday somebody must have poured gold and silver out of a leathern purse into their ancient fists, for they had their beer and skittles presumably of an evening. An unending stream of gold and silver, I thought, must have flowed into this court perpetually to keep the stones coming and the masons working; to level, to ditch, to dig and to drain. But it was then the age of faith, and money was poured liberally to set these stones on a deep foundation, and when the stones were raised, still more money was poured in from the coffers of kings and queens and great nobles to ensure that hymns should be sung here and scholars taught. Lands were granted; tithes were paid. And when the age of faith was over and the age of reason had come, still the same flow of gold and silver went on; fellowships were founded; lectureships endowed; only the gold and silver flowed now, not from the coffers of the king, but from the chests of merchants and manufacturers, from the purses of men who had made, say, a fortune from industry, and returned, in their wills, a bounteous share of it to endow more chairs, more lectureships, more fellowships in the university where they had learnt their craft. Hence the libraries and laboratories; the observatories; the splendid equipment of costly and delicate instruments which now stands on glass shelves, where centuries ago the grasses waved and the swine rootled. Certainly, as I strolled round the court, the foundation of gold and silver seemed deep enough; the pavement laid solidly over the wild grasses. Men with trays on their heads went busily from staircase to staircase. Gaudy blossoms flowered in window-boxes. The strains of the gramophone blared out from the rooms within. It was impossible not to reflect—the reflection whatever it may have been was cut short. The clock struck. It was time to find one's way to luncheon.

It is a curious fact that novelists have a way of making us believe that luncheon parties are invariably memorable for something very witty that was said, or for something very wise that was done. But they seldom spare a word for what was eaten. It is part of the novelist's convention not to mention soup and salmon and ducklings, as if soup and salmon and ducklings were of no importance whatsoever, as if nobody ever smoked a cigar or drank a glass of wine. Here, however, I shall take the liberty to defy that convention and to tell you that the lunch on this occasion began with soles, sunk in a deep dish, over which the college cook had spread a counterpane of the whitest cream, save that it was branded here and there with brown spots like the spots on the flanks of a doe. After that came the partridges, but if this suggests a couple of bald, brown birds on a plate you are mistaken. The partridges, many and various, came with all their retinue of sauces and salads, the sharp and the sweet, each in its order; their potatoes, thin as coins but not so hard; their sprouts, foliated as rosebuds but more succulent. And no sooner had the roast and its retinue been done with than the silent serving-man, the Beadle himself perhaps in a milder manifestation, set before us, wreathed in napkins, a confection which rose all sugar from the waves. To call it pudding and so relate it to rice and tapioca would be an insult. Meanwhile the wineglasses had flushed yellow and flushed crimson; had been emptied; had been filled. And thus by degrees was lit, halfway down the spine, which is the seat of the soul, not that hard little electric light which we call brilliance, as it pops in and out upon our lips, but the more profound, subtle and subterranean glow, which is the rich yellow flame of rational intercourse. No need to hurry. No need to sparkle. No need to be anybody but oneself. We are all going to heaven and Vandyck is of the company—in other words, how good life seemed, how sweet its rewards, how trivial this grudge or that grievance, how admirable friendship and the society of one's kind, as, lighting a good cigarette, one sunk among the cushions in the window-seat. . . . The beautiful October day was fading and the leaves were falling from the trees in the avenue as I walked through it. Gate after gate seemed to close with gentle finality behind me. Innumerable beadles were fitting innumerable keys into well-oiled locks; the treasure-house was being made secure for another night. After the avenue one comes out upon a road—I forget its name—which leads you, if you take the right turning, along to Fernham. But there was plenty of time. Dinner was not till half-past seven. One could almost do without dinner after such a luncheon. . . .

A wind blew, from what quarter I know not, but it lifted the half-grown leaves so that there was a flash of silver grey in the air. It was the time between the lights when colours undergo their intensification and purples and golds burn in windowpanes like the beat of an excitable heart; when for some reason the beauty of the world revealed and yet soon to perish (here I pushed into the garden, for, unwisely, the door was left open and no beadles seemed about), the beauty of the world which is so soon to perish, has two edges, one of laughter, one of anguish, cutting the heart asunder. The gardens of Fernham lay before me in the spring twilight, wild and open, and in the long grass, sprinkled and carelessly flung, were daffodils and bluebells, not orderly perhaps at the best of times, and now wind-blown and waving as they tugged at their roots. The windows of the building, curved like ships' windows among generous waves of red brick, changed from lemon to silver under the flight of the quick spring clouds. . . .

Here was my soup. Dinner was being served in the great dining-hall. Far from being spring it was in fact an evening in October. Everybody was assembled in the big dining-room. Dinner was ready. Here was the soup. It was a plain gravy soup. There was nothing to stir the fancy in that. One could have seen through the transparent liquid any pattern that there might have been on the plate itself. But there was no pattern. The plate was plain. Next came beef with its attendant greens and potatoes—a homely trinity, suggesting the rumps of cattle in a muddy market, and sprouts curled and yellowed at the edge, and bargaining and cheapening, and women with string bags on Monday morning. There was no reason to complain of human nature's daily food, seeing that the supply was sufficient and coal-miners doubtless were sitting down to less. Prunes and custard followed. And if any one complains that prunes, even when mitigated by custard, are an uncharitable vegetable (fruit they are not), stringy as a miser's heart and exuding a fluid such as might run in misers' veins who have denied themselves wine and warmth for eighty years and yet not given to the poor, he should reflect that there are people whose charity embraces even the prune. Biscuits and cheese came next, and here the water-jug was liberally passed round, for it is the nature of biscuits to be dry, and these were biscuits to the core. That was all. The meal was over. Everybody scraped their chairs back; the swing-doors swung violently to and fro; soon the hall was emptied of every sign of food and made ready no doubt for breakfast next morning. Down corridors and up staircases the youth of England went banging and singing. And was it for a guest, a stranger (for I had no more right here in Fernham than in Trinity or Somerville or Girton or Newnham or Christchurch[1]), to say, "The dinner was not good," or to say (we were now, Mary Seton and I, in her sitting-room), "Could we not have dined up here alone?" for if I had said anything of the kind I should have been prying and searching into the secret economies of a house which to the stranger wears so fine

[1] TRINITY . . . CHRISTCHURCH: colleges of Oxford and Cambridge Universities.

a front of gaiety and courage. No, one could say nothing of the sort. Indeed, conversation for a moment flagged. The human frame being what it is, heart, body and brain all mixed together, and not contained in separate compartments as they will be no doubt in another million years, a good dinner is of great importance to good talk. One cannot think well, love well, sleep well, if one has not dined well. The lamp in the spine does not light on beef and prunes. We are all *probably* going to heaven, and Vandyck is, we *hope,* to meet us round the next corner—that is the dubious and qualifying state of mind that beef and prunes at the end of the day's work breed between them. Happily my friend, who taught science, had a cupboard where there was a squat bottle and little glasses—(but there should have been sole and partridge to begin with)—so that we were able to draw up to the fire and repair some of the damages of the day's living. In a minute or so we were slipping freely in and out among all those objects of curiosity and interest which form in the mind in the absence of a particular person, and are naturally to be discussed on coming together again—how somebody has married, another has not; one thinks this, another that; one has improved out of all knowledge, the other most amazingly gone to the bad—with all those speculations upon human nature and the character of the amazing world we live in which spring naturally from such beginnings. While these things were being said, however, I became shamefacedly aware of a current setting in of its own accord and carrying everything forward to an end of its own. One might be talking of Spain or Portugal, of book or racehorse, but the real interest of whatever was said was none of those things, but a scene of masons on a high roof some five centuries ago. Kings and nobles brought treasure in huge sacks and poured it under the earth. This scene was for ever coming alive in my mind and placing itself by another of lean cows and a muddy market and withered greens and the stringy hearts of old men—these two pictures, disjointed and disconnected and nonsensical as they were, were for ever coming together and combating each other and had me entirely at their mercy. The best course, unless the whole talk was to be distorted, was to expose what was in my mind to the air, when with good luck it would fade and crumble like the head of the dead king when they opened the coffin at Windsor. Briefly, then, I told Miss Seton about the masons who had been all those years on the roof of the chapel, and about the kings and queens and nobles bearing sacks of gold and silver on their shoulders, which they shovelled into the earth; and then how the great financial magnates of our own time came and laid cheques and bonds, I suppose, where the others had laid ingots and rough lumps of gold. All that lies beneath the colleges down there, I said; but this college, where we are now sitting, what lies beneath its gallant brick and the wild unkempt grasses of the garden? What force is behind the plain china off which we dined, and (here it popped out of my mouth before I could stop it) the beef, the custard and the prunes?

Well, said Mary Seton, about the year 1860—Oh, but you know the story, she said, bored, I suppose, by the recital. And she told me —rooms were hired. Committees met. Envelopes were addressed. Circulars were drawn up. Meetings were held; letters were read out; so-and-so has promised so much; on the contrary, Mr. —— won't give a penny. The *Saturday Review* has been very rude. How can we raise a fund to pay for offices? Shall we hold a bazaar? Can't we find a pretty girl to sit in the front row? Let us look up what John Stuart Mill said on the subject. Can any one persuade the editor of the —— to print a letter? Can we get Lady —— to sign it? Lady —— is out of town. That was the way it was done, presumably, sixty years ago, and it was a prodigious effort, and a great deal of time was spent on it. And it was only after a long struggle and with the utmost difficulty that they got thirty thousand pounds together.[1] So obviously we cannot have wine and partridges and servants carrying tin dishes on their heads, she said. We cannot have sofas and separate rooms. "The amenities," she said, quoting from some book or other, "will have to wait."[2]

At the thought of all those women working year after year and finding it hard to get two thousand pounds together, and as much as they could do to get thirty thousand pounds, we burst out in scorn at the reprehensible poverty of our sex. What had our mothers been doing then that they had no wealth to leave us? Powdering their noses? Looking in at shop windows? Flaunting in the sun at Monte Carlo? There were some photographs on the mantel-piece. Mary's mother—if that was her picture—may have been a wastrel in her spare time (she had thirteen children by a minister of the church), but if so her gay and dissipated life had left too few traces of its pleasures on her face. She was a homely body; an old lady in a plaid shawl which was fastened by a large cameo; and she sat in a basket-chair, encouraging a spaniel to look at the camera, with the amused, yet strained expression of one who is sure that the dog will move directly the bulb is pressed. Now if she had gone into business; had become a manufacturer of artificial silk or a magnate on the Stock Exchange; if she had left two or three hundred thousand pounds to Fernham, we

---

[1] "We are told that we ought to ask for £30,000 at least. . . . It is not a large sum, considering that there is to be but one college of this sort for Great Britain, Ireland and the Colonies, and considering how easy it is to raise immense sums for boys' schools. But considering how few people really wish women to be educated, it is a good deal."—LADY STEPHEN, *Life of Miss Emily Davies.* [Woolf's note.]

[2] Every penny which could be scraped together was set aside for building, and the amenities had to be postponed.—R. STRACHEY, *The Cause.* [Woolf's note.]

could have been sitting at our ease tonight and the subject of our talk might have been archaeology, botany, anthropology, physics, the nature of the atom, mathematics, astronomy, relativity, geography. If only Mrs. Seton and her mother and her mother before her had learnt the great art of making money and had left their money, like their fathers and their grandfathers before them, to found fellowships and lectureships and prizes and scholarships appropriated to the use of their own sex, we might have dined very tolerably up here alone off a bird and a bottle of wine; we might have looked forward without undue confidence to a pleasant and honourable lifetime spent in the shelter of one of the liberally endowed professions. We might have been exploring or writing; mooning about the venerable places of the earth; sitting contemplative on the steps of the Parthenon, or going at ten to an office and coming home comfortably at half-past four to write a little poetry. Only, if Mrs. Seton and her like had gone into business at the age of fifteen, there would have been—that was the snag in the argument—no Mary. What, I asked, did Mary think of that? There between the curtains was the October night, calm and lovely, with a star or two caught in the yellowing trees. Was she ready to resign her share of it and her memories (for they had been a happy family, though a large one) of games and quarrels up in Scotland, which she is never tired of praising for the fineness of its air and the quality of its cakes, in order that Fernham might have been endowed with fifty thousand pounds or so by a stroke of the pen? For, to endow a college would necessitate the suppression of families altogether. Making a fortune and bearing thirteen children—no human being could stand it. Consider the facts, we said. First there are nine months before the baby is born. Then the baby is born. Then there are three or four months spent in feeding the baby. After the baby is fed there are certainly five years spent in playing with the baby. You cannot, it seems, let children run about the streets. People who have seen them running wild in Russia say that the sight is not a pleasant one. People say, too, that human nature takes its shape in the years between one and five. If Mrs. Seton, I said, had been making money, what sort of memories would you have had of games and quarrels? What would you have known of Scotland, and its fine air and cakes and all the rest of it? But it is useless to ask these questions, because you would never have come into existence at all. Moreover, it is equally useless to ask what might have happened if Mrs. Seton and her mother and her mother before her had amassed great wealth and laid it under the foundations of college and library, because, in the first place, to earn money was impossible for them, and in the second, had it been possible, the law denied them the right to possess what money they earned. It is only for the last forty-eight years that Mrs. Seton has had a penny of her own. For all the centuries before that it would have been her husband's property—a thought which, perhaps, may have had its share in keeping Mrs. Seton and her mothers off the Stock Exchange. Every penny I earn, they may have said, will be taken from me and disposed of according to my husband's wisdom—perhaps to found a scholarship or to endow a fellowship in Balliol or Kings, so that to earn money, even if I could earn money, is not a matter that interests me very greatly. I had better leave it to my husband.

At any rate, whether or not the blame rested on the old lady who was looking at the spaniel, there could be no doubt that for some reason or other our mothers had mismanaged their affairs very gravely. Not a penny could be spared for "amenities"; for partridges and wine, beadles and turf, books and cigars, libraries and leisure. To raise bare walls out of the bare earth was the utmost they could do.

So we talked standing at the window and looking, as so many thousands look every night, down on the domes and towers of the famous city beneath us. It was very beautiful, very mysterious in the autumn moonlight. The old stone looked very white and venerable. One thought of all the books that were assembled down there; of the pictures of old prelates and worthies hanging in the panelled rooms; of the painted windows that would be throwing strange globes and crescents on the pavement; of the tablets and memorials and inscriptions; of the fountains and the grass; of the quiet rooms looking across the quiet quadrangles. And (pardon me the thought) I thought, too, of the admirable smoke and drink and the deep armchairs and the pleasant carpets: of the urbanity, the geniality, the dignity which are the offspring of luxury and privacy and space. Certainly our mothers had not provided us with anything comparable to all this—our mothers who found it difficult to scrape together thirty thousand pounds, our mothers who bore thirteen children to ministers of religion at St. Andrews.

So I went back to my inn, and as I walked through the dark streets I pondered this and that, as one does at the end of the day's work. I pondered why it was that Mrs. Seton had no money to leave us; and what effect poverty has on the mind; and what effect wealth has on the mind; and I thought of the queer old gentlemen I had seen that morning with tufts of fur upon their shoulders; and I remembered how if one whistled one of them ran; and I thought of the organ booming in the chapel and of the shut doors of the library; and I thought how unpleasant it is to be locked out; and I thought how it is worse perhaps to be locked in; and, thinking of the safety and prosperity of the one sex and of the poverty and insecurity of the other and of the effect of tradition and of the lack of tradition upon the mind of a writer, I thought at last that it was time to roll up the crumpled skin of the day, with its arguments and its impressions and

from A Room of One's Own

its anger and its laughter, and cast it into the hedge. A thousand stars were flashing across the blue wastes of the sky. One seemed alone with an inscrutable society. All human beings were laid asleep— prone, horizontal, dumb. Nobody seemed stirring in the streets of Oxbridge. Even the door of the hotel sprang open at the touch of an invisible hand—not a boots was sitting up to light me to bed, it was so late.

Insight
1. Woolf begins by asking what women and fiction have to do with "a room of one's own." In the course of the selection what answers does she suggest?
2. What experiences does Woolf encounter at Oxbridge? To what extent are those experiences dictated by the fact that "I was a woman"?
3. Contrast the quality of the meals at Oxbridge with those at Fernham. What effect on the "seat of the soul" does each meal have?
4. Describe the history of Fernham. How does its background differ from that of Oxbridge? What is meant by the line, "The amenities will have to wait"?
5. Woolf ponders "what effect poverty has on the mind; and what effect wealth has on the mind." How does this thought relate to the question with which Woolf opens the selection?

iN SUMMARY

Insight and Composition

1. Susan in "Titty's Dead and Tatty Weeps" attempts to break free from her life and from the role thrust upon her by her sister and friends. From what does each main character in the other short stories in this unit attempt to break free? Which characters do you feel have been most successful in actually breaking free? Which, least successful? Explain.

2. Often the act of attaining one's independence is accomplished only by paying a great price as does Hetty in "An Old Woman and Her Cat." What other characters in these selections appear to have paid a great price for their independence? In terms of the independence gained do you think the price has been too high?

3. The desire to break free often stems from one's dreams and goals. What dreams and goals motivate the characters in this unit? In each case how realistic do you think have those dreams proven to be?

4. Breaking free implies an attempt at self-fulfillment. To what extent do you think the characters in these selections have found self-fulfillment? Which one, do you feel, has most nearly attained his or her self-fulfillment?

5. By definition fiction means not true. Virginia Woolf more directly states that "lies" will flow from her lips. Yet, paradoxically, she advises the reader to seek the "truth" within the fiction, the "lies." Looking at the fiction as a whole in the unit, what "truths" appear to emerge?

biographical NOTES

biographical NOTES

Bella Akhmadulina (born 1937).   The author of *Struna (The Music Chord)*, "Poems to Pasternak," and "Rain," Bella Akhmadulina was born in Moscow to middle-class parents. She attended the Gorky Institute, the Soviet Union's leading school for literature. There she met the poet Yevgeny Yevtushenko and married him. At first she was allowed to join the Writers' Union only as a translator, not as a poet, but now her poems are widely read and she has become something of a glamorous celebrity in the Soviet Union. During the 1960s she acted in a movie and her picture frequently appears in magazines. After her divorce from Yevtushenko she married Yuri Nagibin, a writer of short stories and motion picture scenarios, and they now divide their time between an apartment in Moscow and a dacha in the country. Akhmadulina is outspoken, anxious for contact with foreigners, and in her poetry, reveals a sense of inner freedom.

Anna Akhmatova (1889–1966).   Considered by many to be the most important woman poet in Russian literature, Anna Akhmatova expressed a personal romantic vision in modern unrhetorical style. She was the daughter of a merchant navy officer and was educated in St. Petersburg and Kiev. While at school she met the poet Gumilev and married him. She began to write poems for publication in magazines and gave occasional readings until in 1922 Gumilev was executed for involvement in an anti-Bolshevik conspiracy. Even though she had divorced her husband before his arrest, she was denied publication in any Soviet magazine. Her reputation was briefly restored during World War II because her poems were thought to express the Russian people's struggle for survival. But in 1946 her poetry was again condemned by the Communist government and she was expelled from the Soviet writers' association. Much of her poetry concerns ill-fated love and personal struggle for survival against fate. Religious images play an important role especially in her later poetry.

Margaret Atwood (born 1939).   "My life really has been writing since the age of sixteen; all other decisions I made were determined by that fact," says Margaret Atwood. Born in Ottawa, Canada, she has lived all over Canada as well as in the United States and England. Educated at the University of Toronto and Radcliffe College, she has taught at the University of British Columbia in Vancouver and at Sir George Williams University in Montreal. She has published a novel, *The Edible Woman,* and several books of poetry of which *The Circle Game* received the Governor-General's Award in 1966.

Aphra Behn (1640–1689).   Aphra Behn was the first woman to earn her living by writing and as such became a celebrity and a curiosity. She wrote seventeen plays, twelve novels, short stories, poetry, letters, and did translations. She was innovative in her experiments with realism and courageous in her defense of her own work and that of other women writers. She is buried in Westminster Abbey.

Louise Bogan (1897–1970). Born in Livermore Falls, Maine, Louise Bogan was educated at Boston Girls' Latin School and Boston University. She served as Consultant in Poetry to the Library of Congress from 1945 to 1946. For over twenty years she was poetry critic for *The New Yorker* magazine and also taught as Visiting Professor at a number of universities in the United States and Austria. In addition to her poetry, for which she received the Bollingen Prize, she wrote several volumes of criticism.

Elizabeth Bowen (1899–1973). A prolific writer of both novels and short stories, Elizabeth Bowen was born in Ireland. She was educated in England, married a professor, and during World War II worked for the Ministry of Information in London and in a shell shock hospital near Dublin. Considered at first to be a writer of social comedy, her talent matured to make her capable of the illumination of human relations in an allusive prose style as subtle and carefully wrought as that of Henry James. Bowen considered the object of the novel to be "the non-poetic statement of a poetic truth." She also believed that a character must be shown to feel "the play and pull of alternatives." "It is in being seen to be capable of alternatives that the character becomes, for the reader, valid." Among her short story collections are *Joining Charles, Ivy Gripped the Steps,* and *A Day in the Dark.* Her novels include *The House in Paris, The Death of a Heart, A World of Love,* and *The Little Girls.*

Anne Bradstreet (1612–1672). Born in England, Anne Bradstreet came to the Massachusetts Bay Colony in 1630 with her father's family and her husband, Simon Bradstreet. The mother of eight children, Anne Bradstreet published her first volume of poetry in 1650 in London—*The Tenth Muse Lately Sprung Up in America.* A Boston printer brought out a second edition, with revisions and additional poems, in 1678.

Emily Brontë (1818–1848). An introverted girl, who at first deeply resented disclosure and publication of her poems, Emily Brontë built a major literary reputation on a dozen or so poems and one astonishing novel, *Wuthering Heights.* She was born in Hartshead, Yorkshire, England and spent most of her life at Haworth where her father was rector. With her sister Charlotte she attended a repressive school which might have been responsible for instilling in Emily her fear of restraint and regimentation. Emily kept her poems secret until Charlotte discovered them and insisted that they be published along with her own and those of their younger sister Anne. *Poems by Currer, Ellis, and Acton Bell* was published in 1846. About this time Emily wrote her only surviving prose work, *Wuthering Heights.* She suffered when the novel was indifferently received, or perhaps, as some have said, from the self revelation contained in the novel. She died a year later, refusing medication.

Gwendolyn Brooks (born 1917).   Awarded the Pulitzer Prize in 1950 for *Annie Allen,* her second book of poetry, Gwendolyn Brooks is also a fine novelist. Both her fiction and her poetry are characterized by a directness and restraint that make all the more moving the seemingly uneventful lives she explores. Although her own life has been comfortable, she writes frequently and sympathetically of the poor, doomed to squalor while dreaming of something better. Her verse, as one critic has noted, draws on the world she understands but records insights about that world in such a way that they become "not merely personal or racial, but universal in their implications."

Elizabeth Barrett Browning (1806–1861).   From childhood Elizabeth Barrett was devoted to literature despite her lack of a formal education. She managed to gain a knowledge of Greek, Latin, and the modern languages through her brother's tutor. In 1846 she married Robert Browning and the couple settled in Florence where she lived until her death. In addition to her numerous volumes of poetry, Elizabeth Barrett Browning was a champion of the Italian struggle for freedom from Austria and wrote against child labor and slavery.

Constance Carrier (born 1908).   Constance Carrier is known both as a poet and a translator of Latin poetry. She was born in Connecticut, attended Smith College, and received her M.A. from Trinity College. She has taught Latin at a Connecticut high school and at the Classics Workshop of Tufts University. Her first book of poetry, *The Middle Voice,* brought her the Lamont Poetry Prize. Her translations include *The Poems of Propertius* and *The Poems of Tibullus.*

Willa Cather (1873–1947).   Born in Virginia, Willa Cather moved at an early age to Nebraska. Her grandmothers taught her Latin and the classics at home and she later attended the University of Nebraska. She worked on the *Pittsburgh Leader* as copy, music, and drama editor. She also taught school and became managing editor of *McClure's* magazine. She retired her post to write short stories and novels and she received the Pulitzer Prize in 1922.

Margaret Cavendish, Duchess of Newcastle (1624–1673).   Margaret Cavendish was one of the first Englishwomen to publish her work. She wrote poetry, plays, orations, biography, autobiography, letters, philosophical works, and scientific treatises. She attempted to get her works accepted by the universities and she hoped very much to teach. Her desire was not, however, realized. She was considered an eccentric, often appearing in outlandish costumes. Her contemporaries called her "Mad Madge." She is known mostly for her biography of her husband.

Diana Chang (born 1934).   Diana Chang was born in New York, but before she was a year old she was taken by her Chinese father and Eurasian mother to China to live for several years in Nanking, Peiping, and Shanghai.

At the end of World War II they returned to the United States and Diana graduated from Barnard College. A John Hay Whitney Foundation fellowship allowed her to complete her first novel, *The Frontiers of Love*. Other novels followed: *A Woman of Thirty, A Passion for Life,* and *The Only Game in Town.* Her poems have appeared in numerous magazines including *Poetry.*

Kate Chopin (1851–1904). Born in St. Louis, Kate Chopin met Oscar Chopin, her husband-to-be and moved to Louisiana. After his death in 1883, Kate Chopin began to write professionally. In the remaining sixteen years of her life she produced two novels and a vast quantity of short stories. Focusing primarily on the Creole and Acadian societies she knew in Louisiana, she wrote of the intricacies of marriage and love. She is best known for her novel *The Awakening.*

Sidonie-Gabrielle Colette (1873–1954). A desire for freedom and independence pervades the romantic novels of Colette and is revealed in titles such as *Claudine s'en va* (Claudine goes away), *La Vagabonde,* and *L'Entrave* (the fetter, or shackle). Remarkably, her prolific career as a writer of novels and short stories spanned over fifty years, from the turn of the century to her death in 1954. She grew up in Burgundy and her first four novels, built around a character named Claudine, draw upon her childhood experiences. Under the influence of her first husband, a failed author, she wrote the Claudine novels and after divorcing him, performed in music halls as a dancer and mime. During her second marriage she devoted herself to journalism and novels, creating the characters Mitsou and Chéri which were to make her famous. She became a prominent figure in Paris society and achieved an important literary reputation. In 1935 she was elected to membership in the Académie Royale de Belgique and in 1944 to the Académie Goncourt. Among her later novels are *Gigi, Le fanal bleu, Paradis terrestre* and *La Fleur de l'âge.*

Patricia Cumming (born 1932). Patricia Cumming's poems have appeared in a variety of magazines and journals including *Shenandoah, Hanging Loose,* and *The Little Magazine.* Her volume of verse, *Afterwards,* was published by Alice James Books, Cambridge, Massachusetts, a cooperative with an emphasis on publishing poetry by women. She teaches in The Writing Program at the Massachusetts Institute of Technology and is presently co-authoring a book tentatively entitled *Write, Write, Write.* She was one of the founders of The Theatre Company of Boston and co-producer its second year. Several of her plays were produced there and elsewhere in the Boston area.

Babette Deutsch (1895–1974). Born in New York City, Babette Deutsch was educated at Barnard College. She taught at the New School for Social Research and at the School of General Studies at Columbia University. She was an Honorary Consultant in Poetry to the Library of Congress and with her husband, Avraham Yarmolinsky, did translations from German and Russian, mostly of poetry. She was a member of the National Institute of Arts and Letters and served as its secretary from 1969 through 1971.

Emily Dickinson (1830–1886).   Except for a few brief trips to nearby cities, Emily Dickinson spent her life in the New England village of Amherst, Massachusetts. She lived much to herself, and when asked who her companions were, she would reply, "Hills, sir, and the sundown, and a dog as large as myself." Her thoughts, too, were her companions. "How do most people live without any thoughts?" she once asked a friend. Emily Dickinson wrote hundreds of poems, often jotting them down on any available piece of paper: a brown paper bag, a used envelope, the back of a recipe. All of them she saved in little packets and tied with ribbon, tucked away in boxes and drawers. The poems were discovered and published shortly after her death, but forty years passed before their excellence was recognized.

Isak Dinesen (1883–1962).   Isak Dinesen was the pen name chosen by Baroness Karen Blixen, a member of a Danish land-owning family, and the daughter of a writer who had lived for several years as a trapper with the Pawnee Indians in Minnesota. After her marriage to Baron Blixen, Karen went to Kenya to manage a coffee plantation, remaining after her divorce to run the plantation for ten years. Her book *Out of Africa* records many of her experiences there. While in Kenya she also worked on a collection of stories called *Seven Gothic Tales*, written in English. That and her next volume, *Winter's Tales* are written in the manner of a romantic storyteller and reflect certain qualities of myths and fairy tales; but she adapts this chivalric mode to the needs of the modern psychological story. Returning from Kenya, she took up residence at her father's estate in Denmark where she continued to write both in Danish and English throughout her life. Her other books in English include *Anecdotes of Destiny*, *Shadows on the Grass*, and *Last Tales*.

Hilda Doolittle (1886–1961).   Hilda Doolittle spent her early years in her native Pennsylvania. She attended Bryn Mawr College. In 1911 she went abroad for what she expected to be a short visit. Traveling first to Italy and France, she arrived eventually in London, where she joined the poet Ezra Pound in organizing the Imagists. The Imagists were American and British poets of the pre World War I era who believed that poetry should be written in concrete language and figures of speech should be about modern subject matter. They scorned the old adherence to strict meter and the use of romantic and mystic themes. Ms. Doolittle's work which she signed "H.D.", first appeared in magazines and was so well received that H.D. soon became known not just as the leader of the Imagists but as perhaps the only true Imagist. She published several collections, the first of which was *Sea Garden*, appearing in 1916. Except for one brief visit to California, H.D. continued to make her home in Europe, settling down finally in Switzerland where she lived for nearly forty years.

Mari Evans.   A native of Toledo, Ohio, Mari Evans was a John Hay Whitney Fellow, 1965–66, a Consultant for the National Endowment of the Arts, and producer/director of a weekly television series. Her poetry has been used extensively in textbooks and anthologies, and a collection of her poems, *I Am a Black Woman* (Wm. Morrow, 1970) received the Black Academy of Arts and Letters poetry award in 1971. Author of several children's books, she is associate professor and Writer-in-Residence at Indiana University, Bloomington.

Anne Finch, Countess of Winchelsea (1666–1720). Anne Finch is known chiefly to be the forerunner of romanticism. She wrote love, nature, and religious poetry, plays, satires, parodies, fables, translations, and criticism. She often wrote about women and the prejudice against the woman as writer. Her first volume of poetry was published anonymously.

Mary Wilkins Freeman (1852–1930). The New England village in which she was born and grew up provided Mary Wilkins Freeman with material for a lifetime of writing. She chronicled the lives of New England villagers in some two hundred short stories, novels, poems, and children's books, prompting Hamlin Garland to praise her for having created "an unparalleled record of New England life." Two of her recurrent character types are the solitary who enjoys a serene life and the strong-willed, resolutely individualistic New England woman. Mary Wilkins Freeman was the first woman to be elected to the National Institute of Arts and Letters.

Charlotte Perkins Gilman (1860–1935). Not long after she was married Charlotte Perkins Gilman began to experience depressions on which she based "The Yellow Wallpaper." After a period she described as "absolute incapacity. Absolute misery," she left her home for California where she taught, edited newspapers, and became a leading feminist lecturer and speaker. *Women and Economics* is probably her best-known work.

Nikki Giovanni (born 1943). "I write what I see, and I take responsibility for it," says Nikki Giovanni, who often writes of her own anguish and bitter experience. A popular poet who has read her poetry on television and put out a best-selling record album, Giovanni continues to search for individual values in the black community. "Who am I?" and "What am I?" are questions of profound concern for her. She was born in Knoxville, Tennessee, studied with John Killens at Fisk University, and attended the University of Pennsylvania school of social work, and Columbia University. She is an assistant professor of English at Rutgers University. Family love is one of the values she has defined for herself and she believes that good family spirit produces healthy communities and should produce a strong black nation. Her books of poetry include *Black Feeling, Black Talk, Black Judgment, Spin a Soft Black Song,* and *My House.* She has also published a collection of essays called *Gemini,* written poems for children, and biographies of Langston Hughes and Nina Simone.

Susan Glaspell (1882–1948). Born in Davenport, Iowa, Susan Glaspell was educated at Drake College in Des Moines and later worked for the *Des Moines Daily News,* covering local and state politics and human interest stories. Leaving journalism she devoted herself full-time to writing fiction—short stories, novels, plays. In 1931 she received a Pulitzer Prize for *Alison's House*, a play based on the life of Emily Dickinson. She is best known for her plays and her work in founding the Provincetown Playhouse.

Nadine Gordimer (born 1923).   Nadine Gordimer writes of the conflicts, injustices, and tragedy of her native country, South Africa. She was born in Springs, South Africa, the daughter of a jeweler, attended private schools and the University of Witwatersrand. She now lives in Johannesburg with her husband and two children. In 1961 she visited the United States under a Ford Foundation Visiting Professor Fellowship. Her stories first appeared in the *Times Literary Supplement* and her first novel, *A World of Strangers* established her as a writer of stature. Her short story collections include *Friday's Footprint, Six Feet of the Country*, and *Not for Publication and Other Stories*. Her most recent novel is entitled *The Late Bourgeois World*.

Lorraine Hansberry (1930–1965).   March 11, 1959 was an important day for Lorraine Hansberry and for the American theater. On that day her play *A Raisin in the Sun* opened on Broadway, the first play by a Negro woman to be produced there and one so outstanding that it won the New York Drama Critics Circle Award. Lorraine Hansberry was born in Chicago, the daughter of a prosperous real estate broker who had once carried a civil rights case to the Supreme Court and won. She attended public schools in Chicago and got involved in theater in high school. During her two years as a student at the University of Wisconsin she took a course in stage design. Later she tried painting at the Art Institute in Chicago and Guadalajara, Mexico, but gave it up and moved to New York. There she began to write plays and stories while working on and off at a variety of jobs. A reading of her first version of *A Raisin in the Sun* by her husband, Howard Nemiroff and some of their friends led to its eventual production. She has said of her play "The thing I tried to show was the many gradations in even one Negro family, the clash of the old and the new, but most of all the unbelievable courage of the Negro people." Later she wrote *The Sign in Sidney Brustein's Window* and after her death a collection of her writings was put together and produced under the title *To Be Young, Gifted, and Black*.

Sister Juana Inés de La Cruz (1651–1695).   Sister Juana Inés de La Cruz was a self-educated Mexican woman of the seventeenth century who wrote extraordinary poems, composed music, and argued cogently with Jesuits on matters of theology. Juana Inés learned to read at the age of three and began her self education with the books available. By the age of thirteen she could read and write Latin and Aztec and had studied literature, science, and history. Her family sent her to the court of the Spanish Viceroy of Mexico. After a time at court however, she resolved to enter a convent "to live alone, to refuse all forced occupation that encumbered the liberty of [her] studies. . . ." During her twenty years as a nun at the convent of San Jerónimo in Mexico City, Juana Inés collected a library of books and musical and scientific instruments, wrote treatises on architecture and harmony, painted, solved mathematical problems, and observed the stars. She also maintained contact with the court and continued to write poems for court occasions.

Sarah Orne Jewett (1849–1909).   Sarah Orne Jewett is known primarily as a regional writer who depicted the people, customs, and landscape of her home in South Berwick, Maine. She wrote that her "local attachments [were] stronger than any cat's that ever mewed," and despite European travel in later life, she did all of her writing in her home village. Her father was a doctor and he took her with him on his calls about the countryside. It was from these trips that she received her real education, the knowledge of a place and time which she was to record so clearly and precisely in her writings. She published stories first in juvenile magazines and then in the *Atlantic Monthly*. When these stories were collected and published under the title *Deephaven* they brought her immediate success. Among her short story collections are *The Country of the Pointed Firs*, *The King of Falls Island*, and *A Native of Wimby*. A novel called *A Country Doctor* presents a portrait of her father.

Fanny Kemble (1809–1893).   Fanny Kemble was born into a London theatrical family—her father managed the Covent Garden Theatre and her aunt, Sarah Kemble Siddons, was a famous actress. Fanny was educated in Boulogne and Paris where she learned to sing and dance. She was persuaded to play Juliet in a family production of *Romeo and Juliet* and was an immediate success. She went on to play a variety of successful roles and at seventeen joined her father and aunt for an American tour. She was acclaimed in New York, Boston, and Philadelphia and remained to marry a Philadelphian, Pierce Butler. Giving up the stage, she turned to writing which she considered a superior endeavor. She wrote plays and poems and published a journal in which she criticized Americans and their customs. A visit to her husband's plantation in Georgia filled her with indignation at the institution of slavery and when the Civil War broke out she published her *Journal of a Residence on a Georgia Plantation,* hoping to lessen Confederate sympathies of the English. After her husband's death she lived on a small farm in Pennsylvania near her daughter and wrote her autobiography, published in three volumes.

Carolyn Kizer (born 1925).   Currently poet-in-residence at the University of North Carolina, Chapel Hill, Carolyn Kizer was born in Spokane and educated at Sarah Lawrence College and Columbia University. She was the founder and for seven years the editor of *Poetry Northwest* in Seattle. After having lived for a year in Pakistan as poet-in-residence for the U.S. State Department, she returned to the United States to act as director of literary programs for the National Endowment for the Arts, under the Johnson administration. Her books include *The Ungrateful Garden, Knock Upon Silence, Midnight Was My Cry,* and *New and Selected Poems.*

Maxine Kumin (born 1925).   Maxine Kumin received both her B.A. and her M.A. from Radcliffe College and returned there as a scholar at the Radcliffe Institute for Independent Study. Born in Philadelphia, she has taught at Tufts University, Newton College of the Sacred Heart, and the University of Massachusetts. Her poems have won her two awards from the Poetry Society of America and a grant from the National Council for the Arts. Besides poems and fiction, she writes books for children. *Through Dooms of Love, The Passions of Uxport,* and *The Abduction* are her novels. Her poems have been published in volumes entitled *The Privilege, The Nightmare Factory,* and *Up Country.*

Dilys Laing (1906–1960).   Although she began to publish poems at the age of twelve and produced four books of poetry and a novel during her lifetime, Dilys Laing was not known to a wide audience. It was only after her death in 1960 that she began to receive the recognition from the reading public which her fellow poets had accorded her during her lifetime. She suffered from two diseases which left her feeling somewhat isolated from the rest of the world, polio and a mastoid infection which left her partially deaf. At fourteen she edited the children's page of the *Vancouver Daily Sun* and a few years later worked on the staff of the *Victoria Daily Colonist.* Marrying a poet, Alexander Laing, she moved to Vermont in the 1940s and bore a son. Here she enjoyed her most productive period of writing despite a constant awareness of the conflicts between artistic creation and domestic duties and restraints. Following her death from acute asthma, much of her unpublished work began to appear in literary magazines and to be known to a new generation of readers.

Doris Lessing (born 1919).   Born of British parents in Iran, Doris Lessing grew up in Southern Rhodesia. Her writings express her concern with two major issues: the conflict between the races in Africa and the problems of an intelligent woman seeking to maintain her identity in a man's world. Her *African Stories,* according to one reviewer, are beautifully wrought "by a sensitive and thoughtful but fiercely honest writer. . . ." Playwright, poet, journalist, writer of fiction, Doris Lessing has been called by the *London Times* "not only the best woman novelist we have, but one of the most serious, intelligent, and honest writers of the whole post-war generation."

Denise Levertov (born 1923).   British-born, Denise Levertov settled in the United States in 1948 and is married to the novelist Mitchell Goodman. Her vivid, impressionistic poems reveal the ability to capture the essential details of sensuous experience and to so portray them as to generate insight and emotional response. In addition to being the author of eight volumes of poetry—including *The Jacob's Ladder, Sorrow Dance,* and *Relearning the Alphabet*—Ms. Levertov is a teacher and lecturer.

Amy Lowell (1874–1925).   The Lowell family of Massachusetts was an illustrious one. In addition to the famed James Russell Lowell, the family included the astronomer Percival Lowell and Harvard President Abbott

Lawrence Lowell, Amy's brothers. Amy Lowell was educated privately. After several years of studying poetry and the techniques of verse, she decided to become a poet. Her first collection *A Dome of Many-Colored Glass,* appeared in 1912. It was not very well received. But her second volume *Sword Blades and Poppy Seeds* (1914) met great enthusiasm. Amy Lowell's fame as a poet grew rapidly. But her experiments in form and technique first attracted attention to her, and it is for them that she is still known best. She died in 1925. One of her posthumous works *What's O'clock* won the Pulitzer Prize.

Paula Ludwig (1900–1974). Paula Ludwig was born in Verarlberg, Austria. In 1926 her collection of poetry, *The Divine Mirror,* was published and made her famous. In 1931 she received a grant from the Abraham Lincoln Foundation for her writing. She also won the George Trakl Literature Prize. In 1938 she fled Austria as the German troops advanced. She spent many years of her life in companionship with her son, whom she bore in 1917 and to whom she addressed a number of her poems directly.

Ursula MacDougall. No biographical data is available.

Katherine Mansfield (1888–1923). "I want to write simply, freely," Katherine Mansfield said, "so as to catch the significance of the fleeting moment." Her best stories do so with notable success. Her real name was Kathleen Beauchamp, and she was born and reared in New Zealand. Most of her adult life, however, was spent in England. In 1921 her collection *Bliss and Other Stories* made her famous. Despite rapidly failing health, she followed that success with *The Garden Party and Other Stories* in 1922 and *The Dove's Nest* in 1923.

Mary McCarthy (born 1912). Known for her acute observations and occasionally biting satire, Mary McCarthy shows her writing skill equally in critical essays and fiction. She was born in Seattle, taught at Bard and Sarah Lawrence Colleges, and now lives in Paris. Her fictional works include *The Company She Keeps, The Groves of Academe, The Group,* and *Birds of America.* Among her nonfiction publications are *Memories of a Catholic Girlhood, Venice Observed,* and *The Stones of Florence,* the latter two being long essays which try to isolate and define the essence of those two cities. In addition, she has written a number of political studies, including *Vietnam, Hanoi,* and *Medina.*

Carson McCullers (1917–1967). Carson McCullers began writing when she was sixteen. She had wanted to be a concert pianist, but then, greatly admiring the playwright Eugene O'Neill, she tried writing a play. It was later performed by and for her family. Carson then went to New York where she worked during the day and went to school at night. She was not able to concentrate on her studies, however, for she found New York a fascinating place, very different from her native Georgia. Soon one of her short stories was published in *Story* magazine. It was the beginning of her long career as an author. Her best-known works include *The Member of the Wedding* and *The Heart Is a Lonely Hunter*.

Phyllis McGinley (born 1905). Phyllis McGinley born in Ontario, Oregon, was educated at the University of Utah and the University of California. She taught school in Utah and New York, wrote copy for an advertising agency, and was a staff writer for *Town and Country* magazine. Her selected poems, *Times Three*, received the Pulitzer Prize. Her other collections of short verse include *On the Contrary*, *A Pocketful of Wry*, *A Short Walk from the Station*, and *The Love Letters of Phyllis McGinley*.

Charlotte Mew (1869–1928). Little is known about the life of Charlotte Mew except that it was filled with poverty, adversity, and personal sorrows that were finally too much for her. Her first volume of poems appeared in 1916 and contained only seventeen poems. Only one other volume of her poetry was published in her lifetime. Although Ms. Mew did not enjoy great renown during her lifetime, she did have the high esteem of Thomas Hardy, Walter de la Mare, and John Masefield, among other notables of that time. Indeed, Thomas Hardy considered her the best woman poet of her day.

Josephine Miles (born 1911). A critic and scholar as well as a poet, Josephine Miles is a professor of English at the University of California, Berkeley. She was born in Chicago, attended the University of California, Los Angeles, and earned her PH.D. at Berkeley. She has written extensively on the language of poetry in such volumes as *The Vocabulary of Poetry: Three Studies*. Her own poems have been published under the titles *Poems 1930–1960*, and *Kinds of Affection* and have won the National Institute of Arts Award and the Blumenthal Award from *Poetry*.

Edna St. Vincent Millay (1892–1950). By the time she was twenty, Edna St. Vincent Millay had achieved fame with her poem "Renascence." The poem marked the beginning of a career that was to see her become probably the most popular poet in America between the two World Wars. Her poems expressed the disillusionment of the postwar generation and struck a tone that appealed to public tastes. Although usually working within traditional stanza forms, she often expressed a romantic protest against traditions and conventions. Her early concern with her own identity—her relationship to others and to the universe—gradually shifted to a concern with broader social issues.

Gabriela Mistral (1889–1956). As the daughter of a country school teacher in Chile and as a school teacher herself, Lucila Godoy Alcayaga developed a concern for children and for the social condition of the Chilean workers, particularly the Indians. She was to maintain this sympathy throughout her lifetime and to support their causes in her writings as well as the cause of social emancipation of women. When she began to write poems she adopted a pen name from the names of two poets she admired, Gabriele D'Annunzio, and Frédéric Mistral. In 1914 her book of poems *Sonetos de la Muerte* (sonnets on death) won a literary prize. She went to Mexico for a while to take part in school reform, but in 1922 the publication of her book *Desolación* made her famous. *Ternura* and *Tala* were published soon after. She agreed to serve her country as consul in Lisbon, Madrid, Nice, Brazil, and the United States. In 1945 Gabriela Mistral was awarded the Nobel Prize for Literature.

Marianne Moore (1887–1972).   Born in St. Louis, Marianne Moore attended Bryn Mawr College, taught typing and bookkeeping, worked in the New York public library, and for three years served as a magazine editor. Originally she had hoped to be a painter, but as she once explained, she had "a passion for rhythm and accent, so blundered into versifying." Her first volume of poetry entitled simply *Poems* appeared in 1921. Her *Collected Poems* was awarded the 1952 Pulitzer Prize. Her vivid and original images frequently derived from her astonishing range of interests: baseball, popular magazines, zoology, motion pictures, boxing, and Oriental art—to name only a handful of her many enthusiasms.

Anaïs Nin (born 1903).   At the age of eleven, Anaïs Nin began to keep a diary which was to bring her literary fame. The diary has been called one of the richest and most illuminating accounts of a woman artist ever written. Anaïs Nin was born in France, the daughter of a celebrated pianist and composer. In the 1920s she became part of a literary group which included Henry Miller, Antonin Artaud, and Lawrence Durrell. With the outbreak of World War II, Ms. Nin left France for the United States where, unable to find a publisher, she bought a printing press and published her works herself. Besides the diary, her writings include short stories, criticism, and novels including *The House of Incest*, *Seduction of the Minotaur*, and *Collages*.

Joyce Carol Oates (born 1938).   Joyce Carol Oates, born in New York, is currently associate professor at the University of Windsor, Ontario. She has published two volumes of poetry and numerous collections of short stories, including *By the North Gate* and *The Wheel of Love*. Her novel *Them* won the National Book Award and *A Garden of Earthly Delights* won an award from the National Institute of Arts and Letters. "All of my writing is about the mystery of human emotions," says Ms. Oates. She further characterizes the mode in which she writes as "psychological realism" combining symbolic and mystical vision with the realistic.

Flannery O'Connor (1925–1964).   Sometimes called a writer of the "Southern Grotesque" school, Flannery O'Connor partially characterized her own talent in her remark "I doubt if the texture of Southern life is any more grotesque than that of the rest of the nation, but it does seem evident that the Southern writer is particularly adept at recognizing the grotesque." Her writing is marked by the inclusion of violence, often unexplained, but also by authentic humor and an accurate rendering of southern country dialect and attitudes. She was born in Savannah, Georgia, and grew up in Milledgeville where she attended Georgia Woman's College. She received a fellowship for study at the University of Iowa and began to publish stories there while earning her M.A. She moved to New York to continue her writing but was forced to return to Milledgeville when she was discovered to be suffering from lupus, a serious blood vessel disease. She was very ill from the disease, most of the time under drug treament, until her death from it in 1964. Her works include the novels *Wise Blood* and *The Violent Bear It Away,* and a collection of short stories *A Good Man Is Hard to Find.* A second collection, *Everything That Rises Must Converge* was published after her death.

Tillie Olsen (born 1913). Tillie Olsen's stories have appeared in *Best American Short Stories of 1951* and *1961* and in *The Fifty Best American Stories 1915–1965.* She has won the O'Henry Award for the best American short story of 1961 for "Tell Me a Riddle" and several of her stories have been recorded by WBAI, a New York radio station. She was born in Omaha, Nebraska, worked for a time as a typist-transcriber, is married and has four children. In 1955 she won the Stanford University creative writing fellowship for study there, and in 1959, a Ford grant for literature. From 1962 to 1964 she worked under a fellowship from the Radcliffe Institute for Independent Study. She now lives in San Francisco.

Grace Paley (born 1922). Grace Paley teaches writing at Sarah Lawrence College near New York City where she was born. She studied at Hunter College and New York University and has taught at Columbia and Syracuse Universities. Her short stories have been published in such magazines as *New American Review, Atlantic,* and *Esquire* and have been collected in a volume entitled *The Little Disturbances of Man.* She began to write poetry on a trip to Vietnam and for many years spent much of her time writing about the Vietnam war, participating in peace demonstrations, and working for anti-war organizations.

Dorothy Parker (1893–1967). Although she was celebrated for her humor and witty remarks, Dorothy Parker was a serious person whose satire was often bitter and whose outlook was sardonic and sympathetic toward suffering. "The humorist has never been happy, anyhow. Today he's whistling past worse graveyards to worse tunes," she has said. She began writing for *Vanity Fair* as drama critic, but was fired for writing unfavorable reviews of important plays. She joined the staff of *The New Yorker* where she wrote a column, "Constant Reader." Her first book of verse *Enough Rope* was an immediate success, and from then on she was only a contributor to the magazine. More verse and short stories followed and several unsuccessful plays. During the 1930s she lived with her second husband, an actor, in Hollywood and wrote screenplays for movies. Both her poems and short stories have been published in collected volumes.

Ann Petry (born 1912). "Slowly, over the years, I have become convinced . . . that the most dramatic material available to a writer in this country is that which deals with the Negro and his history in the U.S.," writes Ann Petry. Her views have not led her, however, to write about Negroes as "types" but rather as full human beings, "as people with the same capacity for love and hate, for tears and laughter, and the same instincts for survival possessed by all men." She attended the College of Pharmacy of the University of Connecticut and worked in drugstores in Connecticut. She married and went to live in Harlem for ten years where she worked on two Harlem newspapers and wrote short stories. After the publication of her first story in *Crisis*, she began a novel, prompted by the suggestion of entering the Houghton Mifflin Fellowship Award Contest. The novel, *The Street*, won the award and her career was launched. Her other fictional works are *Country Place*, *The Drugstore Cat*, and *The Narrows*, and she has written a biography of Harriet Tubman for young people.

Sylvia Plath (1932–1963). During her early years in the Boston suburbs of Winthrop and Wellesley Sylvia Plath began to write poems and draw in pen and ink. By the time she was seventeen her writing had become disciplined and controlled and, after forty-five attempts at publication in *Seventeen* magazine, her first story was accepted. Many of her poems were published in *Seventeen* and *Mademoiselle* and in the summer before her senior year at Smith College she was chosen to be guest editor for the *Mademoiselle* college issue. After her return from this assignment, she suffered the mental breakdown described in her autobiographical novel, *The Bell Jar*. She later returned to college to graduate *summa cum laude* and accept a Fulbright grant to study at Cambridge University in England. There she met and married the British poet, Ted Hughes. She returned to the United States for a year to teach at Smith College, but decided to go back to England and devote herself full time to writing. In a London flat with her two children in the winter of 1962–1963 she began to write at a rapid pace the poems to be published later in the volume *Ariel*. That February she took her own life. Three volumes of her poems have been published, *The Colossus*, *Ariel*, and *Uncollected Poems*.

Katherine Anne Porter (born 1894). Katherine Anne Porter grew up in Texas and has lived in Mexico, Europe, New Orleans, and New York. Before she saw her first story published when she was thirty, she had worked for a newspaper in Chicago, played bit parts in movies, and gotten involved in a Mexican revolution while studying Mayan art. At first she wrote in imitation of great past writers, but she found her own style in the stories published in the volume *Flowering Judas and Other Stories*. Her collection of three novellas, *Pale Horse, Pale Rider*, prompted the *Saturday Review* to place her "in the illustrious company headed by Hawthorne, Flaubert, and Henry James." Her novel, *Ship of Fools*, based on a voyage Porter took from Veracruz to Bremerhaven in 1931, won both the Pulitzer Prize and the National Book Award. Speaking of her writing she says "I have never known an uninteresting human being and I have never known two alike;

there are broad classifications and deep similarities, but I am interested in the thumbprint."

Adrienne Rich (born 1929). Adrienne Rich's first book of poems, *A Change of World*, was published in the Yale Younger Poets Series in 1951, the year she graduated from Radcliffe College. She is a native of Baltimore but lived in Cambridge, Massachusetts for thirteen years writing and trying to think her way through the "woman-writer-wife-mother tangle." She spent a year in Holland learning Dutch and translating Dutch poetry before returning to New York to teach poetry workshops at Columbia University and to help with the SEEK program at City College of New York. While in New York she also worked with a tenants' squatters' movement and on a committee for women prisoners. Her books of poetry include *The Diamond Cutters, Snapshots of a Daughter-in-Law, The Will to Change,* and *Leaflets.*

Elizabeth Madox Roberts (1885–1941). Mastery of the poetic speech patterns of her native Kentucky and accurate observation of her fellow Kentuckians brought Elizabeth Madox Roberts recognition as a poet and novelist. She was born in Perrysville and lived most of her life there. She attended the University of Chicago where she won the Fiske prize for poems. The publication of her first novel, *The Time of Man*, brought critical praise. It was followed by numerous other novels including *Black Is the Color of My True Love's Hair*, and *Not By Strange Gods*. Her poems were published in two volumes: *Under the Tree* and *Song in the Meadow.*

Christina Rossetti (1830–1894). Christina Rossetti was born in north London, of Italian parents. She, like her brothers and sisters, was bilingual and was taught to read and write at home by her mother. When her brother Dante Gabriel Rossetti formed the Pre-Raphaelite group and started a magazine called *The Germ*, several of her poems were included. Although she associated with members of this group and engaged in a brief romance with one, she was never a follower of their dictates. She developed her own visionary lyric style and is considered by some to be one of the finest writers of sonnets in English. The family was poor and Christina taught Italian and tried unsuccessfully to operate a day school. She was deeply religious and a good deal of her literary output consists of religious prose, Anglican tracts, and books of devotion. Ill most of her life, at forty-three she contracted Graves' disease and, turning inward to her religious life, became something of a recluse until her death.

Muriel Rukeyser (born 1913). A poet, prose writer, and teacher, Muriel Rukeyser was born in New York and attended Vassar College and Columbia University. Before the publication of her first volume of poetry, *Theory of Flight*, in 1935, she had worked as a statistician, and taken the ground course at Roosevelt Aviation School. She has published numerous volumes of poetry, including *Beast in View, Orpheus,* and *Waterlily Fire*, as well as children's books, a novel, *The Orgy*, and a biography of the scientist Willard Gibbs. Since 1956 she has taught at Sarah Lawrence College.

Sappho (c. 600 B.C.).   Sappho, one of the greatest lyric poets of antiquity, wrote poems of deep personal feeling expressed simply but with grace and delicacy. Her skill at handling meter was such that Plato later called her the "tenth muse." The poets of her age were turning away from epic poems to choral and solo songs, characterized by a more personal tone and greater variety of meter, and Sappho was in the forefront of this movement. Of her life little is known for certain. She was born on the island of Lesbos and grew up in Mytilene, one of its cities. Historians believe that she and her prominent noble family were exiled to Sicily briefly. She is said to have married a wealthy man and she does write of a daughter, Cleis. She maintained a circle of young girls to whom she addressed poems expressing her emotions, sometimes love. Some have characterized these relations as sexual in nature, while others have maintained that Sappho ran a school for girls or headed a religious group sacred to Aphrodite. Sappho's works filled nine books when they were collected in the third century B.C., but most of them have been lost. Only two of her odes and fragments of a thousand or so lines survive.

May Sarton (born 1912).   May Sarton left her birthplace in Wondelgen, Belgium to come to the United States with her parents during the German invasion of 1914. She attended Shady Hill School in Cambridge, Massachusetts, where her interest in poetry was encouraged by her teacher Agnes Hocking. For a time after graduating from high school she worked in the theater as an apprentice, and she later founded the Associated Actors Theatre. During the 1940s she was a script writer for the Overseas Film Unit in New York, and wrote a play, *Underground River*. She has lectured and taught in many universities and academic programs including Harvard, the Bread Loaf Writers' Conference, the Boulder Writers' Conference, and Wellesley College. Among her novels are *The Single Hound, The Small Room,* and *Mrs. Stevens Hears the Mermaids Singing.* Her poetry has been published in volumes entitled *Encounter in April, Cloud, Stone, Sun, Vine,* and *A Private Mythology.*

Anne Sexton (1928–1974).   Winner of the Pulitzer Prize for Poetry for her collection *Live or Die,* Anne Sexton began writing seriously while she was recovering from a mental breakdown. She called it "a rebirth at twenty-nine." She was born in Newton, Massachusetts, grew up in Wellesley, and lived as a wife and mother in Weston. She was educated at Garland Junior College, Boston University, and Brandeis University. She taught English at Wayland High School and creative writing at Harvard and Radcliffe while she was a scholar at the Radcliffe Institute for Independent Study. In 1960 she held the Robert Frost Fellowship at the Bread Loaf Writers' Conference. She is often grouped with W. D. Snodgrass and Robert Lowell as a "confessional" poet who writes of personal experiences and feelings in a very frank manner. At first friends tried to discourage her from writing so openly about herself. "But then I saw Snodgrass doing what I was doing, and it kind of gave me permission," she said. In September of 1974 she committed suicide. Her collections of poems include *To Bedlam and Part Way Back, All My Pretty Ones, Love Poems,* and *Transformations.*

Edith Sitwell (1887–1964).   A member of a famous literary family, Edith Sitwell was born in Scarborough, England where she was privately educated. She served for several years as an editor of the anthology *Wheels* which protested against the formalities of the Georgian school of poets. In 1954 she was created Dame, Commander Order of the British Empire the first poet so honored. In addition to her poetry, Edith Sitwell wrote biographies and criticism.

May Swenson (born 1919).   Although May Swenson lives in New York, she was born in Logan, Utah, and has served as Poet-in-Residence at Purdue University. During a distinguished career she has been honored by many grants and awards, including both Guggenheim and Ford Fellowships. Her first collection of verse appeared in 1954, *Another Animal;* since then she has published several other volumes, including *A Cage of Spines* and *Half Sun Half Sleep.* May Swenson says that she has written many of her poems "directly on the scene . . . in much the same way a painter sketches from life."

Sara Teasdale (1884–1933).   Because of ill health, Sara Teasdale received part of her early education in her St. Louis home. Later she was sent to a private school where she and her friends founded and edited a literary magazine. Travel in Europe and the middle east stimulated her imagination and visits to Chicago introduced her to a new literary group which included Vachel Lindsay, the poet. Lindsay began an ardent courtship, but Sara, after some indecision, refused him in favor of a St. Louis businessman. With her new husband she moved to New York and began her most productive period of writing. *Rivers to the Sea, Love Songs, Flame and Shadow* were published and were climaxed by *Dark of the Moon,* a more somber and subtle collection. In 1926 she divorced her husband and began to live a somewhat isolated life. Vachel Lindsay's suicide in 1931 affected her severely. On January 29, 1933 she was found dead in her apartment from an overdose of barbiturates. A final volume of poetry, *Strange Victory*, appeared after her death.

Teresa of Avila (1515–1582).   Teresa Sánchez Cepeda Dávila y Ahumada, a Carmelite nun from Avila, Spain, worked for reform within the Roman Catholic Church. She also wrote poems derived from her mystical experiences but used simple metaphors of daily life to express their meaning.

Marina Tsvetayeva (1892–1941).   Born in Moscow, the daughter of a professor of art and philology, Marina Tsvetayeva was educated mostly abroad, at Lausanne and Freiburg, and at the Sorbonne where she studied Old French literature. In 1922 she left Russia to live in Prague, Berlin, and Paris. Later she returned to Russia and committed suicide. Her poems received little attention until several volumes were published almost simultaneously in the 1920s. Her early volumes such as *An Evening Album* and *The Magic Lantern* and the mature works such as *Poems to Blok* and *Bold Fellow* reveal her sensitivity to sound and her ability to handle rhythm, sometimes recalling the inflection of the Russian folk song.

Mona Van Duyn (born 1921). Mona Van Duyn was born in Waterloo, Iowa and attended Iowa State Teachers College and the State University of Iowa. She has taught at the University of Iowa Writers' Workshop, the University of Louisville, and Washington University in St. Louis. With her husband, she is co-founder and editor of *Perspective, a Quarterly of Literature*. In 1970 her collection of poems *To See, To Take* won the National Book Award and the Bollinger Award. Her other publications are *Valentines to the Wide World* and *A Time of Bees*.

Diane Wakoski (born 1937). Diane Wakoski was born in Whittier, California and received her B.A. from the University of California, Berkeley. After moving to New York she worked in a bookstore and taught English at a junior high school. Publication of her first book of poetry, *Coins and Coffins*, in 1962 prompted LeRoi Jones to include her work in a collection he edited called *Four Young Lady Poets*. A later volume, *Discrepancies and Apparitions*, led to a Robert Frost Fellowship in poetry from the Bread Loaf Writers Conference. Since she has become known as a poet, Ms. Wakoski has taught at the University of Virginia and been poet-in-residence at Willamette University in Oregon. Married to the poet Michael Watterlond, Ms. Wakoski edits *Dream Sheet* and *Software*.

Margaret Walker (born 1915). In 1942 Margaret Walker burst into prominence with her first book of poetry, *For My People*, which won the Yale Younger Poets award. She was born in Birmingham, Alabama where her father was a minister and was educated there and in Mississippi and Louisiana before earning her PH.D. from the University of Iowa. After her schooling she worked as a newspaper reporter, social worker, and English teacher in North Carolina and West Virginia. For a period of about twenty years after her poetry collection appeared she occupied herself with bringing up four children and college teaching, until, in 1966 she published her novel, *Jubilee*. The book concerns the decade of the Civil War; it was carefully researched and allowed her to bring her own experiences to bear on the historical material she gathered.

Sylvia Townsend Warner (born 1893). For Sylvia Townsend Warner, an early interest in music gave way to a vocation for poetry and novels, but only after she had helped edit a ten-volume work entitled *Tudor Church Music*. Her father was a school teacher in Harrow-on-the-Hill, Middlesex, England, and Sylvia was educated at private schools. Her poems, published in *The Espalier* and *Time Importuned*, are marked by graceful wit, and her story collections and novels, such as *Lolly Willowes* and *The Cat's Cradle Book* are often touched with fantasy. In 1927 she came to New York to be guest critic of the Herald Tribune and worked for the Loyalists in Spain during the Spanish Civil War, but she returned to London to occupy a Victorian house, work on a biography, and pursue her interest in the occult.

Eudora Welty (born 1909). Eudora Welty has lived most of her life in Jackson, Mississippi where she was born. She attended Mississippi State

College for Women, the University of Wisconsin and the Columbia School of Business. Her short stories, which have appeared in numerous magazines, have been collected in three volumes, *A Curtain of Green*, *The Wide Net*, and *The Bride of Innisfallen*. The Rockefeller and Merrill Foundations have awarded her grants, and she has held a Guggenheim Fellowship. Her novel *The Ponder Heart* was awarded the Howells Medal for Fiction by the American Academy of Arts and Letters. Ms. Welty has recorded experiences and feelings of her fellow Mississippians not only in fiction, but also in a collection of photographs called "One Time, One Place" which she took for the Works Project Administration during the 1930s. Her most recent novel is *The Optimist's Daughter*.

Jessamyn West (born 1907). A rural childhood in Indiana and a Quaker upbringing were reflected in Jessamyn West's first and highly successful collection of stories, *The Friendly Persuasion*. Educated at Whittier College and the University of California, Ms. West also studied in England. As an author she has taught at numerous writers' conferences, including Bread Loaf and Indiana University. Her collections of stories include *Love, Death and the Ladies' Drill Team*, *Except for Me and Thee*, and *Crimson Ramblers of the World, Farewell*. Among her novels are *Leafy Rivers*, *Cress Delahanty*, and *South of the Angels*. When *The Friendly Persuasion* was made into a movie Ms. West wrote the screenplay for it and later wrote other movies including *The Big Country*. In 1970 she spent several months in seclusion in a house trailer writing a book of reflections and recollections of her life entitled *Hide and Seek*.

Phillis Wheatley (1753–1784). Phillis Wheatley was brought to Boston, Massachusetts from Africa as a slave when she was seven years old. She was bought by John Wheatley, a tailor, to act as servant to his wife, Mary. Mary Wheatley taught Phillis to read and write English and some Latin and encouraged her talent for poetry. She was fond of English and classical literature and when she was thirteen, began to write poems modeled on those of the English poets of the time, particularly Pope and Gray. She was considered a prodigy by the Boston intellectuals and several of her poems were published. Some of her poems were published in a volume, *Poems on Various Subjects, Religious and Moral*. After Mr. and Mrs. Wheatley died Phillis was forced to support herself. In 1778 she married John Peters, a free Negro, but financial difficulties and unhappiness followed. Her husband was imprisoned for debt and she was forced to work in a Negro boarding house. Two of her three children died in infancy and she herself died in poverty at the age of thirty-one.

Virginia Woolf (1882–1941). English novelist, essayist, and critic, Virginia Woolf, along with such writers as Proust and Joyce, created the modern novel. Born Adeline Virginia Stephen in London, she was educated at home by her father, a distinguished man of letters. In 1912 she married Leonard Woolf, a critic and writer on economics and politics. She was a ceaseless experimenter in the novel and short story, continually searching for new techniques to replace conventional narrative methods. In such distinguished novels as *Mrs. Dalloway* and *To the Lighthouse* she revealed her characters' lives not as a single straight line of experience but as a web—intricate and complex, reaching out simultaneously in many directions of the past, present, and future. Her essays, while displaying everywhere the same curiosity that her novels exhibit to peer beneath the surface of life and literature, are in style uncomplicated and straightforward. On March 28, 1941 Virginia Woolf drowned herself leaving her husband a farewell note explaining that she feared she was going mad and having previously suffered two mental breakdowns, feared she would not recover. The shock of her suicide was the greater because her difficulties were not generally known and because it seemed to negate the positive values that distinguish her writing.

Elinor Wylie (1885–1928).   Married to the poet William Rose Benét, Elinor Wylie established her reputation as an American poet and novelist. Noted for its vivid imagery and its intense emotion, her poetry reflects a strong influence from the medieval English and French ballads and the metaphysical poets of England. Most of her literary production was concentrated in the last nine years of her life, during which time she wrote four volumes of verse reprinted in *Collected Poems,* four historical novels all reprinted in *Collected Prose,* and a number of short stories and essays.

Marya Zaturenska (born 1902).   Marya Zaturenska was born in Kiev, Russia but, at the age of seven, immigrated to the United States with her family. She worked in a factory at the age of fourteen and attended Valparaiso University and the University of Wisconsin. She married the poet and critic Horace Gregory and edited several anthologies with him. Her second volume of poetry, *Cold Morning Sky,* won the Pulitzer Prize. Her other volumes include *Golden Mirror* and *Terraces of Light.*

iNdEx

By Women

By Women

index of literary terms

Acknowledgments (continued):

"There's Been a Death in the Opposite House," "I Heard a Fly Buzz," "This Is My Letter to the World," "I Like a Look of Agony," by Emily Dickinson. Reprinted by permission of the publishers and the Trustees of Amherst College from Thomas H. Johnson, editor, *The Poems of Emily Dickinson*, Cambridge, Mass.: The Belknap Press of Harvard University Press. Copyright, 1951, 1955, by the President and Fellows of Harvard College.

"The Ring," by Isak Dinesen from *Anecdotes of Destiny* by Isak Dinesen. Copyright © 1958 by Isak Dinesen. Reprinted by permission of Random House, Inc.

"The Pear Tree," by H. D. (Hilda Doolittle), *Selected Poems*. Copyright © 1957 by Norman Holmes Pearson. Reprinted by permission of New Directions Publishing Corporation.

"The Alarm Clock," by Mari Evans from *I Am a Black Woman*, published by William Morrow & Company, 1970, by permission of the author.

"A New England Nun," by Mary Wilkins Freeman. Reprinted by permission of Harper & Row, Publishers, Inc.

"Nikki-Roasa," by Nikki Giovanni from *Black Feeling, Black Talk, Black Judgment*. Copyright © 1968, 1970 by Nikki Giovanni. Reprinted by permission of William Morrow & Co., Inc.

"Trifles," by Susan Glaspell. Reprinted by permission of Dodd, Mead & Company, Inc. from *Plays* by Susan Glaspell. Copyright 1920 by Dodd, Mead & Company, Inc. Copyright renewed 1948 by Susan Glaspell.

"My First Two Women," by Nadine Gordimer reprinted from the author's collection *Six Feet of the Country* © 1955 by Nadine Gordimer. Permission granted by Shirley Collier Agency.

A Raisin in the Sun by Lorraine Hansberry. Copyright © 1958, 1959 by Robert Nemiroff as Executor of the Estate of Lorraine Hansberry. Reprinted by permission of Random House, Inc.

"I Can't Hold You and I Can't Leave You," by Sister Juana Inés de La Cruz. Text copyright © 1974 by Judith Thurman. Used by permission of Atheneum Publishers.

"Amusing Our Daughters," by Carolyn Kizer. Copyright © 1963 by Carolyn Kizer from *Knock Upon Silence*. Reprinted by permission of Doubleday & Co., Inc.

"May 10th," by Maxine Kumin from *Up Country* by Maxine Kumin. Copyright © 1964 by Maxine Kumin. Originally appeared in *The New Yorker* and reprinted by permission of Harper & Row, Publishers, Inc.

"The Double Goer," by Dilys Laing from *The Collected Poems of Dilys Laing*, © 1967 by David Laing. Reprinted with permission of David Laing.

"An Old Woman and Her Cat," by Doris Lessing. Reprinted by permission of John Cushman Associates, Inc. First published in *New American Review*. Copyright © 1972 by Doris Lessing.

"In Mind," by Denise Levertov from *O Taste and See* copyright © 1963 by Denise Levertov Goodman. First published in *Poetry* and reprinted by permission of New Directions Publishing Corporation.

"Patterns," by Amy Lowell from *The Complete Poetical Works of Amy Lowell*. Copyright 1944 by Ada B. Russell. Reprinted by permission of Houghton Mifflin Co.

"To the Dark God," by Paula Ludwig. Translated by Candice L. McRee. Reprinted by permission of Langewiesche-Brandt.

"Titty's Dead and Tatty Weeps," by Ursula MacDougall. Every effort has been made to locate the holder of this copyright. The publishers would be glad to arrange for and pay an appropriate permissions fee when the holder is located.

"Her First Ball," by Katherine Mansfield. Copyright 1922 and renewed 1950 by John Middleton Murry. Reprinted from *The Short Stories of Katherine Mansfield*, by permission of Alfred A. Knopf, Inc.

Art Credits

Frontispiece: George Sakmanoff; p. x: Arthur Tress; p. 15: Duane Michals, "Death Comes to the Old Lady"; p. 28: Barbara M. Marshall; p. 43: Dorothea Lange; p. 52: Martha Mount; p. 59: Lady Hawarden "At the Window" c. 1864, Gernsheim Collection; pp. 63, 68, 78: Edith Allard; p. 85: Shirley Borella; p. 97: Imogen Cunningham, "Martha Graham"; p. 104: Harry Callahan, "Eleanor, 1948"; p. 115: Barbara M. Marshall; p. 124: Shelley Rotner; p. 133: Dorothea Lange; p. 158: Shelley Rotner; p. 175: Ken Regan from Camera 5; p. 194: George W. Gardner; p. 206: Marisol (Marisol Escobar) *The Family* (1962) painted wood and other materials in 3 sections, 6' 10⅝" x 65½". Collection, The Museum of Modern Art, New York. Advisory Committee Fund; p. 220: Lewis Carroll, "Alice Liddell" c. 1859. International Museum of Photography at the George Eastman House; p. 224: Kenneth Josephson, "Matthew, 1963"; pp. 236, 237: Molly Bang; p. 249: These illustrations are reproduced from *Memories of a Catholic Girlhood*, © 1957 by Mary McCarthy, by permission of Harcourt Brace Jovanovich, Inc.; pp. 252, 257, 264: Robin Freedenfeld; p. 274; Imogen Cunningham; p. 282; Morgan Reese; p. 293: Dorothea Sierra; p. 302: Mary Austin; p. 306: Georgia O'Keefe, *Blue Lines*, Metropolitan Museum of Art, Alfred Steiglitz Collection, 1949; p. 310: Daniel S. Brody from Editorial Photocolor Archives; p. 317: Emanuel Kelly, "Stacie, 1969"; p. 320: Imogen Cunningham; p. 324: Jerry N. Uelsmann, "Poet's House" 1965; p. 327: Morgan Reese; p. 332: Edith Crane Lisle; p. 338: Jon Albertson; p. 342: Eric Myrvaagnes; p. 345: T. A. Rothschild from Stock Boston; p. 349: Charles Harbutt from Magnum; p. 355: Morgan Reese; p. 360: Jerry N. Uelsmann; p. 364: Margaret Bourke-White from Time-Life Picture Agency; p. 374: Nicholas Sapieha from Stock Boston; p. 384: Shew, William ("Mother and Daughter") 1845–1850. Daguerrotype, sixth-plate, 3⅛" x 2⅝". Collection, The Museum of Modern Art, New York. Gift of Ludwig Glaeser; pp. 390, 404: André Kertész from Magnum; p. 414: Hakim Raquib; p. 424: Boston Redevelopment Authority; p. 430: Larry Nelson; p. 439: Andrick Tong, "For the Dynamite Lady"; p. 448: Arthur Tress.
Cover: Dorothea Sierra.